Resistance to the Shah

Resistance to the Shah

Landowners and Ulama in Iran

Mohammad Gholi Majd

University Press of Florida

Gainesville/Tallahassee/Tampa/Boca Raton

Pensacola/Orlando/Miami/Jacksonville

05 04 03 02 01 00   6 5 4 3 2 1

Library of Congress Cataloging-in-Publication Data
Majd, Mohammad Gholi, 1946–
Resistance to the Shah : landowners and ulama in Iran / Mohmmad Gholi Majd.
p.   cm.
Includes bibliographical references and index.
ISBN 0-8130-1731-9 (alk. paper)
1. Land tenure—Political aspects—Iran—History—20th century. 2. Iran—History—
Pahlavi dynasty, 1925–1979. 3. Landowners—Iran—Political activity—History—20th
century. 4. Majd, Mohammad Ali, 1891–1978. 5. Agriculture and state—Iran—
History—20th century. 6. Ulama—Iran—Political activity. I. Title.
HD1333.I7 M35 2000
333.3'0955–dc21   99-058586

The University Press of Florida is the scholarly publishing agency for the State
University System of Florida, comprising Florida A&M University, Florida Atlantic
University, Florida International University, Florida State University, University of
Central Florida, University of Florida, University of North Florida, University of
South Florida, and University of West Florida.

University Press of Florida
15 Northwest 15th Street
Gainesville, FL 32611-2079
http://www.upf.com

CONTENTS

ILLUSTRATIONS

Maps

Figures

TABLES

Dedicated to Zohreh, Ali, and Sudabeh

PREFACE

This study is made possible by and relies extensively on the memoirs and private papers of my father, Mohammad Ali Majd, Fatn ol Saltaneh (1891–1978). Its genesis goes back to 1996, when the Islamic Revolutionary Court in Tehran was investigating his record. As in these cases, the court's main purpose was to review his political record and to determine if his wealth had been acquired by corrupt means. If they determined he had acquired his wealth by corruption, it would be confiscated from his heirs. As part of the investigation, my siblings and I were summoned to the Central Revolutionary Court in Khiaban Moalem, Tehran. The examining magistrate, a relatively young man, had some vague ideas that Majd had been involved in the opposition to the shah in the early 1960s, but he was unfamiliar with the details. He asked for a list of property owned by Majd at the time of his death or inherited by his heirs. The list was brief and inconsequential. Convinced that the heirs were attempting to hide their inheritance, the magistrate became irritated and remarked with obvious vexation, "How could a person who was so influential in his lifetime and held important government positions have so little at the time of his death?" We explained that the bulk of his property had been confiscated under the shah's land distribution program, and the rest was used to pay off his creditors, so that at the time of his death he owned practically nothing. Not satisfied with our explanation, the magistrate undertook his own investigation. After a year, he concluded that what we had told him was correct, and he recommended that the dossier on Mohammad Ali Majd be closed. Upon review of the case by the Revolutionary Prosecutor General, the investigation was declared complete and the file was "closed." Of course, as far as I was concerned, the case had just been "opened."

I had just found the unpublished memoirs of my father, who died on 2 April 1978. He had composed his memoirs between 1966 and 1968, and there had been a minor revision in 1971. His memoirs, consisting of five volumes, spanned 1916–68, from his entry into government service until the "defeat" of movements that had opposed Mohammad Reza Shah's "White Revolution," and set forth my father's final observations on the consequences of the shah's land distribution of 1962 through 1971. The first two volumes covered 1916–43; volume 3, 1944–53; volume 4, 1954–58; and volume 5, 1959–68. Just before his death, a version of volumes 1 and 2 been published at his own expense.

However, I soon realized that the published version in 1978 and the original version that I had found were vastly different. The reason was that the reviewers in Savak (the acronym for the secret police) had found some of the material to be unpublishable and had deleted the offending parts. The deleted material was, of course, the most interesting, and it often related to matters of land, landowners, and Reza Shah's land acquisition. A comparison of the two versions shows how censorship can change the nature of a work and present it in a manner totally different from the author's intention. In short, a fascinating part of the material had been left out. The last two volumes of his memoirs, which covered the period when he was a senator, 1954–58, and the subsequent period when he was involved with and was a leader of the opposition to the shah's "White Revolution," could not have been published while the Pahlavis remained in power. Given my own background and interest in matters of landownership and land tenure, the part of the memoirs that most interested me was the land story. In addition to being a politician who held such posts as governorship of Gilan and Mazandaran during the critical years of 1941–43, Majd was also related to landowners and was himself a landowner. He had seen firsthand and had taken part in events that had shaped the agrarian history of Iran during the twentieth century; namely, the land acquisitions of Reza Shah during the 1930s, the land sales of Mohammad Reza Shah during the 1950s, and the land distribution of Mohammad Reza Shah during the 1960s. His entire political career had been shaped by his role as a landowner. Majd's memoirs and private papers provide fresh insights into Iran's agrarian and political history during the twentieth century.

I was aware that my father had been active in the resistance to the shah's land distribution of the 1960s. But I learned from his memoirs and the documents found in his papers that he had been a leader of the landowners who had organized to oppose the shah and that his group had been closely allied with the *ulama*, including Ayatollah Khomeini. As I was examining his papers one day, I found an open envelope marked *"fatwa."* To my astonishment, I saw that the envelope contained numerous original fatwas, including that of Ayatollah Khomeini, in Imam's own handwriting, bearing his signature and personal seal. I knew that I had made an immensely significant discovery.

From these memoirs and documents one comes to conclude that the entire Pahlavi period was characterized by an incessant struggle between the two Pahlavi Shahs on one side (and Iran's landowning class, which was a remnant of the old Qajar landed aristocracy) and the ulama on the other side. It appeared that the Pahlavis had emerged victorious in 1964. But the victory was shortlived. In reading Majd's memoirs thirty-five years later, one begins to understand why Mohammad Reza Shah was not able to broaden the base of his regime. In all, from the material on land and landownership in Majd's memoirs and his private papers, a fascinating account could be constructed, one that provides new insights and necessarily leads to a new interpretation of events in Iran's agrarian and political history in the twentieth century. The account given in this book constitutes an important but little-studied part of Iran's agrarian and political history. It is my duty and privilege to be able to tell this story.

I have also been fortunate to have access to the declassified records of the State Department in the National Archives of the United States. These records clarify the crucial role of the United States in determining Iran's land policy between 1951 and 1971. They provide much insight and information on events and personalities. The consular reports from Tabriz and Mashhad provide vital documentation to many crucial points. In short, the book has greatly benefited from these records.

Acknowledgments

This book has also benefited by help from several individuals. I would like to express my sincere gratitude to several persons at the Institute for Contemporary Historical Studies in Tehran. Abdollah Shahbazi, former director of the institute, provided me with the opportunity in 1996 to examine and study the *Register of Names of His Exalted Imperial Majesty's Private Properties*. This immensely significant document contains a listing of villages, hamlets, and pastures that were acquired by Reza Shah. I also would like to thank Mr. Shahbazi's successor, Seyed Sadeq Kharrazi, for once again placing the register at my disposal and for the courtesy and assistance extended to me. I would also like to thank Safaed-din Tabaraian and Hosein Kalateh for the help and consideration they provided me. Maryam Imaniyeh supplied the photographs of the ulama that are produced in this book. I also wish to thank Reza Azari Shahrezaii, formerly at Iran National Archives Organization, for bringing numerous documents to my attention and making them available to me. My brother,

Mohammad Hosein Majd, searched and found many photographs, including most of those of the leadership of the Agricultural Union of Iran. In addition, Maryam Ghoreishi supplied a photograph of her grandfather, Mohammad Ghoreishi. Nasir Assar provided generous assistance in deciphering some of the original Persian documents. Hilda Pring, librarian at the University of Pennsylvania, permitted me to make generous use of the resources of the library. John Washburn read an earlier version of the manuscript and provided valuable suggestions and comments for which I am most grateful. An earlier version of chapters 3 and 4 was also improved as a result of comments by Professor Shaul Bakhash. The manuscript benefited enormously from the detailed comments by one of the anonymous reviewers, and I take this opportunity to thank that individual.

Finally, I am immensely indebted to my wife, Zohreh, and my children, Ali and Sudabeh, for their understanding and assistance in completing this task. The timely submission of the manuscript to the University Press of Florida was made possible thanks to Ali's computer skills.

Map of Iran. Habib Ladjevardi, *Labor Unions and Autocracy in Iran*, Syracuse University Press, 1985. Reprinted by permission of the publisher.

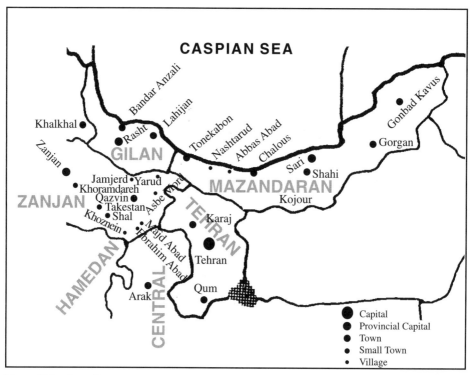

Map of Northern Iran.

1

Brief Historical Survey and Introduction

Historians believe that from the second half of the nineteenth century, Iran, which was ruled by the Qajar dynasty (1779–1925), was subjected to increased penetration by and rivalry between Russia and Great Britain, the imperial powers to its north and south.[1] The Constitutional Revolution of August 1906 was the result of complex social and political forces, including rising nationalism, a desire to establish a constitutional monarchy with limited powers, and parliamentary rule fashioned after the European models. Its success was also facilitated by the 1905 constitutional revolution in Russia. Two events doomed the initial experiment in constitutional rule: the Anglo-Russian Entente of 1907, which divided Iran into "spheres of influence," and the death of the shah. Mozzafar ad Din Shah died in January 1907, five days after granting a constitution and allowing the election of an elected parliament, the Majlis. With Russian support, his son and successor, Mohammad Ali Shah, set about undoing what had been gained by the revolutionaries. In June 1908, the Majlis building was bombed by the shah's Persian Cossack Brigade, led by a Russian officer. Some of those active in the movement were arrested and executed, and others fled the country. The shah's actions and the subsequent uprising in Tabriz by Sattar Khan and Baqer Khan resulted in a strengthening of the constitutional forces, which were now joined by some prominent personalities who had been opposed or lukewarm to the establishment of a constitutional government. In July 1909, an army from Gilan under the command of Mohammad Vali Khan Tonekaboni, Sepahdar Azam, and another army from Isfahan under the command of Ali Qoli Khan Bakhtiari, Sardar Asad, marched on Tehran. They occupied the capital, deposed Mohammad Ali Shah, put his young son, Ahmad Shah (1909–25), on the throne, and restored constitutional rule. Shortly thereafter, the second Majlis was elected.

Once again, the functioning of a constitutional order became a victim of Anglo-Russian intrigue and rivalry. In 1907, Britain and Russia agreed to divide Iran into spheres of influence. When the native government tried to collect taxes from powerful officials allied with the Russians in December 1911, Russian troops shut down the Majlis. World War I brought about increased foreign penetration and both direct and indirect foreign occupation. Russia and Turkey occupied western and northern Iran, while in the south, Britain established the South Persia Rifles to protect its interests. The Iranian government was greatly weakened, a separatist movement developed in Gilan, and a Soviet Socialist Republic of Gilan was established. The Russian Revolution of 1917 ended Russian interference in Iran for twenty-five years, and Britain emerged as the sole imperial power. Britain attempted to gain complete control of Iran through the abortive agreement of 1919 by which Iran would have become a British protectorate similar to Egypt. Historians believe that after the British failed to gain direct control of Iran, they set about achieving their aims by establishing a friendly "strong" government that was anti-Soviet. The outcome of this policy was the coup d'état of 21 February 1921, which brought a newspaper editor, Seyed Zia Tabatabaii, and an obscure Persian Cossack Brigade colonel, Reza Khan (1877–1944), to the scene. They marched on Tehran and forced Ahmad Shah to appoint Tabatabaii prime minister and Reza Khan commander of the army. These two reportedly had not even met before the night of the coup. It had all been arranged by the British. In May 1921, Tabatabaii was sent into exile. Reza Khan became minister of war in 1921, and the following year Ahmad Shah agreed to appoint Reza Khan prime minister and go into exile in Europe. In December 1925, a constituent assembly "amended" the Constitution by removing the Qajar dynasty and giving the throne to Reza Khan and his descendants. Reza Khan was crowned as Reza Shah Pahlavi in April 1926.

Few characters in Iran's history are as controversial as Reza Shah Pahlavi (1926–41). Many have portrayed him as a true reformer who brought Iran into the twentieth century and laid the foundation for Iran's economic development. But to others he was a monstrous tyrant who unleashed a cruel military dictatorship on Iran, murdered his opponents, suppressed all freedoms, and made a mockery of Iran's legislative body and Constitution. In the twenty years that he controlled Iran, he became the wealthiest man in Asia, at least on a par with the Japanese Imperial house, which had ruled Japan for over a thousand years. Chapter 3 will show how Reza Shah acquired this wealth.

In retrospect, Reza Shah's foreign policy brought disaster and foreign occupation to Iran and nearly resulted in the calamitous loss of the provinces of Azarbaijan and Kurdistan after World War II. Although he had come to power with British assistance, Reza Shah became increasingly enamored of Hitler and Nazi Germany. The result was much commerce and "cultural exchange" and the employment of German nationals and experts in Iran. It has been suggested that Reza Shah's German policy was to counter British and Soviet influence in Iran. It was more than this. Reza Shah appears to have genuinely admired Hitler's Germany.[2] When the Allies attacked Iran in August 1941, their excuse was that the shah had refused to expel German nationals from Iran.

Iran's strategic position changed following the German invasion of Russia in June 1941. Iran was a vital link and apparently the only year-round supply route to the besieged Soviet forces. Convinced of an imminent German victory against the Allies, Reza Shah ignored Allied demands that the German nationals working in Iran be expelled. In the early hours of 25 August 1941, Soviet and British forces invaded Iran from the north and west. The Soviet forces met practically no resistance in Azarbaijan and Khorasan. Only in Gilan did the Iranian army make a stand and halt the Soviet advance for four days. Even then, on the third day, the army in Gilan received orders from Tehran that it was to cease resistance. In fairness, Reza Shah's army was neither equipped nor designed to fight a determined attack by two super powers. It was an instrument of domestic rule and security. Within three weeks, Reza Shah abdicated in favor of his son and went into exile, where he died in August 1944. The removal of Reza Shah delighted the general population and heralded a period of freedom of expression and political activity. Newspapers that had been banned under Reza Shah resumed publication, and political parties were free to organize. One such newly formed party was the Tudeh (Masses) Party, which was communist in ideology and allied with the Soviets. It became highly active in the northern provinces that were under Soviet occupation. The war years saw the beginning of U.S. involvement in Iran.

The opening skirmish of the cold war took place in Iran. According to the Tripartite Treaty of January 1942 between Iran, Britain, and the Soviet Union, the Allies agreed to withdraw their forces from Iran within six months of the end of the war. In the Tehran Declaration of December 1943, Roosevelt, Stalin, and Churchill reiterated their respect for the independence and territorial integrity of Iran. In August 1945, with Soviet assistance and protection, members of the Tudeh Party in Azarbaijan took over government buildings in Tabriz. When the Iranian army was dispatched to put down the uprising, the Soviets stopped the army in Qazvin, some three hundred miles from Tabriz. With Soviet assistance, the Tudeh Party in Azarbaijan was renamed the Democratic Party, and in December 1945 it proclaimed an Autonomous Republic of Azarbaijan, with its own army commanded by a Soviet general. A similar autonomous republic was proclaimed in the province of Kurdistan. Iran protested the violation of its sovereignty and filed a complaint with the brand-new Security Council of the United Nations. By 2 March 1946, the British and American forces had left Iran, but the Soviets refused to go. They withdrew in May 1946 but left only after extracting four concessions from Prime Minister Ahmad Qavam. First, Qavam recommended to the Majlis the approval of a joint Soviet-Iran oil company to develop the northern oil resources. Second, he promised to appoint three Tudeh ministers to his cabinet. Third, he agreed to recognize the Autonomous Republic of Azarbaijan. Fourth, he promised to withdraw Iran's complaint with the Security Council. In practice, none of the undertakings was fulfilled. The elections to the Fifteenth Majlis were to be held in early 1947. Qavam tried in vain to fill the Majlis with leftist deputies who would willingly approve the Russian oil concession. The impending elections brought the Azarbaijan crisis to a speedy conclusion. In December 1946, the Iranian army finally moved to retake Azarbaijan and Kurdistan. Abandoned by the Soviets, the republics quickly collapsed. In October 1947, the newly convened Fifteenth Majlis overwhelmingly rejected the Soviet oil concession. Qavam resigned shortly thereafter. For Iran this was an extremely critical period during which it came close to being dismembered. Thereafter, with the onset of the cold war, U.S. involvement in Iran increased considerably.

With the solution of the Azarbaijan and Kurdistan crisis and Qavam's departure, Mohammad Reza Shah began consolidating power in his own hands. He also showed that he was Reza Shah's true heir. One of his first acts was to reclaim ownership of lands and property that had been acquired by Reza Shah. As outlined below, these lands had been assigned to the government for restoration to the previous owners. By such actions, Mohammad Reza Shah eroded his own popularity and legitimacy. He was thus unable to survive the oil nationalization crisis of 1950–53 without the assistance of the U.S. government. Having defeated the Soviet oil concession request in the north, the oil commission of the Majlis, which was under the leadership of Dr. Mohammad Mossadeq, began to push for the nationalization of the Anglo-Iranian Oil Company, which operated the southern oil fields and the refinery in Abadan. This was an enormously popular action with the people of Iran, and those politicians who had opposed the wisdom of outright nationalization or were at all doubtful about it were driven from office. Some were even murdered. The most prominent victim was Prime Minister Haj Ali Razmara, who was assassinated on 7 March 1951. At this time, the shah attempted to regain control by appointing a prime minister, Hosein Ala, who was one of his most trusted associates. On 27 April 1951, the British closed the refinery in Abadan, and Ala resigned. Mossadeq became prime minister the next day, and the Majlis voted unanimously to nationalize the oil industry. The shah signed the bill on 2 May 1951. There ensued a two-year tumultuous struggle with Britain that ended with the CIA-supported coup of 19 August 1953, which overthrew Mossadeq and was to determine the path of Iran's history.

Unquestionably, Mossadeq was a genuine national leader whom the people of Iran trusted and wished to follow. He tried to free Iran's resources from foreign control. He also attempted to curb the power of Mohammad Reza Shah and turn him into a constitutional king similar to the European monarchies. However, Mossadeq's inability to settle the oil dispute prolonged the crisis. Deprived of oil revenues, the economic and political situation deteriorated. He resorted to unconstitutional and dictatorial measures. These actions further alienated some of his supporters. Increasingly abandoned by his allies and associates, he became more reliant on the Tudeh Party. Meanwhile, the country sank into turmoil. Greatly alarmed by the situation in Iran, the U.S. government engineered a coup that toppled Mossadeq and restored the shah to power. It is an indisputable fact that the coup succeeded with relative ease because most conservative politicians and many among the *ulama* were anxious to be rid of Mossadeq. Just as it had happened in 1921, a foreign-instigated coup was to unleash a prolonged period of dictatorship on the Iranian people.

Once restored to power, Mohammad Reza Shah consolidated all power into his own hands. Just as his father had done, he forcefully carried out a series of "reforms" that were deeply resented by large segments of the population and the ulama. He set about acquiring more wealth. The lessons of Reza Shah's experiment were completely lost on his son. Mohammad Reza Shah was oblivious to the fact that his father undertook a series of "reforms" that were profoundly unpopular. He chose to ignore the outpouring of popular joy that greeted Reza Shah's departure for exile. He thought that the same could not happen to him. He was sadly mistaken. By far the most important of these "reforms" were the land distributions that were undertaken between 1962 and 1971. In this book I examine the nature and consequences of these land distributions, as well as the manner in which hundreds of thousands of petty landowners were expropriated and deprived of their means of livelihood and their life sav-

Fig. 1.1. *From left to right:* Ali Qoli Khan Bakhtiari, Sardar Asad, Prince Abdol Hosein Mirza Farmanfarma, and Mohammad Vali Khan Tonekaboni, Sepahdar Azam, after the liberation of Tehran, 1909.

ings. In reality, what the shah did to small landowners in Iran was similar to what Stalin had done to the kulaks in Russia in the late 1930s.

The army from Gilan that marched on Tehran in July 1909 was commanded by Mohammad Vali Khan Tonekaboni, Sepahdar Azam (1844–1926). Sepahdar and his ancestors were courtiers who had been intimately associated with the Qajars since the 1770s (see chap. 3). He was also one of the largest landowners in Iran. The army from Isfahan was commanded by Ali Qoli Khan Bakhtiari, Sardar Asad, who was also a large landowner. In this early resistance to royal tyranny, landowners had taken the lead. Mohammad Vali Khan became the first prime minister after the restoration of the constitutional government, and Sardar Asad became interior minister. The Second Majlis was elected during this government. Forty years later, the fierce and ultimately unsuccessful resistance of 1951–53 to royal tyranny was led by another landowner, Dr. Mohammad Mossadeq. His successor as prime minister, General Fazlollah Zahedi, was also a landowner. He was soon dismissed and sent into exile. This book describes another challenge to royal arbitrary power and tyranny that was mounted by Iran's landowners in cooperation with the ulama between 1959 and 1964. The alliance of landowners and ulama had deep roots. As described in this study, the history of Iran during the entire Pahlavi period (1926–79) was characterized by a struggle between the two Pahlavi shahs and Iran's landowners and ulama. The struggle greatly weakened the Pahlavi regime and contributed to its overthrow in 1979.

Background to Land Distribution

During the cold war years following World War II, the U.S. government and international agencies such as the World Bank and the Food and Agriculture Organization of the United Nations strongly advocated and pushed for land reform in countries that were under U.S. influence. Examples of American-sponsored reforms include the land distribution programs in Japan, South Korea, Taiwan, South Vietnam, the Philippines, and El Salvador as well as in Iran. Land reform in Iran (1962–71) consisted of taking land from landowners and presenting it on highly favorable terms to the tenants who already cultivated the land. By giving the land to the "landless" tenants, it was believed that a communist revolution or takeover would be avoided and greater political and social stability achieved. The U.S. government had pushed for a land distribution in Iran since the 1940s. It aided Mohammad Reza Shah in setting up Bank Omran in 1952 to supervise the sale and distribution of the villages that his father had acquired. Following intense government pressure, the Majlis finally passed a moderate land distribution law in May 1960, and this was duly approved by the shah. But the newly elected administration of President John F. Kennedy was not happy with this law. In May 1961, the "reform" cabinet of Ali Amini was appointed, and the shah dismissed the Majlis. No new elections were announced.

In January 1962, the land reform law of May 1960, which had been approved by both houses of parliament and duly signed by the shah, was "improved and amended" by a cabinet decree. Thereafter, on the basis of a series of cabinet decrees, a most radical land distribution was implemented between 1962 and 1971. Given that legislation or amendment of an existing law was the constitutional right of the elected parliament and not that of the shah's cabinet, the decrees were a grave violation of Iran's Constitution and laws. It is highly lamentable that writers and researchers in the West have been unaware of, or have chosen to ignore, this grave subversion of the legal process and violation of Iran's Constitution.[3] The 1962 decree and the subsequent ones, including the Additional Articles to the Amended Land Reform Law of January 1963, also known as Phase Two, were apparently the work of one man: Hasan Arsanjani. Thus, the

actions that were destined to determine the fate of 3 million rural households, or 15 million people, were implemented by mere "cabinet decrees"
that were prepared and issued overnight. One could hardly expect intelligent and compassionate policy under such circumstances.

Land distribution in Iran did not result in the political stability predicted in the theoretical literature. The Pahlavi regime was unable to
strengthen and enlarge its political base, and a monarchical system that
had lasted for 2,500 years was overthrown shortly after the completion of
a major land distribution. It is the purpose of this book to describe what
transpired in Iran during the land distributions of 1962–71. One of my
main findings is that Ann K. S. Lambton's long accepted views on landownership in Iran were in serious error. Contrary to Lambton's belief that
most of the land was owned by large landowners, much of the agricultural land in Iran was the property of small landowners, whose numbers
were far greater than has been realized. Moreover, since the U.S. government policy on land appears to have been based on Lambton's erroneous
views, American policy with respect to the land question was fundamen-
tally flawed. Because land distribution in Iran transferred the ownership
of land to the cultivating tenants, it resulted in the expropriation and disenfranchisement of a large group of people who were deprived of their
livelihood with little compensation. In addition, large numbers belonging
to the urban professional classes, middle classes, and lower middle
classes lost their life savings, retirement nests, their inheritance, and often
their only source of income. In the final phase of land distribution, the
number of landowners expropriated exceeded that of the peasant beneficiaries.

In response, landowners were able to forge an effective and powerful
alliance with the ulama, including Ayatollah Khomeini, who had the political acumen and courage to seize the leadership of the religious opposition in Qom as early as 1961. By its adversarial land policies, the Pahlavi
regime may have gained the allegiance of some of Iran's peasants, but in
the process it alienated important groups, including the ulama. The alliance of the landowners with the ulama was actually much older, extending at least to the time of Reza Shah (1926–41). He had begun the attack on
traditional landowners and the ulama, and it was simply being continued
by his son. Faced with powerful opposition, the Pahlavi regime resorted
to force and intimidation and the silencing of the opposition. It then tried
to cover up the extent of the confiscation under land distribution. It delayed the publication of the 1960 census of agriculture for a decade, and
then it suppressed useful data on landownership and put out conflicting
and inconsistent data on landowners expropriated. But it was all to no

avail. The uprising of 5 June 1963 marked the beginning of the Islamic Revolution.

Memoirs of Mohammad Ali Majd, Fatn ol Saltaneh

This study is made possible and draws heavily on the private papers and unpublished memoirs of my father, Mohammad Ali Majd, Fatn ol Saltaneh (1891–1978). Majd was a landowner who held numerous government posts and was a Majlis deputy and a senator. In 1956–57, he incurred the shah's displeasure and was forced out of the Senate. He never held public office again. In 1959, following rumors of an impending land distribution, he began organizing Iran's landowners and founded the Agricultural Union of Iran. Its leaders included former cabinet ministers and Majlis deputies, as well as members of the senior ulama. Majd knew

Fig. 1.2. Mohammad Ali Majd, Fatn ol Saltaneh, 1950.

that he was participating in events that were likely to have far-reaching consequences for Iran. Following the silencing of the opposition in 1964, he began writing his memoirs. He was careful to preserve important documents such as the original fatwas by the ulama against land distribution, including that of Ayatollah Khomeini. Thanks to him, a new and more accurate account of the events of this period can be given. This study also makes use of declassified State Department records held in the National Archives. The material clarifies the role the United States played in shaping Iran's land policy between 1951 and 1971.

Landowners and the ulama were actively allied from the beginning of the resistance to the shah in 1959, and important personalities had declared their opposition to the proposed land confiscation-distribution policy as early as 1960. Landowners quickly became victims of the government's propaganda and the open encouragement given to peasants to seize land by violence and drive out the owners. The small landowners who resided in the villages fled the countryside. They took refuge in urban areas, where they lived in poverty. They lost access to their property and means of livelihood. Many people's savings and retirement funds were wiped out. In short, as the consequence of the "reform," more than 5 million individuals were reduced to poverty. These disenfranchised people were to be heard from in June 1963 and again in 1978.

Overview

Chapter 2 follows Majd's political career from 1932 until 1957. Chapter 3 describes the manner in which Reza Shah acquired vast areas of Iran and the often tragic consequences for those who happened to own the land that Reza Shah coveted. Chapter 4 recounts what became of the lands acquired by Reza Shah and the land sales and distributions by Mohammad Reza Shah. It thus provides a background to the land distributions of the 1960s. The chapter also describes the events that led to the emergence of Mohammad Ali Majd as one of the most important landowners in Iran.

Chapter 5 describes the founding of the Agricultural Union of Iran in 1959, a pioneering political organization of landowners, and its first skirmish with the government over the passage of the land reform law that was eventually approved by the Majlis and the Senate in May 1960. In this initial fight, the landowners sought the help of the senior ulama, especially Ayatollah Borujerdi, who responded with a fatwa. The opposition's initial appearance of success greatly annoyed the shah. The chapter then gives an account of the appointment of the Amini-Arsanjani government, the vicious propaganda campaign and violence against landowners, and the approval of the 1962 cabinet decree that "amended" the 1960 land reform law. It is shown that as a consequence of Arsanjani's policies, both large and small owners were driven from the countryside. While it may not have been the original intention to expropriate the small owners, they too were dispossessed of their land. Thereafter, the government lost initiative, and its policy became one of response to the prevailing situation it had created. Phase Two and Phase Three of land distribution were simply "legalization" of the prevailing conditions. It is also shown that because the government incited the peasants, it was forced to distribute villages that had been endowed for charitable and religious purposes (*vaqf-e amm*), thereby further alienating the religious establishment.

Using State Department records, chapter 6 examines American land policy in Iran between 1951 and 1963. After supporting land distribution in the early 1950s, the U.S. embassy and the State Department became fearful of the potential political and economic hazards. The State Department decided that there was no pressing need for land distribution in Iran and concluded that the greatest danger facing the shah's regime was a "hasty and thoughtless" policy. Faced with domestic opposition, and urged by the U.S. embassy to exercise caution, even the shah himself decided to proceed slowly and carefully with the implementation of the 1960 land distribution law. The records reveal that in early 1961 there was a complete reversal in American policy concerning land distribution in Iran, and the shah was pushed to proceed at full speed. The evidence leaves no doubt that the shah was pressured by the U.S. government to adopt policies that were against his better judgment and that were ultimately disastrous to Iran as well as the Pahlavi regime. Shortly before the uprising of 5 June 1963, the U.S. government realized that things had gone terribly wrong, but by then it was too late. Thereafter, the U.S. government distanced itself from land distribution, and by late 1968 it was criticizing the shah for his "hasty and ill considered" actions.

Chapter 7 gives the main publications, bulletins, and position papers of the Agricultural Union of Iran between 1961 and 1963. The position papers describe the actual agricultural conditions in Iran, the structure and nature of landownership, the role of landowners in digging and maintaining irrigation systems (*qanats*) and building new villages,[4] and the relationship between landowners and tenants. The material provides fresh insight and describes the manner in which the government violated Iran's Constitution and religious laws. It also describes publications that were put out by organizations of small landowners. These publications point to a part of land distribution that has remained completely unexplored, namely, the expropriation and plight of the huge class of small landowners. It is only after examining this evidence that one begins to understand some of the political and social consequences of land distribution.

Chapter 8 describes the landowners' appeal to the ulama in Najaf and Qom and the alliance that was established between landowners and the ulama from the very beginning of the resistance in 1959. The material is clearly of historical significance. The ulama's opposition to the land confiscation-distribution policies was far greater than has been described in the literature. After the death of Ayatollah Borujerdi in March 1961, no supreme Source of Emulation emerged. Consequently, there was some disarray within the ulama, and the response to the landowners' appeal was far from united. The evidence indicates that the Najaf-based ulama responded with a series of fatwas that declared the shah's land confiscation policies to be in conflict with the laws of Islam. In Qom, only Ayatollah Ruhollah Khomeini responded to the landowners' appeal, and he was the first alem (cleric) in Qom who after the death of Ayatollah Borujerdi had issued a fatwa denouncing the proposed land confiscation policies. By his early and courageous action, Ayatollah Khomeini was to emerge as the leader of the religious opposition. Eventually, in response to government actions and outright provocation, including the attempt by the government to portray the ulama as supporters of land distribution, the remaining ulama declared their opposition to the land confiscation policies. The fatwas and declarations against land distribution by the ulama were obtained by the Agricultural Union of Iran, printed as pamphlets, and distributed.

The large landowners were not the only ones to appeal to the ulama. By its land distribution policies, the Pahlavi regime also alienated petty landowners and much of the urban middle class. In this situation of profound turmoil and unease, many looked to the ulama for guidance and protection. Consequently, rather than having been weakened by the expropriation of the religious endowments, the ulama were vastly strengthened. The historical role of Ayatollah Khomeini was to seize control of the opposition early on.

Not realizing that U.S. policy was based on a dogged disregard for and ignorance of conditions in Iran, the opposition was convinced that land distribution was an American plot designed to destroy Iran's agriculture and force her to import food in exchange for oil. In this "satanic" conspiracy, the United States collaborated with the shah and his government. Chapter 9 recounts my father's dealings with two senior members of the U.S. legation in Iran, senior diplomat James C. O'Neil and Gen. John C. Hayden. Majd's emergence as an opposition politician attracted the attention of American and British officials, who initiated contacts with him.

Hoping to be able to influence U.S. policy, Majd responded to the overtures and met with O'Neil and Hayden. The British ambassador, Sir G. W. Harrison, and his wife visited Majd's estate in Mazandaran. Majd's friendly dealings with American officials, however, were short-lived. A few months after O'Neil left Iran, Majd and his associates were betrayed by the American embassy, and their supposedly confidential letters were given to Arsanjani, as well as to the domestic and foreign press.

Chapter 10 describes the manner in which the opposition was suppressed and eventually silenced. With other forms of political activity barred, the opposition resorted to street protests between 1961 and 1963. The government responded with violence. The timing and force of the protests of 21 January 1962 and the violent upheavals in the spring of 1963, which culminated in the protests of June 1963, reflected the anger of the urban middle class, who were faced with the loss of their savings and livelihood, and the desperate plight of the petty landowners, who had been driven from the villages and had lost everything. In addition, the tribal rebellions in the spring of 1963 reflected a futile attempt by the tribes to resist the confiscation of their lands. All were brutally suppressed. But for the Pahlavi regime, it was the beginning of the end. The uprising of 5 June 1963 is now commemorated as the beginning of the Islamic Revolution. Government retaliation against the opposition included personal vilification, libel, confiscation of property, intimidation, and detention. Authoritarian regimes do not tolerate independent political organizations. Under the prevailing conditions, the Agricultural Union of Iran was forced to discontinue its open political activities. The chapter also contains an account of Majd's legal challenge to the shah's land policies, the outcome of the suit, and the shah's referendum of 26 January 1963.

Chapter 11 discusses the modern theory of land reform, and it is shown that many of the theory's conditions and assumptions were absent in Iran. Consequently, a land distribution that simply gave the land to the tenants and removed the owners was unlikely to result in greater output and efficiency. Such distribution had adverse long-term economic and social consequences. The chapter then gives case studies of landownership, landlord-tenant relations, investment role of landowners, and the actual practice of land distribution in numerous regions of Iran. The firsthand account of landownership and land distribution in these villages, the investment role of landowners, landowner-tenant relations, discussion of rural taxation, the valuation of the land on the basis of the land tax, and the inequities and absurdities of the regulations that were prepared and issued overnight—all provide new insights into this important episode in Iran's agrarian and political history. It is only by studying such detailed and documented case studies that one begins to understand some of the consequences of land distribution in Iran. The chapter also describes and documents grave violations of the land distribution regulations that were committed by the government. The chapter also gives a detailed account of how land distribution affected an elderly widow who was a small land-owner in Mazandaran. Her property was systematically confiscated, and she was reduced to poverty. This is a particularly important case study because it documents the manner in which small landowners, those who owned a few hectares or a small fraction of a *dang*,[5] were systematically deprived of their means of livelihood with little compensation.

Chapter 12 gives a statistical account of the winners and losers under land distribution. More than half of the land was owned by small land-lords, and land "reform" resulted in the expropriation of at least 1.3 million persons. Overall, 1.8 million tenants on private, government, and endowed land benefited and received land. Thus, while land distribution benefited a huge number of people, it also resulted in the financial ruin of nearly as many others. Chapter 13 discusses a theory of landownership in an Islamic system, one that explains the coexistence of large, medium, and small ownerships. This ancient system was efficient, dynamic, and equitable. Its demise resulted in the neglect and ruin of many qanats and the transformation of Iran into one of the largest agricultural importers in the world. In addition, the disenfranchisement of Iran's landowners was clearly of immense political and social significance. The dissatisfaction weakened the Pahlavi regime and contributed to its overthrow. Chapter 13 also summarizes the main findings and raises some issues concerning the land policies of the Islamic Republic. Despite the pronouncements of the ulama before coming to power, the Islamic Republic has continued to confiscate and redistribute land. Moreover, these policies have conflicted with the fatwas and declarations by the ulama, particularly those of Ayatollah Khomeini himself between 1961 and 1963. This raises sensitive issues of religious law and dogma as well as public policy that need to be explored in other studies.

2

Political Career of Mohammad Ali Majd, Fatn ol Saltaneh

From Supporter to Opponent of the Pahlavis

My father, Mohammad Ali Majd (1891–1978), gives an account of his early years in his memoirs. He was born in Qazvin into a religious family. His father, Sheik Mohammad Majd ol Kottab (also known as Shali), founded Majdieh School in Rasht in 1906. This was the second "modern" school in Rasht, the first being established in 1899 by my maternal great-grandfather, Mohammad Vali Khan Tonekaboni, Sepahdar Azam. In 1908, Sheik Mohammad became head of Omid School in Qazvin, the only school in Qazvin, a post that he held until his death in 1918. He was an established calligrapher, and his work, dated 1890, adorns the front of the Shrine of Shahzadeh Hosein in Qazvin. On the paternal side, Majd was a descendant of the Shia Mojtahed and Source of Emulation Sheik Abd ol-Al Karaki, whose title was Khatam ol Mojtahedin (the Ultimate Mojtahed).[1] Karaki had come to Iran at the invitation of the Safavi Shah Tahmasb I (1524–76). On the maternal side, Majd was a great-grandson of Hamid Khan of Azarbaijan, one of the political notables during the reign of Fath Ali Shah (1797–1834), and Mohammad Shah (1834–48). After the Russo-Persian Wars of 1828, Hamid Khan moved to Qazvin where he later participated in an unsuccessful rebellion against Nasser ad Din Shah (1848–96). He was put to death, and all fourteen of his sons fled or were exiled. Eventually, his sons were pardoned, and one, Kazem Khan, returned to Qazvin. One of his daughters became Majd's mother.

Although he came from a strict religious background, Majd attended the Russian school in Qazvin, and upon graduation, he and Abdol Samad Kambaksh were granted scholarships to study in Russia. Because his mother opposed the idea, Majd reluctantly declined the offer, and in his place Hedayatollah Khan Samii was sent to Moscow. Samii was killed during the Russian Revolution, and Kambaksh returned as a dedicated communist and served on the Central Committee of the Tudeh Party. In 1911, Majd entered the elite School of Political Science for a five-year program. His instructors included two future prime ministers, Mohammad Ali Foroughi and Ali Mansur. An excellent student, Majd also studied French. His fluency brought him to the attention of Ahmad Qavam, a capable politician and future prime minister, who needed someone to help him sharpen his French language skills. Majd entered government service in 1916 on the strength of a recommendation from Qavam. As his first government post, he was placed in charge of the confidential communications of the cabinet. He held this post for nearly three years, during which time there were five prime ministers: Ala ol Saltaneh, Ein ad Dowleh, Samsam ol Saltaneh, Vusuq ad Dowleh, and Mostofi al Mamalek. Between 1918 and 1928, his career advanced rapidly. In 1918, he became deputy head of the Bureau of Agriculture. In 1919, he was appointed supervisor of the Office of Trade, Industry, and Licenses. In 1920 he was given the title of Fatn ol Saltaneh by Ahmad Shah. The following year, he was appointed the government representative to the Caspian Fisheries, and in 1922, he became head of the Office of Trade, Industry, and Licenses. In 1923, in recognition of his services as a government employee, he received from Ahmad Shah the Order of Lion and Sun (2d class). In 1926, he was appointed head of the Bureau of Commerce in the Ministry of Public Interest (subsequently renamed Ministry of Industry and Mines).

In 1928, he married my mother, Shams ol Moluk Khalatbari Tonekaboni, Amir Banou (1909–1990). She was a daughter of Mohammad Qoli Khan Tonekaboni, Amir Entesar (1874–1936), and a granddaughter of Mohammad Vali Khan Tonekaboni, Sepahsalar Azam (1844–1926). A brief history of the Khalatbaris of Mazandaran is given in chapter 3. At this point, suffice it to say that by marrying Amir Banou, Majd had joined the remnants of the Qajar landed aristocracy. Thereafter, Majd's advancement slowed considerably. He was appointed head of the Karaj Agricultural College in 1929 and head of the Office of Pest Control in Lorestan the following year. In 1932, he directed the Bureau of Mines, Fisheries, and Licenses, and in 1933, he became head of the Office of Government Factories. Evidently, his connection with the Khalatbaris, who were perceived as opponents of Reza Shah, had damaged his prospects. His rapid political rise resumed in 1935. Reza Shah sent word that he wished to acquire the estates of Zavar in Tonekabon. Zavar was mostly the property of my maternal grandfather. Having seen firsthand Reza Shah's brutality in matters related to land and property, Majd offered the property to His

Left: Fig. 2.1. Shams ol Moluk Entesar Khalatbari, Amir Banou Majd, circa 1930.

Below: Fig. 2.2. Prince Adl ol Mamalek *(front left)*, Moham- mad Qoli Tonekaboni, Amir Entesar *(center)*, and Hasan Tonekaboni, Amir Momtaz *(front right)*, Qazvin, 1905.

Majesty without hesitation. This act greatly pleased the shah, and Majd's political career resumed its rapid advancement.

In 1936, Seyed Mehdi Farrokh became governor-general of West Azarbaijan, and he selected Majd as deputy governor. In October 1936, Reza Shah visited West Azarbaijan, and it became clear that Majd's political fortunes were on the rise. In the following year, Farrokh became minister of industry and mines, and Majd was appointed undersecretary of state. A year later, Reza Shah chose Majd to lead Iran's economic mission in Europe. Since Reza Shah and the Iranian government were engaged in large-scale purchase of factories and machinery, this was a significant mission. Majd spent large sums buying industrial equipment and factories. In 1939, following a dispute with the new minister of industry, he was recalled from Europe. After Reza Shah reviewed the case himself, the minister was dismissed, and Majd was reinstated. However, as a clear sign of his unhappiness with the state of affairs and with his treatment, Majd resigned and went to Europe with the intention of leaving Iran permanently. His career in the Pahlavi system appeared to be at an end. His time in Europe was cut short by the outbreak of war. Following the first bombing of Berlin in September 1939, he returned to Iran.

Fig. 2.3. Reza Shah (*right, hand extended*) on an inspection tour of West Azarbaijan, October 1936. Also seen are Hosein Shokuh ol Molk, chief of Reza Shah's Special Bureau (*far right*), and Mohammad Ali Majd (*center*).

Governor of Gilan, 1941

Despite all that had transpired a year earlier, Majd was invited to rejoin government service, and he became governor of the province of Gilan in February 1941. Given Gilan's proximity to the Soviet Union and the war in Europe, this was a sensitive appointment. In addition, given that nearly all commerce and travel to Europe and pilgrimage to Mecca and the holy shrines of Iraq passed through Gilan, the population of Gilan was relatively cosmopolitan and cultured.[2] Before the 1917 revolution, many in Gilan traveled regularly to Russia and even beyond. Moreover, located on the Caspian coast and with an annual rainfall of nearly two meters, Gilan was a land of dense forests, rivers, and fertile farmlands. It produced much of Iran's rice. It was also a region where Reza Shah wished to acquire more land. It turned out that Majd's appointment was a wise choice. Speaking Russian, he was the right man for the job. With his appointment as governor of Gilan, and his subsequent actions as governor before, during, and after the Russian occupation of Gilan and the neighboring province of Mazandaran, Majd was transformed from a senior civil servant into a person of national standing. Majd was to win election to the Majlis and the Senate with large majorities. It began with his appointment as governor of Gilan.

Majd recalls his audience with the shah on the occasion of his appointment as governor of Gilan. What he noticed was that Reza Shah said nothing about conditions in Gilan or what Majd's duties were. Instead, he questioned Majd for half an hour about his mission to Europe some three years earlier and the prices that had been paid for the various factories and machinery, some of which had been purchased for Reza Shah and were his personal property, especially the factories in Mazandaran and some near Tehran. Two months later, in April 1941, Reza Shah was on one of his regular visits to Gilan and Mazandaran, and again his preoccupation was to acquire more land, specifically the estates of Ashraf Amini, Fakhre ad Dowleh, daughter of Mozzafar ad Din Shah and mother of Ali Amini, a future prime minister. Thus, with the world at war, on the very eve of the German invasion of Russia, and just before the Allies invaded Iran, a main preoccupation of Reza Shah, and by implication those who served under him, was to expand his already vast holdings. No wonder that the entire edifice collapsed like a house of cards after the Red Army invaded northern Iran. As it became clear from the torrent of newspaper articles that were printed following the removal of Reza Shah, and the brief period of press freedom between 1941 and 1947, the reason Reza Shah had not spoken to Majd about his mission and duties as governor was simple. All provincial governors were supposed to know what their duties were. They were to be instruments of a harsh and authoritarian system. They arrived with empty pockets and left with immense wealth.

In Majd's private papers, there are numerous clippings from *Badr Monir*, a newspaper published in the city of Rasht, the capital of Gilan. From these clippings one gains insight into the conditions that prevailed under Reza Shah, the "thick wall of hatred and mistrust" that separated government officials and the people of Gilan, and the suffering of the people during the twenty years that Reza Shah ruled Iran. The existing literature on Reza Shah has dwelt on the positive side, the building of railways and factories, institutional reforms, and "modernization." These articles present a side that has been badly neglected. One learns of the tyranny and the grim conditions that had prevailed under Reza Shah. They also describe the reasons why Majd became such a popular governor.

From the beginning he had set about reversing the existing ways. He quickly established cordial relations with the Soviet officials. He records in his memoirs that when he arrived in Gilan, government officials seemed duty-bound to mistreat Soviet officials and violate their obvious rights. In one particularly nasty incident, two women from the Soviet consulate in Pahlavi had been insulted (or assaulted) on the streets by thugs, and the previous governor had not taken any steps to punish the offenders. Majd reversed the policy, and in the process he incurred Reza Shah's displeasure. Upon arrival in Gilan, Reza Shah's first action was to question Majd about the close relationship that he had established with the Russians. It had required two hours of explanation and reasoning by Majd to satisfy Reza Shah that the previous policy of deliberate mistreatment of Soviet citizens and officials was not in the interest of the country or of its monarchy. Iran shared a border of 2,800 kilometers with the Soviet Union. Previous governors had alienated a powerful neighbor and had in no way served the nation's interests.

Majd also changed the ways government functioned in Gilan. He initiated an "open door" policy. He did not use his office for personal enrichment. Instead, he set an example for other government officials to follow. For the people of Gilan, Majd represented a side of government that had long been forgotten. They grew to trust him. When the British and Soviet armies simultaneously invaded Iran on 25 August 1941, many government officials, from the provincial governors and army commanders to the lowly district administrators, abandoned their posts and fled. According to *Badr Monir*, they used government trucks to transport all their belongings, including the smallest morsel of charcoal, to Shiraz and Kerman. It is not clear whom they feared most, the local population or the Soviets. In any event, they abandoned the people when they were needed most. In contrast, Majd had no reason to run. He remained at his post and gained the love and gratitude of the people. After the government and the army disintegrated, the people's only source of assurance and security was to see the governor in their midst.

Soviet Invasion of August 1941

In the early hours of 25 August 1941, my father was awakened by telephone and informed that the Soviet army, navy, and air force had attacked Gilan at several points, and the Russians were landing troops at Bandar Pahlavi. Majd provides a detailed account of events in Gilan during that critical week and his actions as governor. It was his initial response and his subsequent actions during the months following the occupation that endeared him to the people of Gilan and gained him national stature. His reports and telegrams to the central government during this period are maintained in Iran's National Archives. Some of these reports were recently published in a wartime documentary volume on the years 1939–45.[3]

Majd reports that under the command of Brigadier Qadar, whom Majd calls a brave and patriotic soldier, the Eleventh Army was immediately mobilized. He was witness to the outpouring of patriotism by the four thousand soldiers of the Eleventh Army, whose only weapons against Russian tanks and armor were rifles and machine guns. At this time, Majd had learned that the Eleventh Army's supplies of ammunition were very limited and that some of the artillery shells were actually the wrong kind, there were no tanks or armor, and there was no air protection.[4] Nevertheless, troops were well positioned to defend Gilan because of a topography that consisted of dense forests, flooded rice fields, marshes, and numerous rivers. Under these conditions, the Soviet tanks and armor did not count for much because they could only operate on the few roads that could be defended by infantry and artillery. Majd reports that the Soviet advance was halted at Gorgan Rud by the courageous resistance of the Eleventh Army, several other Soviet landing attempts were driven off by the shore batteries, and the Eleventh Army quickly secured its rear by occupying the heights of southern Gilan. At the same time, all heads of government bureaus were warned that any dereliction of duty or cowardice would bring dire consequences. Thus, what transpired in Gilan in the days following the Soviet invasion was completely different from what took place in Azarbaijan and Khorasan where there was no organized resistance by the Iranian army. Later, it became known that as soon as the

Soviet army entered Azarbaijan, the governor and the commander of the Iranian army fled to Tehran. Both had used army trucks to transport all their belongings, including the commander's flock of turkeys. Similarly in Khorasan, the army commander had escaped as soon as the Russian forces had entered the province. It thus appears that only in Gilan had the Iranian army put up any resistance to the enemy and had actually halted the Soviet advance. In contrast, the commanders of the army in Khorasan and Azarbaijan had run away.

After the Soviet advance was halted in Gilan, urgent appeals for reinforcement and air cover were sent to Tehran. Tehran replied that none was available. On the night of 26 August, there was a probing attack by the Eleventh Army. The Soviets had taken a defensive posture and were not in a position to break out. The military situation had apparently stabilized by the third day. After three days of successful and courageous resistance by the Eleventh Army, word came from Tehran that because Tabriz had fallen and the Russian army was advancing on Qazvin, the Eleventh Army was to abandon Gilan and take up a defensive position in Mazandaran. This order, which did not make sense, was disobeyed by Brigadier Qadar and the other officers of the Eleventh Army. To Majd's dismay and disgust, on 28 August, Tehran again ordered the abandonment of Gilan and the redeployment of the Eleventh Army to Mazandaran. An hour later, Tehran ordered cessation of resistance and asked that the Soviet army be so advised. On 29 August, the Eleventh Army ceased resistance. With the de facto dissolution of the Eleventh Army, the Soviet army was finally able to take Bandar Pahlavi, and its tanks moved toward Rasht. For Mohammad Ali Majd, Brigadier Qadar, and the inhabitants of Gilan, the hour of crisis had arrived.

Despite the declaration of a cessation of resistance, and the return of the soldiers of the Eleventh Army to the barracks, on the morning of Friday, 29 August, twenty-seven Russian aircraft bombed Rasht and several other cities, killing several hundred and injuring many more. It was clearly intended to terrorize the population. Majd heard the cries of the defenseless people of Rasht. As the bombs fell and the streets were strafed, all he could do was to maintain a visible posture by walking the streets between the governor's office and the telegraph office to reassure the people of Gilan that he remained in their midst and that they should remain calm. Having reached the telegraph office, he found the doors locked. With great difficulty he located the telephone and telegraph operator and persuaded him to come and open the doors. He then telephoned Interior Minister Ameri. Learning that Ameri had gone to Shemiran, he telephoned Prime Minister Foroughi's house to ask for instructions. Unable to reach Foroughi, he left a message with his son. An hour later, Foroughi instructed Majd to contact Reza Shah's office. Majd continues:

> In desperation, I telephoned Saad Abad Palace and asked for Mr. Shokuh ol Molk, Chief of His Majesty's Special Bureau, and with great difficulty explained the situation in Gilan. After two hours of waiting and repeated attempts to telephone Saad Abad Palace, eventually at around one in the afternoon, Mr. Shokuh ol Molk replied that His Majesty was informed, but did not say anything.[5] In the meantime, the telegraph office was repeatedly attacked and strafed by aircraft. Having lost hope, and in total isolation and greatly saddened, I walked back to my house. Having received no instruction and cut off from the rest of the world, for half an hour I paced up and down the living room. I was wondering whether I should get into the governor's car bearing the number plate "Gilan 1" and escape to Tehran. Or should I risk my life for the sake of duty, the defense of life and property of the people of Gilan, and the honor and dignity of the government? I thank God that I chose the second path. I then went to inform my wife, Amir Banou Majd, of my decision to stay in Gilan, and to suggest to her that she should save herself and leave immediately for Qazvin and then go to Tehran. She was at prayer in her room. She carefully listened to what I said, and then tearfully informed me that she was not going to leave Gilan. She said that our destinies were joined. If we lived, then we lived together, and if we died, then we would die together. Martyrdom in the service of the country was a supreme honor, and if we lived and Gilan was saved, it would also be an honor for us and our descendants.

Certain events in the life of each individual and the responses to these events are so significant that they are said to constitute a defining moment. For Mohammad Ali Majd, that defining moment came in the days following the Soviet invasion. It is a matter of record that of the provincial governors, only two remained at their posts during the Soviet attack and thus fulfilled their duty to their country in its hour of greatest need. They were Mohammad Ali Majd of Gilan and Fatollah Pakravan of Khorasan. Baqer Aqeli quotes Foroughi as saying that in the days following the invasion, "government representatives and agents have abandoned their posts from fear. As the result, government authority has vanished in most towns and cities. Of the governor-generals, only Pakravan has remained in Mashhad, and of the governors, only Fatn ol Saltaneh Majd has remained in Rasht and is negotiating with the Russians."[6]

Governor of Second Province:
Struggle for Control of Mazandaran and Gorgan

Based on his record in Gilan, Majd was appointed by Ahmad Qavam to the post of governor-general of the Second Province in January 1943. The province consisted of the following regions: Mazandaran, Gorgan, Shahrud, Damghan, and Semnan. Located east of Gilan and bordering the Caspian Sea, Mazandaran and Gorgan were among the most important agricultural regions of Iran, producing most of Iran's rice, cotton, and citrus fruit. Similar to Gilan, the latter two regions consisted of dense forests, rice fields, and rivers. As Qavam put it, Majd's mission was "to try to bring back to Iran the region of Mazandaran and Gorgan." In effect, his task was to restore the authority of the Iranian government in an area under full Russian control, a dangerous mission. He arrived in Sari, the administrative capital and largest city in the Second Province, in mid-January 1943. He found a desperate situation in which for nearly two years the Soviets and their Tudeh Party allies had had a free hand to organize. With no government, the province was plagued by insecurity, lawlessness, and bloodshed. He describes the situation in Iran's Second Province.

> Unfortunately, the situation in the Second Province was far worse than what I had been told in Tehran by Mr. Qavam Saltaneh, Mrs. Fakhre ad Dowleh, and others. The Russians were in complete control of all government bureaus, and interfered in all the details of government, including tax collection and school curriculum. They controlled all the railways and rail stations. They had complete supervision of all the factories. There were a large number of persons from the Caucuses, pretending to be Iranians. For example, an individual by the name of Hosein Nouri inspected the government offices and issued orders, and for all practical purposes, he was the governor of Mazandaran. After some investigation, it was learned that he was from Georgia, and his real identity was Julien Eliassof. The Tudeh Party had established a wide-ranging and intricate relationship in all the factories in Shahi and Behshahr, the railways, and the other industrial establishments. On the one hand, they had di-

rect contact with the Russians and were in constant touch with the Central Committee of the Tudeh Party in Tehran. They generally wore the Order of Stalin, and in public places such as the rail stations, portraits of Lenin and Stalin had replaced that of the Holy Prophet and that of His Majesty, Mohammad Reza Shah Pahlavi.

According to reliable sources, the membership of Tudeh Party in Mazandaran was eleven thousand. They controlled all the factories and the railroads. They were engaged in three principal tasks. First, publicity against the government. Second, publicity in favor of the Soviet Union. Third, creating anarchy in Gorgan, Mazandaran, Semnan, and Damghan. In their secret meetings, the Soviet Commissars were frequently present. Hosein Nouri, or more appropriately, Julien Eliassof, issued direct orders or conveyed the orders of the Soviet leadership. In a large gathering in Shahi, Hosein Nouri had given a speech in which he had stated that Iran was dead and had been divided between Russia and England. He had also stated that the emblem of Lion and Sun belonged to Armenia and would be restored to its rightful owner. The audience, consisting of Tudeh Party members as well as immigrants from the Caucuses, had applauded and cheered loudly. In short, the same plan for the dismemberment of Iran that I had witnessed and neutralized in Gilan was openly and furiously being implemented in Mazandaran and Gorgan. The people of Gorgan and Mazandaran were naturally very unhappy with the state of affairs, but they dared not protest or do anything. Any protest was dealt with and silenced by the Tudeh Party. If necessary, the Russian army intervened directly on behalf of the Tudeh.

Reports came in every day from the police, the gendarmerie, and the administrators stating that the Tudeh was interfering in all the affairs and creating problems for the people. If government agents or the police attempted to prevent Tudeh meddling, they were insulted and often beaten up. On 20 November 1942, members of the Tudeh had ransacked the Art School in Shahi, beating up the students, fifty-three of whom were injured, two seriously, and had plundered the furniture and the contents of the building. There had been no response whatsoever from the authorities on the scene, and the government agents had acted as spectators. The Tudeh and Russian plan was to demonstrate the government's weakness by such actions and to humiliate government officials.

Arrest of the Tudeh Party Leadership and the Crisis

Majd's mission had been the restoration of the power of the Iranian government in the Second Province. With his mandate and faced with the desperate situation, he was required to act. But what to do was up to him. His most urgent task was to deal with the Tudeh threat. The problem of banditry and lawlessness could be addressed later. Courageously, he decided to meet the Tudeh Party head on and break up its organizational setup in Mazandaran. This was a difficult task in an area under direct Soviet military occupation.

Using the remnants of the gendarmerie and police, on 26 February 1943, Majd struck back by arresting the leadership of the Tudeh Party in Mazandaran, including "Hosein Nouri," who was a Soviet citizen. As described by Ramazani,[7] the arrests initiated a crisis with the Soviets in Mazandaran and with the Tudeh Party in Tehran. Backed by the government of Ali Soheili, Qavam's successor, Majd stood up to the Soviet pressures. Thereafter, the Soviets gradually abandoned their Tudeh Party allies, and Majd was able to restore the authority of the Iranian government in the Second Province.

The Fourteenth Majlis and the Azarbaijan Crisis, 1944–46

The historian Ervand Abrahamian has described the elections to the Fourteenth Majlis as "the most prolonged, the most competitive, and hence the most meaningful of all elections in modern Iran."[8] The Fourteenth Majlis is considered to have been the most free and democratically elected Majlis during the Pahlavi era. In recognition of his services in northern Iran between 1941 and 1943, and in what was a fierce electoral contest, Majd was elected from Qazvin to the Fourteenth Majlis in March 1944. The issue that preoccupied the Fourteenth Majlis was that of the Soviet-Iran relationship. After the war, the Soviets refused to leave Iran. The Tudeh Party in Azarbaijan was reconstituted into the Democratic Party of Azarbaijan, and it set about separating Azarbaijan from the rest of Iran. In the summer of 1945, the Democrats set about disarming the Iranian army garrisons and took over the government offices. When a force was dispatched from Tehran, it was stopped by the Soviet army near Qazvin, about 300 miles east of Tabriz. The separation of Azarbaijan was becoming a reality, and Iran was faced with the gravest crisis in its modern history. Iran was indeed fortunate that at this critical juncture in its history, thanks to the Fourteenth Majlis the leadership of the government was placed in the hands of the likes of Mohammad Saed, Mohsen Sadr (Sadr ol Ashraaf), and Ahmad Qavam (Qavam Saltaneh).

For Mohammad Ali Majd the gravity of the situation was driven home when as a Majlis deputy he was visiting his electoral district in the fall of 1945. On a stretch of road between Takestan and Qaraveh to the west of Qazvin, he saw a large sign in Russian stating "Granitza," meaning frontier.

At about the same time, a large fire consumed the Bazaar district of Qazvin. Majd was convinced that the fire had been set by the Tudeh Party and Russian sympathizers. Meanwhile, the situation in Tehran became desperate. It appeared that the government was powerless to prevent the separation of Azarbaijan. Mahmood Khan Zolfaqari, a landowner in Zanjan, secretly obtained some arms from the government and began to resist the Russian agents and the Democrats. Majd was convinced that if it were not for this brave and patriotic fight, the Democrats would have occupied Qazvin and threatened Tehran itself. Subsequently, they could have pressured the government into whatever they wanted and forced it to grant autonomy to Azarbaijan.

Encouraged by the example set by Zolfaqari, Majd spent all of his time and energy in organizing guerrilla movements to fight the Democrats and procuring arms from the army for delivery to the resistance. Procuring and delivering arms in areas that were under direct Russian occupation was risky. He was able to acquire several truckloads of arms for delivery to Jaffar Khan Rashvand, a landowner in the Rudbar Alamut region of Qazvin, and also to Hedayatollah Khan Yamini, a landowner in Hamedan. Together with Zolfaqari, Majd reports that these brave patriots were able to secure the northern and western regions of Qazvin and thus deny them to the enemy. In the fall of 1946, the Iranian army finally moved to retake Azarbaijan from Pishevari and the Democrats. In his memoirs, Majd includes letters written to him by his friend Seyed Haj Lotf Ali Khan Tabatabaii, who led the resistance against Pishevari. His account shows that well before the arrival of the army in Tabriz in December 1946, the people of Tabriz had risen up against Pishevari and had captured or put to flight most of his supporters. Thus, Tabriz was liberated before the arrival of the army.

Election of Hasan Arsanjani to the Fifteenth Majlis, 1947

With the solution of the Azarbaijan crisis, the tension between Qavam Saltaneh and the conservative politicians erupted. Qavam Saltaneh was deeply distrusted because he was perceived as pro-Russian. Convinced that Qavam would prevent his reelection, Majd decided not to run for reelection in the Fifteenth Majlis. He continued his opposition activities from outside the Majlis. An issue that had greatly upset the conservative politicians was the election to the Fifteenth Majlis of Hasan Arsanjani, a leftist newspaper editor. Arsanjani had written opinions in *Darya* that appeared to favor the continued Soviet occupation of northern Iran. In particular, one piece in the issue of 17 September 1945, no. 106, right at the height of the Azarbaijan crisis, had greatly offended and inflamed the conservative and nationalist opinion. In the article, Arsanjani argued that although the Soviet Union was to leave Iran in March 1946, the continued military occupation of Iran after that date was justified under the provision of article 5 of the 1921 Soviet-Iranian treaty. The conditions in Iran were such that the Soviet Union felt threatened and could thus invoke article 5. This editorial caused an uproar. When the Soviets refused to leave Iran, they gave the same reason as the one suggested by Arsanjani. They invoked article 5 of the 1921 Soviet-Iranian treaty. To make matters worse, in the pages of *Darya*, Arsanjani also advocated the confiscation of all privately owned agricultural land and its distribution among the tenant cultivators. According to Arsanjani, under Islam all land was owned by all the people, and private ownership of land constituted unlawful usurpation by the owner (*tasarof-e odvani*). Confiscation without compensation was thus justified under Islam.

Despite the fact that Arsanjani had no connection to Gilan, as a protégé of Ahmad Qavam he had been "elected" to the Fifteenth Majlis as the representative from Lahijan, Qavam's home base. It was clear to all that the election had been fixed. In what must be considered a stunning rebuke to Qavam Saltaneh and a humiliating defeat, the Majlis rejected Arsanjani's credentials and barred him from taking his seat in the chamber. In particular, citing Arsanjani's past writings, the Majlis branded him a traitor. The depth of anger and hostility toward Arsanjani can be seen by the front-page article in the newspaper *Keshvar*, dated 4 September 1947, no. 270. The headline read: "Rejection of Arsanjani's Credentials Is Demanded by Public Opinion. Arsanjani Is Not Qualified to Represent the People." Arsanjani's "thesis" was that the foreigners could continue to maintain their armies in Iran. At a time when treason in Azarbaijan was increasing, Arsanjani was demanding changes in the Constitution. The article stated that the Majlis contained several representatives who, like Arsanjani, had been forced upon the people. Unlike Arsanjani, none had taken any action against the independence and integrity of Iran.

Arsanjani was appointed minister of agriculture in Ali Amini's cabinet in 1961 and placed in charge of the shah's land distribution. Given that the deputies from Azarbaijan had led the movement to reject Arsanjani's credentials, it was not surprising that Azarbaijan was the first region where land distribution was carried out in 1962. In at least one of his books, Arsanjani falsely stated that he had been elected to the Majlis in 1947 and had served as a deputy.[9]

Royal Rebuff, 1949

Between 1947 and 1949, following the resolution of the Azarbaijan crisis and the removal of Ahmad Qavam, Mohammad Reza Shah began to gain some measure of control. In January 1949, he vetoed Majd's appointment as interior minister in the cabinet of Mohammad Saed. As outlined in much greater detail below, following the downfall of Reza Shah in 1941, Majd had sued in the Court of Assigned Estates for the recovery of land that the shah had confiscated. My mother had also sued for the recovery of property belonging to her grandfather, Mohammad Vali Khan Tonekaboni, Sepahsalar Azam. That is, even the governor of Gilan and Mazandaran and his wife had sued the Pahlavi estates for the recovery of land taken by Reza Shah. Not surprisingly, the shah's veto was related to this lawsuit.

Mossadeq and the Oil Nationalization Crisis, 1950–1953

Following this rebuff, Majd was without government employment and was tending to his private affairs. In June 1950, he was appointed governor-general of Gilan. In February 1951, he was dismissed at the insistence of Dr. Mohammad Mossadeq.

Majd writes that with the loss of oil revenues, the economic and political situation deteriorated rapidly after 1951. Mossadeq's inability to settle the oil dispute caused the situation to become more desperate. Abandoned by some of his associates, such as Ayatollah Kashani, Mossadeq became increasingly dependent on leftist groups, including the Tudeh Party. He also resorted to increasingly dictatorial and unconstitutional measures. He demanded plenary powers, including the power to legislate. He also dissolved the Supreme Court, abolished the Senate, and called a "referendum" to dissolve the Majlis. In this referendum, 99 percent of the electorate voted in the affirmative. There were two voting booths, one for the supporters and one for the opponents. No one dared to enter the negative booth. By October 1952, the situation had grown so desperate that men who had tried to stay on the sidelines were forced to make a choice.

Convinced that Mossadeq's policies were ruinous, Majd and a group of conservative politicians became active in support of the shah and General Fazlollah Zahedi, leader of the opposition and a landowner in Hamedan. Majd acted as liaison, and he and Zahedi became good friends.

Premiership of Zahedi and Majd's Election to the Senate

The American-sponsored coup d'état of 19 August 1953 succeeded easily because Mossadeq was opposed by a coalition that included practically all of Iran's large landowners, business interests, and the senior ulama. When General Zahedi became prime minister, those politicians who had opposed Mossadeq and backed the shah and Zahedi were rewarded with government positions and parliamentary seats. At the suggestion of General Zahedi, Majd ran for the Senate and was elected from Qazvin in April 1954. Many of his landowning friends were also elected to the Majlis and the Senate. However, the alliance of landowners with the shah was short-lived, and it broke down after the dismissal and exile of General Zahedi in April 1955. Thereafter, both the Senate and the Majlis became centers of opposition to the shah. As described in chapter 6, by the summer of 1955, many senators and deputies had become profoundly unhappy with the shah and his style of politics. In particular, parliament deeply resented the shah's appointment of Hosein Ala as the titular prime minister while the shah became his own prime minister. As the conversations between the U.S. diplomats and Iranian politicians show, many deputies and senators were unhappy with most of the shah's policies and with the rising levels of corruption and inefficiency in his government.

Majd had also become disillusioned with the shah by 1955, and as his Senate speeches show, he became an open opponent of Ala's government. Of course, such "loyal opposition" was not looked upon kindly by the shah because it was common knowledge that the real prime minister and the person who appointed all the ministers and determined policy was the shah himself. Determined to rule as well as reign, the shah once again set about packing parliament with supporters and driving out those politicians opposed to his style of government.

In March 1957, the shah was presented with an opportunity to get rid of some of his Senate opposition. According to the Senate regulations, the Senate's term was six years, and half of the sixty senators were elected and half were appointed by the shah. Halfway through the Senate's term, half of the senators would exit through lottery. If they were elected senators, they could stand for reelection, and if they were appointed senators, the shah could reappoint them or someone else. Majd's name came up in the lottery, and the shah blocked his reelection. The Senate changes were duly observed by the U.S. embassy.

In a confidential report on the outcome of the Senate drawings (Foreign Service despatch 841, dated 19 March 1957), John W. Bowling, second secretary at the American embassy in Tehran, reported with sarcasm that

Fig. 2.4. Group of senators visiting "Atom for Peace" exhibit, Tehran, 14 March 1957. *Left to right:* Mohammad Ali Majd, S. Hasan Taqizadeh, Jaffar Sharif-Emami, Mohammad Saed, Mohammad Ali Varasteh, unidentified man, Dr. Amir Aalam (*dark glasses*), unidentified man, Hosein Dadgar, Ali Mansur, Mohammad Sajadi, unidentified man (*white beard*).

the shah had not been "lucky," because only some of the opposition senators had been eliminated. The shah's "most persistent critic," Jamal Emami, had retained his seat for another three years. Bowling indicated that several of those senators whose names had been drawn were open critics or covert opponents of the government. Bowling reported that of these, "Majd had worked closely with Jamal Emami for the past six months of the current Senate session." Bowling also noted that since the shah was unlikely to permit the reelection of the opposition senators, the shah was well on his way to packing the Senate with people who in the opinion of the embassy were "politically undistinguished supporter[s] of the Government and the Shah." Many of these "supporters" became active opponents of the government by 1960.

Majd believed that the shah's displeasure was primarily due to his intervention on behalf of forty-two officers condemned to death. During 1954–55, some 600 army officers had been arrested on charges of belonging to the Tudeh Party. Twenty-seven had been executed. Another forty-two were awaiting execution. One of the condemned officers was Hosein Qoli Heshmati, son of Sohrab Heshmati, Majd's friend and constituent. Majd went to see the shah and asked that the officers be granted a royal pardon and that their sentences be commuted to prison terms. Reluctantly, the shah consented, but he was greatly displeased by Majd's intervention. Another reason for the shah's displeasure was that Majd had become known as an opponent of the sale and distribution of Pahlavi estates.

Having been forced out of the Senate, Majd was about to open a new chapter in his political career, one that would prove to be of lasting significance. In 1959 he founded the Agricultural Union of Iran (Etehadieh-e fellahati-e Iran) and served as its executive secretary. This was a political organization that came to organize and lead much of the resistance by Iran's landowners to the land confiscation policies of Mohammad Reza Shah during the "White Revolution" of the 1960s. It was also the organization that was allied with the senior ulama of the time, including Ayatollah Khomeini, in the joint struggle against the shah. To give additional background to this fascinating tale, it is necessary to give an account of the emergence of Mohammad Ali Majd as a large landowner during the time of Reza Shah.

3

Acquisition of Land and Wealth by Reza Shah

In the two decades that he was the real ruler of Iran (1921–41), Reza Shah amassed an immense fortune. He became the largest landowner in Iran's 2,500-year history.[1] A glimpse of his wealth is provided by Donald Wilber, an American intelligence agent who was posted in Iran between 1941 and 1945. Since a great deal of Reza Shah's domestic banking and financial records had been preserved in the Pahlavi Foundation, the material fell into the hands of the revolutionaries. After the Islamic Revolution, the assets and records of the Pahlavi Foundation were transferred to the newly established Alavi Foundation. The evidence indicates that Wilber's figures are not exaggerated. Moreover, as an avowed admirer of Reza Shah, Wilber was unlikely to exaggerate. Wilber reported that, upon his abdication in 1941, Reza Shah had 680 million rials on deposit at the Bank Melli.[2] This was a vast sum at a time when the entire Iranian government revenue (exclusive of oil income, which in any case was relatively small) was 1,250 million rials. At the prevailing exchange rate, 680 million rials was equivalent to $42 million. At 1999 prices, this would be approximately equal to $500 million.[3] This sum represented about one year's income from Reza Shah's domestic assets.

This sum did not include Reza Shah's foreign bank accounts for which documentary evidence exists. In 1952, Prime Minister Mohammad Mossadeq alleged that Reza Shah had diverted much of Iran's oil income to his personal bank accounts in America and Europe on the pretext of buying arms. He named a German employee of National Bank of Iran, a Dr. Lindenblatt, as the one handling the shah's early transfers. Lindenblatt's name and signature appear frequently in the documents. Another person whose name appears is a Colonel Amir-Khosrovi, whose post was that of director-general of Bank Pahlavi, the shah's private bank. Later in Reza Shah's reign, Amir-Khosrovi was appointed minister of finance, and he "sold" Reza Shah rural estates and urban properties that belonged to the government. As the documents illustrate, there was a great deal of activity with foreign banks in 1931–32, and each deposit to Reza Shah's various accounts was $150,000.[4] By the standards of the time, this was a great deal of money. On the basis of the American Consumer Price Index, $150,000 in 1931–32 would be equivalent to $2 million in 1998. The chain of instruction concerning two deposits of $150,000 each at the Westminster Bank in London is most revealing (see appendix A). Not surprisingly, the instructions came from Reza Shah himself. By 1931, he also maintained bank accounts in Germany and Switzerland. It is significant that these deposits were made well before Reza Shah acquired the bulk of his property and before Iran signed the 1933 oil agreement with Britain. By this agreement, Iran's oil revenues increased substantially.

Sporadic but revealing evidence of the shah's wealth is found in the literature and in the British and American diplomatic reports. In September 1941, the British Broadcasting Corporation (BBC) announced that Reza Shah had deposited enormous sums in foreign banks. When informed of these broadcasts, according to Wilber, Reza Shah smiled bitterly and said, "I have a little over three pounds in a Swiss bank which is the balance remaining from the money I sent there for the education of my son." On the way to Bandar Abbas, Reza Shah complained to the British Consul in Kerman, "I have not five rials in my pocket." Shortly thereafter, Reza Shah and nine of his children boarded the British ship *Bandra* for Bombay, supposedly on their way to South America. In Bombay, Reza Shah was informed of his new destination, the Indian Ocean island of Mauritius, and he was also informed by Sir Clarmont Skrine that the royal party would not be allowed to disembark in Bombay. In 1954, Skrine described this affair in *Blackwood's Magazine*. Based on Skrine's account, Wilber gave the following description: "The royal children had looked forward to shopping at Bombay, but were reduced to giving their orders to the British official. Their extensive purchases were financed from funds that Riza Shah had transferred just prior to his abdication to the Bombay branch of a British bank: these funds totaled at least £35,000."[5] In dollars, this was about $175,000. The existence of these funds goes a long way toward explaining the precipitous departure of Reza Shah for exile in 1941 and the sudden flight of his son in August 1953.

Reza Shah died in August 1944, and his money in foreign banks was divided among his children. Even before his father's death, Mohammad Reza Shah's foreign financial dealings had caught the attention of the British envoy in Tehran. Sir Reader Bullard reported to London that in March 1943, Mohammad Reza Shah transferred $500,000 from New York to Tehran for the purpose of influencing the outcome of the elections to the

Fourteenth Majlis.[6] In December 1943, Ambassador Bullard reported that based on a "completely reliable source," the shah was looking for a "safe investment" in the United States.[7] Additional insight is also provided by American diplomatic and consular dispatches during the 1950s. In a conversation between the American embassy attaché in Tehran and Massoud Foroughi, the person in charge of managing Princess Shams's affairs, Foroughi had admitted that reports concerning the shah's "vast" bank balances in America and Europe were accurate (Foreign Service despatch 805, dated 5 March 1956).

A confidential State Department report concerned part of the shah's inheritance from his father. On 9 October 1957, Reza Afshar, managing director of Iranian Airways, met in Washington with three State Department officials, Murat W. Williams, Grant E. Mouser, and Howard J. Ashford. One of the topics they discussed was the purchase of new aircraft for Iranian Airways, the predecessor of Iran Air. The report stated that Afshar "bitterly noted that he would be forced to accept three Vickers Viscount aircraft purchased on the Shah's account in Great Britain. He said this account, amounting to as much as £20 million, was blocked by the British except for purchases of British-made equipment." The money was blocked because of the British restrictions on exchange and capital transfers that had been imposed since the beginning of World War II. By purchasing British airplanes and paying in pounds, the shah would be reimbursed by the Iranian government in dollars or another fully convertible currency, such as Swiss francs. Given the timing of the conversation, and given that Britain had imposed exchange restrictions since 1939, there can be no doubt that this money had been part of Reza Shah's transfers. At the exchange rate that prevailed during Reza Shah's period (£1=$5), £20 million would have been $100 million. Majd reports that during the height of his struggles with the shah (1952–53), Mossadeq claimed that Reza Shah had stashed away $500 million in foreign banks. Given that Reza Shah also maintained bank accounts in Geneva and New York, and given that he was survived by ten children, each of whom would have inherited part of his fortune, it is evident that Mossadeq's allegation cannot be dismissed. Moreover, even a cursory analysis of Reza Shah's assets and income in Iran indicates that Mossadeq's claim was essentially accurate.

Mossadeq also claimed that Reza Shah received $25 million after signing the 1933 oil concession and that the shah transferred abroad most of the income from the properties that he had confiscated. Majd states that the income from Reza Shah's agricultural land in Mazandaran alone was reputed to be 200 million rials ($12 million) per year. In addition, since he had acquired most of the rice-producing areas of the country—Gorgan,

Mazandaran, and Gilan—he almost monopolized the market for rice and citrus fruits. It is also clear that Reza Shah extracted a heavy payment in kind and cash from the peasants. Contracts drawn up in 1940 between the Office of Royal Estates and the tenants in the villages of Zavar, concerning the planting of new orchards and the division of the orange crop, are presented and discussed in appendix A. The contracts show that Reza Shah's share was to be half of the crop, and any neglect on the part of the peasants was subject to stiff fines. It should also be noted that Reza Shah was relieved of many of the "normal" expenses of production. Gorgani cites British consular and diplomatic reports that describe the use of army trucks to transport Reza Shah's rice and wheat crop to the markets in Tehran and elsewhere.[8] Thus, Reza Shah's annual income could have easily reached $30–40 million during the last decade of his rule. The 680 million rials ($42 million) found in his account with Bank Melli in 1941 was equivalent to one year's income.

In addition to farmland, Reza Shah acquired commercial establishments, such as hotels and shops, and industrial establishments. During Majd's audience with the shah on the occasion of his appointment as governor of Gilan, the entire conversation centered on Reza Shah's questions concerning the purchase price of factories and equipment. Many of these factories were part of the shah's personal industrial holdings. It is also recorded in the literature that Reza Shah acquired vast amounts of prime urban real estate. As described by Sattareh Farmanfarmaian, soon after ascending the throne, Reza Shah sent word to the Qajar prince, Farmanfarma, that the prince should "donate" his home and garden so that His Majesty could build a new palace. Without hesitation, the wise old prince gave up his home and garden and moved into smaller quarters.[9] Farmanfarmaian also describes instances when Reza Shah confiscated automobiles and jewelry.

Land Acquisition by Reza Shah

Some of Reza Shah's money came from the rural land and urban real estate that he acquired during his reign. Lambton notes that although these lands were frequently "legally purchased" or "exchanged" for other property, the procedure amounted to confiscation. Given that "the holder was forced to exchange his property for property elsewhere, not always of equivalent value," the whole exercise "was merely a cloak for virtual confiscation."[10] The most reliable information on the extent of land acquisition by Reza Shah is contained in a remarkable document discovered after the revolution in the records of the Pahlavi Foundation. The voluminous document is entitled *Register of Names of His Exalted Imperial Majesty's Pri-*

vate Properties, and it is now the property of the Alavi Foundation. I inspected this document in 1996 and 1997, and its authenticity is indisputable. This thick leather-bound volume is written in exquisite calligraphy. It is divided by regions in which Reza Shah acquired land, and the last entry and closure of the book is in 1941. It appears that the entries were made as Reza Shah expanded his holdings. The authenticity of the document is also confirmed by the fact that the information on the three adjoining estates in Tonekabon with which the author is familiar, namely, Nashta, Zavar, and Vali Abad, is entirely accurate, including the list of villages, the date of acquisition by Reza Shah, the manner of acquisition, and the identities of the previous owners. The register lists three principal categories of property: *qar-yeh* (village), *mazra-e* (hamlet), and *martah* (pasture). Many items consist of shops, hotels, and qanats. The register comprises 651 pages and 6,126 entries. However, many entries consist of multiple items, which make the computation difficult. These indicate that the amount of property acquired by Reza Shah was, in fact, much greater than a simple addition of the entries in the register.[11]

Table 3.1 provides the location of the properties contained in the document. It is certain that the actual extent of Reza Shah's land acquisition was considerably greater than is indicated by this register. There must be another register that has not been located or identified. For instance, according to my father's memoirs, Reza Shah also acquired large areas of Gilan, all the way from Ramsar to Lahijan. The register contains nothing on Reza Shah's acquisitions in Gilan, the most productive rice region in Iran. Another notable omission from the register consists of some villages that were sold by the shah in the 1950s, such as the village of Takestan near Qazvin. Takestan was among the property acquired by Reza Shah, and it was sold by his successor in 1954. Yet Takestan is not listed in the register. Either the pace of Reza Shah's land acquisition was such that the recorders had some difficulty in keeping up, or there must be another register that has not been located. It is also clear that the bulk of the land acquired was in Gorgan, Mazandaran, and Gilan.

The magnitude of Reza Shah's land acquisition is truly astonishing. It included a 1,000-mile stretch from Fariman near the Afghan border in the east to Lahijan, Gilan, in the west. Reza Shah acquired practically all of the land in Gorgan, Mazandaran, and Gilan, the most fertile regions of the country. His acquisition consisted of 3,500 villages and 4,000 pastures and forests. As an indication of Mohammad Reza Shah's sensitivity on this issue, in his 1961 book he has only one brief sentence on the acquisition of land by his father.[12]

Table 3.1. Villages, Hamlets, and Pastures Cited in the Register of Reza Shah's Private Property

Location	Villages and Hamlets	Pastures
Kojour, Mazandaran	192	486
Tonekabon, Mazandaran	689	872
Amol, Mazandaran	241	197
Ashraf, Mazandaran	202	58
Noor, Mazandaran	44	132
Remainder of Mazandaran	499	1,132
Gorgan	293	255
Bojnurd, Khorasan	175	-
Fariman, Khorasan	38	-
Gharb (Western Iran)	247	286
Varamin, Tehran	30	-
Farah Abad, Tehran	1	-
Damavand, Tehran	12	2
Qazvin, Zanjan, Karaj	14	19
Total	2,677	3,439

Source: *Register of Names of His Exalted Imperial Majesty's Private Properties,* Institute for Contemporary Historical Studies in Tehran.

Majd's Comments on Land Acquisition by Reza Shah

Mohammad Ali Majd recorded information on land acquisition in his original and unabridged memoirs. Here he recalls the changing borders of Gilan during Reza Shah's rule.

> The eastern border of Gilan had always consisted of the river Chabok Sar. But from 1930 when His Majesty purchased the estates of the late Sepahsalar Azam [Mohammad Vali Khan Tonekaboni] in Shahsavar, the entire area consisting of the tri-region of Tonekabon was either purchased or confiscated from their owners and made part of his private property. He then turned his attention westward, and nearly all of the estates in Rankuh, Lange-Rud, Rudsar, and parts of Lahijan were either purchased or confiscated in the name of His Majesty. Land that was purchased or confiscated in Gilan was then separated from Gilan and made part of the governorate of Shahsavar [Mazandaran]. As I wrote above, when I went to Gilan in 1941, the eastern border of the governorate of Gilan was only three kilometers from the eastern gates of Lahijan. All regions to the east

of Lahijan, that is, Rankuh, Rudsar, and Lange-Rud, had been separated from Gilan and added to Mazandaran. After the events of August 1941, I gradually separated these parts from Mazandaran and restored them to Gilan, and for each region, I appointed and sent special government agents. Once again, I made Chabok Sar the eastern border of Gilan.

Although Majd clearly admired and supported Reza Shah, soon after the shah went into exile, Majd set about undoing some of his work. Clearly, such actions could not have endeared Majd to Reza Shah's son and successor. It is also noteworthy that up to the very end of his rule, Reza Shah was accumulating additional land. The events during the April 1941 inspection tour of Mazandaran and Gilan by Reza Shah provide insight into his process of land acquisition. The following is a translation of Majd's account.

His Imperial Majesty purchased much land from ordinary people and the government in Gorgan, Mazandaran, Gilan, Tehran, Kerman, Khorasan, and western Iran. The system of purchase was as follows. A representative of the Office of Royal Estates, say, in Mazandaran, would approach a landowner and suggest that the landowner should offer to sell his estate to His Majesty. If the landowner accepted the suggestion, the Royal Estates would take immediate possession of the land, and from the date of the offer of sale, the revenue from the land belonged to His Majesty. The Office of Royal Estates would then appraise the property, and usually the land would be appraised at 40 percent of its value. The system was known as *fard-e amal*; that is, if the revenue from the land was 100 tomans per year, instead of pricing the estate at 1,000 tomans, it would be appraised at 400 tomans. After two or three years, the revenue from the land would accumulate to this sum, and the landowner would be paid this sum and the Estates would acquire the deed. The other and less frequently used system was the exchange method. The government would be required to exchange government-owned estates [*amlak-e khaliseh*] for private land, and then sell the exchanged land to His Majesty. During his travels in the north, the governors usually told His Majesty that the rural estates in the area were in a state of ruin and begged His Majesty for permission to purchase the estates for His Majesty. His Majesty usually consented, and this created enormous hardship for the inhabitants of the region.

On the afternoon of 15 April 1941, His Majesty left his place of residence in Rasht for Mianposhteh. During the audience of 16 April, His Majesty had mentioned that the rural estates in Gilan, and in particular the estates of Lashte Nesha and Hasan Kia, were in a state of ruin. For some time, it had been rumored that His Majesty wished to purchase the estates of Lashte Nesha and Hasan Kia, property of Mrs. Fakhre ad Dowleh [Ashraf Amini], daughter of Mozzafar-ad Din Shah and wife of Amin ad Dowleh. The owner of these estates was not willing to part with them for any price. It had even become clear that she had prevented the construction of a road to Lashte Nesha in order to reduce its value to His Majesty. In reply to His Majesty's remarks, I had responded that in contrast to what His Majesty had been advised, Gilan is well developed, and that under the guidance of His Majesty, the landowners are rapidly undertaking more development. My remarks had angered His Majesty. His Majesty angrily asked me, "On what basis do you say Gilan is developed and becoming more developed?" I presented the agricultural statistics for the years 1938, 1939, and 1940 and informed His Majesty that rice cultivation was at a high of 250,000 hectares, and production had reached 130,000 tons, and I described the increase over the years. An hour later, Mr. Shokuh-ol Molk took me to a corner and informed me that His Majesty requires concrete proof that Gilan is developed and becoming more developed by the day. I prepared and presented a short report to His Majesty. In short, the expansion of the royal estates was halted at Lahijan, and the people of Gilan were spared additional trouble.

The Aminis were ultimately saved by the Allied invasion in August 1941.

Khalatbaris of Mazandaran

The Khalatbaris of Mazandaran were prominent victims of Reza Shah's land acquisition, and as members of the ruling class under the Qajars, they were subject to persecution by the new Pahlavi dynasty. The most prominent member of the family during the latter years of the Qajar era was my maternal great-grandfather, Mohammad Vali Khan Tonekaboni, Sepahsalar Azam, a statesman, constitutionalist, and prime minister. In 1925, his youngest and most capable son, Colonel Ali Asghar Khan Khalatbari Tonekaboni, Saed ad Dowleh, died under mysterious circumstances outside Tehran, the victim of a "hunting accident." Shortly thereafter, Mohammad Vali Khan committed suicide by shooting himself in the head. The process of land acquisition in Mazandaran by Reza Shah inevitably resulted in conflict with the Khalatbari family, one of the most ancient families of Persia. A brief account of the history of the family given here is based on the material in Amir Abdol Samad Khalatbari.[13]

Long a warrior tribe, the Khalatbaris wielded power and influence in the northern and southern slopes of the Elburz Mountains, and their seats of power consisted of the Tonekabon, Kelarestaq, and Kojour regions of Mazandaran, as well as Qazvin. In modern times, it appears that the wars of Nader Shah Afshar (1736–48) had provided the Khalatbaris with new opportunities. They took part in the conquest of India, and some of the members of the clan had decided to remain in India. During the reign of the Zand Dynasty (1750–79), the head of the clan, Mehdi Khan Tonekaboni, Sardar (commander), had been formally appointed by the shah as governor of Tonekabon and Kelarestaq. His astute son and successor, Hadi Khan Tonekaboni, Sardar (died ca. 1810), had thrown in his lot with the rising power of Agha Mohammad Khan Qajar, who succeeded in uniting the Qajars of Mazandaran and established the Qajar Dynasty (1779–1925). Thereafter, Hadi Khan and his descendants became intimately associated with the Qajar dynasty. Two of Hadi Khan's sons, Fath Ali and Mohammad Vali, had risen to positions of power and wealth in the courts of Fath Ali Shah (1797–1834) and Mohammad Shah (1834–48). While it is recorded that Mehdi Khan had owned a considerable amount of land in Tonekabon, the position of Khalatbaris as landowners in Tonekabon, Kelarestaq, and Kojour was consolidated and expanded during the early 1800s. In an Imperial Farman (edict) dated 1831, Fath Ali Shah had bestowed the ownership of the village of Siarestaq to Fath Ali. The stated basis of the land grant was the ownership of the village by Fath Ali's father, Hadi Khan Tonekaboni, Sardar. In a Farman dated 1834, Mohammad Shah had given control of Tonekabon, Kojour, and Kelarestaq to Fath Ali Tonekaboni.

Whereas Fath Ali became head of the tribe, his brother Mohammad Vali had risen in the military ranks and had taken part in Persia's foreign wars. Abbas Mirza (died 1832), the heir to the throne and chief of Iran's armed forces, had thanked Mohammad Vali in his will and testament for his bravery and dedicated service. Mohammad Vali was subsequently killed in 1837 during the Herat wars of Mohammad Shah. He was given the ultimate honor of burial in the shrine of Imam Reza in Mashhad on the orders of Mohammad Shah. In a decree dated 1837, Mohammad Shah declared Mohammad Vali a hero and a martyr who had sacrificed his life for his country, and he had ordered that all parts of Mohammad Vali's will would be honored. In 1838, a grateful Mohammad Shah had appointed Mohammad Vali's most capable son, Habibollah Khan, as governor of

Tonekabon, Kojour, and Kelarestaq in place of Fath Ali and had bestowed the title of Saed ad Dowleh on him. Fath Ali was given a large annual pension and the village of Akuleh Sar in Tonekabon.

Habibollah Khan, Saed ad Dowleh (died ca. 1900), is said to have been one of the shrewdest and most capable leaders of the Khalatbaris during the nineteenth century. He rose to a position of considerable power and wealth in the court of Mohammad Shah and Nasser ad Din Shah (1848–96). His governorship expanded to include eastern Mazandaran and Gorgan. He was also given the title of Tarkhan Sardar, one of the select few who had access to the shah at all times. He named his oldest son Mohammad Vali (1844–1926) and another son Abdollah. At the age of twelve, Mohammad Vali was taken from Tonekabon by his father and presented

Fig. 3.1. Mohammad Vali Khan Tonekaboni *(left)* and Habibollah Khan Tonekaboni, Saed ad Dowleh *(center)*, with an unidentified child and attendant, circa 1875. Photo courtesy of Mohammad Khalil Akbar.

Fig. 3.2. An unidentified child and Jamshid Khan Tonekaboni, Sardar Kabir (brother of Habibollah Khan), ca. 1900.

to the court of Nasser ad Din Shah in Tehran. Like his grandfather, for whom he was named, Mohammad Vali had a distinguished military and political career. He was named Sepahdar Azam (c. 1906) and given the highest rank of Sepahsalar Azam in 1910. He was not only the most important member of the Khalatbaris during the last decades of the Qajar rule but also an important historical personality. His political career culminated during the constitutional struggles of 1906–9 when, as the head

Fig. 3.3. Mohammad Vali Khan Tonekaboni, Sepahdar Azam, when he served as head of the first government after the restoration of the Constitution. Sepahdar Azam, 1910.

of the constitutionalist army in Gilan, he had marched on Tehran and occupied the capital in 1909, along with Ali Qoli Khan Bakhtiari, Sardar Asad. The two had proclaimed the deposition of Mohammad Ali Shah in favor of his son, Soltan Ahmad Shah (1909–25). In 1910, the newly re-opened Majlis had passed a resolution thanking Mohammad Vali Khan for his part in restoring the Constitution. He served four terms as prime minister.

Mohammad Vali Khan Tonekaboni, Sepahsalar Azam

Majd gives an account of Sepahsalar's political career and provides a measure of his importance as a politician and statesman:

The late Mohammad Vali Khan Khalatbari, Sepahsalar Azam, was one of the great statesmen of this country during the past century. On the occasion of formal court receptions during the Qajar period, it was customary that officers of the same rank gathered and were served in the same hall. Mohammad Vali Khan had served for ten years as the senior colonel from Tonekabon. On the occasion of Nasser ad Din Shah's birthday, there was a reception at the Golestan Palace. As usual, Mohammad Vali Khan had entered the colonels' room. But at that time, he was told by an officer that he had been promoted to a brigadier (*sartip*), and he was to go to the brigadiers' room. This account was given to me by the late Amir Entesar, Mohammad Vali Khan's nephew and son-in-law.

From then on, Mohammad Vali Khan rose rapidly. The late Mirza Hosein Khan, Sepahsalar Qazvini, was instrumental in Mohammad Vali Khan's rapid advancement. He became minister of post and telegraph, and for a while he was in charge of customs. For a considerable period he was in charge of the country's treasury and coin issue. For years, the entire postal service and telegraph had been leased from the government by the late Mokhber ad Dowleh. Mohammad Vali Khan had wrested control of the post and telegraph by offering the government a sum that was double that paid by Mokhber ad Dowleh. In 1901, there was a revenue shortfall of 300,000 tomans in the postal service. Mohammad Vali Khan paid his debt to the government by the sale of his house and by revenues from his estates. When I was governor of Gilan, the aged ulama and the old men all recalled the governorship of Mohammad Vali Khan and the enormous power he wielded. For instance, the Russian head merchant had committed a murder in Rasht. The Russian consul had gone to extreme lengths to save the merchant. Despite the consul's efforts, the head merchant had been hanged. Whenever the Turkomans in Mazandaran resorted to banditry, hostage taking, and plunder of the pilgrims to Mashhad, to restore security and suppress the Turkomans, the governments appealed to Mohammad Vali Khan.

In 1909, during the uprising of the constitutionalists in Azarbaijan, Mohammad Vali Khan, who had been named Sepahdar Azam, was dispatched to Azarbaijan by Mohammad Ali Shah for the purpose of crushing the rebellion by Sattar Khan and Baqer Khan. Once in Azarbaijan, Mohammad Vali Khan refused to fight the constitutionalists on the grounds that it amounted to fratricide, and he returned to Tehran. Having incurred the shah's wrath, he went to Tonekabon. In the meantime, the constitutional movement had reached Gilan. A delegation of constitutionalists went to Tonekabon and invited Sepahdar Azam to become the leader of the freedom movement. He went to Gilan and marched on Qazvin and occupied it. Thereafter, he marched toward Tehran. Among the papers of Mohammad Vali Khan, there is this letter. It is a telegram from the Russian foreign minister in St. Petersburg to the Russian embassy in Tehran. The content is as follows:

Please inform His Excellency Sepahdar Azam that if he and his army peacefully march on Tehran, and then proceed to the house of Saad al Dowleh, then on the authority of this telegram, Sepahdar Azam and all his relatives and kin will be placed in the protection of the Tsarist government. The Tsarist government will pay him a sum of 6 million gold menats.

The telegram is in French, and a Persian translation is given, at the end of which it is stated that "the copy is forwarded for the information of His Excellency Sepahdar Azam, so that if agreed by him, the Tsarist government will fulfill its undertaking."

The document bears the official seal of the Russian embassy. The comments that Mohammad Vali Khan made in the margins of this letter provide the best evidence of his patriotism and generosity: "The Russian government believes that I have done all this for personal gain. For Iran's freedom and independence, I will sacrifice my life and property and those of my children."

Mohammad Vali Khan subsequently marched on Tehran and occupied it. Mohammad Ali Shah had taken refuge in the Russian embassy in Zargandeh and then left Iran. At that point, he could easily have seized the throne and made himself king. As an expression of the nation's gratitude, the newly reopened Majlis passed a resolution in 1910, thanking Sepahdar Azam for his services and sacrifices.

With the advent of Reza Khan in the 1920s, Mohammad Vali Khan was placed under increased financial and political pressure. First, his property was seized by the government. Then his favorite son, Colonel Ali Asghar Khan, Saed ad Dowleh, was killed in 1925 in Jajerud outside Tehran. Although his death was officially attributed to a hunting accident, it was widely believed that he had been poisoned by agents of Reza Khan. On 16 July 1926, Mohammad Vali Khan, Sepahsalar Azam, committed suicide. His last note to his oldest son read: "Amir Asad, right away take my body to the shrine for cleansing and burial next to my son Saed ad Dowleh. Do it now. For after having lived for over eighty years, no mourning or tears are needed for me."

Although Mohammad Vali Khan had played a central part in establishing Iran's Constitution, he was nearly forgotten during the Pahlavi period. Even the historical name of Tonekabon was changed to "Shahsavar." The hostility of the Pahlavis was based on two facts. First, Mohammad Vali Khan had staunchly opposed the rise of Reza Khan to the throne. Second, much of his property was subsequently acquired by Reza Shah. With the overthrow of the Pahlavis, some of the victims of Reza Shah are now being posthumously rehabilitated. Judging by the frequent articles that have appeared in the Iranian press and journals praising Mohammad Vali Khan, especially for his role in establishing a constitutional government, and for his services during his governorship of Gilan, Mazandaran,

Fig. 3.4. Col. Ali Asghar Khan Tonekaboni, Saed ad Dowleh, circa 1920.

and Azarbaijan, it is evident that Mohammad Vali Khan, Sepahsalar Azam, is finally receiving the proper recognition and respect denied to him under the two Pahlavis.

Acquisition of Property of Sepahsalar by Reza Shah

Shortly after Sepahsalar committed suicide, Reza Shah acquired his property. The manner in which this occurred can be reconstructed from my father's memoirs. Since the material is pertinent to the land story and is also of interest to historians, a detailed account is given here. In 1926, Majd was involved in some bureaucratic intrigues, and he backed the wrong side. He was relieved of his duties and placed "on the service waiting list." He used his time to help the heirs of Sepahsalar in their dispute with the government, thereby further incurring the government's wrath. Majd's involvement gave him insight into Sepahsalar's affairs. Majd gives the following account of Sepahsalar's wealth.[14]

> The late Sepahsalar was one of the wealthiest men in Iran during the twentieth century. He owned much property from Talesh in Gilan to Alamdeh in Mazandaran, and this included Siarsataq, Tonekabon, Chalous, Noor, as well as estates in Tehran, Bijar, Arak, Qom, and Qazvin. The revenue from these estates was said to be 750,000 tomans per year (about $1–2 million). With the price of rice at 25 rials (2.5 tomans) per kharvar (300 kg), and price of wheat 80 rials per kharvar, and the price of barley 20 rials (2 tomans) per kharvar, one can imagine the real value of this sum. The sharecroppers in the villages owned by Sepahsalar were among the most comfortable and prosperous peasants in Iran. For example, in Gilan the landowners levied a rent of 22 boxes of rice from each hectare of land. Sepahsalar levied only 11 boxes per hectare. In addition to rice, the peasants in Gilan also rendered garlic, onions, beans, and other products to the landowners. Sepahsalar had exempted his peasants from these additional dues. Before his suicide in 1926, as described above, his property had been seized by the government for taxes owed and for his debt to the Russian Bank, and the government was deriving the income from these properties.

Majd provides an account of the stated reasons for the seizure of Sepahsalar's property:

> Toward the end of the reign of Mozzafar ad Din Shah (1896–1907), security deteriorated throughout the country. In Astarabad (present-day Gorgan), the Turkomans frequently closed the high-

ways to the pilgrims bound for Mashhad, robbed them, and even took them hostage. To suppress the Turkomans and restore security, the government chose Mohammad Vali Khan, whose title at the time was Nasr ol Saltaneh Amir Akram. To raise and equip an army and undertake a campaign, large sums were needed. And the government had no money. To maintain the government's dignity, and based on his own personal pride, Mohammad Vali Khan had borrowed from the Russian Bank and given the deeds to his properties as collateral for the loan. After the Russian Revolution and based on the provisions of the treaty of 26 February 1921, the Russian Bank and all of its assets were transferred to the Iranian government. After the Russian Revolution, the value of the Russian menat sank to 1/100th of its previous value. Since all the debts to the Russian Bank were in menats, subsequently, many of the bank's debtors were able to buy the depreciated menats and repay their debts to the bank, and thus had recovered their deeds. It was repeatedly suggested to the late Sepahsalar that with a payment of 30,000 tomans he could settle the debt and recover the deeds and documents. But Sepahsalar had replied that the debt in truth was the obligation of the government. It was known to all that he had incurred the debt for the purpose of war and the pacification of Astarabad. In addition, the late Sepahsalar had pointed out that during the brief life of the Gilan Republic, the Bolsheviks had plundered a great deal of his property, including much rice and livestock in Gilan and Mazandaran. The value of the plundered goods far exceeded the Russian claims on him. Consequently, he was not responsible for the debt.

After his arrival in Iran, Dr. Millspaugh was placed in charge of the newly named Bank of Iran (the old Russian Bank). Millspaugh began to pressure the late Sepahsalar. Eventually, on the basis of the effort by the late Saed ad Dowleh, an agreement was reached with the government by which Sepahsalar's debt to the bank was set at 650,000 tomans, and Sepahsalar's debt to the government for alleged unpaid taxes was set at 400,000 tomans. Despite the accord, all of Sepahsalar's property was seized by the government in 1923, administrators were posted, and the government derived the income from these properties. The practice continued after the suicide of Sepahsalar, and all the revenue accrued to the government.

All subsequent attempts by Majd as representative of Sepahsalar's heirs to restore the property had been unsuccessful. Majd reports that the minister of finance, Nosrat Dowleh, had tried to reach an amicable settle-

ment with the heirs. Majd was convinced that Nosrat Dowleh's intervention contributed to his dismissal and eventual arrest by Reza Shah on
trumped-up charges.[15] Majd describes the eventual "settlement" that was
reached in 1930 between the government and the heirs of Sepahsalar:

> The late Mirza Reza Khan Naini, the chief prosecutor general,
> was placed in charge of Bank of Iran (the old Russian Bank). It was
> his intention to settle and regulate all the affairs of the bank in a fair
> and equitable manner. That is, repay all the bank's debts and receive
> all of its claims. The two largest debtors to the bank consisted of the
> heirs of Mohammad Vali Khan, Sepahsalar Azam, and Haj Amin ol
> Zarb. The settlement with Haj Amin ol Zarb consisted of the follow-
> ing: the government acquired Abbas Abad and Yusef Abad, and the
> remaining 300,000 tomans of debt were to be paid over ten years
> with the revenues from Haj Amin ol Zarb's estates in Zanjan, and
> was underwritten by Haj Moin ol Tojar-e Bushehri. Mirza Reza
> Khan intended to reach a similar settlement with the heirs of Sepah-
> salar. He had even suggested that the heirs should approach the
> bank's creditors, including Sa-ad ad Dowleh, and acquire his notes
> and claims on the bank, and then exchange the claims so acquired as
> settlement of their debts with the bank. I recall one day we were at a
> meeting with Mirza Reza Khan and Sa-ad ad Dowleh. I suggested
> that in exchange for Sa-ad ad Dowleh's notes, he be given the houses
> in Tighestan at a price of 3,000 tomans per house. He had objected
> in earnest that he was only ninety-five years old, and since these
> houses yielded no income, how was he to provide for himself dur-
> ing the next twenty-five years!
> When the government learned of Mirza Reza Khan's plan to
> settle the matter, and given that His Late Majesty had his eyes on the
> estates of the late Sepahsalar in Tonekabon, Siarestaq, and Kelares-
> taq, Mirza Reza Khan was quietly told to resign, and this honorable
> man resigned as manager of the Bank of Iran. In his place the gov-
> ernment appointed Hasan Moshar, Moshar ol Molk, who suggested
> to Sepahsalar's heirs that the matter be entrusted to a committee of
> three arbitrators. The arbitrators selected consisted of the late Sheik
> Noor ol Din Khalatbari, representing the heirs; Mirza Hasan Khan
> Kia, an official of the Ministry of Finance, representing the govern-
> ment; and Haj Moin ol Mamalek-e Rashti. These three people trav-
> eled to Tonekabon, and an initial suggested appraisal was 1.8 mil-
> lion tomans. But Sheik Noor ol Din, an honest and respected person,
> had refused to go along on the basis that since the annual revenues

were 750,000 tomans, the value of the estates was at the very least 5 million tomans. Haj Moin ol Mamalek had then secretly sent a telegram to Moshar ol Molk and had informed him that he had suggested a price of 1.8 million tomans, but the arbitrator representing the heirs was unwilling to sign. Moshar ol Molk had then replied that Haj Moin had no authority to place a value of 1.8 million. The appraised value was to be only 710,000 tomans. If Sheik Noor ol Din was not willing to sign the appraisal, the arbitrators were to return to Tehran. The arbitrators returned to Tehran, and Sheik Noor ol Din was forced to sign the appraised value of 710,000 tomans. I would like to add that Sepahsalar's debt to the Russian Bank was settled at 650,000 tomans. Although the government had derived the revenues from these estates for several years, they were considered part of the interest on the debt. In this manner, the property of the late Sepahsalar was acquired by the government and the deed of transfer was drawn up. One by one, his heirs were taken to notary office number 10 in Tehran, and they were made to sign.[16]

Although Majd does not provide details, a similar "settlement" was imposed on the heirs of Sepahsalar concerning his alleged 400,000 toman tax debt. The entire affair was part of a ploy by Reza Shah to acquire these properties. The villages and estates so acquired by the government were then "purchased" by Reza Shah. In the *Register of Names of His Exalted Imperial Majesty's Private Properties,* it is recorded that the villages had been purchased from the Bank of Iran or the Ministry of Finance. The "price" paid by Reza Shah was equivalent to the land's revenue for one year. There was still another method. Having acquired the estates of Tonekabon, Kelarestaq, and Siarestaq, Reza Shah had then set about acquiring the estates of Kojour to the east. Reza Shah's "purchase" of some seventy villages and hamlets and 140 pastures and forests in Kojour, Mazandaran, from the heirs of Mohammad Vali Khan, Sepahsalar Azam, is described in my father's unabridged memoirs, and I can do no better than to offer a translation:

Shortly after [the suicide], the heirs were approached by Mirza Karim Khan Rashti, and Amir Akram, and it was suggested that the heirs should sell the estates of Kojour to His Majesty. The heirs of Sepahsalar consisted of two sons, Amir Asad and Sardar Eqtedar, and three daughters, Amir Zadeh Khanum, Gohar Saltaneh, and Taj ol Moluk Akbar. It was suggested that in exchange for the estates, Amir Zadeh and Gohar Saltaneh each be given 2,500 tomans, and Amir Asad and Sardar Eqtedar each be given 5,000 tomans. And Taj ol Moluk and Soghra Khanum, the widow of Sepahsalar, should each be given 10,000 tomans. In those days, there were no official registration offices. The most important religious notary office was that of the Emam Jomeh Khoii. The estates of Kojour consisted of 150 items of villages, hamlets, and winter and summer pastures and forests. The deed of transfer from Amir Zadeh and Gohar Saltaneh to His Majesty for a sum of 5,000 tomans was drawn up and signed by them. But since no money had been exchanged, the Emam Jomeh refused to record and recognize the transaction, and insisted that 5,000 tomans in cash be given to the two sisters. Amir Akram and Mirza Karim Khan left the notary office and returned half an hour later, and gave 2,500 tomans to each of the two sisters. Upon receipt of the money, Amir Zadeh Khanum gave 300 tomans of her share to the notary office of the Emam Jomeh. Upon leaving the office, the two representatives, Mirza Karim Khan and Amir Akram, immediately demanded the return of the money. Gohar Saltaneh surrendered 2,500 tomans and Amir Zadeh Khanum the remaining 2,200 tomans. That same afternoon, two individuals were sent by Mirza Karim Khan to Amir Zadeh's residence, demanding the remaining 300 tomans. To raise 300 tomans, Amir Zadeh Khanum had to pawn her diamond ring with Ebrahim Qadiri. Later, Mirza Karim Khan had borrowed the 10,000 tomans due to Taj ol Moluk, and had given her only 300 tomans.

Another rural acquisition was the estates (*amlak*) of Valiabad in western Mazandaran, which were "purchased" from Sepahsalar's son, Amir Asad Khalatbari. A legal document of transfer dated 19 February 1934 refers to Valiabad as "the amlak of His Imperial Majesty purchased from Mr. Amir Asad." It should be added that there were many others from whom Reza Shah "purchased" land. For instance, in 1932 he took more than 1.6 million hectares of land from landowners and tribesmen in Turkoman Sahra.[17] Even a cursory examination of the *Register of Names of His Exalted Imperial Majesty's Private Properties* shows that many of the villages acquired by the shah had been "purchased" from petty landowners (*khorde-malekin*). The consequences for many were tragic.

The Tragedy of Amir Nasri and Amir Zadeh

One of Sepahsalar's closest relatives was Mohammad Qoli Tonekaboni, Amir Entesar (1874–1936), son of Abdollah Khan, Sepahsalar's brother. In addition to being his nephew, Mohammad Qoli was married to Sepahsalar's eldest daughter, Amir Zadeh (1877–1933). Amir Entesar was a

Fig. 3.5. Amir Entesar *(center)*, wearing a white hat and holding a rifle, with fellow free-dom fighters (Mujahedin) in 1909. The original caption reads: "This is a photo of the War Commission taken in Rasht in the year 1327 [1909] during the revolution, in the company of His Excellency Amin ol Molk, Haji Mir Panj, and other fighters from Georgia and Cau-cuses. Mohammad Qoli Tonekaboni."

graduate of Dar ol Fonoun, the elite institution of the day. He was elo-quent and well versed in history. Amir Entesar was active in the constitu-tional movement of Tonekabon and governor (farmandar). He took part in the constitutional war of 1909. He also accompanied Sepahsalar during the latter's governorship of Azarbaijan, 1919–20. With the overthrow of the Qajars and the advent of Reza Shah, Amir Entesar left Tonekabon and settled in Qazvin, where he maintained a home. His oldest son, Hosein Qoli Tonekaboni, Amir Nasri (1905–32), however, remained in Tone-kabon. Amir Nasri was married to Soghra, daughter of Massoud ol Molk Tonekaboni (died between 1925 and 1930). Massoud ol Molk was the owner of the neighboring estates of Nashta and a friend of Amir Entesar. Nashta and Zavar shared a river for their common irrigation needs. It is said that the marriage was arranged, intended to reduce conflict over water between Nashta and Zavar.

Fig. 3.6. Amir Entesar and notables in Tabriz, 1920. Also seen is Hedayatollah Khan Massoud ol Molk Tonekaboni *(front row left)*. The original caption reads: "This photo was taken in the noble Tabriz in the year 1339 [1920] during the governorship of the late Sepahsalar Azam, may his soul be blessed, and in the company of the late Movasaq ol Molk, Mr. Aalam ol Molk, Dr. Shokuh, and Mr. Massoud ol Molk-e Hezar Jaribi (of a Thousand Jaribs), and a group of others. Mohammad Qoli Tonekaboni, may he be forgiven."

If they thought that they had purchased a measure of security by donating Kojour to Reza Shah, the descendants of Sepahsalar were sadly mistaken. Soon after the acquisition of Kojour, the estate of Valiabad in Mazandaran was similarly "purchased" by Reza Shah from Amir Asad, Sepahsalar's oldest son and brother of Amir Zadeh. Inevitably, Zavar was next. Zavar had been the property of Abdollah Khan Tonekaboni (died ca. 1900), brother of Mohammad Vali Khan. It passed to his children, Fatemeh, Mohammad Qoli (Amir Entesar), Fakhre Zaman, and Hasan (Amir Momtaz). Having become convinced that surrender and nonresistance only invited greater transgression by Reza Shah, it appears that Amir Entesar, Amir Momtaz, and a group of landowners in Tonekabon decided to resist. Majd reports that a group of landowners in Tonekabon organized for the purpose of preventing additional "encroachments" on their land by agents of Reza Shah. On 21 March 1932, the first day of the Iranian New Year (Nowruz), Reza Shah's police struck. As reported in Majd's memoirs and confirmed by documents discovered after the revolution in the archives of the Pahlavi Foundation, fifty-eight individuals were arrested on that day in Tonekabon. In the words of Majd, the detainees were transported like sheep in open trucks across the snow-covered Elburz Mountains to the notorious Qasr Qajar Prison in Tehran. Others were arrested in Mazandaran and Tehran. All were arrested on the ludicrous charge of "Bolshevism." It is now clear that the police reaction was particularly severe because it was intended to serve as a lesson to would-be recalcitrant landowners and those who resisted Reza Shah's land acquisition. Reza Shah used the affair to acquire the property of those arrested as the price of their release from prison or of a posting to a more favorable place of exile. The names of these unfortunate individuals, which included several members of the ulama, numerous merchants, and even heads of government bureaus, were preserved in the records of the Pahlavi Foundation and were duly examined by this author. There is also a separate list giving the names of forty-one individuals and the places to which they and all their kin were exiled. The dependents consisted of 318 persons, giving a total of 359 individuals who were to be exiled. Many were sent from Mazandaran to the coastal regions of Kerman and Bam in the south. The "lucky" ones were exiled to Kermanshahan and Kurdistan.

Fig. 3.7. Hosein Qoli Khan Tonekaboni, Amir Nasri, circa 1930.

In some instances, it is noted in the margin that the person remained in jail, but his dependents had already been sent to the place of "migration." The "unlucky" ones died in prison. All were victims of Reza Shah's tyranny and insatiable greed. Of course, it should be noted that the above took place in a tiny corner of Mazandaran. Given that Reza Shah's acquisitions extended from Fariman in Khorasan to Gilan in the north and included many other regions of the country, and Reza Shah confiscated houses and even shops, large numbers of people were imprisoned or exiled, and many died. The following is a documented case of a death in prison.

Those arrested in Tonekabon on 21 March 1932 included my uncle, Hosein Qoli Khan, Amir Nasri (number 48 on the list). Another detainee was his paternal uncle, Amir Momtaz (number 51 on the list). In addition to Amir Nasri, all six of Soghra's brothers were arrested at the family's New Year's celebration. Since Amir Nasri himself owned no land, his arrest constituted hostage taking in order to intimidate his parents and his wife. My father recalls the events leading to the arrests and what happened thereafter, including Amir Nasri's death in prison:

The property of the late Sepahsalar was acquired by Reza Shah in two stages. The eastern limit of these estates consisted of Alamdeh in Mazandaran and the western limit was Bahar Taq in Gilan. In between, many individuals such as Montazem-ol Molk, the heirs of Massoud ol Molk, Amir Entesar, and many others owned property. The officials of the Office of Royal Estates not only prevented the landowners from collecting rent but would also encroach on their land and property. In response, the landowners had little choice but to organize and hold meetings for the purpose of defending their rights and property. In return, the officials of the Office of Royal Estates, who were mainly military or police officers or members of the Ministry of Agriculture, were also active and had reported to Tehran that the landowners had become communists. On the morning of 21 March 1932, about sixty landowners in Tonekabon were arrested by the police, transported to Tehran like sheep in open trucks, and delivered to the Qasr Qajar Prison in Tehran. Those arrested included Hosein Qoli Khan, Amir Nasri, the only son of Amir Entesar and Amir Zadeh. In prison, Amir Nasri fell ill, and as his condition was deteriorating, I contacted Mr. Abol Hasan Ebtehaj, chief inspector of the Imperial Bank at the time, and a close friend of General Ayrom, chief of police. By this intervention, Amir Nasri was moved to the police hospital. Early on the morning of 15 May 1932, there was loud knocking on the door. I was informed by the prison officials that Amir Nasri had died, and I was told to go to the prison in person in order to collect the body. What a tragedy! Amir Nasri was buried in Emamzadeh Saleh in Tajrish, next to his grandfather, the Sepahsalar, and uncle Saed ad Dowleh. For two months the death was hidden from Amir Zadeh and Amir Entesar. Since Amir Zadeh and Amir Entesar resided in Qazvin, I had instructed the servants to open all letters and telegrams and not to deliver the ones conveying condolence. Gradually, the detainees were released, and every day Amir Entesar and Amir Zadeh telephoned from Qazvin to find out if Amir Nasri had been released. My wife, Amir Banou, and I were in a very difficult situation. On the one hand, we had lost an innocent youth, and on the other, we did not know how to convey this tragic news to his parents. Eventually after two months, one day when Amir Entesar was at the gate of his house, the postman had delivered a letter to him. The writer had sworn by the spirit of Amir Nasri, and Amir Entesar had learned of the death. We were telephoned from Qazvin, and my wife and I left immediately for Qazvin. May God spare all of the tragic sight we witnessed. Amir Entesar was weeping, while Amir Zadeh was praying and murmuring that the Lord giveth and the Lord taketh, and she was asking the Lord's forgiveness for having mourned for her beloved son.

Amir Nasri was twenty-eight. His death was a bitter blow to his parents. No one saw his parents smile again. Soon thereafter, Amir Zadeh's life was extinguished, and she passed away on 19 August 1933. She was buried in the terrace of the Shrine of Shahzadeh Hosein in Qazvin. After the death of Amir Nasri and Amir Zadeh, Amir Entesar completely gave up on life. At first, he had decided to stay in Jamjerd, but with the cold weather in Jamjerd, he returned to Qazvin. He spent much of his time by the grave of Amir Zadeh. In February 1936, news came from Qazvin that Amir Entesar was ill. I went to Qazvin and persuaded him to come to Tehran. He was better for a while, but sadly, he passed away on the night of 27 February 1936. I took his body to Qazvin and had him buried next to Amir Zadeh. As I revise these memoirs (1972), it is now thirty-six years since his death. Each year, on 27 February, if we are in Iran, my wife and I travel to Qazvin to be at his side.

It is noteworthy that Majd's account of what transpired after Amir Nasri's death in prison is similar to the account given by Sattareh Farman Farmanfarmaian following the 1938 murder of her brother Nosrat Dowleh in prison. In both instances, there was an early morning visit by prison officials bearing the news of the death. In each case, the body was to be claimed in person, and there was to be no announcement of the death or formal mourning.[18] While it has not been claimed that there was a systematic policy to eliminate the remnants of the Qajar ruling class, the fact remains that in the nine years since the advent of Reza Shah, this branch of the Khalatbaris was decimated. The record speaks for itself. Sepahsalar committed suicide, his youngest son was murdered, his grandson Amir Nasri died in prison, his daughter Amir Zadeh and her husband, Amir Entesar, died of grief. Sepahsalar's oldest son, Amir Asad, was declared legally insane and was institutionalized. His other son, Sardar Eqtedar, suffered a complete nervous breakdown and lived in a continuous state of anxiety. The destruction of the Khalatbaris by Reza Shah and their uprooting from Mazandaran were clearly processes of enormous political and social importance. The Khalatbaris had wielded influence and control in Tonekabon from at least since the time of Nader Shah (1736–48). Their destruction was part of Reza Shah's tribal policy and subjugation, consolidation of power, and acquisition of wealth. I noted above that during the struggle over the establishment of a constitutional government in 1909, two armies marched on Tehran. The first from Gilan was commanded by Mohammad Vali Khan Tonekaboni, Sepahdar Azam, and the other army from Isfahan was commanded by Ali Qoli Khan Bakhtiari, Sardar Asad. The fate of Mohammad Vali Khan and that of his kin was described above. Unlike Mohammad Vali Khan, who opposed Reza Shah to the end, Sardar Asad was initially a leading supporter of Reza Shah. However, he suffered a worse fate. Mohammad Vali Khan took his own life. He died with his honor and reputation intact. In contrast, Sardar Asad's son was arrested by Reza Shah and murdered in prison.[19]

Property Registration by Reza Shah: A Case Study in Royal Extortion

A nationwide system of property registration and deeds was enacted in 1928, and the Bureau of Registration was established. Clearly, this was a much needed measure.[20] However, the cynical and gross misuse of the new laws by Reza Shah made a mockery of both the institutions and the new laws from the very beginning. A case in point is the matter of ownership registration for a pasture and a village in Kojour, Mazandaran. Under the new property laws, before obtaining an ownership deed, the owner or owners of a property first had to register with the Bureau of Registration. This required announcement and publication of each owner's name, the amount of property, and the location and description of the property in the official provincial newspaper published by the Ministry of Justice.

The process was repeated four times in sixty days. If there were no objections or competing claims on the property, then the ownership would be registered, and the owners could obtain an ownership deed. If there were objections, the matter had to be resolved between the parties outside the judicial system or settled by a court ruling.

Among my father's private papers, I found an issue of the *Official Newspaper of the Ministry of Justice, Mazandaran Branch,* dated 1 October 1932. As the date, the stamp, and the address on the front page indicate, it had been mailed to a grieving Amir Entesar following the death of Amir Nasri in prison a few months earlier. That tyrannical and lawless regimes leave ample evidence of their misdeeds is well known. Reza Khan's regime was no exception. For two-thirds of a century, this damning piece of evidence lay among the papers of Amir Entesar and subsequently those of Mohammad Ali Majd, finally to be discovered in 1997.

On the front page there are two registration announcements. The first is for a pasture by the name of Vatehayn in the district of Kalege in Kojour. The second is for Farash Kalay-e Sofla, a village in the district of Kacheh Rastaq, also in Kojour. In the case of the pasture, the announcement contains the names of three individuals declaring ownership on the basis of actual possession of the land. First is His Most August Imperial Majesty, Reza Shah Pahlavi, the Shahanshah of Iran. His Majesty is represented by Brigadier Karim Aqa Khan Bouzarjomehri. His Majesty's ownership is said to consist of 3 dangs (3 shares out of 6 shares). The other two owners named are Mirza Ebrahim Khan Deev Salar, whose title was Zayghom ol Soltan, and Mirza Yahya Khan Deev Salar, each with 1.5 dangs (1.5 shares out of 6 shares). There follows a description of the property, dimensions, and the proposed value of the property (in this case 1,300 rials, or $80). Anyone wishing to register an objection to the ownerships had ninety days from the date of the first publication to submit his objection with the Ministry of Justice and to obtain a receipt (very important)! In the case of the village, His Most August Imperial Majesty is again represented by Brigadier Bouzarjomehri, and His Majesty's ownership is declared to be 4.5 dangs (4.5 shares out of 6). However, this time the situation of the other owners is more complicated. One dang (1 share out of 6 shares) has been endowed in equal amount for the benefit of two brothers, Mirza Esmail Khan Shaygan and Mirza Ali Akbar Khan Shaygan. The remaining half dang (.5 share out of 6 shares) was owned by three brothers: Rahman Qoli Khan Darvish, Yazdan Qoli Khan Darvish, and Qassem Khan Darvish. The "value" of the village was declared at 14,500 rials ($900). Again it was announced that those who wished to object had ninety days from the date of the first publication to register their objections.

How had Reza Shah acquired this pasture and village? Who were these landowners who had become His Majesty's "partners"? In finding an answer, one gains more insight into Reza Shah's rule. In discussing the tragedy of Amir Nasri and Amir Zadeh above, I noted that on 21 March 1932, fifty-eight individuals were arrested in Tonekabon, and others were arrested elsewhere. Documents released and published after the Islamic Revolution show that nine were arrested in Tehran and sixteen in Kojour, Mazandaran. An examination of the list of those arrested shows that nearly all the landowners whose names appear with Reza Shah in the above two registration announcements had been arrested on 21 March 1932, sent to Qasr Qajar Prison in Tehran, and then exiled to distant places. Released documents after the Islamic Revolution show that the two Deev Salars cited in the first announcement had been sent to Kerman. The three Darvish brothers had been exiled and banished to Kashan. Clearly, to gain their release from prison and escape a fate similar to that of poor Amir Nasri, these unfortunate individuals had donated part of their property to Reza Shah. In accordance with the new "modern" laws, His Majesty was in the process of registering his ownership and obtaining a title deed.

The Zavar Exchange, 1935

Amir Entesar's passive resistance to the takeover of Zavar by Reza Shah continued after the death of Amir Nasri and Amir Zadeh. Having suffered the ultimate misfortune, it appears that he was now less susceptible to pressure and intimidation, and he continued to refuse to give up this land to Reza Shah. Although exiled and banned from Tonekabon, Amir Entesar remained the legal owner of Zavar. On 18 February 1934, in what must be seen as a remarkable act of defiance (and outright danger) by Amir Entesar and Mohammad Ali Majd, as well as the notary public, Mohammad Baqer Moussavi Iravani, Amir Entesar transferred the legal ownership of Zavar to his son-in-law, Mohammad Ali Majd. Although such legal maneuvers were unlikely to deter Reza Shah, the transfer to Majd ultimately resulted in "exchange." In 1935, Zavar was "exchanged" for a group of government-owned villages. The legal basis of the exchange, it appears, was a series of laws enacted between 1932 and 1934, permitting the transfer of khaliseh (government-owned) land to persons who were exiled from their original homes in exchange for their original estates.[21] On the practical side, the account of the events leading to the exchange is given by Majd. Majd's account illustrates the direct role played by Reza Shah himself, and in the interest of historical accuracy, Majd's account is given in full:

In 1929, six dangs (six shares out of six shares) of the village of Mo-hammad Abad in Zarand were presented as a gift to my wife and me by the late Amir Zadeh Khanum. After the transfer of the property of Sepahsalar in Tonekabon, the rest of his property was freed by the government, including the three dangs (three shares out of six shares) of twenty-five villages located in Arak, Rajerd, Qom, Fara-han, and Borujerd, which were part of Amir Zadeh's inheritance. From the revenue of these estates, I provided all their living ex-penses and settled all their debts. One evening in February 1934, the late Amir Entesar asked me to accompany him to a place the next afternoon. At 4 P.M. the next day, we got into the car, and he in-structed the driver to go to the notary office of Iravani. On the way, he quietly murmured to himself and played with the white beads that he usually carried. At the notary office, Amir Entesar asked the secretary if the papers were ready, to which the secretary replied that the contents had even been entered into the register. Then Amir Entesar turned to me and said, "It was God's will that we lost our son. Amir Zadeh and I had agreed that her property should pass to our two daughters, Ashraf Dowleh and Amir Banou, and my prop-erty should pass to Amir Nasri. On her deathbed, Amir Zadeh asked me that you should take the place of Amir Nasri, and all of my prop-erty should go to you." Tearfully, I had resisted. Amir Entesar in-sisted that what happened was God's will and cannot be resisted, and it was incumbent that I should accept. The papers were signed, and by the document outlined below, with the exception of 1,370 jarib, the ownership of the estate of Zavar was transferred to me. That day, I became one of the most important landowners in Iran. The estates of Arak, Zarand, Tonekabon, and Amir Zadeh's share in the rest of the property that were subsequently freed by the govern-ment were under my management. After my return from Europe in 1935, I spent most of my time in the management of these estates and traveled frequently to these spots in the company of Aman Ollah Safari [Baha ol Saltaneh] and Rasouli.

In 1933, with the sole exception of the estate of Zavar, the remain-der of Tonekabon had been purchased by His Majesty, or if not pur-chased, the landowners had no control or say in the management of their estates. The sole exception was Zavar. Without hindrance, I continued to collect the revenues of the estate. One day I went to Zavar, and I was truly puzzled by the fact that Zavar had been left alone by the agents of the Office of Royal Estates, and they had not created any problems for me or the cultivators. On a trivial excuse one day, I visited the Office of Royal Estates. The head of the Office was a man by the name of Engineer Halati. He showed me great respect, left his desk, and sat by the door. I soon learned that while I was the head of the Karaj Agricultural College, this gentleman was a student at the college. To show his respect and gratitude, he had left my property alone.

One day while I was away, I was summoned by telephone to the accounting department of the Special Imperial Bureau. Immediately I returned to Tehran, and the following day, I went to the accounting department at 8 A.M. I was informed by General Bouzarjomehri that His Majesty wished to purchase the estates of Zavar. By this time, I realized that the atmosphere had changed, and that those in the office spoke very quietly. I said to General Bouzarjomehri that everything ultimately belonged to His Majesty, and I was very happy to present them to His Majesty. The General said, "His Majesty does not accept presents, and he will pay the price." I said, "One hundred and fifty people derive their livelihood from these estates. We beg His Majesty to provide for these people in any way he deems appropriate." The general said, "You shall have your answer." On the way out of the office, I realized that during my conversation with General Bouzarjomehri, His Majesty was standing behind a partially open door and listening to the conversation.

Soon after, Mr. Latifi telephoned me. Accompanied by Amir Entesar, I went to the Special Imperial Bureau. Mr. Latifi informed us that His Majesty had referred to us as good people and had ordered that our estates be exchanged. After much coming and going, it was eventually agreed that Zavar would be exchanged for the following villages: Khoramdareh, Ebrahim Abad, Khoznein, Nowdeh Lakvan, Najaf Abad, Ardagh, Asb-e Mord, Yarud, Ebrahim Beigi, and the garden and residence of the late Sepahsalar in Qazvin. Davar,[22] the minister of finance, summoned me to his office and told me that Ashtiani, the head of the office of the Ministry of Finance in Qazvin, insisted that the garden and house of Sepahsalar be excluded because it was badly needed by the Ministry of Finance. As the late Davar was insistent, I gave in, and the garden was excluded. The following document of exchange was drawn up and signed. It should be added that, although I was the formal owner of Zavar, it was decided that my name should not in any way be involved, because I was a civil servant. The deed of exchange was drawn up under the names of Amir Entesar, Amir Momtaz, Eqtedar Soltan, and Fakhr-e Zaman Khanum. I vividly recall that Amir Entesar and others all wept openly during the formal signing of the exchange document.

Shortly after the exchange, I drew up a formal acceptance letter and confirmed the exchange in the notary office number 10 in Tehran.

The document of exchange, the original of which I found in my father's private papers, is of great value to historians. It is prepared by the Ministry of Justice, Department of Registration of Documents, dated 26 July 1935, and it is signed by Ali Akbar Davar, minister of finance, acting on behalf of the Iranian government, and signed by Amir Entesar and Amir Momtaz, both duly shorn of their titles, Jahanshah Massoudi Tonekaboni, representing his mother-in-law, Fakhr-e Zaman, and Gholam Hosein Akbarpour, Eqtedar Soltan (son of Fatemeh). By this document, the estates of Zavar in Tonekabon were legally ceded to the government in exchange for land elsewhere in the country.[23] (The text of this document is given in appendix A.) The area that was ceded is in the 40-kilometer stretch between Zavar in the west and the town of Chalous to the east. As Majd noted, since the rest of Tonekabon had already been acquired by Reza Shah, it appears that the "exchange" completed the confiscation of

Fig. 3.8. View of mountain village of Yarud, circa 1935.

the entire 50–60 kilometers between Tonekabon and Chalous. The document also demonstrates one of the "legal" ways in which the "exchange" took place. Villages that were owned by the government were exchanged for private land. Immediately thereafter, the land newly acquired by the government through the exchange would be "sold" to Reza Shah. Majd reports in his memoirs that the estates of Zavar were "purchased" by Reza Shah from the Ministry of Finance for 300,000 rials (about $17,000). In fact, the transfer of Zavar to Reza Shah took place on the same day in which the "exchange" had taken place. In the register containing the list of Reza Shah's properties, it is recorded that Zavar had been "purchased" from the Ministry of Finance for an undisclosed amount, and the date of purchase is given as 26 July 1935. Thus, the transfer to Reza Shah took place in the same notary office and on the same day as the transfer of the property from the owners to the government.

Majd gives the basis of the exchange. The Ministry of Finance had determined that the yearly income from the estates of Zavar consisted of 1,500 kharvar of rice, 120 putts of dried tea, and a certain amount of dairy products. These were converted into a monetary equivalent. Supposedly, the government villages that were exchanged for Zavar had total annual

Fig. 3.9. Gholam Hosein Akbarpour, Eqtedar Soltan, in Najaf Abad during the spring of 1936.

Fig. 3.10. Neglected Safavi bridge over Khar Rud River, circa 1935.

revenues that were equal to the revenues that it had determined for Zavar, hence the number and composition of the exchanged villages that were received for Zavar. In reality, the Zavar "exchange" was a very uneven exchange. The most productive and fertile agricultural land in Iran was "exchanged" for villages located in semi-arid areas on the edge of the desert or in remote mountain regions. Two of the villages, Yarud and Asbe-mord, were remote and inaccessible mountain villages that had little or no agriculture. The rest were mostly badly neglected government-owned villages in a semi-arid region. For example, Khoznein and Ebrahim Abad were located on the edge of Iran's central desert and did not even have a working qanat. In the case of Ebrahim Abad, Majd reports that its qanat had been destroyed by a flood in 1921. These villages consisted of a group of "ruins" that were subsequently developed by Majd, after the expenditure of much money and effort. In addition, in contrast to the Zavar villages that border each other, the exchanged villages were widely scattered over a large region. And the transportation was extremely poor. The "roads" that linked Ebrahim Abad and Khoznein to Qazvin and Karaj were nothing more than dirt tracks until the 1960s, becoming impassable during the winter and spring flooding of the Khar Rud River. Asbe-mord and Yarud were accessible only by horses and mules, and then only during part of the year when the winter snows had melted. The lack of transportation and access made management of these estates very difficult. Since Amir Entesar's eldest daughter, Ashraf Dowleh, was childless, he had decided that most of the exchanged villages should pass to his youngest daughter, Shams ol Moluk, and her husband, Mohammad Ali Majd, who became the legal owner of Khoramdareh and other exchanged villages.

Amir Entesar, Amir Momtaz, and Fakhre-Zaman were members of a prominent Mazandaran landowning family with deep roots that extended over several generations. As the names of the villages in Tonekabon bear testimony, the Khalatbaris had established and played a significant part in the development of most of these villages. In contrast, they had no connection to the Tati- and Turkish-speaking villages of Qazvin and Karaj, which they had acquired. To the peasants who sharecropped their new land, they were an alien group with little local standing. Thus, Reza Shah's land policy combined personal enrichment with the destruction of local leadership in regions of Iran. As a politician and an influential civil servant, as well as a friend of Davar, Majd's intervention undoubtedly resulted in a better deal for the landowners, although he denies this in his memoirs. This point needs to be qualified, however. Although Davar was supposedly a "friend" of Majd, it is clear from Majd's account that until the final stage of the deal, Davar was trying to reduce the property to be given to the expropriated landowners. For instance, although

Fig. 3.11. Iranian landowners and peasants, circa 1930. Gholam Hosein Akbarpour, Eqtedar Soltan, stands in the front row, fifth from the left.

originally Sepahsalar's house in Qazvin was to be returned as part of the exchange, Davar "persuaded" Majd to forgo the house.

Confiscation of Nashta, 1932

As painful and uneven as the Zavar exchange was, it was infinitely better than the deal obtained by many other landowners. In fact, Majd points out that the "exchange" transaction was rare. The usual mode of land acquisition by Reza Shah was the "purchase" method. This was how he acquired the estates of Nashta in 1932. These estates were located east of Zavar and shared an irrigation source with Zavar. Nashta was mostly owned by Hedayatollah Khan Tonekaboni, Massoud ol Molk (died ca. 1925), neighbor and friend of Amir Entesar. Hedayatollah Khan, who was also known as Massoud ol Molk of a Thousand Jaribs, was a large land-owner active in politics. The 1911 photo taken in Tabriz (fig. 3.6) shows that, like Amir Entesar, Hedayatollah Khan had accompanied Moham-mad Vali Khan, Sepahsalar Azam, to Azarbaijan during the latter's gover-norship. As members of the aristocracy, the families of Amir Entesar and Hedayatollah Khan were also closely related by marriage. Hedayatollah had three wives and was survived by six sons and eight daughters. One of his daughters, Soghra Khanum (1900–1975), was married to Amir Nasri. Her brother Jahanshah Massoudi Tonekaboni (died 1976) was a signatory to the Zavar document of "exchange" given above. He had signed on behalf of his mother-in-law, Fakhre-Zaman Khanum, Amir Entesar's sis-ter. On his death, Hedayatollah Khan's children inherited Nashta. In 1932, Reza Shah confiscated Nashta, and the owners were exiled from Tonekabon. Moreover, as outlined in this chapter, the events preceding the confiscation of Nashta and the neighboring Zavar were brutal, result-ing in the death of Amir Nasri in prison and the early death of his parents, Amir Zadeh and Amir Entesar.

Following the overthrow of Reza Shah, many sued for the recovery of their land. In 1942, the descendants of Hedayatollah Khan sued in the Court of Assigned Properties for the recovery of Nashta. In 1944, the court ruled in favor of the plaintiffs, and Nashta was restored. The court's ver-dict included an account of the manner in which Nashta had been "pur-chased" by Reza Shah, who paid less than the land's revenue for one year. Moreover, the restoration of Nashta was possible because Mohammad Reza Shah had not yet consolidated power. No compensation was paid to the owners for thirteen years of lost income and for the pain and suffering inflicted because of Amir Nasri's wrongful death and the exile of the oth-ers. Very few restorations took place after 1946. In 1949, the lands that had been confiscated by Reza Shah became the property of his son, and they were subsequently sold between 1951 and 1962. Hedayatollah Khan's estate was owned by some sixty descendants. This provides an outstanding example of the manner in which large estates were broken up under an Islamic system. In just two generations, the descendants of Hedayatollah Khan had become small landowners. They were expropriated under the three phases of land distribution during the 1960s. A nearly identical case concerned the village of Golsefid, also in Mazandaran.[24] As described by Adib-Saberi, Reza Shah acquired Golsefid during the 1930s. After the shah's downfall, the owners sued and the village was restored. Adib-Saberi reports that before land reform, the village of Golsefid was owned by forty-six individuals; all were expropriated under Phase Three. Between 1932 and 1962, Nashta and Golsefid were confiscated twice by the Pahlavi regime.

Reza Shah as Source of Corruption

Until the very end of his reign, Reza Shah was amassing wealth. A case in point is Reza Shah's acquisition of a large amount of property, including villages, gardens, houses, mills, shops, caravanseries, and stables in Bojnurd, Khorasan. The text of the deed of sale by the Ministry of Finance to Reza Shah appears in appendix A. This document demonstrates why it is so difficult to obtain an accurate figure on the amount of property obtained by Reza Shah. Many entries consist of numerous items, for example, a village, eighteen gardens, and a mill all under one entry. Others include shops, houses, and a hamlet, all mixed together. However, similar to the Zavar document of exchange, this document is of enormous interest to historians. And it is very revealing. It shows Reza Shah's income was so large by the standards of the day because he left practically no source untapped. Why was the shah acquiring houses, shops, flour mills, inns, and even a stable in Bojnurd? The answer is to be found in the geographical location of Bojnurd. It is located on the route to Mashhad, and practically all Iranian pilgrims passed through the town on their way to and from Mashhad. Shops, bakeries, and inns did brisk business all year. And houses could be turned into inns. Reza Shah was anxious to tap into this lucrative business. Historically, the pilgrim route between Gorgan and Bojnurd had been infested by bandits. After the common bandits were suppressed, a far more powerful, dangerous, and sinister bandit had emerged.

It can safely be concluded that these estates in Bojnurd had been acquired by the government from the owners through force and fraud, and they were then "sold" to Reza Shah. How had the government acquired the shops and the houses and gardens in the town of Bojnurd? Evidently,

Reza Shah did not take only from landowners; even shopkeepers and ordinary people were not safe. The deed of sale is dated 13 February 1940. The seller was Brigadier Reza Qoli Amir-Khosrovi, minister of finance, representing the government of Iran. The purchaser was His August Imperial Majesty, Reza Shah Pahlavi, who was represented by a Hosein Sheibani. We are told that the price was 1,718,759 rials, which was "all deposited in the country's treasury." It was noted above that Amir-Khosrovi's name and signature had appeared in some of the correspondence and deposits with foreign banks. It is highly revealing that the same person who had handled Reza Shah's foreign bank deposits was now the country's minister of finance and was selling government property to the shah.

Inevitably a question arises. To what extent were individuals like Brigadier Amir-Khosrovi and General Bouzarjomehri able to emulate the example of Reza Shah and accumulate land and property for themselves? Having arranged and participated in the confiscation of these villages, houses, and even shops from their unfortunate owners, and then having "sold" them to His Majesty, could the servant "purchase" a few villages and houses for himself from the Ministry of Finance? Naturally not in Mazandaran, Gilan, Bojnurd, or other places that were of interest to the shah. But perhaps in Qom, Qazvin, or Saveh, locations that were not too far from Tehran, or even in the official's home province? Could Reza Shah continue to accumulate wealth in this manner without keeping these brigadiers and generals happy? Could he ask his servants to take the vows of poverty while he himself accumulated so much wealth? Of course not. To become and remain instruments of brutality and force, these individuals expected to receive adequate compensation. Once having acquired a few villages themselves, to what degree did these high government and military officials emulate some of the royal practices of demanding half of the crop and regular forced labor from the peasants?

These are important questions because of the enormous scale and potential for corruption and brutality. We have identified a few of the many individuals, both military and civilian, who were instrumental in helping Reza Shah to acquire and manage this wealth. They ranged from senior army officers such as General Bouzarjomehri and Brigadier Amir-Khosrovi, to a Lieutenant Majlisi, and the lowly former police and gendarme officers who acted as bailiffs in the villages of Zavar. They included a cabinet minister, Ali Akbar Davar, a senior bureaucrat, Hasan Moshar, head of the Bank of Iran, and a midlevel bureaucrat, Engineer Halati, head of the Office of Royal Estates in Tonekabon. Did these individuals faithfully serve their master in his accumulation of wealth, or did they also emulate his example? In their dealings with the peasants, did they just take what "rightfully belonged to the shah," or did they take a little extra for themselves? Clearly, the answer is important, because if each of these individuals became even a minuscule version of Reza Shah, the cumulative effect would have been enormous. Reason as well as evidence indicate that many if not all of these individuals were following the shah's example. In the case of the "purchase" of Kojour by Reza Shah, we saw what became of the money that was supposed to go to the unfortunate landowners. The money was appropriated by His Majesty's two representatives, Mirza Karim Khan Rashti and Amir Akram. To compound the injury, we saw how one of the landowners, Amir Zadeh, even lost her diamond ring! Clearly, the subject is a fertile one for in-depth research.

The depth of anger that was expressed in the pages of the Rasht newspaper, *Badr Monir,* in 1942–43 was a reflection of the hostility caused by the misdeeds of government agents. The newspaper described how government officials came with empty pockets and left with wealth and all its trappings. The newspaper also noted that on the path to the acquisition of these riches lay the remains of many ruined families. Following the removal of Reza Shah, the Tudeh Party had established in Mazandaran an organization called the Union of Iranian Cultivators and had published and distributed its manifesto. This manifesto outlined Tudeh's demand for a land distribution, and the practical measures it proposed are given in appendix A. Unquestionably, the manifesto contained much propaganda, but it was not all lies and falsehoods. The Tudeh pamphlet contained the following:

Peasants and Cultivators of Mazandaran

For twenty years reactionary agents have plundered the innocent cultivator without leaving him the barest necessities needed to survive. The landowner, the bailiff, the gendarme, the tax collector, in short, whoever arrived first at the harvest took all he could from what rightfully belonged to the cultivator. . . . All this wealth and goods that you have been deprived of have been created by your blood, suffering, and effort. Do you recall the black period of Reza Khan when you grew the tastiest and best citrus fruits, but the agents of Reza Shah plundered your fruits and did not permit your children to even taste this fruit? Do you recall how your wives and children were forced to plant rice in the malaria-infested swamps and under the burning sun? They produced the best rice that was plundered by lackeys of Reza Khan, and you had to make do with the crumbs and the inferior champa rice. Often even these crumbs were not available. Do you recall when the bailiffs and the butchers of Reza Khan took your daughters and wives for forced labor, separated them and forced them to sleep in the stables, and did not spare them of all dishonor and rape? Do you know that the same system is in place? Do you know that unless you do something now, the past will come again?

Reza Khan robbed you and is gone. He left these lands which must now be distributed to you who have been so robbed. But now a group of large landowners, the same people who were representatives of Reza Khan, want to devour this land like a dragon, and deprive you of your livelihood, and once again take the place of Reza Khan in perpetuating tyranny. Brothers! At no time have the people of Mazandaran been so oppressed and exploited. Your ancestors did not have to submit to this indignity and poverty. You too must not submit to this poverty and degradation. Do not let the estates of Reza Khan be stolen by parasites and plunderers. Destroy these cursed dragons. These properties must be distributed among you the people who work this land and water this land with your sweat. To make sure that the estates of Reza Khan are distributed among you the people, and the hands of plunderer and parasite are forever cut off, you must unite! You must join hands. One hand does not make a sound. But a thousand hands do. One twig is easily broken, but even Rostam and the White Ogre cannot break a thousand twigs. If you unite, no one can deprive you of your rights and impose tyranny on you. Never again will a second Reza Khan come to life! Long live the Union of Cultivators–Tudeh Party!

4

Background to Land Distribution

Sale and Distribution of Pahlavi Estates, 1951–1962

In his memoirs, my father discusses the history of lands acquired by Reza Shah. On 14 September 1941, in the city of Isfahan, shortly before leaving for exile, Reza Shah transferred the ownership of his lands to his son and successor, Mohammad Reza Shah. One week later, Mohammad Reza Shah signed an imperial order, transferring these lands to the government for return to the previous owners. In June 1942, the Thirteenth Majlis enacted the Law of Transferred Estates. The law set up a special court or land tribunal, the Court of Transferred Estates, and the previous owners were given six months to file their claims and the supporting documents. In June 1949, as one of its last acts, the Fifteenth Majlis passed a law to the effect that in those cases where the government prevailed against the previous landowners in the Court of Assigned Properties, the villages would be given to Mohammad Reza Shah. With the approaching elections for the Sixteenth Majlis, many deputies had voted for this law in order to curry favor with the shah and ensure their reelection. Two individuals in the cabinet of Mohammad Saed were particularly important in facilitating the transfer of these lands to the shah: Abbas Qoli Golshahian, minister of finance, and Amir Assadollah Alam, minister of agriculture. Not surprisingly, Alam was subsequently placed in charge of the management and sale of these estates. The villages so acquired by the shah were formed into a private endowment (*vaqf khass*) called the Pahlavi Vaqf.

On 27 January 1951, the shah issued an edict instructing the director of Pahlavi Endowments, Jalal Shademan, to arrange for the sale of the Crown lands to the peasants residing on and cultivating these lands. The shah's edict also called for the formation of a commission that would be responsible for the details of the sales. On 30 January 1951, the membership of the commission was announced. According to a confidential report by J. J. Wagner of the American embassy (no. 593, dated 31 January

1951), the commission was chaired by Hosein Ala, minister of court, and its members were Amir Assadollah Alam, Habibollah Amuzegar, Jamal Akhavi, Amir Alai, Shahab Khosravani, Abdollah Moazami, Ibrahim Zand, and Sadeq Shafaq. Sale and distribution were begun in May 1952 when twelve villages in Varamin, near Tehran, were distributed. As described below, from the beginning the distribution and sale of Pahlavi estates were assisted by the U.S. government through its Point Four Program. Evidently, there was a clear and fortunate convergence of U.S. foreign policy considerations and the financial interests of the Pahlavis. Prime Minister Mossadeq stopped the sales on the grounds that these lands had been illegally acquired by Reza Shah, and hence they did not belong to Mohammad Reza Shah. Moreover, the sales were technically illegal, since a vaqf was supposedly inalienable and could not be sold. In his book, Mohammad Reza Shah displayed great bitterness toward Mossadeq for halting his land distribution.[1] He accused Mossadeq of being jealous of his popularity and of being a reactionary landowner himself. Mohammad Reza Shah finally obtained possession of these lands after the August 1953 coup, which restored him to power. Sales resumed following the overthrow of Mossadeq, and were completed in 1962. The ownership of these villages, however, was subject to dispute. Ann Lambton noted that despite "unresolved legal issues" concerning the disposition of these lands (for example, the status of ouqaf, or endowed properties immobilized for charitable or other purposes), the shah proceeded to sell these lands to peasant cultivators as well as to entrepreneurs during the 1950s.[2] It was also reported by the American embassy that some of the land was given to friends and supporters of the shah (confidential report by R. W. Dye, Foreign Service despatch 419, dated 1 February 1961).

There were striking differences between the way land reform was implemented on the royal estates and the way it was implemented on private land. In the case of royal estates, the land was carefully parceled, and each parcel was valued by "expert" appraisers and then sold at favorable market prices. Information on the sale price of royal lands is provided in a confidential report by T. O. Engebretson, agricultural attaché at the American embassy (Foreign Service despatch 204, dated 21 October 1961). The purpose of the report was to discuss ways to compensate landowners in the forthcoming land distribution program. The report contains the following observation: "Where private individuals have bought and sold land there is some historical precedent for the valuation of land (villages) on the basis of 10 times its annual yield of crops. In the distribution of Crown lands and Public Domain lands the valuation key used has been 8 to 10 times the annual productivity." In "Distribution of Public

Domain Lands in Azarbaijan" (Foreign Service dispatch 107, dated 21 June 1961), Martin Polstein, American vice consul in Tabriz, reported that the price of government land distributed to peasants in Azarbaijan was 20,000 rials ($267) per hectare. In the case of the Pahlavi lands, an additional 15 percent service charge and the value of the cultivator's house and facilities were added to the cost of the land. Consequently, the price charged for the shah's land was in essence the market price of land, notwithstanding the shah's claims of "benevolence." It is also noteworthy that in his 1961 book, the shah was adamant that his land should not freely be given to the cultivators because it would send an inappropriate "psychological" message. Attempts to give land away at no cost were strongly discouraged on the grounds that it was socially "disruptive." In contrast, when it came to the distribution of private land, the land was summarily confiscated with only a token compensation and given to the cultivators at practically no cost.

The shah also claimed that he had not benefited financially from the sale of Pahlavi estates. However, Thomas J. Scotes, second secretary of the American embassy, noted in a confidential report (Foreign Service dispatch 695, dated 30 March 1959) that "many people believe that the Shah is using this way to sell his land while he can, for as much money as he can." The skepticism was related to the shah's purchases of real estate in Europe while he was selling his lands in Iran, thereby giving the impression that he was exchanging lands confiscated by Reza Shah for more valuable and secure real estate in Europe. In a confidential report to the State Department (Foreign Service dispatch 275, dated 5 May 1959), the American representative to the United Nations Organization in Geneva, Henry S. Villard, described the shah's May 1959 visit to Geneva:

> This is the Shah's second visit to Geneva in recent months. Press reports indicate that on May 4 he inspected a villa situated at 27, Chemin du Velours, in the Chene Bourgeoisie district, which has been bought in his behalf by General Zahedi. Other press reports indicate that the Shah consulted with Geneva bankers handling his financial interests. According to earlier, private reports, the Shah has been purchasing apartment houses in Geneva through General Zahedi, and has rented some as furnished apartments (a more highly profitable operation than unfurnished rental) while leaving others unoccupied.

In 1952, Bank Omran (Development Bank) was established for the express purpose of selling these lands and handling the finances. Much information on the sale of the Pahlavi estates can be obtained from two reports produced in the 1950s. First, there is a 1955 report by Ali Moarefi given at an FAO conference in Salahudin, Iraq.[3] The second is an undated Bank Omran report on the sales (most likely, the report was put out in 1958). Bank Omran is described as "His Majesty's private bank," with capital of 100 million rials. Of this, 15 million rials had been deposited by the shah and 18 million rials by the Point Four Program (U.S. government). The rest was obtained from the government of Iran (Plan Organization and Bank Melli) and from the installment payments obtained from the land sales. The International Cooperation Administration (U.S. government), the Ford Foundation, and the Near East Foundation provided technical assistance.[4]

Understandably, information on the amount of land that remained in the possession of Mohammad Reza Shah and the sale of this land has been sketchy. However, it is possible to reconstruct a broad outline. In a 1951 speech to a land reform convention in Madison, Wisconsin, Assadollah Alam stated that of the 45,000 villages in the country, 3,000 were owned by the shah.[5] As a member of the imperial commission for the distribution of the Crown lands, Alam was in a position to know. Alam's figure indicates that of the 3,500 villages acquired by Reza Shah, about 500 had been restored to the previous owners by the Court of Assigned Properties. However, Alam was silent on the subject of 4,000 pastures and forests acquired by Reza Shah. Ali Moarefi reported in 1955 that the shah's distribution of his private property involved "more than two thousand totally or partially owned villages and almost two thousand parcels of pasture lands located in six out of eleven Iranian Ostans." Moarefi did not mention the "other" 2,000 items, and the wording indicates that not all of the property was available for sale. The Bank Omran report stated that in the summer of 1958, of the 2,100 villages in the Pahlavi estate, 120 had been sold and the remaining 1,980 villages were to be distributed during the next three or four years (Bank Omran 8). In terms of hectares, the Bank Omran report stated that potentially 1–1.5 million hectares of the shah's property were available for sale and division and were "among the most fertile cultivated lands in Iran." Most significantly, the report also states that as of 1958, the ownership of at least one-third of the Pahlavi land was subject to litigation in the courts. That is, well after the establishment of the shah as the undisputed ruler, the landowning classes were trying to recover the land taken by his father. It is also noteworthy that the Bank Omran report does not even acknowledge the existence, let alone the disposition, of some 4,000 "other" pieces and "pastures." None of these documents give any clue as to what became of the many shops, houses, hotels, and other such properties that were acquired by Reza Shah. Another piece of the

puzzle concerns the discrepancy between Alam's 1951 figure of 3,000 villages and Bank Omran's estimate of 2,100 villages. Some of the discrepancy can be explained by the restoration of land to the previous owners or
their descendants in the 1950s after the overthrow of Mossadeq. The restored land was promptly reconfiscated by the Pahlavi regime, this time
under land reform—but this is getting ahead of our story. In all, the data
show that the shah sold at least 2,000 villages, consisting of 1–1.5 million
hectares of land.

Sale of Pahlavi Estates: Two Case Studies

Concerning the conditions and terms of the sale and distribution of the
Pahlavi estates, all land to be sold was surveyed and appraised. It was
then sold to the cultivators and, in the case of excess land, to other "qualified" individuals as well. The price charged to the buyer was the appraised price less 20 percent discount granted by the shah. A 15 percent
service charge was then levied. The net price to the cultivator came to 92
percent of the appraised price. The price for the land was payable in
twenty-five yearly installments, and the 15 percent service charge was
payable over fifteen years. The land could not be sold or leased out until
all installments had been paid off. Concerning the cultivator's house and
the land on which the building was located, each person's residence was
to be appraised, and the property was to be sold to the occupant at 25
percent of the appraised value, payable in cash. A rare glimpse of the
prices charged for the Pahlavi estates is given in the paper by Moarefi,
which contains a report by Assadollah Alam on the sale and distribution
of land in the village of Khanlogh, near Tehran, in 1954, and another report by Habibollah Amuzegar on the sale of land in Takestan, Qazvin,
also in 1954.

The land area of Khanlogh was 1,610 hectares. Of this, 960 hectares
were divided among 120 cultivators, each receiving 8 hectares (consisting
of three plots, each plot being of a different quality). Alam reports that
another 150 hectares were prepared and distributed later. The 960 hectares had been appraised at 1,440,000 rials, and with 20 percent discount
this amounted to 1,155,000 rials ($32,000), or 1,200 rials ($33) per hectare.
If the remaining 650 hectares were sold under similar terms, then the
sums received for the sale of this village would have amounted to $53,000
payable over twenty-five years ($2,100 per year), and $8,000 in 15 percent
service charge, receivable over fifteen years ($530 per year). The sum of
$61,000 in 1954 would be equivalent to $400,000 in 1998 prices. Alam does
not give any indication of the amounts to be received from the sale of the
houses occupied by the cultivators.

A report by Habibollah Amuzegar on the sale and distribution of land in Takestan, Qazvin, in 1954 is also given in Moarefi. Located 30 kilometers southwest of Qazvin, agricultural land in Takestan receives irrigation water from the Khar Rud River. According to Amuzegar, the total land area in Takestan was 18,000 hectares. Of this, 10,800 hectares had been distributed among 1,600 households, of whom 400 were not previously cultivators. Amuzegar also points out that the 2,000 hectares of vineyards and orchards, the most valuable part of Takestan, were not included in this sale. The total value of the land sold was appraised at 33 million rials ($917,000 at the 1954 exchange rate), but with the 20 percent discount granted by the shah, the price charged was 26.4 million rials ($733,000), payable over twenty-five years. The price per hectare, inclusive of the 15 percent service charge, was $78. Assuming that the 5,200 hectares were sold at the same price, the total cropland in Takestan was sold for $1.25 million. If the sales of the 2,000 hectares of vineyards and orchards are included, the sum would have easily surpassed $2.5 million at 1954 prices (including the 15 percent service charge). This was a vast sum by the standards of the time. In terms of 1998 prices, it amounted to at least $15 million, and the annual installment amounted to at least $100,000 at 1954 prices, or about $600,000 at 1998 prices. The sums did not include amounts received from the sale of residential properties to the cultivators.

Given that over 2,000 villages were sold under these conditions, the sale of the lands that had been confiscated by Reza Shah, the Pahlavi estates, was an immensely lucrative affair. In his 1960 book, the shah denied any financial benefit from the sale of these lands. He stated that all profits had been ploughed back into the development of these villages. Unfortunately, the total amount from the sale of these lands may never be known because the subsequent reports on the matter, such as the undated Bank Omran report, and several other reports by Hushang Ram, the person who was subsequently placed in charge of the sale of the Pahlavi estates, do not contain any financial information. Unlike Alam and Amuzegar, Ram carefully avoided all financial matters in his reports. Furthermore, the most valuable part of the Pahlavi estates was not the semi-arid lands of Khanlogh and Takestan about which we have the sales information. The most valuable land consisted of the Caspian rice fields and orange groves of Mazandaran and Gilan and the cotton fields of Gorgan. No information was provided on the prices at which this land was sold. There is also clear evidence that there was a subsequent attempt to mislead future researchers on the extent of the land sales by the Pahlavis. The 1962 report by Hushang Ram, given in the presence of the shah in Marble Palace on the occasion of the announced completion of the sale of the Pahlavi estates, stated that 42,000 households had received 200,000 hectares of land under the program for the distribution and sale of the Pahlavi estates. Prior reports by Bank Omran had mentioned 2,000 villages, and 1.5 million hectares were available for distribution. No attempt was made to explain this discrepancy. That this is a gross understatement can be seen from the following. The 1955 report by Moarefi reported that by October 1955, agricultural land in sixty villages belonging to the Pahlavi estates had been sold and distributed. The total land area in these villages was 100,812.8 hectares. Of this, 56,492 hectares (56 percent of the area) had been sold and distributed to 8,251 households. Given that over 2,000 villages were sold and distributed, the reported figure of 42,000 total households is simply not credible. The actual figure was many times higher. Furthermore, all these discrepancies and the absence of financial data cast further doubt on the assertions by the shah that he was in no way a beneficiary of these sales. If not, why the misleading data and secrecy?

My father gives the following account of the distribution and sale of the village of Takestan:

> During the fall of 1956, accompanied by some of my children, I was returning from Ebrahim Abad to Qazvin. On the way, we stopped in Takestan to get some water. When the inhabitants found out that I had arrived, they gathered around me. At that time, on His Majesty's order, Takestan had been distributed among the cultivators. I praised this action, but the cultivators were deeply unhappy. It turned out that without taking into consideration the actual holding and cultivation of the land, the surveyors had drawn lines and had divided the land into plots, and the land had been distributed by drawing lots. Consequently, land previously cultivated by Hosein had been allotted to Taqi. Taqi would not come forward to take possession of the land, nor would Hosein permit Taqi to approach the land. In short, the whole process was defective, and the village was in turmoil. The right way was that each person should have been given the land he previously cultivated. I learned that Mr. Amuzegar had been involved in the division of Takestan, and in Tehran I spoke to him privately during a meeting of the Joint Commission on Justice and Treasury. I suggested to him that in the future, land distribution should be on the basis of existing land holding and not on the basis of the surveyor's drawings.

Majd reports that Amuzegar became upset and subsequently portrayed him as an opponent of land distribution.[6]

Restoration of Zavar, 1955

Some of the lands acquired by Reza Shah were eventually returned to the original owners during the 1940s and 1950s following litigation. Zavar was returned after lengthy litigation against the Pahlavi Foundation. The restoration of Zavar was part of the settlement between the government and the heirs of Sepahsalar, much of whose property had been seized by the government during the 1920s and subsequently acquired by Reza Shah. The details of the restoration are described by Majd and will be given here. As noted earlier, in 1942 the Majlis enacted a law that enabled the landowners whose lands had been expropriated by Reza Shah to file suit in the newly formed Court of Assigned Properties. On the basis of this law, the descendants of Sepahsalar petitioned the court on the grounds that their father's property had been forcibly and unlawfully seized. Despite the evidence and the testimony in support of the plaintiffs by people such as Prime Minister Sadr-ol Ashra-af, the court ruled against the plaintiffs in 1945. Majd reports that he filed a separate complaint concerning the estates of Zavar with the court, and in 1947 the court ruled in his favor. However, the government appealed, and most of the ruling was overturned. With the exception of the villages of Mazibon and Talusarak, the rest of Zavar was returned to the government. In 1949, the Fifteenth Majlis passed a law that gave the shah all contested properties over which the government had been victorious in the tribunal. Under the law's provisions, Zavar became the property of the shah.

Fig. 4.1. Rural house and barn, presumably in the village of Moalem Kuh, Nashta, Tonekabon, circa 1950.

Having lost in the land tribunal, the heirs filed a civil suit. Majd hints that by 1954, the plaintiffs commanded considerable political muscle. One of the plaintiffs, Abol Hasan Amidi-Nuri, was a Majlis deputy and deputy prime minister to Zahedi. Another, Arsalan Khalatbari, was a Majlis deputy and a foremost attorney. Two others, Mohammad Ali Varasteh and Mohammad Ali Majd, were influential senators. The complainants then authorized Seyed Mehdi Farrokh to reach a settlement with the Pahlavi estates. The settlement consisted of 9 million rials for each male descendent and 4.5 million rials for each female descendant. In 1954, the shah consented to giving each descendant an equivalent amount of land. Although Majd does not say so, it appears that the shah's generosity was in return for the support he had received from Amidi-Nuri, Arsalan Khalatbari, and Majd during his battle with Mossadeq. According to the settlement with the Pahlavi estates, as the sole surviving child of Amir Zadeh, the eldest daughter of Mohammad Vali Khan, my mother was to receive 4.5 million rials in land. The settlement had nothing to do with the 1935 exchange between Amir Entesar and the government in which Zavar had been exchanged for a group of villages in Qazvin, Zanjan, Arak, and Karaj. My father gives the following account:

In 1935, the government had exchanged the estates of Zavar. Since prior to the exchange the late Amir Entesar had transferred Zavar to me, after the passage of the Law of Assignment, I filed suit in the court, and I prevailed in the initial ruling. But on appeal, due to Tudeh Party intrigues, with the exception of two villages, Mazibon and Talusarak, I was defeated on the other villages. In 1955, that is, ten years after the adverse court ruling, on the basis of His Majesty's order, and as part of the legal settlement [with the Pahlavi estates], Amir Banou Khanum was to receive property as her inheritance from her mother, the late Amir Zadeh Khanum, daughter of the late Sepahsalar Tonekaboni. One day, I had been invited to a luncheon party by General Zahedi at his residence in Qeitarieh. Mr. Assadollah Alam was also a guest. I asked him if, as part of the settlement with Mrs. Majd, she would be given the estates of Zavar. He consented and informed His Majesty. Immediately, an imperial order was issued stating that since Zavar had been the property of the late Amir Entesar, father of Amir Banou, its ownership had been granted to the same. But since each female inheritor was to receive 450,000 tomans, and the six-dang of Zavar exceeded this amount in value, the Pahlavi estates were willing to sell the remainder and receive the price in ten yearly installments. But Mrs. Majd would not accept, and consequently, she became owner of 3.5 dangs of Zavar. In this manner, the exchanged Zavar was restored.

At my mother's insistence, the remaining 2.5 dangs were transferred to her aunt, Taj ol Moluk, Mansur Saltaneh, the youngest daughter of Sepahsalar. Following the transfer of 3.5 dangs of Zavar to my mother, and the continued ownership of the exchanged villages, my father undoubtedly became one of the most important landowners in Iran. Majd points out that the Zavar restoration was unrelated to the 1935 exchange with the government. At the time of land distribution in 1962, Hasan Arsanjani had repeatedly claimed, in speeches and newspaper articles, that my parents had unlawfully acquired both the original and the exchanged land. By this he implied that the confiscation of my parents' property was justified. The reality was very different. The 1935 Zavar exchange was related to the property of Amir Entesar, my maternal grandfather. The 1955 Zavar restoration was in the context of the property and inheritance of my maternal grandmother.

The restoration of Zavar was bound to infuriate the shah. Although the restoration constituted royal generosity to those who had stood by him in his battle with Mossadeq, the shah viewed the restoration as an undoing of his father's work and legacy. Moreover, there were financial consider-

Fig. 4.2. Zavar, circa 1955. Rice field and wilderness at the foot of Elburz Mountains.

ations. The restored Zavar could have been sold to its cultivators at lucrative rates. The shah had blocked Majd's ministerial appointment in 1949 over matters relating to land and Zavar, and he was unlikely to forgive Majd's role in the Zavar restoration. He soon found other reasons to dislike my father.

Peasant Disturbances in Zavar, 1955–1956

The return of Zavar and other parts of Tonekabon to the heirs of Mohammad Vali Khan resulted in severe disturbances, and the events that followed can be described as a peasant rebellion in the winter of 1955. The origins of the disturbances can be traced to the acquisition of this land by Reza Shah in the 1930s and the land sales by his son twenty years later. The evidence shows that peasants on lands that were acquired by Reza Shah were exploited by the representatives of the Office of Royal Estates. Whether this was done on the shah's instructions is irrelevant. The fact is that the peasants came to feel the heavy hand of the shah's bailiffs, who were mostly former military or police officers. It is highly doubtful that the previous owners could have exerted this degree of control. A case in point is the "contractual" agreements that were drawn up between the Office of Royal Estates and the individual cultivators in Zavar for the establishment of new orange groves. I found a few of the original duplicates of these contracts in my father's private papers, and the terms are very revealing. The contracts, which are dated 1940, show that in return for a small sum as advance and aid, the peasants were obligated to clear jungle areas and plant orange trees within a prescribed period. In return for the financial "assistance," half of the crop was owed to the Office of Royal Estates (see appendix A). The contracts also stated that any neglect of the new orchards by the peasants or violation of the terms of the contract would be punishable by stiff fines. The cultivators of this land had briefly enjoyed independence after the downfall of Reza Shah. Between 1941 and 1946, when the area was under Soviet occupation and the ownership of these lands was in dispute and in limbo, the sharecroppers had paid little or no rent to anyone. But the harsh conditions had returned with the effective restoration of Zavar to the shah in 1949. That the shah's bailiffs had practiced much oppression is also reported by Lambton.[7] In 1955, Zavar had been restored to the Khalatbaris, who inherited the prevailing conditions that had grown under the Office of Royal Estates. For example, citing the precedent set by Reza Shah, the Khalatbaris could similarly demand half of the orange crop. They could also claim a rent of 55 kilos of rice per jarib (1,000 square meters) of rice field, on the grounds that this was the prevailing rent as determined by His Majesty's office. It appears that, to the cultivators, this was a heavy burden.

Moreover, the Tudeh Party had been active in rural Mazandaran since at least 1941 and had put out inflammatory pamphlets stating that the lands claimed by Reza Shah rightfully belonged to the tenant cultivators and must be distributed. The pamphlets had attacked and condemned in no uncertain terms the previous owners' attempts to win back the land. With the onset of the distribution of the Pahlavi estates in 1954, this dream appeared to be within the peasants' grasp. With the return of Zavar to previous owners, things could revert back to the conditions that existed under Reza Shah. Moreover, the tenants in Zavar felt aggrieved and cheated. By this time the Pahlavi villages were being divided and sold to the cultivators. The report by Moarefi indicates that several Pahlavi villages in Tonekabon had been sold and distributed by this time. The cultivators of Zavar similarly expected to be included in the distribution program. Their hopes had been dashed by the restoration to the previous owners.

Trouble broke out in Tonekabon as soon as the newly restored owners tried to exert their ownership rights. Majd cites some of the incidents. For example, in the village of Toshgoon, Tonekabon, in December 1955, the representative of the newly restored owner, Rahman Qoli Khan Khalatbari, was assaulted by the cultivators and chased out of the village. He complained to the gendarmerie.[8] When the gendarmes arrived to investigate, they were attacked by the villagers and chased away. In January 1956, representatives of the Registration Office arrived in the village of Aghouse Kaleh, Tonekabon, at the request of the newly restored owner, Haidar Qoli Khan Khalatbari, brother of Rahman Qoli. The purpose was to map and measure the land. They were attacked by the villagers. The chief cartographer was badly beaten, and the rest were put to flight. The troubles in Zavar were also serious.

Given that the total rent was based on area of land cultivated, it was the practice to measure the land cultivated by each sharecropper for the purpose of determining the rent due from each cultivator. Upon assuming ownership of Zavar, Majd ordered a measurement of all the rice fields in November 1955. This aroused intense and vociferous opposition on the part of the large cultivators who, according to Majd, held 50 percent of the total land. They sent telegrams to the shah and other notables, claiming that they were being oppressed and exploited by a powerful senator, and they staged sit-ins at the local telegraph office in Tonekabon (or Shahsavar, as it was known under the Pahlavis). Majd wrote:

In response to these provocations, the supervisor of the estates, Mohammad Saleh Ghaffari, brought in some twenty persons from the
village of Shal in Qazvin, and placed one or two Shalis in each village for the purpose of advising the Zavar cultivators and bringing
the troubles to an end. Unfortunately, the peasants were further enraged by this action, and a crowd of 1,500 wielding clubs, sickles,
and even guns attacked the house in which the Shalis were staying
in the village of Pelet Kaleh. After breaking the doors and the win-
dows, they brought cans of kerosene and intended to burn down the
house with the occupants therein. Faced with the threat of arson, the
Shalis exited the house, and in the ensuing fight, shots were fired,
two were injured, and the cultivators fled the scene. At this time, the
gendarmes arrived and arrested the Shalis and a group of the Zavar
cultivators. The old diehard members of the Tudeh Party seized
upon this affair to settle their account with me. They encouraged the
detainees to send numerous telegrams against me to His Majesty,
and copies were widely distributed. During the session of 26 January 1956, the text of a telegram was read on the Majlis floor by
Mohammad Derakhshesh. The Majlis deputies then protested Mr.
Derakhshesh's action.

Although the fellow senators were supportive, Majd records that the affair was very damaging politically. Majd also reports that the shah became upset over the affair, thereby hastening the end of Majd's political
career.

The significance of Mohammad Derakhshesh's attacks on landowners,
and Majd in particular, was not lost on the Majlis deputies nor on John W.
Bowling, second secretary at the American embassy. In a confidential report (Foreign Service dispatch 260, dated 22 October 1955), Bowling described Derakhshesh's attacks on landowners. He portrayed Derakhshesh as:

a man with former Tudeh affiliation who in the past has been used as
stalking-horse for the Shah. . . . Derakhshesh heaped abuse on the
landowning class, and bandied the name of the Shah freely as an
example of the reforming zeal which he admired. . . . Most of the
deputies understood it as a gesture by the Shah. They interpret it as
a kind of declaration of war by the Shah. . . . The development appears to be very significant. At the very least, it would appear that
the incident presages another undercover bitterness between the
Shah and the Majlis, with concomitant dangers and uncertainty.

In another confidential report (Foreign Service despatch 661, dated 7 February 1956), Bowling reported that during the Majlis session of 26 January 1956, "Deputy Derakhshesh caused a stir when he read a telegram from farmers in Qazvin alleging that the employees of Senator Majd (a big landowner in the area) were oppressing the villagers." That the alleged "telegram from farmers in Qazvin" was a forgery can be seen from the fact that the actual disturbances had occurred in Mazandaran and not in Qazvin.

The forgery of the telegram notwithstanding, the affair and the other disturbances in Tonekabon were bound to be seen by the shah and the pro-distribution faction in the U.S. embassy as yet another indication of the need for land distribution. However, the landlord-tenant relations had broken down in Tonekabon because of the special circumstances created by the actions of the two Pahlavi shahs since the 1930s. Moreover, there were sharp differences in climate and topography between the small Caspian region and the rest of Iran. It did not follow that landlord-tenant relations were similar in the rest of Iran.

Land Distribution in Vardavar, Karaj, 1958:
A Case Study of Private Initiative

In his writings and speeches during the 1960s and 1970s, Mohammad Reza Shah had often castigated Iran's landowners for not following his lead in land distribution. This was not strictly true. My father sold and distributed two hamlets in Khoramdareh, Zanjan, to the cultivators in 1953 (see chap. 11). Moreover, as described in this case study, rhetoric notwithstanding, the shah and his government were actually hostile to any private initiative in land distribution. The point is illustrated by a revealing episode concerning the village of Vardavar located halfway between Tehran and Karaj.

The village was actually a landmark because of an old stone-made caravanseray. The village had three sources of irrigation water and one main qanat. It also drew water from the Karaj and Qouri Chai Rivers. It had twenty-five sharecropping cultivators. The village was owned by Prince Shahroukh Firouz, the youngest son of Prince Nosrat Dowleh Firouz. As noted in chapter 3, Nosrat Dowleh was murdered in prison and was a prominent victim of Reza Shah. Shahroukh Firouz was also a brother of Mozzafar Firouz, a bitter foe of the Pahlavis who served in the cabinet of Qavam Saltaneh as a leftist minister during the Azarbaijan crisis of 1945–46. What follows was recounted to me by Shahroukh Firouz himself. In the late 1950s, Shahroukh Firouz was employed by the U.S.

Point Four Program. Having witnessed the unrelenting American pressure for a land distribution, and convinced that a land distribution was inevitable, he decided to distribute his estates in a manner that would be beneficial to himself and the cultivators. In addition to the village of Vardavar, he owned several villages in the Maragheh region of Azarbaijan, the first region where land distribution was implemented in 1962. The agricultural estates in Azarbaijan were particularly valuable because the land was irrigated by the waters of Zarin Rud River. He had tried the project first in Vardavar. In 1957–58, the agricultural land in Vardavar had been surveyed and mapped by engineer Jaffar Yekta, a retired employee of the Registration Bureau. Subsequently, the land that was cultivated by the twenty-five tenants was transferred to the tenants at no charge. In addition, the landowner undertook to maintain and clean the qanat and the irrigation canals as in the past. In exchange, the cultivators renounced all claim to the remaining land that was not cultivated by them. The transactions were completed in Notary Office 3 in Tehran, located in Hasan Abad Square notary public, Hasan Enayat. The attorney was Ali Oveissi. He was also the attorney in Majd's 1962 test case lawsuit against the government in which Majd challenged the legality and constitutionality of the 1962 land distribution cabinet decree.

As freely admitted by Shahroukh Firouz, his generosity was based on his personal interest. On the one hand, the cultivators received land and water at no cost. On the other hand, all land not held by the cultivators became the recognized and secure property of the landowner. This was supposed to be a pilot project for the much larger distribution program in the estates of Azarbaijan, where the land was irrigated by the waters of Zarin Rud River. Having separated the land in Azarbaijan, Firouz intended to undertake large-scale commercial farming. Since the land was in the vicinity of the sugarbeet mill in Miandoab, he intended to specialize in sugarbeets, grains, and livestock. However, it was not to be. As soon as the land was transferred to the cultivators in Vardavar, General Baqaii, the owner of the village of Qaleh Hasan Khan to the south of Vardavar, objected and complained to the shah that this was a "communist" act. The general claimed that Shahroukh Firouz had become a communist like his brother Mozzafar. Subsequently, Shahroukh Firouz was arrested by Savak and jailed for one week. He was released only after giving a written guarantee that he would not repeat the action in his other villages located in East Azarbaijan. It appears that the shah's displeasure was related to the sale of the Pahlavi estates. During this time, the shah himself was in the process of selling the Pahlavi estates at lucrative prices. Rhetoric aside, he did not look kindly on those who gave land to the peasants free of charge. It is also remarkable that while one landowner, my father, had been driven out of the Senate because he was perceived as an opponent of land distribution, another landowner, Shahroukh Firouz, had been jailed for distributing land. Unquestionably, Firouz's experiment was an interesting one. It showed that private land could have been surveyed and distributed in an orderly fashion to the cultivators. It safeguarded the qanats, and it could have been a model for land distribution in the rest of Iran.

5

Founding of the Agricultural Union of Iran,
1959, Land Reform Law of May 1960,
and Cabinet Decrees of 9 January 1962
and 17 January 1963

After leaving the Senate, Mohammad Ali Majd embarked on a new chapter in his long political career, one that would have lasting significance. He gradually became an active opponent of Mohammad Reza Shah and played an important part in the resistance to the shah's "White Revolution." In his memoirs, my father states that upon hearing widespread rumors of an impending land redistribution in the late 1950s, he began organizing Iran's landowners, and in 1959 he founded and was executive secretary of the Agricultural Union of Iran (Etehadieh Fellahati-e Iran). This was a political organization whose purpose was to influence public opinion, parliamentary debate, and government action and to defend the interests of the landowning class. Its means consisted of publishing information bulletins and commentaries in the national press. It also formed an alliance with the ulama, including Ayatollah Khomeini. By Iranian standards, this was a pioneering organization, one that could have evolved into a political party had it not been forcibly suppressed by the government.

Majd states on numerous occasions that the foundation of sound agriculture in Iran was cooperation between the cultivator and the landowner. Addressing the economic and political role of landowners, Majd asks, "How were villages established in Iran?"

For the villages of Iran, there is no recorded history stating in what year and how a village was established. But this information is evident from the names of the villages. For example, when an individual named Hasan has developed previously unused land by establishing a qanat and has constructed the homes to house the cultivators, the village is named Hasan Abad after its founder. Wherever a landowner has established a village, that village has taken the name of its founder. In particular, whenever a village has a qanat, for sure it has been established by an owner and named after him, such as Ebrahim Abad, Majd Abad, and Fatn Abad. The last two villages were recently established by me. I dug the qanat and built the houses, and the villages are named after me. For example, traveling eastward from Shahsavar, the first village is called Abdollah Abad, established by Abdollah Khan, a brother of Mohammad Vali Khan Khalatbari, Sepahsalar Azam. Then it is Mohammad Hosein Abad, established by Mohammad Hosein Khan Entesar ol Dowleh, another brother of Sepahsalar. Then Haji Mahalleh, established and developed by an individual named Haji. Then there is Vali Abad, established by the same Vali Khan Khalatbari. The point is that most of the villages of Iran were established and developed by the landowners. I recall that one night after Arsanjani's anti–land reform decree was approved by the cabinet of Ali Amini, I had a conversation with Mr. Ameri, one of the most respected landowners in Kerman. He told me that he knew of a landowner who had spent 15 million rials ($200,000) on a qanat, but the qanat was still not fully productive. After the Arsanjani decree, he had given up digging and had written off the cost. Later, I learned that the landowner was Mr. Ameri himself.

The following duties and tasks are generally performed by landowners and their representatives:

1. Construction of qanats and canals and the distribution of water.
2. Construction of houses for the cultivators at the time of establishment of the village. Thereafter, if a new cultivator wished to settle in the village and undertake cultivation, the owner would either build a house or would permit and help the cultivator to build.[1]
3. Provision of primary capital such as plough animal and seed and the living expenses of the cultivator in the first year of establishment and settlement. If necessary, the owner would also provide the cultivator with a few sheep, or its equivalent in money.
4. Provide help to the cultivators in years of drought, crop failure, or locust infestation. To enable the survival of the cultivators,

the owner provided assistance in cash and in kind until the next crop year.[2]
5. Investigation and resolution of local disputes.
6. Construction of a mosque and water storage.
7. Help the cultivators in their dealings with the gendarmes and government agents.
8. Supervision of cultivation and agricultural tasks. The land-owner or his representative supervised each individual cultivator during the planting and harvest. At dawn after the morning prayers, the bailiff went to each door and sent each cultivator to perform his daily tasks.
9. Ensure village security, evict undesirable individuals, or place them in the custody of the authorities.

Majd then stresses the political and military role played by landowners especially since the sixteenth century. Since the Safavi era, Iran's landowners have provided the bulk of its military and senior statesmen. The Ottoman Wars of the Safavids and the Russian and Afghan Wars of the Qajars are examples of the military role of landowners in the defense of the kingdom. Defense of the borders of the kingdom was always the responsibility of the landowners.

History shows that landowners have been at the forefront of all the progressive upheavals in this country. The Barmakis were among the most important landowners of their period. The Seljuk minister, Khajeh Nezam ol-Molk, and his family were also among the largest landowners. In the famous Battle of Chaldaran, all the leaders and generals of the army of Shah Esmail were landowners. All were killed and not one was taken prisoner. With only 27,000 men they fought a much bigger Ottoman army of 250,000 men that was the bravest and best equipped army of its time. Their bravery was based on two principles: their devotion to the Shia faith, and the love of the land they owned. During the Herat wars, the father of Habibollah Khan, Saed ad Dowleh, and grandfather of Mohammad Vali Khan, Sepahsalar Azam, Mohammad Vali, who was killed on the day of the battle, was among the largest landowners of the day. In more recent times, the victors of Tehran in 1909 were Mohammad Vali Khan Khalatbari (then Sepahdar Azam), and Ali Qoli Khan Bakhtiari, Sardar Asad, who were among the largest landowners of Iran. After the conquest of Tehran, they deposed Mohammad Ali Shah, installed Ahmad Shah, and established constitutional rule. One of those who bore arms in the ranks of Mohammad Vali Khan's army and fought was Mirza Hasan Sheik ol Eslam-e Qazvini, who was also a landowner.

Between 1901, when the oil concession was given to D'Arcy during the reign of Mozzafar ad Din Shah, and 1932, the most the Anglo-Persian Oil Company paid to Iran was £500,000. It was the likes of Teymourtash, Sardar Asad, Nosrat Dowleh, Hosein Ala, and Davar (the late Ali Akbar Davar had been sent to study in Europe at the expense of the Panahi family, a large landowner in Azarbaijan), all landowners, who brought the importance of oil to Reza Shah's attention. Consequently, Reza Shah tore up the oil agreement, and under the new agreement, Iran's revenue increased to £5 million. In 1946, such individuals as Zolfaqari, Hedayatollah Yamini, Reza Qoli Khan Burandi, and Jalil Khan Rashvand, who rose up and fought the Russians and the Communist Party, were all landowners. The late Dr. Mossadeq, who repealed the oil concession in 1951, and the late General Zahedi, who negotiated the current agreement, were also landowners. As the result of this agreement, Iran's oil revenue has reached $800 million. History has shown that landowners have been in the front ranks of those who served this country. In my opinion, the destruction of the landowning class was a historic mistake.

Founding of the Agricultural Union of Iran and the First Skirmish with the Shah

Majd describes the establishment of the Agricultural Union of Iran in his memoirs:

From the year 1959 when there were rumors of an imminent distribution of estates between the cultivators, I began organizing Iran's landowners for the purpose of defending our rights. For this purpose, I gradually invited the landowners to my house, and we had regular meetings. The aim was to influence public and parliamentary opinion by publishing a regular bulletin and articles in the press. The main core of the group that regularly met in my house two or three times each week consisted of the following:

1. Mr. Ayatollah Nasrollah Bani Sadr, a respected and highly informed person who is in the front ranks of the learned ulama and a major landowner in Hamedan. 2. Mr. Hosein Khakbaz, son of the late Haj Aqa Araki, a former Majlis deputy, a solid and clear thinking individual, and a landowner of premier rank in Arak. 3. Mr. Mohammed Ebrahim Amir-Teimur-Kalali, long a Majlis deputy, deputy chief and chief of police, and minister of the interior

under Mossadeq, a respected statesman, and a major landowner in Khorasan. 4. Mr. Mohammad Ghoreishi, former Majlis deputy, and among the largest and most respected landowners in Khorasan. 5. Mr. Abol Hasan Amidi-Nuri, Majlis deputy, seasoned attorney, deputy prime minister under Zahedi, and editor of the newspaper *Dad*. 6. Mr. Mahmoud Fateh, agronomist and head of the Karaj Agricultural College, former minister of agriculture, and a landowner in Isfahan. 7. Mr. Abu Taleb Shirvani, former Majlis deputy and a landowner in Varamin and Fars.

These gentlemen formed the intellectual core of the Agricultural Union of Iran. From Azarbaijan to Fars and from all over Iran, landowners consulted with this group. As I shall describe below, we tried to prepare and print as many articles and bulletins as possible.

Majd, Khakbaz, and Ayatollah Bani Sadr led the Union. Bani Sadr and Khakbaz were particularly important because of their close relationship with the senior ulama, including Ayatollah Borujerdi and Ayatollah Khomeini. Majd and Khakbaz also had a long and close friendship. Both had been deputies to the Fourteenth Majlis. Numerous letters from Hosein Khakbaz to Majd written after the final suppression of the Agricultural Union of Iran in August 1964 testify to their friendship.

Fig. 5.1. Ayatollah Nasrollah Bani Sadr, circa 1960.

Fig. 5.2. Hosein Khakbaz, circa 1985.

Fig. 5.4. Amir-Teimur-Kalali, circa 1955.

Fig. 5.3. Mohammad Ghoreishi, circa 1930.

Fig. 5.5. Abol Hasan Amidi-Nuri, circa 1970.

Fig. 5.6. Arsalan Khalatbari, circa 1970.

Mohammad Ghoreishi and Mohammad Ebrahim Amir-Teimur-Kalali were also highly effective members of the Agricultural Union of Iran and known to the American consulate in Mashhad. Excerpts from a conversation between Amir-Teimur-Kalali and Consul Thomas A. Cassilly are given in chapter 6. In another confidential report by American Consul Edward H. Thomas (Foreign Service despatch 39, dated 25 June 1960), Mohammad Ghoreishi, former Majlis deputy, is described as "one of the few big landlords of this area who has made a genuine effort to improve the condition of his villages for the benefit of his peasants as well as himself." His son, Ali Ghoreishi, a Majlis deputy, was described as an outspoken opponent of the proposed land distribution law.

Soon after its establishment, the Agricultural Union of Iran met its first challenge and seemingly emerged victorious. Following the submission of a land distribution bill to the Majlis by the government of Manucher Eqbal in 1959, the Agricultural Union of Iran appealed to Grand Ayatollah Borujerdi, the most eminent Shia alem and Source of Emulation. Ayatollah Borujerdi responded with a fatwa against land distribution. He categorically declared that any such measure was contrary to the laws of Holy Islam. He also asked Ayatollah Behbahani to bring the matter to the attention of the government. Ayatollah Behbahani had written an "open letter" to Reza Hekmat, Sardar Fakher, the speaker of parliament (see chap. 8). The letters were read in a closed session of the Majlis. The effect of the letters on the deputies, many of whom had wept openly during the session, was decisive. Majd reports that after much debate, a commission of twenty-five men was selected and entrusted with the task of purging the proposed law of provisions contrary to Islam.

The chairman of the Majlis commission was Arsalan Khalatbari, a Majlis deputy and a foremost attorney. He had also served as mayor of Tehran and governor-general of Gilan. Khalatbari was a grandson of Mohammad Vali Khan Tonekaboni, Sepahsalar Azam, and a landowner in Mazandaran. In a confidential report on his conversation with Khalatbari (Foreign Service despatch 179, dated 28 September 1955), John W. Bowling, second secretary at the American embassy, wrote: "Khalatbari is one of the best all-round men in the Majlis. He has a good political record, is a very able lawyer, and is regarded as very honest by Iranian standards. He has considerable standing among the various groups of intellectuals, and is a very prolific contributor to newspapers. At one time, he was considered as a 'Shah's man' in the Majlis, but, like many of his friends, he has drifted to a conservative position in reaction to what he considers to be the Shah's dangerous leftist tendencies. . . . There is more than a grain of truth to his allegations as to how the anti-corruption campaign was carried over by some elements in the Government and the press to an attack on the landowning class as such, an almost totally unrelated subject."

The deputy head and spokesman of the Majlis commission was Abol Hasan Amidi-Nuri, an active leader of the Agricultural Union. In a confidential report on his conversation with Amidi-Nuri (Foreign Service Despatch number 192, dated 3 October 1955), Bowling described him as an influential newspaper editor who was "direct, sincere, and anti-communist." Amidi-Nuri was said to be a member of the strongly pro-Zahedi Mosavat faction and a bitter foe of Abol Hasan Ebtehaj, the shah's protégé and chief of plan organization. Bowling also observed: "Despite protestations of loyalty to the Shah, Amidi-Nuri must be counted among the most determined opponents of the Shah as a de facto Prime Minister."

The land reform law that was reluctantly passed by the Majlis and ratified by the Senate on 16 May 1960, and subsequently signed by the shah, was the work of the Khalatbari commission. Suffice it to say that the law did give land to the peasants, while it had the appearance as well as some substance of a "democratic" land reform. The 1960 land reform law also contained a provision whereby prior to implementation, the Ministry of Agriculture had to submit to the cabinet a list of implementation regulations (ayin-nameh ejraii). As the head of the Agricultural Union, Majd was invited by Ebrahim Mahdavi, the minister of agriculture in the government of Sharif-Emami, to submit a proposal and help draft the regulations (see chap. 6). He reports that a set of regulations was prepared and submitted to the minister. But the government of Sharif-Emami resigned shortly thereafter. Despite this setback, in the opening skirmish with the shah, the landowners, backed by the ulama, had prevailed. The victory was short-lived. A clearly angered shah vowed in his book, "As a class, the large feudal landowners are parasites, and as I shall indicate shortly, their days of feudal control are numbered."

Majd reports that, although the Sharif-Emami government was proceeding to implement the 1960 land reform law that had been passed by the Majlis and duly signed into law by the shah, neither the American government nor the shah was happy with the law. The Sharif-Emami government thus became a victim of intrigue by the shah and his American supporters, who actively promoted Ali Amini to be prime minister (see chap. 6). It is also noteworthy that Majd's account is at sharp variance with the one given by Ann Lambton in her 1969 book. Lambton claims that the 1960 land reform law was "aborted" and became a "dead letter," owing to the opposition of the ulama.[3] In actuality, the law passed three months after Ayatollah Borujerdi's fatwa, and the law that had been

Fig. 5.7. Ali Amini, 1960.   Fig. 5.8. Hasan Arsanjani, circa 1962.

drawn up by the agricultural commission of the Majlis and subsequently approved by the Majlis and Senate had addressed some of the concerns of the religious opposition. The account given by Majd is also confirmed by Floor.[4] Majd states that the law became a victim of intrigue by Mohammad Reza Shah, Ali Amini, and their American supporters.

Government of Ali Amini and Hasan Arsanjani

During the crucial first quarter of 1961, Majd was sidelined by an operation.[5] In May 1961, Sharif-Emami resigned and Amini became prime minister. Amini presented his cabinet on 6 May. The Majlis and the Senate were dismissed on 9 May on the orders of Mohammad Reza Shah, and no plans for a new election were announced. The minister of agriculture in the new cabinet, and the spokesman for the government, was Hasan Arsanjani, a former newspaper editor, an attorney by training, and a controversial figure. Lambton hints that Arsanjani may have been connected with the communist Tudeh Party in his youth.[6] Katouzian calls Arsanjani a Tudeh Party "sympathizer."[7] Whatever his affiliation, Arsanjani had written editorials in 1945 defending the Allied military occupation of Iran. Specifically, he had argued in *Darya* that the continued military occupation of northern Iran by the Soviet Union was justified under Article 5 of the 1921 Iran-Soviet nonaggression pact. To say this at the time of the Azarbaijan crisis was highly controversial, to say the least. Although Arsanjani had no roots in Gilan, as a protégé of Ahmad Qavam he was subsequently elected in 1947 to be a deputy to the Fifteenth Majlis from

Lahijan, Gilan. However, citing his 1945 article and his lack of connections in Gilan, the Majlis prevented Arsanjani from taking his seat in the chamber.

Arsanjani had also long advocated the confiscation of *all landlords* and distribution of the land to peasants. In 1951, he wrote that "in an Islamic country cultivated land, forests, and mines belonged to the people and ought to be held by the government; and that the ownership of land by large landed proprietors was nothing but usurpation. The government should therefore expropriate all landlords and place the land, which belonged to the people as a whole, at the disposal of the peasants who actually cultivated it, or were prepared to do so."[8] Although from widely differing social backgrounds, Ali Amini and Hasan Arsanjani had been friends for many years. Both had been protégés of Prime Minister Qavam. Amini had served as Qavam's deputy in 1942–43, and Arsanjani had

Fig. 5.9. Mohammad Reza Shah *(center, in uniform)*, Hasan Arsanjani *(kissing the shah's hand)*, Ali Amini *(far right)*, and Queen Farah, 1962.

worked as Qavam's deputy for parliamentary affairs in 1952. Arsanjani's appointment to the cabinet greatly alarmed and angered the Agricultural Union of Iran. It was an open declaration of war against landowners.[9]

Lawlessness and Violence in Rural Iran

The situation deteriorated rapidly for landowners after May 1961. Majd reports that from the beginning, the entire government publicity and propaganda apparatus was placed at the disposal of Arsanjani, who launched a virulent campaign of vilification against all landowners. More ominously, on the national radio, also dubbed "Radio Arsanjani," he continuously encouraged the "dear peasants" to seize the land and drive the landowners from the villages. Majd reports that as a consequence of Arsanjani's incitement to violence, absentee landowners were too fearful to go to rural areas. The small landowners who resided in the villages were driven out, their land and property either seized or burned. Peasants stopped paying rent. Majd also records that the police and gendarmes did nothing to stop this officially sanctioned lawlessness. Landowners' complaints to the law enforcement agencies were simply ignored. Moreover, although the shah's anger was directed at large landowners, a situation was created whereby the large and the small would burn together. It is clear from Majd's account that even before the actual land distribution, the landowners had been de facto deprived of their property and driven from the countryside. Majd gives the following account:

> Mr. Sharif-Emami was in office for eighteen months. He proceeded wisely and cautiously, and he set about implementing the land reform law that had been passed. Since the law was not to the liking and the designs of the Americans, and since the cabinet of Dr. Ali Amini was 100 percent willing to carry out their orders, thus under incessant intrigue and pressure by the Americans and Amini himself, Mr. Sharif-Emami resigned, and Dr. Amini became prime minister. Dr. Amini constantly gave speeches on the radio, day and night, and portrayed the country as bankrupt. Hasan Arsanjani, whom I have introduced earlier in reference to the 1945 events, was appointed minister of agriculture. Despite the existence of a land reform law, the cabinet approved a decree and called the decree the Amended Land Reform Law, which was much worse than the original defective law. It is simply unprecedented that the cabinet should repeal an existing law and in its place approve a decree without any

parliamentary process and approval and call it a "law." This outrage was perpetrated by Arsanjani and Ali Amini. On 9 January 1962, they approved a decree that I shall discuss later.

In the history of Greece, it is written that after Alexander the Great conquered Iran, he invited the nobility of Iran to collaborate with him in the governance of the country. When the nobility refused, Alexander warned them that since they were not willing to assist him, as punishment for them, he would find the most unscrupulous and the most corrupt people, select the lowest of the low among them, and then entrust the affairs of the state to such people. Then Iran would be truly destroyed. In selecting Arsanjani, Amini was following in the footsteps of Alexander. He could find no one else who, apart from Arsanjani, was so willing to make a mockery of the laws of the country, the Constitution, and the laws of Islam.

From the first day of his appointment as minister, Arsanjani's mode of operation was one of vilification and propaganda against landowners in conjunction with incitement, exhortation, and violence by peasants against landowners. Without justice or justification, he accused the landowners of outrageous sins. The reader will agree that in each group of people, there are good and bad. If one person in a group is bad, this does not make everyone in that group similarly bad. As the result of Arsanjani's incitement and secret orders to government agents, a situation was created in the villages where the ignorant and ungodly peasants did not desist from any evil and abuse, including rape and dishonor, against landowners and their relatives. Those small landowners who owned a few hectares or a few dangs and resided in the villages totally and without exception abandoned their homes and property and sought shelter in the towns. Those landowners who resided in the towns, neither they nor their representatives dared to go to the villages, because if they were not assaulted and beaten up, at the very least they were insulted and abused. In order to hear Arsanjani's speeches, the peasants sold their rugs and household goods to buy transistor radios. In order to demonstrate the operation of the radio, it would happen that the seller would tune in to music being broadcast by Tehran radio, whereupon the peasant buyer would become angry and demand a radio that broadcast only Arsanjani's speeches and not music. In his speeches and in his radio and television interviews, he often singled me out, claiming that I had gained the original and the exchanged land.

Meanwhile, Majd reports that as the result of government encouragement, landowners both large and small were driven from the countryside, and their lands and homes were seized by peasants. He provides the following account.

An Overview of Iranian Villages in 1962

Arsanjani spent all of his time on the following actions:

1. Vilifying and insulting the landowning class. 2. Incitement of ignorant peasants against landowners, and encouragement to peasants to assault the landowners, drive them out of the village, and seize their property. 3. Most government agents followed Arsanjani's example and created difficulty for the landowners.

Day and night on the radio and in news conferences, he would heap insults on the landowners and incite the peasants to plunder the landowners' property. In one of his visits to Azarbaijan, he was met by a large welcoming group of peasants in one of the villages. The cultivators complained of the landowners to Arsanjani. Next, Arsanjani asked how many resided in the village. The cultivators stated one thousand. Next, Arsanjani asked how many owners did the village have. They had replied eleven. Arsanjani then declared to the peasants that they should be ashamed of themselves. Why couldn't a thousand people take care of a mere eleven? And he departed. Ultimately, because of the propaganda and actions, nearly all landowners, both residing in the villages and in the towns, abandoned the villages and were scattered in various towns. They lived in total poverty. Their homes were demolished by the cultivators and the trees in their gardens were cut by the peasants, or water was diverted from their orchards. A totally unprecedented situation was created.

Decree of 9 January 1962 and Subsequent Decrees: Arsanjani's Legacy

On 11 November 1961, in what must assuredly be one of the defining moments of Pahlavi rule, the shah issued an edict ordering the cabinet of Ali Amini to "amend" the land reform law that he himself had signed into law. The text of the edict as provided by the American embassy (Foreign Service despatch 256, dated 22 November 1961) was as follows: "Land reform and limitation must be enforced. The land reform law has been found impractical. The government should amend it in any way deemed necessary as soon as possible, and make arrangements for its complete and correct enforcement."

On 9 January 1962, the cabinet of Ali Amini "improved and amended" the 1960 land reform law, which had been passed by the Majlis and the Senate and signed by the shah. Thus, what came to be known as the 1962 land reform "law" was a cabinet decree that allegedly "amended" the existing law. The shah and his cabinet usurped the power of legislation, and the entire affair constituted a grave and blatant violation of Iran's Constitution. In her 1969 book, Lambton completely disregarded the grave constitutional violations that were associated with the 1962 cabinet decree.[10] Lambton fails to mention that, under Iran's Constitution and system of constitutional monarchy, the shah's cabinet could not legally promulgate legislation, nor could cabinet ministers sign a bill into law or decree a bill. At this point in his memoirs, Majd does not mince words: "Although the land reform law had been approved by the houses of parliament and had received the royal signature, the cabinet of Dr. Amini approved a decree under the name of the Amended Land Reform Law, containing the following provisions, and implemented them. It was both betrayal and a crime."

There has never been a satisfactory explanation of why the 1960 law could not have been implemented. Lambton's reasoning does not bear closer scrutiny. She suggested that the 1960 law would have required cadastral surveys and land measurement and would have taken many years to complete. In the meantime, the opposition could have organized and prevented the measure. Another reason she gave is that under the 1960 law, landowners had the right of appeal to the judiciary and the courts. That is, in the event of disagreement over the price of land between a landowner and the government, the landowner could file a complaint, and the outcome would be determined by the courts. Lambton argues that the judicial process slowed the pace of land distribution. Under the 1962 and subsequent decrees, landowners were denied access to the courts. This was a huge violation of the Constitution, which had "guaranteed" every citizen access to courts and the protection of law. Praising the supposed "simplicity" of the amended land distribution decree, Lambton declared that the "law" had elements of "genius."

Lambton's praise notwithstanding, it is clear that the new "amended law" consisted mostly of measures that had been tried in Egypt during Nasser's 1952–61 land distribution program. In many ways, Arsanjani's "genius" was simply copying Nasser. For instance, the initial setting of a maximum limit on ownership, and the "purchase" of the "excess" land had been tried in Egypt. So had the valuation of the land on the basis of the land tax, and the payment in the form of bonds with a nominal interest rate, in lieu of cash. As described by Abdel-Fadil, the use of land tax as a basis for land valuation was a disguised form of confiscation.[11] Subsequently, the repayment period in Egypt was raised from thirty to forty years, and in the same manner, it was raised from ten to fifteen years in Iran. In Egypt, under the second stage of land distribution, the maximum ownership was again reduced and the small ownerships were leased to the tenants for long periods. The leases were practically irrevocable and inheritable. The same provisions are contained in the cabinet decree known as the Additional Articles to the Amended Land Reform Law, also known as Phase Two, which were issued in January 1963 when Arsanjani was still the minister of agriculture and thus the author of the "Additional Articles." Of course, in many ways, conditions in Iran and Egypt were very different. But, given the official animosity that prevailed between Iran and Egypt in the early 1960s, and given the fact that Arsanjani did not speak Arabic or have much knowledge of the Arab world in general and of Egypt in particular, how had he gained such intimate knowledge of the Egyptian land reform?[12] Many officials of the Ministry of Agriculture had been sent to Israel, not to Egypt, for training in matters of land and rural cooperatives.[13] Thus one arrives at the interesting conclusion that an Egyptian-style land reform was implemented by a Tudeh Party "sympathizer" and by officials who had received their training in Israel.

Arsanjani repeatedly claimed that the new "law" was the same as the existing law but with some "improvements." However, as Lambton noted, the "amended law" was completely different. The subsequent decrees "amended" the existing "amended law." That is, the government simply improvised as it went along. First, under the original 1960 law, maximum landownership per person had been set at 400 hectares of irrigated or 800 hectares of nonirrigated land, and maximum per family had been set at 600 hectares of irrigated and 1,200 hectares of nonirrigated land. Under the decree, subsequently known as Phase One, maximum ownership per owner was set at one "village" or its "equivalent." Second, under the original law, compensation was to be based on an "equitable and just" price, and landowners were to be paid in cash. Under the decree, the value of the land was assessed on the basis of tax payments, and landowners were to be paid in ten annual installments. Under a subsequent decree, the mode of payments was changed to dastur-e pardakht (promissory note issued to landowners in lieu of money), which were given the label of "land reform bonds" by western writers and which bore a 6 percent rate of interest. Another cabinet decree increased the redemption period to fifteen years. Third, the law had stipulated that if a landowner disputed the appraisal of his land, the owner had recourse to the courts and the judicial system. Under the decree, landowners had ten to fifteen days to appeal the decision of the Land Reform Ministry to a "commission" consisting of officials of the same ministry. The commission's ruling was final and without judicial recourse or other appeal.

Moreover, if a landowner refused to sign the documents transferring his land to the government for distribution, on the basis of Article 14 of the decree, the Ministry of Agriculture was empowered to act as the owner's "representative" and sign the documents on his "behalf" and notify the public prosecutor. Another disturbing feature of the "amended law" concerned land subject to a lien. Under the original 1960 law, if a landowner used his land as collateral for a loan *after* the date the law took effect in 1960, and subsequently the amount owed on the land exceeded that land's value as appraised by the Land Reform Organization, the landowner would be responsible for the balance of the loan. For loans contracted before 1960, the landowner would not remain responsible if valuation was less than the loan's balance. Under the 1962 decree, the time distinction was eliminated. In the case of land subject to a lien or mortgage, irrespective of the date the loan had been contracted, if the assessed value of the land by the government was less than the mortgage or the loan, although the land would be confiscated, the balance of the loan remained the obligation of the ex-landowner. The creditors were then able to seize the landowner's home and other belongings. Given that land was appraised on the basis of tax payment, the previously incurred obligations far exceeded the assessed "price" of the land. Consequently, many landowners lost everything to creditors.

With the benefit of hindsight, it is clear that the decree which came to be known as the "amended law" was a recipe for disaster. The amended regulation can be criticized on numerous other grounds. Following Arsanjani's line, Lambton and others had claimed that using a hectare as the measure of land was not "practical" for Iran; instead, using the "village" as the unit of account eliminated the need for cadastral surveys and land measurement. Otherwise, land distribution would have taken many years to complete. It is again pointed out that some 2,000–3,000 villages and hamlets which had been the property of the shah had been distributed during the 1950s following careful cadastral survey. This land was sometimes divided into parcels, always appraised by experts, and then sold to cultivators. Clearly, cadastral surveys and the use of hectares in land measurement did not constitute a barrier to the sale and distribution of land that had been owned by the shah. In addition, the findings of the 1960 census of agriculture are all given in hectares. Second, from a legal as well as a practical side, the "village" was by no means an unambiguous entity. What was known as one "village" and recognized in the registration documents as one village often consisted of several villages and hamlets. This resulted in all kinds of inequities. As described in chapter 11, often enterprising landowners had dug new qanats and had established new settlements on land that had been part of an existing village, so that numerous villages existed in what was legally recorded as "one" village. These "excess" villages were summarily confiscated under land distribution. Moreover, the newly established villages had neither a separate tax status nor even a separate registration record. This had been overlooked in the original decree. An additional decree was needed to rectify this omission. The decree of 27 August 1962 showed that Arsanjani and the government were initially unaware that many villages did not have a tax record. Thus landowners who had been enterprising and had invested in new irrigation channels and established new villages were heavily penalized.[14] Moreover, a "village" could be anything from a small cultivated area on the edge of the desert with three cultivators to a large settlement with several hundred cultivators in a high precipitation area.

Third, under the decree, each owner was supposedly able to retain a "chosen" village. This measure was clearly intended to result in rural lawlessness and violence. The cultivators of the "chosen" village were justifiably aggrieved and angered by their "chosen" status, because they had not received land. Thus, with the government slogan that land belongs to the cultivator, and given the condition that the cultivators in other villages had received land, while those of the "chosen" villages had not, the peasants were likely to react violently, and they did. At the very least, they refused to pay the owner's rent. Most often, the landowners were chased out of the village and their houses set on fire, their orchards cut, and machinery broken. The decree resulted in serious breakdowns in law and order, and the landowners lost everything.

Fourth, the proposed compensation was based on the annual land and agricultural taxes, and landowners were to be paid in long-term "bonds" and not in money. However, Binswanger and Elgin note that practically nowhere in the world are agricultural taxes even remotely related to the value of the land, nor is agricultural income subject to any real taxation. On the contrary, agricultural income is subsidized. Land taxes are low everywhere because it is recognized that heavy taxes discourage agricultural development and reduce land values. In addition, in the case of Iran there were other reasons that historically resulted in low taxes on land. One was the high degree of risk associated with semi-arid agriculture and the frequency of crop failures and drought years. High taxes in years of crop failure could have resulted in financial ruin. A common form of rural taxation had consisted of a lump sum payment by landowners to the government for the purpose of reducing future tax payments. This system, known as *baz-kharid*, was advantageous to both sides. For the landowner, the reduction in future tax payments increased the value of the land and reduced the risk of insolvency in the years of crop failure. It was also advantageous to the government in the short run because it enabled the government to access a sum that was equivalent to several years of future tax revenues.[15] Moreover, taxes were low in many villages because they had been initially owned by the government.[16] The point is that taxes had been low for various economic and historical reasons, and the use of taxes to establish compensation was a deliberate act of confiscation. In any case, the "compensation" to the owners was in the form of "land reform bonds," bearing a 6 percent interest and redeemable over fifteen years. However, in a country where the nominal interest rate in the market was at least 24 percent per year, bonds with a mere 6 percent interest rate were heavily discounted. Consequently, the actual compensation to the landowners under Phase One was about 30 percent of the nominal compensation.[17] That is, landowners were penalized on two counts. The land was appraised at a small fraction of its value, and the bonds they received as "payment" were heavily discounted. Given that most of the landowners were deep in debt, most were financially ruined.[18] Not only was the use of taxes to determine compensation to the owners a deliberate act of disguised confiscation. It was in stark contrast to the manner in which land distribution had been implemented on land owned by the shah. In the case of the Pahlavi estates, the land had been carefully parceled and appraised by "experts" and then sold at market prices.

Middle Class as Landowners

A significant factor that has been completely ignored in the literature is that of the structure and composition of the landowning class. In a country with rudimentary industry and few commercial investment possibilities, agricultural land constituted the most desirable and often the only source of investment for the upper, middle, and lower middle classes. Even those described as "industrialists" often held much of their assets in the form of land. Both the modern and traditional middle classes in Iran invested their life savings in land. Thus, many of those who were described as "feudal landlords" were actually members of the modern professional class and bazaar merchants. Even in the first stage of land distribution, which was supposed to get at the "feudal oppressors," many of the direct victims were middle-class professionals. It was not only the modern middle class who had put their savings in land. The traditional bazaar merchants, religious classes, shopkeepers, petty bureaucrats, army officers, university professors, and teachers invested their savings in land. All of this is readily recognized in a confidential American embassy report on land distribution that is discussed in chapter 6. Moreover, for many the tiny sums they derived from their tiny estates were all they had.

In short, many people were faced with the loss of their livelihood or life savings or both. In addition, many petty landowners resided in the villages. Their plight is described in a lengthy report by the American consul in Tabriz, John M. Howison. These petty landowners were driven from the villages and their property was seized by the peasants (see chap. 12). The middle-class component of the "landowning class" is illustrated with examples from East Azarbaijan, the first province where land distribution was implemented, and from Isfahan.

In a secret report (airgram A-35, dated 9 November 1962), Howison stated: "Disaffection of landlord class, including many conservatives whose landowner status has in the past been partially obscured by their prominence in other fields (professions, civil and military service, and so on) has now reached an advanced stage. Although from force of habit they tend to be monarchists, they are privately bitterly critical of Mohammad Reza Shah." In another report (airgram A-51, dated 25 January 1963), it is mentioned in passing that one of these landowners whose property had been "reformed" was Eng. Gholam Hosein Fotuhi, dean of the agricultural faculty of the University of Tabriz. In another case described in chapter 9, a Tehran University professor, Ali Pasha Saleh, complained to a visiting American academic, Dr. George A. Meyer of Utah State University, "that he and his wife had put all their life savings in a relatively small piece of land to which they wanted to retire after his services at Tehran University ceased. But the Land Reform Program was taking it from them at a ridiculously low figure, and none of his appeals had received any response." From the date of the letter, 2 June 1963, Saleh's property was to be seized under Phase Two. The modern and professional middle class was not the only group that had invested in land. Even those described as "industrialists" held much of their assets in land.

In February 1962, Consul Howison solicited the views of a Tabriz industrialist, Ahmad Sadaqiani, which he reported in Foreign Service despatch 60 (17 February 1962). Howison wrote, "Sadaqiani is a member of the younger generation of the large and influential Sadaqiani family, which initially acquired its wealth in commerce, began acquiring land about a century ago, and ultimately became industrialists (tanning, textile). The family's fortune is believed to be more or less equally divided between land and industry at present. Their reputation as landlords is fair; as shrewd businessmen, they supervise their villages (irrigated villages near Miandoab and dry-farming villages near Bostanabad) closely." Sadaqiani told Howison that "Arsanjani's land reform program will be an unmitigated disaster for Iran." However, the consul concluded, "Sadaqiani's rationalization of the land reform program which directly threatens the interests of his own family is neither internally consistent nor factual."

In a confidential report on landownership in the province of Isfahan (Foreign Service despatch 695, dated 30 March 1959), Consul Franklin J. Crawford reported that the bulk of the agricultural land in Isfahan was owned by petty landowners. He also stated: "Another phenomena which has occurred is the acquisition of agricultural land by urban industrialists and bazaar merchants. As these people have made fortunes from wartime commodity speculation, from the textile industry, and from urban real estate speculation, they have purchased villages, or shares in villages. There are two reasons for this. Landholding provides prestige in Isfahan. It is also a good investment which appreciates in value along with the general land inflation."

In another confidential report (airgram A-63, dated 12 March 1963), Howison described the composition of the absentee small landowners affected by Phase Two: "Absentee smallholders are of such groups as minor bureaucrats, petty merchants, and schoolteachers. They have in the past had money to invest, and not having confidence in the security of investments in industry or business, have purchased lands." Howison's description is supported by Lambton's findings. Lambton had noted that most of the villages near the towns were owned by shopkeepers, minor bureaucrats, army officers, and members of the religious classes.

What these examples clearly establish is that in the absence of industrial and commercial investment opportunities, the middle-class professionals and the lower middle classes had put much of their savings into land. Even industrialists and large bazaar merchants had invested in land. We are just beginning to understand some of the damage wrought by the so-called land reforms. Thus, the shah deprived the middle classes of their inheritance, life savings, retirement nests, and often their only source of income. Howison, however, quickly reassured himself and his superiors in Washington that despite their rage, there was little the landowners could do because they lacked power, and "landlord-clergy coalition cannot be independently developed in this district."

Compensation and Composition of Landowners in East Azarbaijan

With Phase One of land distribution approaching completion, on 10 December 1962, Archie M. Bolster, U.S. vice consul in Tabriz, visited Parviz Behbudi, director general of agriculture for East Azarbaijan, and had "gleaned some interesting facts about the land distribution program in this province." Fortunately, what he had learned was included in a report (airgram A-40, dated 14 December 1962). Bolster noted, "Behbudi gives the impression of a man wholly at ease in his difficult job. Although himself a minor landowner (he owns a village near Mianeh) and sympathetic with that group to the extent that landowners' normal lives are being disrupted, he is gently forceful in requiring landowners to comply with the provisions of the land reform program."

Bolster had learned of the total "compensation" paid to Azarbaijan landowners under what subsequently became known as the first phase of land distribution. He had duly included the information in his report without any comment. Bolster reported, "Behbudi stated that a total of twenty million rials ($263,160) had been paid to provincial landowners for the areas they had sold to the government for distribution." Under the provisions of Phase One, one-tenth of the appraised value was paid in cash, and the remainder ($2.368 million) was paid in land reform bonds, bearing 6 percent interest and redeemable over fifteen years. Since the "bonds" were heavily discounted on the financial market, actual compensation was at most 35–40 percent of the nominal compensation. Consequently, the actual payment to landowners under Phase One in East Azarbaijan, Iran's "bread basket," was at most $1 million. The number of landowners in the eleven separate townships (shahrestan) of East Azarbaijan who were "included" in Phase One is not given. However, a detailed list of such landowners who were subject to Phase One in the township of Maragheh is provided in a consular report by Bolster (Foreign Service despatch 68, dated 19 March 1962). Forty-eight landowners in Maragheh were subject to the provisions of the decree and were ordered to complete and submit the "declaration forms." Twenty-three others were not affected, but they "voluntarily filled out land declaration forms and requested that their lands be divided." That is, in Maragheh alone, there were seventy-one landowners whose property had been acquired by the government. Given that there were ten other townships in East Azarbaijan, it can be confidently claimed that at the very least 500 landowners in East Azarbaijan had been subject to the "law." On average, a landowner received $2,000 to $3,000 as "compensation" for his or her land. It is noteworthy that the total amount paid to East Azarbaijan landowners was less than what the shah had received from the sale of just one village. The shah's sale of the village of Takestan in Qazvin in 1954 was described in chapter 4. Moreover, similar to the practice under Reza Shah, "compensation" for land seized was a small fraction of the land's revenue for one year.

While Bolster was sitting in Behbudi's office, another visitor appeared. He was Manucher Diba, "cousin of Queen Farah and former owner of some twenty villages near Ardebil." Diba, who was also photographed in a meeting of the Agricultural Union of Iran (fig. 5.10), is described by Bolster as a Francophile Tabrizi who was educated in Switzerland and married to a Swiss woman. Bolster gives an account of the conversation:

> Diba professes to approve of land reform but complains that the program is hastily-conceived and is being carried out in a ruthless manner. (His ire is primarily directed at Minister of Agriculture Arsanjani; he praised Behbudi in a subsequent chat with the reporting officer as a considerate and fair person who is doing his best in a difficult job.) Although professing to be satisfied with the amounts he received for his villages, Diba had several complaints to take up with Behbudi and painted a discouraging picture of the situation in which landowners find themselves. He claimed that most landowners in this area, far from being wealthy, had been saddled with so many expenses in improving their lands that they borrowed money for such purposes. Diba said some landowners were so far in debt that low valuation of their lands for purposes of sale to the government had ruined, or could ruin, them financially. Behbudi agreed with this analysis, and commented that valuation of the lands being sold to the government was difficult because taxes which had been paid on those villages in the past were often ridiculously low or even nonexistent.

The content of an earlier conversation between Manucher Diba and consular officials Howison and Bolster is given in a confidential report (airgram A-19, dated 28 August 1962). "Manucher Diba whose relative-by-marriage the Shah obliged him to begin selling his own lands to his peasants without waiting for the reform law to be applied in his area, has given up pretending that he enjoys his role. 'My ancestors risked their lives to acquire land and worked hard to exploit it; what have the peasants done to deserve wealth?'" The report had also included the following observation about two other landowners. "A recent visitor to the home of former land tycoon Jamshid Esfandiari reported him to be extremely depressed and bereft of his former arrogant reassurance that things would come out well for him sooner or later. Seyed Hasan Adl recently bemoaned 'the loss of the fruits of a lifetime of hard work.'"

Peasant Violence Against Landowners

For months before and after the promulgation of the decree, Agriculture Minister Hasan Arsanjani had spearheaded a propaganda campaign that openly encouraged peasants to seize land by violence. Thus, with government encouragement and protection, the peasants had driven out the landowners, who were now scattered in the towns. This political folly would come back to haunt the regime fifteen years later. It is difficult to understate the damaging consequences of the government incitement to peasants to seize the land by violence and drive out the landowners. It resulted in the de facto and ultimately de jure confiscation of the petty landowners. In short, the government instigated a total breakdown in law and order. With government incitement, the small landowners too became early victims. Their land was seized by peasants, and they could no longer collect rent. By the summer of 1962, the traditional landlord-tenant relationship had ceased to exist. Although the small landowners were supposedly "exempt" from the provisions of the 1962 decree, they had been "included" in the program. Thus, while the initial intention of the U.S. government and the shah may have been to distribute the property of the large landowners, as the result of Arsanjani's actions, the small owners were also effectively expropriated. With the expectations created by the government publicity that all land belonged to the cultivator, it was no longer possible to restrict land distribution to only those villages that were owned by large landowners and exclude the majority of the villages that were owned by small owners. The second phase of the land distribution was the inevitable outcome of the atmosphere and facts that had been created under Phase One. It should also be noted that in his early writings, Arsanjani had advocated the confiscation of all private land, because such ownerships constituted "usurpation." Such land was to be confiscated and given to the cultivators. As minister, Arsanjani had implemented his plan.

American Consular Reports on Peasant Violence in Azarbaijan

Initially, American consular officials John Howison and Archie Bolster had written very favorable reports on the land distribution program and had urged the U.S. government to give land distribution its fullest support. In a secret report entitled "Tentative Evaluation of Land Reform Program" (State Department airgram A-9, dated 27 March 1962), Howison had concluded his observations with the following:

Land reform is rare, even unique phenomenon in modern Iranian history, in that it is constructive domestic program Iranians are carrying out themselves. Failure of this first hopeful effort, so bravely begun, could do much damage to national morale. From vantage point Tabriz, program thus appears to deserve fullest U.S. support, discreetly rendered to avoid damaging Iranian sense of responsibility for program. Such discretion is not incompatible with the harvesting of good will accruing to us from our visibly sympathetic relations with government responsible for this program.

It was not surprising that at first they had tried to minimize and mitigate reports of peasant violence against landowners and their families. In a confidential report (Foreign Service despatch 53, dated 29 January 1962), Bolster reported in passing that in the village of Varjui, which was owned by Jamshid Esfandiari, the villagers "had several times beaten up his son." In another confidential report (airgram A-8, dated 27 March 1962), Howison stated, "Reports that many landlords in Azarbaijan now cautious about entering their own villages, and in certain cases do not actually dare to do so, can no longer be dismissed as rumor. Within past few days, agents of landlord Esmail Hamidieh expelled from Keshavar in Zarineh Rud valley; interestingly, peasants did not attempt to confiscate landlord's tractors. In another village, pranksters dressed and painted donkey in caricature of landlord during Now Ruz celebrations. Maragheh resident declared prestige of mollahs in decline. Sounding like Marxist, this Iranian informant stated peasants, despite piousness, resented clergy as allies of landlords."

In another report (Foreign Service despatch 84, dated 28 May 1962), Bolster recounted the events in the village of Arbat Sofla in Miandoab. The landowner, Ahmad Kazemi, "selected the village of Arbat Sofla as the one he desired to retain, but whom the villagers refused to allow in the village. In response to Kazemi's request, five gendarmerie soldiers arrived to protect the Kazemi family, one member of which was injured before they arrived. The source said the death of a three-year-old village girl, who some say was killed by the villagers themselves, was blamed on Kazemi, and in the ensuing disturbance the five gendarmes were trapped in a house for several hours. Kazemi left the village, and when later gendarme reinforcements arrived they found not one man in the village. Later, ten villagers were arrested. Portions of this account were confirmed by a news item in the May 19 issue of *Etela-at*. In yet another case, a minor landowner from Solduz told the reporting officer that when he went to the beet sugar processing plant at Miandoab a few days ago he met some inhabitants of a village near Miandoab who had forced their landowner Yusuf Kalantari to leave the village and had come to negotiate for the processing of their crop on their own behalf."

By April 1962, Howison and Bolster were also becoming doubtful of the "reassurances" given by government officials. On 3 April 1962, Bolster met with Engineer Manucher Khalkhali, described as the "czar of land distribution in Azarbaijan," and Nosratollah Riazi, governor of Maragheh (Foreign Service despatch 71, dated 6 April 1962). They discussed the matter of rural violence. Khalkhali assured Bolster that the recent incidents "were no more serious than incidents which happened almost every year." Bolster, nevertheless, made the following observation:

> Some indication of the seriousness with which government officials really regard the recent landlord-peasant incidents can be gained from the following observations made during the reporting officer's April 3 trip to Maragheh: (1) General Hasan Mehrdad, Savak Chief for Eastern Azarbaijan, was in Maragheh that day, (2) Colonel Hasan-Ali Tabatabaii-Vakili, Gendarmerie Commander for Eastern Azarbaijan, was seen at the Agricultural Office in Maragheh, (3) during the morning Engineer Khalkhali was not available for an interview due to his presence at the Third Division Headquarters, and (4) the reporting officer was accorded a correct, but cooler than usual, reception at the Agricultural Office.

With reports of violence continuing to come in, Howison reluctantly showed some concern over "agrarian unrest" in his area, but he was not unduly worried. By July 1962, however, reports of violence in rural areas could no longer be taken lightly. In a confidential cable (State Department airgram A-9, dated 30 July 1962), Howison wrote the following (no editorial change by this author):

> Habib Amiri, Shakkak Kurd formerly employed by USG in Iran, alleges land reform having disruptive impact on Kurdish areas south of Miandoab. Peasants refusing pay legitimate dues to landowners, including small holders. Says fabric of social discipline breaking down to point burglary and other lawlessness at highest since Mahabad Republic days. Amiri claims to have witnessed several crop burnings near Kurdish village outside Miandoab land reform area July 26. U.S. being blamed and compared to post-war Russian occupiers by landowners and even by small holders and peasants.

Although Amiri inclined use extravagant language, have little doubt his report bears relation to truth. His further claim that land reform officials complacent and even pleased by illegal anti-land-lord activity hardly worth serious consideration, although such activity might stimulate some landlords to surrender their lands to Government without fight.

That Howison was covering up the complicity of land reform officials in peasant violence can be seen from the following. In despatch 84 of 28 May 1962, Vice Consul Bolster reported on his conversation with Parviz Behbudi, chief of the Agriculture Ministry in Azarbaijan. According to Bolster, "Behbudi indicated that even in the villages not distributed peasants would be permitted to cease payment of shares of their crops to their landowners, and that this weapon would help to persuade the recalcitrant landowners to yield to the inevitable and comply with the Law." By late August 1962, Howison and Bolster could not even try to mitigate and minimize rural violence and lawlessness. Their confidential report (airgram A-19, dated 28 August 1962) included the following:

The Consulate with increasing frequency hears reports that peasants on undivided lands, both within and near current land reform areas, are refusing to pay their dues to their landlords. (Although peasants whose land has been designated for distribution have been authorized to withhold payment of landlords' shares on this year's crop, the situation of other peasants is legally unchanged.) If all of these reports are to be believed, some scores of landlords, large and small, are being illegally deprived of their rents by peasants who choose to interpret the government's land reform policies in their own way. A village north of Miandoab, Molla Shahabeddin, belonging to the Sadaqiani family of Tabriz industrialists, had at last report resisted all efforts at rent collection. At Baruq [Paruh?] east of Miandoab, which was to have been retained by the Molavi family under the provision of law that each landowner can keep the equivalent of one village, villagers are reported to have taken a particularly violent "no pay" stand. When the Molavi family sought legal support from local officials of the Ministry of Justice, the peasants had said flatly: "We are not going to pay. If the landlord or his agent comes to the village to try to collect we shall kill him. Not one, but all of us will kill him. Will you hang six hundred murderers? The product of our farms belongs to us." The Justice official is said to have appealed to land reform czar Manucher Khalkhali for support; Khalkhali is supposed to have gone to the village and told the peasants that the law obliged them to pay, but to have failed to alter their determination. Next steps in this drama cannot be predicted.

The two American officials had also reported on their conversation with General Hasan Mehrdad, chief of Savak (secret police) in Azarbaijan. The Savak chief had expressed sympathy for the villagers attacking landowners because "it was also natural that peasants in non-distributed villages adjoining distributed villages were asking what is our sin that we are not getting water and land?" The governor-general of East Azarbaijan, Ali Dehqan, had similarly stated, with a rueful smile, that peasant violence was to be "expected" on lands not yet divided.
The consuls had also written:

> For the present, such actions merely constitute illegal land seizures by the peasant—a carrying forward of land reform at a pace faster and with a thoroughness greater than foreseen by law. There is no evidence that there is any coordination among the various peasant actions, nor that land reform officials are encouraging them by improper means. However, in the conversation referred to above General Mehrdad avowed that he personally believed that most landlords would feel obliged to give up their remaining holdings in a year or two.

Summing up the situation, the report stated "self-generating agrarian unrest, particularly the refusal of whole villages to pay their shares to landowners is reportedly widespread, notably in Western Azarbaijan. This unrest may contribute to a tendency toward landlords' giving up for distribution lands which they are entitled to keep under present law." In what must be considered a landmark in the annals of American diplomatic reports on Iran, Howison and Bolster stated: "The possibility that such peasant rebelliousness may in fact be widespread need not cause immediate alarm to anyone except the landlords."

While reporting on the violence and lawlessness, the American consulate frowned on the attempts of some landowners to defend themselves. One landowner and member of the Agricultural Union of Iran, Engineer Ahmad Afshar, incurred the intense hostility of the American consulate in Tabriz. Bolster included the following entry in his report (Foreign Service despatch 71, dated 6 April 1962):

> An opponent of the land reform program whose actions are of some political importance is Engineer Ahmad Afshar, former deputy and one of the heirs of Yamin Lashkar, deceased major landowner of the Shahin Dej bakhsh. Afshar wrote an open letter to the Shah in which

he stated that the Land Reform Law is illegal, and he does not recognize the authority of Dr. Arsanjani to implement the law, and that he desires an audience with the Shah to present his views. He is supported by Yusef Eftekhari and (behind the scenes) by other landowners of the Shahin Dej area, and has apparently become their unofficial spokesman. His actions will bear close watching.

On 20 August 1962, Engineer Ahmad Afshar wrote to the Agricultural Union of Iran describing several incidents of peasant violence. Copies of the letter were circulated by the Agricultural Union of Iran.

Agricultural Union of Iran:

I, Engineer Ahmad Afshar recently spent five days in Shahin Dej and Miandoab area. I witnessed some grave incidents, and I feel obligated to provide a short report.

In nearly all parts of Maragheh and Miandoab, those landowners who are subject to land distribution, that is, those who owned more than one village, have been forced to transfer to the government the excess property, and each has retained one village. However, in all of the villages retained by the owners, the cultivators are refusing to pay the owner's legal rent. They say that there is no reason for 20 percent of the cultivators to receive land while the rest got nothing. Consequently, there has been much conflict and disorder in the region. I describe two such incidents that have taken place in Miandoab within five days.

1. The owner of the village of Javad Hesar, near Miandoab, approached the Commission for Settling Disputes in Miandoab and complained that the cultivators of the village were refusing to pay him his share of the crop, despite the fact that they are required by the cabinet decree to give the owner his rightful share. The Commission ordered the gendarmerie in Miandoab to collect and deliver the owner's share to the owner. Accompanied by a few gendarmes, the commander of Miandoab Gendarmerie Station went to the above village, but they encountered strong resistance from the inhabitants. The inhabitants of the neighboring village also came to the assistance of the villagers, surrounding the Gendarmes for one day. After radioing for help, the Prosecutor General dispatched about eighty gendarmes to the village of Javad Hesar. Subsequently, shots were fired, and the inhabitants attacked the gendarmes with clubs and knives, and returned fire, injuring the commander of the gendarmerie. After much firing by the gendarmes, several villagers were injured, and the cultivators re-

treated and surrendered. In the meantime, the crop was plundered, five cultivators died (two on the spot and three at the hospital), 20–30 were injured, and many were arrested. Some gendarmes were also injured.

2. The village of Ghareh Tapeh, near Shahin Dej, is a village retained by its owner. The cultivators harvested and took the crop without paying the owner's share. The owner complained to the gendarmerie in Shahin Dej. The gendarmes went to the village and were met with resistance by the villagers, resulting in some injuries to the gendarmes. With no success, the gendarmes returned to Shahin Dej. That night, the landowner's house, where there were women and children, was pelted with stones and attacked. Informed of the events, the gendarmes sought help from Rezaieh and Miandoab. As I had to leave for Tabriz the next day, I was unable to follow the subsequent events.

By March 1963, Consul Howison could no longer even try to conceal the magnitude of the tragedy that had taken place in Azarbaijan. Howison had felt obligated to report on the plight of Azarbaijan's small landowners who were being "harassed' by peasants and were being driven from their homes and villages. All he could do was to display his belated "sympathy" for the small landowners of Azarbaijan who "had nowhere else to go," except join the ranks of the unemployed in Tabriz and Tehran. He had joined the chief of land reform in Azarbaijan, Engineer Parviz Behbudi, in shedding some crocodile tears and in expressing his hope that the government would undertake construction projects in the cities so that these displaced and disenfranchised people could find employment. Extensive excerpts from Howison's confidential report (airgram A-63, dated 12 March 1963), which was euphemistically entitled "Azarbaijan Smallholders and the Land Distribution Program," are given in chapter 12.

The lawlessness was not confined to Azarbaijan, of course. By January 1963, violence and lawlessness by peasants in Khorasan and the complicity of land distribution officials had reached an advanced stage, thereby prompting a normally pro-government newspaper to write editorials on the subject. The American consul in Mashhad, J. P. Mulligan (airgram A-16, dated 24 January 1963), reported that the newspaper *Aftab-e Sharq* "published an interesting two part editorial addressed to peasants and workers and secondly to the land reform officials of Khorasan. The editorial appeal for greater individual responsibility seems to have been prompted by substantiated reports that various villagers in the Mashhad area are becoming increasingly independent in attitude and have in several cases denied landlords legitimate access to their property, and by a growing realization that certain land reform officials, spurred on by the zeal of the Minister of Agriculture are inclined to act arbitrarily and beyond the law. . . . The publication of this editorial was noteworthy and well regarded in view of the fact that the owner-publisher of *Aftab-e Sharq*, Abol Hosein Amuzegar, has been in the forefront of those liberal citizens of Mashhad who espouse the Shah's reform measures and has most recently been active in promoting support for the coming referendum."

Cabinet Decree of 17 January 1963: The Additional Articles

On 17 January 1963, another cabinet decree called the Additional Articles to the Amended Land Reform Law was issued. This decree, which came to be known as the Additional Articles, or Phase Two, was also initially referred to as the Regulations Concerning Small Landowners. Lambton has claimed that this decree represented a deliberate slowing of the pace of land distribution. The reality was starkly different. The decree formally initiated the de jure confiscation of the small landowners. The decree legitimized what had already taken place, namely, the de facto confiscation of the small landowners. Under this decree, landowners were given the "option" of selling their land to the tenants, or dividing the land with the tenants, provided the tenants consented, or "buying" their own land subject to the consent of the tenants, or "leasing" the land to the tenants for thirty years for cash rents. Cash rents were to be based on the average rent paid between 1961 and 1963, the years when peasants had withheld rent, and were subject to revision every five years. The tenants could not be evicted, and the thirty-year leases were hereditary. That is, the lease would be inherited by the tenant's heirs. As noted by Majd, the thirty-year lease option was a joke. The division option was not even a remote possibility to most landowners. It is noteworthy that the division option was not available in the rice-growing regions of Gilan and Mazandaran. Ownership of rice fields was limited to thirty hectares. The excess was sold to the tenants at terms equal to those of Phase One, and the "retained" thirty hectares were leased to the cultivators for thirty years at a rent that was equal to the average for the years 1961–63 when the cultivators had paid no rent. The sale option on land not taken by Phase One was the most advantageous to landowners. But it was the least advantageous to the cultivators. Consequently, it was not a realistic option for the vast majority of landowners. Hence, only a few were recorded in the data. It is also noteworthy that the government was now using the hectare as the appropriate unit. Arsanjani had previously insisted that the hectare was not the "appropriate and practical measure" for Iran. The only realistic choice facing the vast majority of the landowners was to forfeit ownership at a nominal price (the sale option) or to maintain nominal ownership for a token rent (the lease option). Most chose the latter option and signed thirty-year leases with the tenants. However, although the lease contracts had been drawn up by the Land Reform Ministry and were thus "legally" binding on the tenants, the landowners could not collect rent, because tenants refused to pay and the government could not or would not enforce collection (see chap. 11). In reality, having been told for years by the government that the land belonged to them, the peasants were not about to pay rent to the landowners. Moreover, the refusal to pay rent did not result in any meaningful sanction. A situation was created whereby large numbers of small landowners could not collect rent. The third phase of land distribution was a response to this chaotic situation.

The third and final phase of land distribution was the 1968 Law for the Sale and Division of Rented Estates, also known as Phase Three. Like the Additional Articles, the law legitimized existing reality. Under this law, the landowners were given the "option" of selling the land to the tenants, and the compensation was to be based on the annual rent as specified under Phase Two. However, given that rents were so low, the compensation was a thinly disguised confiscation. The other "choice" was to divide the land with the tenants. However, the law stipulated that all tenants had to be "notified" of the owners' intent to divide the land. And only after all the tenants of a village had affixed their signatures to the green notification certificates would the land be divided. Landowners had desperately tried to get the peasants to sign the notification forms. Finally, after two years of trying, they had settled for the "sale option." The compensation was based on rents that had been established under Phase Two and resulted in a de facto confiscation. Finally, under the 1972 Law for the Sale of Public Endowments, lands that had been endowed for charitable and religious purposes were sold to the tenants who had been given ninety-nine-year leases under Phase Two. Given that an endowment was supposedly inalienable and everlasting, the sales constituted a grave breach of religious practice and tradition. It has been claimed that Hasan Arsanjani was the "architect" of Iran's land distribution. This is essentially correct. While the U.S. government and the shah were in favor of land distribution, it was Arsanjani who determined the practical outcome of land distribution. Although his term as minister of agriculture was relatively brief (May 1961 to March 1963), his actions and words set the course for the remainder of the program.

An American Diplomat's Interview with Hasan Arsanjani

By November 1962, the ulama were united in their opposition to the shah's land distribution. On 20–21 November 1962, both the shah and Alam bitterly complained to the American ambassador, Julius Holmes, about the "unholy alliance" of the ulama with landowners. Holmes's reports on his meetings with the shah and Alam are given in two secret cables (airgram A-318 and airgram A-319, both dated 26 November 1962). The shah and Alam stressed that while the ulama were outspoken in their attacks on the government concerning the "reform" of the electoral laws by cabinet decree, their real hostility was aimed at the land distribution program. Moreover, both informed the ambassador that the land distribution program would be completed by June 1963, after which it would be safe to hold elections and create a Majlis of a "different character." It is clear that even by late November 1962, neither Alam nor the shah had a plan for issuing the cabinet decrees of 17 January 1963. Otherwise, they could not have possibly concluded that land distribution would be completed by June 1963. They had no idea that a "second phase" was to be launched in January 1963. Evidently, it was all done by Hasan Arsanjani.

On 21 November 1962, the same day that Ambassador Holmes met with the shah, Stuart W. Rockwell, minister-counselor of the American embassy, called on Arsanjani. His confidential report on this one-hour conversation is contained in a State Department airgram (A-314, dated 24 November 1962):

> The Minister said that the first stage of the land distribution program would be completed by next March. By this he meant that by that time all the lands belonging to landlords possessing more than one village would be distributed, except for the one village permitted by law to the landlord. The second stage would then begin, which would involve the distribution of the remaining one village still in the possession of the landlords, since the Minister was convinced that, owing to the attitude of the peasants in these villages, the landlords would be unable to hold on to them. The second stage would also see the beginning of the distribution of *vaqf* lands. The Minister maintained that small landowners—those who own less than one village—should have no fear of the present program, especially if they work their lands themselves and have established good relationships with the peasants. It is not the government's purpose to deprive these landowners of their lands.

Dr. Arsanjani said that there had been resistance to his program all along the way. This was principally organized here in Tehran by such people as Sardar Fakher Hekmat and Ghavam Shirazi, the father-in-law of the Prime Minister. Threats had been made to assassinate [him] but he believed that if this should happen peasants all over the country would tear landlords limb from limb, and this was restraining the intriguers.

It is noteworthy that Rockwell ignored the inconsistency and contradiction between Arsanjani's pledge on small landowners and the need to have a second stage of land distribution. Moreover, Arsanjani avoided any mention of the mounting religious opposition. He also tried to mislead the American diplomat by claiming that the opposition was "led" by Hekmat and Qavam Shirazi, who were not very active in the opposition. Most significantly, he also informed the embassy officer of his plan to distribute the endowed lands. But Arsanjani neglected to inform Rockwell that the distribution of the endowed lands was also due to "peasant attitudes." The following is from a confidential report (Foreign Service despatch 447, dated 4 April 1962) from the American embassy in Tehran to the State Department, concerning landlord-peasant relations in an endowed village in Lorestan. The report, by attaché George W. Cave, is particularly valuable because the village in question was a public endowment (vaqf-e amm) that was administered by no less a personality than Ayatollah Seyed Hasan Emami, the Imam Jomeh (prayer leader) of Tehran, a former senator, and a close advisor to the shah himself. Because of his staunch support for the shah when he had been speaker of parliament at the time of Mossadeq, Emami had come close to losing his life in an assassination attempt.[19] It is emphasized that the endowed village was not even subject to the provisions of the 1962 land distribution decrees. This report clearly illustrates why following Arsanjani's incitement of the peasants the government was forced to include the endowed villages in Phase Two of land distribution, thereby further inflaming the religious opposition. According to Cave, the village was managed by Mrs. Emami, the wife of the Imam Jomeh. The plight of Mrs. Emami, as described in the report, is also indicative of the plight of landowners in Iran in 1962.

Conditions in an Endowed Village in March 1962

The reporting officer, accompanied by John Turner, Second Secretary of Embassy, enjoyed an unusual opportunity to see some of the problems of the new land reform program at first hand. The impressions reported in this memorandum were obtained during a hunting trip to Luristan March 7–10. A focal point of the current unrest in Luristan is the village of Darband, situated 18 kilometers from Azna, a rail station with a large NIOC installation. About six years ago, Darband was given to *vaqf* (religious endowment), and since that time the village has been administered by the Imam Jomeh of Tehran, Dr. Seyed Hasan Emami. The proceeds from the village are intended for use by the Imam Jomeh to help defray expenses of the Shah Mosque in Tehran.

On the afternoon of March 8, Mr. Turner and the reporting officer were invited to tea by Mrs. Emami who supervises the property. She and the officers' host, Hosein Khan Fuladvand, said that about six weeks previously the peasants had come to Mrs. Emami and demanded that she give them their lands. According to Mrs. Emami, she told the peasants that any such action required a decision on the part of the government and in any case the land in question was a *vaqf*. Nothing much happened until March 7 when, as a result of a speech by Agriculture Minister Arsanjani on March 6 calling for more rapid implementation of land reform, the peasants in Darband demanded that Mrs. Emami give the lands to them immediately. When she demurred they burned a tractor which had been recently purchased by the Imam Jomeh. With the help of the other landlords in the area she was able eventually to encourage about half the peasants in Darband to go back to work, but the remainder refused to do so.

The gendarmerie colonel in Khoramabad arrived in Darband on March 8, but, according to Mrs. Emami, he offered little but sympathy. He pointed out that he was powerless to make a move which would be interpreted as being counter to government policy. However, he did leave a gendarme to guard her house. In addition, one of Mrs. Emami's faithful retainers armed with a shotgun was assigned to guard the house. The above developments turned the area into an armed camp. All the landlords carried sidearms, and Mrs. Emami kept a loaded .38 caliber pistol handy. Mrs. Emami appeared to be very much afraid, and her attempts to appear calm to the reporting officers only made her more frenetic. It was apparent that the other landlords had prevailed on her to remain in Darband, since if she were to capitulate their hold over their respective peasants would be weakened. One of the local landlords, Manucher Khan, was staying in the house with Mrs. Emami.

At a dinner given by Mrs. Emami on March 9, Hosein Khan Fuladvand, Manucher Khan and Mrs. Emami went into a huddle to make arrangements for a communication system in case of any trouble. At this dinner party, Manucher Khan and Hosein Khan Fuladvand presented the landlords' case as follows: As now constituted, the land reform program is illegal since it has not been ratified by the Majlis. Both stated that the bill approved by the Majlis limiting land holdings to 400 hectares was a bill landlords had little objection to. The current program limiting landlords to a single village is meaningless in Luristan since few landlords own villages outright; most have shares in numerous villages. Both men agreed that the division of lands and the emergence of the peasants as small landholders is inevitable. What the landlords are fighting for now is an equitable price for their land. They stated that most landlords would gladly relinquish their lands for an equitable price, since if they were to lose their lands they would require capital to establish themselves in another business.

It is important to note the general belief among the landlords that the United States Government is backing Arsanjani's land reform program. The reporting officer had a long argument with Hosein Khan Fuladvand on this subject. Fuladvand pointed to Arsanjani's statements of U.S. financial backing for land reform. The reporting officer commented that these statements had been denied by the Embassy. Fuladvand then quoted Mr. Bowles's recent statement to the effect that he was greatly pleased by the progress of the land reform program. The reporting officer pointed out that the U.S. assumes that lands must be divided eventually, but that land distribution is an internal Iranian problem which the Iranians must settle themselves.

Nationalization of Forests and Pastures, 1963

On the same day (and apparently at the same sitting) that the cabinet of Assadollah Alam and Hasan Arsanjani issued the so-called Additional Articles, it also issued a decree nationalizing all of Iran's forests and pastures. Given Iran's vast forests in the north and western parts of the country and the vast areas that consisted of pasture land, this was an immensely important action. It negatively impacted a huge number of people. Surprisingly, it has received no scrutiny or analysis in the literature. The statistics are simply amazing. Iran's total area consists of 164 million hectares. Of this, 19 million hectares were designated as forest, and 10 million hectares consisted of pasture. That is, one-fifth of the country's area was nationalized by a mere "cabinet decree" that was prepared and issued virtually overnight. It will also be shown (see chap. 12) that at least half of Iran's agricultural land was owned by small landowners. These were the same people who were formally expropriated under Phase Two, the subsequent label given to the Additional Articles. We thus arrive at the truly mind-boggling conclusion that in one day, and in one sitting, the government of Mohammad Reza Shah Pahlavi confiscated or dispossessed the owners of about 60–70 percent of the entire land area of Iran, or about 1 million square kilometers, using two cabinet decrees. This has probably no historical precedent anywhere. One gains the impression of a government that was both desperate and completely out of control. It was a regime that was galloping toward a certain suicide. In reviewing these statistics, one begins to understand why Iran exploded a few months later on 5 June 1963, now regarded by scholars as the beginning of the Islamic Revolution.

Concerning compensation for the nationalized forests and pastures, the amounts were so negligible and the conditions so stringent that practically no one received anything. As specified in the nationalization decree that was subsequently "approved" by the referendum of 26 January 1963, annual payment for compensation to the owners of forests and pastures was set at a maximum of 50 million rials ($700,000). It should be noted that the entire annual payment to *all* the former owners of *all* the country's forests and pastures, which amounted to 20 percent of the country's total land area, was less than the partial sale price of just *one* Pahlavi village (Takestan in Qazvin) that was described in the previous chapter. The duration of payments was over ten years. Thus, the potential "compensation" payable for all of the country's forests and pastures was a mere $7 million, payable over ten years. Even assuming an interest rate of 10 percent (actual interest rates were above 20 percent), the present value of $7 million to be received in ten equal installments was only $4.3 million. At 20 percent interest rate, the present value fell to $2.93 million. However, to qualify for any payment, an owner had to present title deeds with certified maps showing the boundaries and accurate measures of the forests and pastures owned. Few possessed these documents. Having declared that measurement of agricultural land and the use of hectares were "inappropriate and impractical" for Iran, the government was now demanding certified maps of forests and pastures, along with accurate measurements. Not having these documents, most owners received nothing. Similar to the provisions of the 1962 cabinet decree, in the event that the pasture or forest had been used as collateral for a loan, while the forest or pasture was lost, the loan remained the obligation of the hapless owner, and the creditor could then recover his claim through "normal" legal channels and seize the debtor's home and belongings. The nationaliza-tion of forests and pastures resulted in an abrupt and cruel loss of income to small landowners. In addition, the "nationalization" of pastures must have created immense difficulty for the tribal and nomadic population. It is noteworthy that those who had received land under land distribution were exempt from the provisions of this decree. Consequently, it appears that the main purpose was to confiscate the remaining property of the landowners.

It is very difficult to find rational justification and reason for national-izing forests and pastures. After all, there were no tenants on this land. The only reasonable explanation is to be found in Arsanjani's earlier writ-ings in which he stated that forests and mines belonged to the people and should be held by the government. Subsequently, as minister of agricul-ture he had implemented his ideology. He appears to have had a free hand as minister. Subsequently, after nationalization, some of the nationalized forests and pastures were "privatized" in that they were distributed among cabinet ministers, high officials, senior and even middle-level military officers, and other supporters of the Pahlavi regime. A similar case of "privatization" in Khoramdareh, Zanjan, will be described in chapter 11.

Meeting with Amini, 9 February 1962: The Final Rupture

Shortly after the 1962 cabinet decree was issued, Ali Amini requested a meeting with the leaders of the Agricultural Union of Iran. Reluctantly, Majd consented to a gathering at the house of Isa Behzadi, an attorney and active Union member. The meeting took place and was photographed (see fig. 5.10). Majd gives the following account:

> I had completely severed all contacts with Mr. Amini, the prime minister. He had repeatedly sent word through Dr. Alamuti, the minister of justice, and through my friends, Mr. Hosein Khakbaz and Mr. Mahmoud Fateh, to meet with him. But I had declined. I had great respect for Mr. Amini's mother, Mrs. Ashraf Amini, Fakhre ad Dowleh, and was friends with her children, especially Ali Amini. During the Fourteenth Majlis, Mr. Amini had been sent to India. He was appointed minister of agriculture by Mr. Mohammad Saed by my request. When his mother found out that the appointment was at my initiative, she asked me not to pursue the matter. Dutifully, I informed Mr. Saed, and another person was appointed. I never ex-pected that Ali Amini, a son of Fakhre ad Dowleh, and a grandson of Mirza Ali Khan Amin ad Dowleh, would so willingly serve and

carry out the orders of the American and British governments. Nor did I expect that he would so blatantly violate and trample on the laws of Islam and the Constitution by approving and issuing the notorious cabinet decree and then name it the land reform law. Besides, his own brothers and sister, Massoumeh Khanum, own the estates of Lashte Nesha in Gilan, one of the best properties in Iran, and they own the village of Kahrizak in Tehran. Although Amini himself possesses large sums in foreign banks and has no interest in the Constitution, the laws of Islam, and the country, at least he should be ashamed in front of his brothers and sister. For the sake of four days of premiership (prime minister in name only), he completely followed the orders of the foreigners.

On 5 February 1962, there was a large gathering of unfortunate and helpless landowners in my house. Mr. Sharif ol Ulama, Amini's minister of religious affairs, arrived and told me that Mr. Amini insisted on seeing me. If I would not go to see him, then he would come to my house. I responded that my house was his house. I then asked about Arsanjani, and told him that I had never met him. He said that I must have seen him in Qavam Saltaneh's house. He usually stood in the hallway in the ranks of Qavam Saltaneh's servants. Two days later, Mr. Sharif ol Ulama telephoned that the prime minister wished to meet with the landowners on 9 February 1962 at the house of Mr. Isa Behzadi, and asked me to come on that day. I did not wish to go, but my friends, Mr. Hosein Khakbaz and Mahmoud Fateh, insisted and took me along. At the appointed hour, Dr. Amini arrived and the meeting began. At first, Mr. Behzadi, Mr. Abu Taleb Shirvani, and Haj Lotf Ali Khan Tabatabaii spoke, and in the interest of historical accuracy, the text of each speech is provided.

In his speech, Abu Taleb Shirvani noted that while he was in the United States for medical treatment, he had traveled extensively and had closely inspected the agricultural situation. In many states he had come across farms greatly in excess of 20,000 hectares. If land distribution was a wise idea, then why was it not implemented in America itself? He had correctly foreseen some of the consequences of Arsanjani's publicity against landowners and some of the end results of the 1962 land decree. Given the structure of landownership, he had correctly suggested that only about 5,000 villages out of 55,000 private villages were subject to the provisions of the decree (see chap. 12). How was the government going to satisfy the cultivators of the remaining 50,000 villages who would not receive land under the decree? Having consumed government publicity for nearly a

Fig. 5.10. Meeting of the Agricultural Union of Iran with Ali Amini at the house of Isa Behzadi, 9 February 1962. *Front row, left to right:* Dr. Amir Aalam, Mohammad Ali Majd, Mohammed Ghoreishi, unidentified man. *Second row, second from right:* Manucher Diba.

year, the cultivators would not be satisfied, and the outcome would be political turmoil with unforeseen consequences. The way out of the impasse was to implement the original 1960 land reform law. After Shirvani, Lotf Ali Khan Tabatabaii, a landowner in Azarbaijan, had made a brief but moving speech:

Mr. Prime Minister, Respected Gentlemen,

First I thank Mr. Behzadi for organizing this gathering and enabling the landowners of Azarbaijan, and specially the landowners of Maragheh, to air their grave difficulties and grievances and bring them to the attention of His Imperial Majesty and the prime minister. I also thank the prime minister for taking the time to come to this meeting and for listening to our statements. We trust that the purpose of this meeting is not merely theatrical but is intended to give the Azarbaijan landowners an opportunity to describe their problems and grievances, and we ask that the laws of religion, the Constitution, and the laws of the country be observed.

Mr. Prime Minister, historians readily agree that Azarbaijan has always been a center of development and civilization. Of the country's 45,000 villages, fully 9,000 are in Azarbaijan, and today, thanks to the efforts of the landowners in Azarbaijan, there is a prosperous village every half a league. From the granting of the Constitution by His Late Majesty, Mozzafar ad Din Shah in the 1324 Lunar [1906], we Azarbaijanis have been at the forefront of movements to preserve the independence and the freedom of the country. We are proud of the fact that the Provincial Assembly of Azarbaijan compiled the Articles of the Constitution that today is the guarantor of the country's independence and its constitutional monarchy. Is it not true that Sattar Khan and Baqer Khan of Azarbaijan sacrificed themselves for the sake of the constitution?

From Shahrivar 1320 (August 1941) to the events of 1325 Solar (1946) we endured the tyranny of Pishevari and other foreign lackeys, and we Azarbaijanis perished in front of their machine guns for the defense of this land, and many died in their prisons. Before the Imperial Army had passed Qoflankuh (in 1946), we in Tabriz rose up and chased the foreign lackeys out of Azarbaijan. After all this patriotism and devotion to the shah, is it justice that our reward should be the confiscation of our property?

Mr. Prime Minister, you are in Tehran, but you cannot imagine the consequences and difficulties suffered by the people of Azarbaijan because of the poisonous words uttered by the minister of agriculture, Mr. Arsanjani. Arsanjani's propaganda has been ten times worse than all the propaganda put out for the past twenty years by Radios Moscow, Baku, and Iravan.

Mr. Prime Minister, we respect and we will obey the Constitution and all laws that are not in conflict with the laws of Islam. In reality, we have been the defenders of the frontiers of this land, and now Mr. Arsanjani wants to confiscate all that we possess. We beg you to issue orders that such unlawful actions in Azarbaijan and specially in Maragheh be terminated.

On behalf of the Union of Azarbaijan Landowners,

Seyed Lotf Ali Khan Tababtabaii,

Tehran, 9 February 1962

The meeting ended acrimoniously with shouting between Amini and Majd. Majd continues:

After Mr. Tabatabaii, Mr. Amini went to the podium, and at this time the microphone was connected to Radio Tehran and his speech was broadcast live. As usual, he spoke at length. The gist of his remarks was that the time had come for some changes in rural affairs and the ownership of land. He then turned his attention to me and embarked on a personal attack. He said, "I have known Mr. Majd and have been his friend. But now Majd is the only person who is resisting and derailing our reforms. A few days ago, Majd went to Gilan and, using his influence with the people of Gilan, has incited the people against the government." I grew upset at this pack of lies because I had not gone to Gilan. I shouted loudly that he was lying and that I had not gone to Gilan for a long time. He responded that if I had not gone personally, then I had sent my representatives to incite the people. He also added that I owned so much land that I had to buy a private airplane just to inspect my properties. In short, a shouting match developed between me and Dr. Amini. I screamed at him that he had betrayed Iran and its people. At the end of the meeting, Dr. Amini came up to me and took my hand as if nothing had happened. He joked that one day even my children would turn against me. I said, "We will see." In this manner, the meeting broke up.[20]

6

The Vagary and Perfidy of American Policy

American policy concerning land distribution in Iran can be divided into three distinct phases. Between 1945 and 1955, the U.S. government actively promoted land distribution, and this culminated with the sale and distribution of Pahlavi estates. The records indicate that between 1955 and 1959, there were extensive discussions between American embassy and consular officials and prominent anti-shah Iranians concerning the issue of land distribution. These conversations revealed serious opposition not only to land distribution but also to the shah himself and his style of rule. Following these conversations, the American enthusiasm for land distribution waned, and a lengthy 1959 confidential embassy report was issued on its dangers and drawbacks. The report concluded that there was neither a need nor a widespread demand for land distribution in Iran. A "hasty and thoughtless" land distribution was seen to be the greatest danger to the shah's regime. The State Department was so impressed by this report that its authors received a meritorious citation from the acting secretary of state.

In the meantime, stung by continuous criticism and unfavorable reports in the American press about the landownership situation in Iran, the shah pushed the May 1960 land distribution bill through a highly reluctant Majlis and Senate. However, faced with domestic and religious opposition, as well as continued apprehension and ambivalence by the American embassy, the shah decided to proceed cautiously.

By early 1961, there was a complete change in American policy. The records show that the U.S. government was not only actively promoting land distribution but actually pressuring the shah. A February 1961 report to the State Department showed extreme unhappiness with the Majlis amendments of the 1960 land distribution law. It considered the appointment of Ebrahim Mahdavi as minister of agriculture as a betrayal and abandonment of land distribution by the shah. Mahdavi had invited the

Agricultural Union of Iran to help draft the implementation regulations for the law. The report criticized the shah's slow pace and recommended "forceful" actions. It discussed the "inevitable" struggle between the shah and the "vested interests" consisting of landowners and the ulama, and declared that in the absence of effective "counter-power" against the vested interests, there would be no "vigorous reform" in Iran. To implement radical land distribution, the report stated that "revolutionary" conditions were needed. In short, the report is a practical blueprint for the appointment of the Amini-Arsanjani government in May 1961 and the subsequent events. It leaves little doubt that the shah was coerced by the U.S. government into adopting measures against his better judgment.

Subsequently, a long parade of senior American officials visiting Iran in 1962, including Vice President Lyndon Johnson, presidential adviser Chester Bowles, and Secretary of State Dean Rusk, declared full support for Arsanjani's policies. Numerous consular reports from Tabriz and Mashhad in 1962 clearly showed the active support and encouragement of the U.S. government for Arsanjani's program and methods. Despite repeated denials by the U.S. embassy that it was not providing financial support for Arsanjani, a confidential embassy report (Foreign Service despatch 352, dated 30 January 1962) revealed that $88 million had been given to the Amini-Arsanjani government during its first six months. By early 1963, however, enthusiasm had waned as American consular officials received reports of peasant violence, the expropriation of the small landowners, and the rising levels of civil and religious opposition. The American consul in Mashhad expressed concern at the gatherings of landowners at the residences of the senior ayatollahs in Mashhad. It is noteworthy that by 1964, American consular reports from Tabriz and Mashhad on land distribution consisted of almost verbatim reproductions of comments by the chiefs of land reform in the respective provinces. It was hoped that by not reporting on the developing crisis, it would somehow go away. Even these sanitized versions could not conceal the gravity of the situation for the small landowners.

By late 1968, the American embassy had adopted the posture of an innocent bystander. When legislation to launch the third phase of land distribution was introduced in the Majlis in October 1968, the shah's "hasty and careless" action was roundly criticized in a confidential embassy despatch. The shah was castigated for "bad faith" with the small landowners whose "plight" and "lingering resentment" had belatedly become a matter of concern and sympathy for the American embassy. The hapless shah was being blamed for the very policies that the United States had pushed him to follow.

Distribution of Pahlavi Estates

In the early years, American policy concerning landownership in Iran was based on outright ignorance of prevailing conditions. An outstanding example is provided by two secret reports on conditions in Azarbaijan that were sent by W. C. Burdett, U.S. consul in Tabriz. In secret report no. 40, dated 20 February 1951, Burdett described landownership in West Azarbaijan in the following terms. "The land is held primarily by large landowners. A feudal type of relationship exists between landlord and tenant. . . . The proportion of small proprietors is highest in the Rezaieh and Shapur areas. Here also was found greater prosperity and intensive cultivation. Historically the concentration on small proprietors is attributed to the Christian minorities who settled down and developed their own land and were later imitated by Moslem communities. The Governor of Maragheh described the solution of the landowning and crop distribution problems as a basic requirement for future progress and well-being of the province. Although cognizant of the great political difficulties involved, the Consulate is in full agreement." In a subsequent secret report on East Azarbaijan (report no. 43, dated 8 March 1951), Burdett wrote, "The Governor of Ardebil had claimed that the greater part of the land was held by small proprietors, but the villagers questioned declared that it is held by large landowners." The consul chose to believe the villagers. It is noteworthy that the consul quickly accepted the view of the governor of Maragheh because it corresponded with his own preconceived notions. He summarily dismissed the view of the governor of Ardebil and sided with the villagers.

It was thus not surprising that American officials welcomed the proposed distribution of Pahlavi estates. In a confidential report (no. 593, dated 31 January 1951), J. J. Wagner, second secretary at the American embassy in Tehran, informed the State Department that 4,000 estates were to be included in the sales: "This constructive proposal on the part of the Shah has come like a breath of fresh air upon the stagnant social situation, and it certainly will be in our interest to do everything possible to strengthen his determination to carry it into effect." Subsequently, as described in a confidential report (Foreign Service despatch 524, dated 20 February 1960), the officials of the U.S. government's Point Four program provided "technical aid" to the shah's sale and distribution of his estates. Although Wagner's report contains several references to the manner in which these lands had been "purchased" by Reza Shah, and shows full awareness that the lands had been acquired by questionable means, it nevertheless frowns on "the attempts of certain persons to recover the lands which they allegedly were forced to sell to the former Shah." Evidently, in the quest for "reform," neither in 1951 nor between 1962 and 1971 did the legal and human rights of the people of Iran carry much weight in the American scheme of things.

In a subsequent secret report (no. 626, dated 9 February 1951), embassy counselor Arthur L. Richards summarized the reason why the U.S. government was so ardently backing the shah's sale and distribution of his estates. It was to be the beginning of a general land distribution in Iran. Richards provides a lucid statement of the rationale for American policy for most of the next decade.

> No single recent occurrence in Iran has been the subject of so much discussion, or is potentially so important from the point of view of the political and economic development of the country, as the Shah's announcement on January 27, 1951, that the Crown Lands are to be divided among the resident peasants. If successful, this program will mean the start of a process designed to improve the lot of a great depressed section of the population. A greater confidence in the government will develop, and a desire for governmental stability will be created in fields now fertile for revolutionary ideas. Furthermore, the position of the Shah, as the originator of a move for the better distribution of wealth, will be enhanced. If unsuccessful, on the other hand, the sense of cynicism and frustration among the people, already great, must be expected to increase; the Shah's position would become less secure; and possibly even violent measures against the Government should be anticipated. Most certainly the depressed classes would then become even more attracted by the subtle and persistent promises of communism.

Conversation between Governor-General Ram of Khorasan and U.S. Consul Cassilly

Following the overthrow of Mossadeq, American embassy and consular officials met repeatedly with politicians who had opposed Mossadeq, including several who were to become active in the Agricultural Union of Iran. They discussed political and economic matters, including land distribution. On the basis of these conversations, American views on landownership were revised, and American enthusiasm for land distribution evaporated. These conversations are extremely informative, and a few are reported here. In early October 1955, the principal officer at the U.S. consulate in Mashhad, Thomas A. Cassilly, met with Mostafa-Qoli Ram, governor-general of Khorasan, at a small dinner given by Ram for George

Hillier of the British embassy. The governor of Mashhad was also present. They discussed land distribution, and Cassilly filed a confidential report (Foreign Service despatch 15, dated 10 October 1955). Excerpts are given here:

The Governor General of Khorasan, Mr. Mostafa-Qoli Ram, former Minister of Interior under Dr. Mossadeq and also formerly Minister of Agriculture and Mayor of Tehran, is one of the handful of senior civil servants who actually govern Iran. . . . Ram prefaced his remarks on land reform by professing admiration for the Shah's program of distributing the royal estates. Everyone in Iran applauded His Majesty's liberal gestures, according to Mr. Ram, but it must be recognized that this was an enormously expensive program that only the Crown could afford. It was illogical to expect private landholders to follow the Shah's example, he maintained, because they had no other means of support once their land had been given away. Since the Government could not afford to buy this land and would not expropriate it "like the Communists," it was wrong even to suggest that private owners should follow the State, any more than they should fulfill any other functions of the State, such as building railroads.

"Americans always assume that Iranian landlords are fabulously wealthy," Mr. Ram contended. Now consider the province of Khorasan; there are only a few really well-to-do landlords here, and all the rest should be considered more as farmers and not rich men. Most of their capital is bound up in the land which is not worth much, although the total number of hectares might seem enormous to a European. Furthermore, these landowners had to provide water, a very difficult undertaking in this part of the world and one which American and European farmers were spared. Asked who the great landlords in this ostan [province] were, the Governor General named, first, the Malek family of which Haji Aqa Hosein Malek is one of the greatest single landholders in the country. Next, Mr. Mohammad Ghoreishi, deputy to the Majlis from Mashhad, who has extensive holdings near the Afghan border. Third, the prominent Alam family, including Minister of Interior Amir Assadollah Alam, who own a large part of the shahrestans (townships) of Birjand and Sistan. And fourth, the Saidi family, with large holdings in the vicinity of Neishabur, whose representative in the Majlis is Mr. Abdollah Saidi. Only these families could be classed as really great landlords here, Mr. Ram maintained.

Of the 6,412 villages in this ostan, only about six hundred are the property of these influential families, according to Mr. Ram, while the other 5,800 were sometimes owned by one individual, but more likely, by several persons or occasionally as many as a hundred different owners. Unfortunately, Mr. Ram observed wryly, most Americans tended to think of the typical Iranian landlord as being like Mr. Haji Malek, who was not very flatteringly described in Anne Sinclair Mahdavi's *Persian Adventure*. Not only was this description exaggerated as far as Mr. Malek was concerned, he protested, but it was as absurd as believing that the average American businessman acted like Mr. Rockefeller.

No, land reform was not the solution to Iran's agricultural problems, Mr. Ram maintained. What was needed was a strong central agricultural bank for which America might be willing to supply the capital. The institution would have branches throughout the country which would make loans at low rates of interest to landlords who wished to improve their property. At present only a few owners could afford to provide electric pumps such as the one Mr. Malek had installed at Chenaran. Few could buy agricultural machinery and repair it, build qanats or storage barns and all the other improvements which were needed to increase agricultural production, according to the Governor General. Gradually, as conditions improve, the peasants will learn from the landlords and eventually be prepared to own land themselves. Mr. Ram reiterated that he wholeheartedly backed the Shah's distribution program and was impressed by the improvement shown in the Fariman district, southeast of Mashhad, where some of the royal estates were broken up two years ago. He pointed out, however, that Point Four (U.S. Government) had spent a great deal of time and money in Fariman helping the peasants, and while this could be done on a small scale as long as ICA functioned, it could never be considered as a model for the country as a whole.

Mostafa-Qoli Ram's interview is an important document not only because of the wisdom displayed but also because of his depth of knowledge. Ram's description of the structure of landownership in Khorasan is confirmed by the findings of the 1960 census of agriculture. What is also truly remarkable about Ram's statements and his opposition to land distribution was the fact that he was the father of Hushang Ram, the person in charge of the sale and distribution of Pahlavi estates. Cassilly was somewhat uncomfortable, however, with Ram's "conservative" views. He made the following observation:

The impression of the Governor General that emerges is one of a man of many qualities including a sincere interest in the welfare of his native province and an apparently warm admiration for the United States. Nevertheless, Mr. Ram also emerges as a man who is essentially a conservative who is not likely to attempt any bold, imaginative action to improve conditions in this province. As such, he finds himself in opposition to most of the younger, educated group in Khorasan as well as some of the liberal policies of the Shah himself. . . . His deference to the religious reaction in Mashhad runs counter to the aspirations of most of the enlightened elements in the city.

Conversation between Majlis Deputy Amir-Teimur-Kalali and Consul Cassilly

On 8 and 16 December 1955, Thomas Cassilly spoke twice with Moham-mad Ebrahim Amir-Teimur-Kalali, deputy from Gonabad and Tabas to the Eighteenth Majlis. A record of their conversations was sent in a confi-dential report (Foreign Service despatch 28, dated 17 December 1955). Amir-Teimur-Kalali was one of the leaders of the Agricultural Union of Iran. In this conversation, he expressed his growing opposition to the policies of the shah:

During the course of the first conversation, the Consul observed that he had recently passed through Fariman where part of the royal estates had been distributed two years ago. He had stopped and talked to some of the officials there and was impressed by the progress that had been made in this area. Did the Deputy feel that the Shah's plan for land reform might serve as a model elsewhere in Iran? Mr. Amir-Teimur-Kalali replied rather definitely that he did not; the land distribution program was part of His Majesty's liberal philosophy which, though well-meaning, was not very profound. He went on to say that the Shah's increasing disposition to take an active part in governing the country had not only caused resentment in the Majlis but was actually a threat to the institution of the mon-archy itself. Other kings realized that it was wiser to reign above the level of politics, but the present Shah was inexperienced and ill-advised. No European monarch acted in this way, Mr. Amir-Teimur-

Kalali contended, and even in the Middle East, other kings were more discreet. It was because the Deputy realized the vital importance of the throne as a symbol in Iran that he was so disturbed by the Shah's recent actions.

When reminded that the monarchy had also played an active role under Reza Shah, he retorted that of course it had, but unfortunately the present King had inherited little of his father's ability or strength. The deputy emphasized that he had nothing against the Shah personally, as he was a pleasant, conscientious young man, but the Court was filled with ambitious sycophants who kept encouraging the King to be a second Reza Shah. This was a dangerous policy, Mr. Amir-Teimur-Kalali contends, since the Shah has sometimes acted on impulse, then seen his mistake and has been too proud to withdraw completely. What the Court needs is sincere steady advisors selected from among the nation's statesmen of long experience. Now, however, such men had little confidence in the Shah or the future of Iran if things continued on their present course.

As for his own feelings on land reform, the Deputy explained that it was a mistake to think of Iran as made up predominantly of the holdings of great landlords. He estimated that 85 percent of the cultivated land belongs to the peasants or small landlords owning one village or less. Another 8 to 10 percent is the property of either the Government or the Crown so that barely 5 percent of the land in Iran is owned by the great landlords. Yet, to listen to some foreigners and a few of the so-called liberals in Tehran, you might think the percentage was exactly reversed.

The peasants in Iran depended on their landlord to repair the qanats and provide seed, animals, and equipment. If they were suddenly thrown on their own resources, these simple, well-meaning people will be lost. In the Deputy's opinion, it would be disastrous for Iran to go about breaking up the big estates.

Since Mr. Amir-Teimur-Kalali had served in eleven out of eighteen Iranian parliaments, the Consul asked whether he intended to run for reelection for the next Majlis. The Deputy replied that he was no longer a young man and that he found he was becoming increasingly depressed by some of the follies of politicians in this country. His friends were urging him to run again, but he felt he was really exhausted now from so many years in the Majlis. Besides, he added, the way things seem to be going now, many persons believed that the new parliament might turn out to be a "rubber-stamp" for the Shah. Mr. Amir-Teimur-Kalali admitted that he did not have much confidence in the bright, young so-called liberals that seemed to be so much in evidence just now. Most of them have had a European education and come back to Iran convinced that they know every-thing, whereas they don't even know conditions in their own coun-try. The Consul noted that there had been reports in the press that the Shah might take an active part in the forthcoming elections; in this event, did Mr. Amir-Teimur-Kalali feel he would have difficulty being reelected? The Deputy replied with a smile that His Majesty had not been enthusiastic about his candidacy for the Eighteenth Majlis either, but that had not prevented a favorable outcome. The people of Khorasan knew him so well and had so much respect for him that he was sure he could win anywhere in a free election.

Cassilly's comments on the conversation included the following:

Mr. Amir-Teimur-Kalali's disapproval of the Shah's policies is well established as is his opposition to the Baghdad Pact in its present form. Although he has represented this province in every election since the Sixth Majlis, it is unlikely that the Deputy will be reelected this time if the Shah decides to take an active part in the elections. His attitude towards land reform is not much different than that of the great majority of landowners in this province. In varying de-grees they look on the Shah's program of distributing his estates as an ill-advised gesture whose implications have not always been thoroughly considered by the royal advisors.

Conversation between Majlis Deputy Said Mahdavi and Consul Cassilly

On 15 and 17 May 1956, Consul Cassilly met with Said Mahdavi, deputy from Quchan, and the content of the conversations was reported in a con-fidential report (Foreign Service dispatch 58, dated 26 May 1956). Deputy Mahdavi was a brother of Ebrahim Mahdavi, a former and future minis-ter of agriculture and was at the time director of Karkeh Dam in Khu-zestan. The appointment of Ebrahim Mahdavi as minister of agriculture in September 1960 was to be denounced by the American embassy as a betrayal of land reform. In addition to being a member of a prominent Khorasan family, Mahdavi was also closely related to Reza Kadivar, a deputy from Mashhad to the Eighteenth Majlis. The following is an ex-cerpt from Mahdavi's reported remarks on land distribution:

When the matter of land reform was mentioned, Deputy Mah-davi began by stating that he was not opposed to the principle of dividing up the Crown lands and was not a great landowner himself. Nevertheless, he felt there was too much reckless talk about land reform by persons who had made no effort to study the situation. Foreigners must understand that Iran is not like France or Denmark, where individual holders can cultivate their own little plots. Because of the qanat system practiced in Iran, a series of large holdings was the only practical solution since obviously each peasant with a hectare or two cannot afford to build his own underground tunnels. Cut this peasant off from the landlord's qanat, and he would be helpless. Landowners in this part of the country should be strengthened, not weakened, he argued; they protect their villagers from the unjust demands of the Gendarmerie and rebuild the qanats when washed out by floods as they were this spring. The landlords in Khorasan have become so discouraged during the past year or two that they are not spending money on improving their estates, Mahdavi declared. Why should they waste money on property they are going to lose anyway? If this trend should continue for many more years, Mahdavi fears the country will be in a very critical condition.

Why is it that "Point Four" refuses to help the landlords, the Deputy asked? Apparently they are prepared to spend thousands of dollars on the peasants' cooperative in Fariman where the Royal lands have been distributed, but nothing to help the landowners to buy tractors and spare parts from the U.S. on easy, long-term credit. Anyone who really knows conditions in rural Iran could tell USOM this, and yet they continue to concentrate on a visionary experiment that will probably collapse anyway as soon as "Point Four" aid is withdrawn.

You know that the people are saying that America is pushing the land reform program, Mr. Mahdavi remarked. The Shah is an inexperienced young man who wants to do the right thing, and if the U.S. keeps on pressing him, he will probably try to push a land distribution program through the Majlis. The parliament cannot stall indefinitely because the King is the dominant force in Iran now, but this would cause a great deal of resentment which could lead to serious disturbances throughout the country.

Reading the material forty-five years later, one is struck by the wisdom of Mahdavi and how his predictions came true. Cassilly had remarked, "As could be expected, the Deputy is opposed to land reform and sensitive to alleged U.S. criticism of the landlords. Although his opinions are similar to those of Deputy Bozorgnia from Sabzevar and others in this ostan, they are repeated as an indication of landlord thinking on this controversial matter." Consul Cassilly continued to hold conversations with landowners and Majlis deputies, and he faithfully reported on them. He met with Reza Kadivar, deputy from Mashhad (Foreign Service despatch 33, dated 12 January 1956). Cassilly reported that although Kadivar had been a chief organizer of the pro-shah demonstrations in Mashhad on 19 August 1953, his reelection chances were not good because of his outspoken opposition to some of the shah's policies. Cassilly had subsequently met with many landowners, including Kazem Malek, Ezatollah Gandji, and Mahmoud Farrokh (Foreign Service despatch 3, dated 26 July 1956). Cassilly concluded, "Among the wealthy landowners in Khorasan there appears to be growing though discreet resentment over some of the liberal policies of the Shah. Since many persons are convinced that American influence is partly responsible for His Majesty's actions, some of this discontent has also been directed against the United States."

Conversation between Majlis Deputy Arsalan Khalatbari and Second Secretary Bowling

Meanwhile, John W. Bowling, second secretary at the American Embassy in Tehran, held a conversation with Arsalan Khalatbari, deputy from Mazandaran, and the contents were recorded in a confidential report (Foreign Service despatch 179, dated 28 September 1955). Khalatbari expressed extreme unhappiness with the shah:

Corruption in government is not uniquely Iranian. I think it is probably just as bad in your country, and is probably worse in France than it is here. In our administration, the basic cause of bribery and corruption is the inflation which has left policemen, for example, with monthly salaries of 100 tomans a month, while the cost of living, profits, and free wages have skyrocketed. The causes of corruption in this country are economic, not moral, and the problem should be attacked on the economic plane. For the Shah and the government to talk about corruption all the time as a moral issue is self-defeating. It just helps the communists and other groups who want to change our form of government and our society. The anticorruption campaign, by some mysterious process, gradually slid into a campaign against the landowning class, which is even more dangerous to the country as a whole.

There are no thousand families in Iran; the landowner performs a vital economic function, and I have yet to see a demonstration of any social or economic organization which can take his place in this country. The landowners are the backbone of the country and of the present regime. They are the people who provide the capital for qanats and other improvements which keep our agriculture in shape. The farmers of this country are not a political force at present; if anyone unites them on demagogic political issues, it might be a great danger for the country. The Shah makes a great mistake when, as at Babolsar in July, he appeals for support to a group of young students at the cost of weakening and antagonizing the landlords, who are his real support.

The Shah is not capable of trying to rule with a strong hand; he should retire from this kind of active politics; he should not continue to make himself minutely responsible for day-to-day administration. I have no doubt that the Shah would like to see this Majlis expire and then elect a lot of young socialists to the Majlis. This plays into the hands of the communists. In this country, unlike Europe, the leftists are not anti-communist. On the contrary they are usually ready to help the communists and work with them. I don't think there is any chance of my being re-elected.

American Embassy Report on Land Reform in Iran

Following such conversations, American resident diplomats in Iran became alarmed. Apparently, the expensive Point Four program of assistance to peasants receiving Pahlavi lands, like the one in Fariman near Mashhad, had not been altogether promising. In November 1958, John W. Bowling, now promoted to first secretary of embassy, advised against land distribution. In a confidential report (Foreign Service despatch 365, dated 19 November 1958), Bowling wrote, "It seems certain that the Shah and the Cabinet are now considering a draft bill which would specify a maximum amount of land which could be held by any one owner, with provisions for the forced distribution of any land over that maximum. The Embassy is not aware of the details of the draft, but knows that a large and influential group of officials is opposed to the introduction of the bill at this time. The Embassy is inclined to agree with those opposed to the bill. . . . A bill limiting the size of individual landholdings would have important and far-reaching effects; it is possible that some of these effects would be harmful."

Bowling advised that it would be best to enforce the existing laws and regulations. "In addition to the bill requiring landlords to construct houses for their tenants, the decree abolishing feudal dues, and the administrative speed-up in the distribution of Crown and public lands, the government has introduced a bill requiring landlords to provide the land and buildings for schools and teachers' housing in their villages, as required by the Ministry of Education."

Bowling reminded the State Department "that the urban middle class, the target of the Shah's reform campaign, was not so much interested in the welfare of the peasant." He concluded, "The Embassy, with the help of the Consulates, hopes to produce an analysis of all the political aspects of land tenure reform in Iran; at present the despatch is scheduled for February 1959."

The confidential report produced by the embassy was entitled "Land Reform in Iran" (Foreign Service despatch 695, dated 30 March 1959). It is an important document. Each consulate submitted a report on its district. By this time Consul Cassilly, who had obviously gained the confidence of prominent Khorasan personalities, had left Mashhad, and the report on Khorasan was prepared by his successor, Robert R. Schott. The section on Azarbaijan was prepared by Harold G. Josif. The section on Isfahan was prepared Franklin J. Crawford. The conclusion was written by Thomas J. Scotes. Crawford's analysis and description of landownership in Isfahan is a competent and accurate piece of reporting and analysis and is given in appendix C. Crawford pointed out that, contrary to Ann Lambton's description of landownership in Isfahan and contrary to foreign and domestic misconceptions, the landownership structure in Isfahan was dominated by a huge number of petty ownerships, often consisting of no more than several square meters. This was the outcome of the Islamic practices of matrimony and inheritance. The largest landowner in the province, Akbar Massoud, Sarem ad Dowleh, controlled only four villages, of which one was owned by his wife, and another was owned by his son. He suspected that the situation in Shiraz and Khuzestan was similar. Josif reported that landownership in Azarbaijan was dominated by "medium ownerships." Schott stressed the importance of qanats in Khorasan and the crucial role of landowners in maintaining and repairing them. A land distribution, he feared, would result in unrest as well as destruction of qanats and an inevitable production decline. The authors of this report received a commendation from the acting secretary of state, Christian A. Herter. Its summary contained the following conclusions:

> After a period of study of land reform in Iran the Embassy and the Consulates have come to the conclusion that there is no widespread, popular demand for land distribution in Iran. Whatever pressure does exist comes primarily from the urban intellectual class and

from external propaganda. That there is dissatisfaction on the land is generally admitted, but this pressure is not so great that it cries for immediate action. Most of the peasants in Iran, if they consider their condition at all, would prefer an amelioration of the status quo, of the life they and their fathers have known and understood for many centuries. While they are not necessarily a stupid group, centuries of passive living have made it very difficult to transform them by fiat into landowners. The Iranian Government, therefore, must not rush headlong into a land reform program without taking this factor into consideration. Land reform in a traditional and feudalist society like Iran is fraught with too many implications to lend itself to facile solutions. Apart from the usual economic and political problems which would be involved, many problems peculiar to Iran would have to be solved. These include such disparate elements as religious holdings, qanat maintenance and tribal structures. The United States should encourage the Shah to make some attempt at reform, but not to the extent of weakening his position by hasty action.

Clearly, what subsequently transpired under Arsanjani must have horrified the authors of the report. The main findings were written by Scotes:

Despite the profound and to some extent destructive changes which have occurred in this country over the last half century or more, Iran in many ways still gives the impression that like Persepolis it consists of a complex, partially ruined, somewhat reconstructed superstructure standing on a base still apparently firm and change-resistant. The cities, particularly Tehran, have been radically transformed, too radically perhaps, but the countryside still remains the same. While the former take on foreign manners and ways, the latter continues to live out its life scarcely affected by the outside world.

It can safely be stated that at present the peasant class is putting no pressure on the Shah to reform in any radical manner the status quo. While there does exist, as has always, the demand that the peasant not be exploited by the landlord, any complaints or demands for changes are still being made from within the system and not against it. The peasant, generally speaking, would be just as happy to continue under the present system if he had the assurance that he could get an equitable return for his labor. Obviously, if someone wants to give him land for nothing, he will accept it with no hesitation. However, it is doubtful if any peasant would voluntarily be willing to assume the problems of a landowner if he felt that he could get his fair share under the present feudal arrangement. If he does any thinking at all on the subject, the peasant appears to ask that the Government act as the protector and arbiter it is supposed to be under the traditional system and not be given land with all the attendant troubles of qanat maintenance, lack of easy credit, and the absence of fairly reliable market.

While the Government has set up the Development Bank, which is supposed to help the new landlord-peasant with these very problems, and which is now supervising the distribution of Crown and public lands, it is still too early to contemplate initiating a nationwide distribution of excess lands under its supervision. The bank is not presently equipped to handle the present program, and an additional hastily organized program could lead to fiasco and even disaster. At the same time, tales of corruption about the bank are already being spread and few people have any confidence in it. Another point which must be considered here in connection with the operation of the Development Bank is that the land is not being distributed free to the peasant; it is not an outright grant. It is expected that he will pay the Shah or the Government, as the case may be, in a series of payments extending over a period of 25 years. This plan has caused much skepticism about the eventual efficacy of the entire program and many people believe that the Shah is using this way to get rid of his land while he can, and for as much money as he can. The peasants, therefore, do not appear to be in a great rush to take on the responsibilities of being landowners, as well as the obligation of being the Shah's debtors.

Of course, this situation varies from area to area, but the peasants in many villages are not as downtrodden by the landowner as one would imagine. Many of the landowners are absent most of the time and have very little idea what goes on on their estates. Their agents very often work very closely with the peasants or at least play one off against the other with the landlord often coming out the loser. Thus many peasants are not necessarily clamoring for a change of their present position. At the same time, for obvious reasons the landowning class is not agitating for a diminution of its holdings. Many landowners fully realize that the situation can get out of hand if reforms are not introduced, but few of them, including their liberal western-educated sons, think that hasty distribution will solve the problem. Some have already voluntarily divided their lands among their peasants, only to see the peasants sell it after a year or two because of inability to handle the selling and purchasing aspects of farming. Granted this result does not derive so much from the stupidity of the peasant as his lack of easy credit and stable market prices, the great majority of landowners would rather try to effect reforms within the present framework in the hope of avoiding the radical solutions which might be imposed on them later.

The Shah, therefore, is not presently confronted with a revolutionary threat from the countryside. In fact, this is the one area in the country which should least concern him in terms of short-range priorities. So long as the landowning class identifies its survival with the maintenance of the present regime and so long as the peasant class feels that its needs and demands can be satisfied by the powers that presently be, the Shah need not worry. For this reason, it is imperative that the Shah not be rushed into some ill-advised land reform scheme which might very easily weaken his position in this area. The landowning class and in a more passive sense the peasants are two important supports for the present regime, and the Shah would be foolish to tamper with them without first securing his position elsewhere.

The lack of pressure for land reform from the groups most directly affected does not mean that agitation and demands for land reform do not exist in Iran. Not surprisingly enough, the most insistent demands for land reform come from those who own no land, know very little about the problems involved, and often even care less about the peasant. As is usually the case in underdeveloped countries trying to cope with the industrialized world around them, the main pressure for land reform, as well as other reforms, comes from that small group of foreign-influenced intellectuals of the urban middle class who have adopted, often without profound thought, "modern" modes of thinking, including much of the claptrap and many of the clichés. Land reform is one of these clichés, which in the opinion of this group, when put into effect, will help transform the country into a modern nation able to hold its own against powers that now surround it and play with it as they like. For many of these urban intellectuals the peasant is merely one factor among many which will have to be manipulated in order to make Iran a modern progressive nation. Another reason, however, for their support of land reform is not so idealistic. As one of them put it, "We agitate for land reform now and press the Shah to start it because we hope thereby to alienate the landowning class from him. If this were to happen, the Shah would not remain in power very long." This statement, if it does nothing else, indicates a good awareness of the power politics which presently run the country.

The Shah, then, should be as concerned with dissatisfaction among the present ruling class as among the other embryonic groups which go by the same names as their more highly developed and more sophisticated western counterparts. Any dissatisfaction among this class, moreover, will most assuredly not be due to lack of land reform. Those dissatisfied with the present regime who do own land or are related in any way to landowning families show a surprising disinclination to support land reform, if it means giving up their own or their family lands. They feel this way despite their enthusiastic espousal of other reform proposals. When these persons talk about land reform, it is usually in general terms. The breaking up of large estates is definitely not contemplated. Rather, under a new regime, as they see it, the peasant would be helped more and protected more, but by and large the landowner would not lose his land, unless he was some particularly evil man. In short, under a new regime, feudalism would be better because the leadership will have been changed and everyone will be working for the good of the country. For many of these aristocratic progressives, the old Iranian saying that "the fish rots from the head" seems to have a particular significance. Cut off the present rotting head and the body politic will remain fresh and unspoiled. However, one should not tamper with the body politic.

Thus, apart from a small though admittedly important group of foreign-influenced, dissatisfied, liberal intellectuals, little other internal pressure for land reform exists in Iran today. The merchant and business class, while beginning to invest its money more in city land and factories, still puts much of its money in agricultural lands, this being particularly true in the provinces. In a country without stable banks and a stock exchange, land is still the only safe investment. This class, therefore, is not overly enthusiastic about too much land reform. However, little love is lost between this class and the aristocratic landowners, and doubtless this class would not mind seeing some of the latter humbled a bit. The labor class, when not contemplating its own problems, is obviously in favor of land reform, but as one reform among others which might mean the overthrow of the entire regime. There is no deep feeling about the problem itself, although the close connections between the worker and the peasant should not be overlooked. Many of Iran's laborers are only too recently off the land, and ties are usually maintained with the old village.

Whatever other pressure for land reform there is on the regime today comes from outside the country. Recent events in Pakistan, Iraq, and the United Arab Republic have caused it much concern. In the long run it may be that this foreign pressure does more to bring about agrarian reforms than any pressure now emanating from within the country. When considering this external pressure, the propaganda attacks of the Soviets are another element which has recently increased in sharpness with the signing of the bilateral agreement with the United States and which has worried the present Government. As mentioned above, this outside pressure might very well stampede the regime into some precipitous action which in turn might bring about the situation so hopefully described above by the Iranian intellectual with regard to the alienation of the landowning class from the Shah. It is this precipitous action which, in the Embassy drafting officer's opinion, appears to be the greatest danger confronting the Shah as far as land reform is immediately concerned. Should the Shah not take any action, or should he fail in what he does undertake, this, too, would be fraught with danger. If the Shah takes his time and thinks out a good program, and if other conditions permit, the Shah can effect some lasting reforms in this area which will rebound to the credit of his regime.

The task facing the Shah and his regime is the effective implementation of the present distribution of the Crown estates and of the public lands. By doing this, the regime can hold out the real hope that changes contemplated for the future will actually happen. If the people as a whole and the peasants in particular can be shown that the Crown lands and the public lands have been distributed and that the peasants on these lands have really benefited with the aid of the Government, then the proper climate can be prepared for further land reform. The upper class would be more receptive to giving up some of their land once it is realized that the Shah was actually succeeding with his program. And at the same time, they would have no other alternative because popular opinion, such as it is, would force them to accede.

The prestige of the United States is already too deeply committed in this country to stand aside and watch while the Shah or his Government makes a failure of a land reform program for various reasons. This is one of the few ways still left to the United States to show the average Iranian that it is not supporting the status quo because it necessarily likes it but because it thinks that the present status quo is only a step toward a better future for Iran. In a country like Iran the control of the capital city often makes the difference between being in power or out of power. The countryside is no longer the important area it once was, that is, if it ever really was important in Iran. However, a relatively contented peasant class is a stabilizing element, and as time goes on the only way to keep this class happy is going to be by visibly improving their lives. The Shah by starting now in a firm and effective manner can ensure that reforms will be initiated under the best possible conditions. A good and carefully planned beginning now may well mean the difference between agrarian progress or agrarian chaos for Iran later.

This report clearly delighted the State Department. In a confidential despatch (State Department instruction CA-9113, dated 22 April 1959), Acting Secretary of State Christian A. Herter wrote:

The Department commends Foreign Service Officers Franklin J. Crawford, Harold G. Josif, Robert R. Schott, and Thomas J. Scotes for their excellent analytical report on land reform in Iran. In a day when the subject of land reform arouses great interest and emotions throughout the world and is frequently used by the Soviet Government in its propaganda, a calm, objective report of this nature is particularly welcome.

The dispatch in question performs a real service in pointing out the complexities of the land reform problem in a country such as Iran and in stressing the reality that it is not an issue which can be couched in black-and-white terms. In recognizing the merits of certain land reform measures, the reporting officers at the same time are not led into the error of recommending land reform for reform's sake. They outline clearly the economic, social, and political dislocations which would inevitably arise if the Iranian Government were to embark upon a land reform program without due regard to these consequences. On the positive side, the reporting officers had offered concrete conclusions and recommendations which merit further careful study. The three consular officers, Messrs. Crawford, Josif, and Schott, showed initiative in not confining their comments to their particular consular districts. Their views on the country-wide aspects of land reform combined to give the report additional perspective.

The reporting officers made a contribution to available material on an exceedingly complex subject which should serve as a basic reference document for some years to come.

Land Distribution Law of 16 May 1960

Despite American misgivings, the shah continued to push for land distribution. The main reason was unfavorable foreign press comments on landownership in Iran. In a secret telegram (no. 1153, dated 1 December 1959), Ambassador Wailes informed the State Department that on 23 November 1959, in the presence of the shah, a comprehensive land distribution bill had been presented to the High Economic Council. The bill was then presented to the cabinet of Manucher Eqbal on 27 November 1959. The bill was sharply criticized by the minister of finance. Most significantly, Ambassador Wailes added, "In discussion with Governor Tootel, U.S. Farm Credit Administration, Shah indicated his primary objective in supporting legislation of this type is to counteract unfavorable criticism both locally and abroad of Iranian land ownership pattern."

The subsequent progress of the bill is reported in an unclassified report by John P. Walsh of the U.S. embassy in Tehran (Foreign Service despatch 367, dated 15 December 1959). On 30 November 1959, the shah informed a group of Majlis deputies that the proposed bill was "just and good." The shah also said that the time had come to reduce the holdings of landowners who "have so much that they cannot remember the names of all their estates and villages." On 6 December 1959, the bill was introduced to the Majlis by Prime Minister Eqbal, who called the bill the most progressive measure ever presented to the Majlis, and he said he hoped that it would be speedily enacted. Eqbal's comments were followed by those of Jamshid Amuzegar. The dispatch included the following:

> Dr. Jamshid Amuzegar, Minister of Agriculture, who had the primary responsibility for preparation of the land measure, stated that is a "Land Reform" and not a "Land Limitation" proposal. In his opinion, the bill is the most radical and far-reaching to be introduced in Iran since the introduction of the Constitution. Asserting that the most successful aspects of land reform measures in nine other countries have been incorporated into the bill, he concluded that any landowner reading the bill would agree that it is fair to all—landowners, peasant farmers, and the government.

This bill encountered strong opposition in both the Majlis and Senate, and it was against this very measure that Ayatollah Borujerdi issued a fatwa. The bill was subsequently amended by the Majlis, passed with great reluctance, and sent to the Senate. On 16 May 1960, fearing for their political futures, the senators voted unanimously to approve the bill, and the shah signed it on 6 June 1960.

Embassy Report on the Bill

While the religious and political maneuverings were taking place, Thomas J. Scotes, second secretary of the American embassy, once again sent a long confidential report to Washington stating that the land distribution law was unwise and dangerous (Foreign Service despatch 524, dated 20 February 1960). He concluded, "The Embassy is of the opinion that the introduction of a land distribution bill has been precipitous on the part of the Shah and that the effects are not going to aid the stability of the Shah's regime." He noted, "While everyone is attributing this bill to the Shah, many Iranians also see the influence of the Americans behind it, particularly in view of Point Four help in the Crown Land Distribution program." The report is long, and I can only offer a summary here. It first examines the effects of the bill on the government, landowners, peasants, urban middle class, the press, and Iran's parliament. It concludes with the embassy comments on the episode.

Land distribution, the report notes, has been a "pet project" of the shah for some years. The shah is pushing land distribution because he "apparently wants to counter foreign press charges of feudalism inherent in the present landowner-peasant relationship and in so doing effect some basic reforms which will redound to the credit of his person and his regime." Nevertheless, Iranians blamed the American government for pushing land distribution. The fact that Jamshid Amuzegar had been educated in the United States further convinced Iranians that this was an "American bill."

Landowners were strongly opposed, and in the opinion of the embassy, their criticisms were "varied and often logical." Landowners regarded compensation over a period of fifteen years as too long and the suggested 3 percent interest rate as too little. The report stated that landowners believed that agriculture had suffered because so much talk about land distribution had already discouraged investment by landowners. The peasants were unable to manage their own affairs and maintain the qanats. Given the importance of agriculture in Iran's economy, the agricultural decline would have serious consequences. Unemployment and discontent in rural and urban areas would increase and thereby weaken the regime.

Scotes also mentioned the rising religious opposition and warned of the dangers of an alliance of landowners and ulama:

> This opposition is still in the formative stages although even the Shah was moved to say recently to the American Ambassador that several landowners are paying out bribes to mullahs so the latter

will oppose the bill. One newspaper reported that Ayatollah Borujerdi, the highest Shia cleric in Iran, is opposing the bill, but this has never been officially admitted by that divine. Should this opposition ever materialize, it could have profound effects, given the rather fanatical character of less-educated Iranians.

Despite their opposition, "there is little that the landowners can do now except hope for delays in the passage of the bill. But even these hopes appear futile in view of the Shah's decision to effect an agrarian reform in Iran as soon as possible." Scotes reported that Iran's urban middle class was extremely unhappy with the bill. Initially, it had been estimated that only 80 to 120 large landowners would be affected by the bill. It was now clear that 2,100 to 2,400 landowners were affected. "Many of these persons are not necessarily large or feudalistic landowners, but rather represent the very sinews of the upper and upper middle class from which the Shah derives much of his support. . . . Many members of the urban middle class are also said to be concerned about the extent to which land distribution may affect their relatively small holdings. These people usually own one or two villages or parts of them which they often use as summer places. For them land is both a prestige symbol as well as a major form of investment. If these holdings are to be affected by land distribution, it could mean the loss of considerable money for this already hard-pressed group and cause further disenchantment with the regime."

The bill's indirect effects on Iran's urban middle class were the most serious. Scotes reportd that, since the introduction of the bill, there had been a precipitous decline in land values. In a country like Iran where there were few commercial possibilities and little industry, urban Iranians had traditionally put much of their savings into land. For Iran's middle class, investment in land was a way to provide for retirement and gain prestige. Many depended on this income. Because of the government's actions and pronouncements, land values declined sharply, wiping out the people's hard earned savings and endangering their retirement nests. What possible political benefit could the shah's government derive from such actions? In addition, the inevitable decline in agricultural production would have a repercussion throughout the economy, increasing poverty and unemployment. The downturn in the economy would further hurt middle-class businessmen and shopkeepers. Although the Persian press had taken a favorable line with land distribution, Scotes noted that the English-language press in Tehran was outright hostile to the bill and had published many articles criticizing it. Tehran economist Mostafa Elm had published a scathing attack.

Scotes pointed out that even the Iranian government expected agricultural production to decline because of this bill. "When applying for wheat under P.L. 480, the Iranian government indicated that it expects a drop in agricultural production because of the land distribution bill." Scotes also noted that the experience with land distribution had not been favorable in Sistan during the 1930s. Nor was the outcome of the distribution of Pahlavi estates any better, despite much expenditure of funds by the U.S. government. Even the few Majlis deputies who actually supported the current land distribution bill such as Qolam Hosein Saremi, deputy from Jahrom in Fars, had admitted to Scotes, "Farmers in Varamin who received Crown land are not doing well. This is true even at Daudabad, one of the richest villages in the area" (Foreign Service despatch 538, dated 27 February 1960). It was not surprising that the Majlis and the Senate were strongly opposed to the bill. Of the twenty-five members of the Majlis special committee on the bill, only four were in favor.

According to one member of the committee, who happens to be for the bill, Qolam Hosein Saremi, pressure is being brought to bear on the committee by outsiders, particularly Senators Hosein Dadgar and Mohsen Sadr, to delay the bill as long as possible.

The latter is reportedly very much against the bill, and since he is the President of the Senate, can be considered quite a formidable opponent. The Speaker of the Majlis, Reza Hekmat (Sardar Fakher), is also reportedly opposing the bill, although his opposition is said to be based on parliamentary and technical considerations rather than emotional and religious ones. By use of parliamentary stratagems, these men and others like them might delay the bill for some time. These tactics, however, could also affect their political futures and it is doubtful if any of them is prepared to go that far.

Scotes also warned about possible peasant reactions once the bill was passed. "Recently certain Iranian government officials have indicated privately that they fear the reaction of the peasants once this law is enacted. What will happen, they ask, when one village gets distributed while a neighboring one does not? Some go even so far as to predict the possibility of peasant uprisings as a result of a land distribution program and the frustrations which will more than likely flow from it."

In his conclusion, Scotes expressed his astonishment at the ignorance of Iran's agricultural realities by those who drafted the bill. The bill contained so many defects indicating "that either the bill will never be seriously enforced, or that a real ignorance of problems obtains among those people charged with the drafting of the bill. In any event, a land distribution is apparently going to be initiated and retreat for the Shah will be difficult if not almost impossible. The Shah himself has been told that the United States is neither for nor against the present bill and considers it an internal Iranian matter. The United States may well have to be prepared to advise this government on the problems which will ensue."

Many persons are saying that this bill is very obviously a political bill and as such its implications will have to be considered from a political point of view. It seems to the Embassy, therefore, that if the Shah is serious about land distribution he may be making a political mistake at this time. Many very influential supporters of his regime are going to be affected by a law of this type. The unrest which will ensue in the thousands of Iranian villages alone should give pause. In short, the Shah will be antagonizing several important segments of the Iranian population and more than likely getting very little in return.

The serious opposition already evinced against the bill leads the Embassy to renote the opinion expressed in Embassy dispatch 695, dated March 30, 1959, to the effect that there was no pressing need for land reform at that time and that the Shah might be better advised to continue at a slow pace with the Crown and Public Lands before embarking on a land reform program fraught with so much danger not only for the agriculture of his country, but also for the stability of his regime.

While the Embassy does not immediately foresee serious troubles in a political sense emanating from the enactment of this bill, it does feel that this bill can only add to the political malaise which presently affects Iran and can, when taken with Iran's other problems, only bode ill for the future.

The profound ignorance of the agrarian conditions in Iran by those who had drafted the 1960 land distribution bill can be seen by their choice of Kurdistan as the first area selected for land distribution. Moreover, this ignorance was fully shared by those who directed American policy after 1961. In the words of a key confidential report discussed below (Foreign Service despatch 419, dated 1 February 1961), the choice of Kurdistan was "based on the fact that the area has an exceptionally large number of absentee landlords, many of whom are not even in Iran. Also the area has a background of political instability." The reality appears to have been completely the opposite. By May 1962, Arsanjani's land distribution in Kurdistan had made no progress. The reason is described by the American vice consul in Tabriz, Archie M. Bolster (Foreign Service despatch 84, dated 28 May 1962):

> Despite Arsanjani's statement during his April 20 visit to the Rezaieh area that land reform would be carried out in Kurdish areas as well as the project areas, there have been no moves to do so. Nevertheless, there is considerable dissatisfaction among Kurds about the prospect of land reform in their areas, primarily on the grounds that there are so few landowners who possess more than one or two villages that land reform there would not be worth the trouble it would cause, but also on the grounds that Kurdish villagers are rather well taken care of anyway and are not oppressed by absentee landlords as peasants in other areas of Iran. According to one source, many Kurds fear that if land reform were carried out the government would eventually deprive them of even the one village which the Land Reform Law allows them to retain. One immediate result of the fears concerning land reform in Kurdish areas has been a marked decrease in land prices.

Opposition by Business Interests

Scotes continued to report on the rising opposition to the bill. On 5 March 1960, he met with a businessman and former Majlis deputy, Hormoz Shahrokhshahi, at the house of Kavus Baqai, the son of Senator Hasan Baqai, secretary of the Senate. The content of the conversation is given in a confidential report (Foreign Service despatch 576, dated 12 March 1960). Shahrokhshahi is described as an individual who was active against Mossadeq, and "in recognition of his help during the fall of Mossadeq," he was elected from Arak to the Eighteenth Majlis. "But because of his opposition to Hosein Ala's government after the dismissal of General Fazlollah Zahedi, he was not returned to the Nineteenth Majlis. . . . Shahrokhshahi was said to be in the Shah's disfavor and word was given that he was not to be employed by any government agency. At present he is engaged in private business."

Shahrokhshahi told Scotes that people believed "this bill, which is against the Constitution as well as Islam, was an American bill." Ayatollah Hosein Borujerdi had issued a fatwa against this bill, and "the Shah was making a big mistake in sponsoring this bill." The bill was so bad that "it will cause agricultural production to fall, and the Americans will get the blame." Shahrokhshahi also told Scotes that "Dr. Jamshid Amuzegar was not in favor of bringing this bill to the Majlis, but he was obliged to do so by the Shah and his American advisors." Ominously, the former deputy told Scotes that "peasants are already saying that the land belongs to them. In the Isfahan area, peasants are refusing to give the landlord his share." Only landowners had the capital and ability to maintain Iran's qanats. Without landowners, agricultural production would fall "and America will get the blame." At the end of the conversation, Scotes tried without success to convince Shahrokhshahi that the United States was not behind the shah's land reform programs.

Ali Ghoreishi, deputy from Khorasan and son of Mohammad Ghoreishi, also expressed extreme unhappiness after the passage of the bill. In a confidential report (Foreign Service despatch 39, dated 25 June 1960), Edward H. Thomas, American consul in Mashhad, quoted Ghoreishi as saying that in much of Iran such as Khorasan, "the state of business and commerce is poor, and that industry (except oil) is making little progress. The only major economic activity which is in a relatively satisfactory condition is agriculture. Now by this land distribution law a blow will be inflicted against agriculture as well. Agricultural production will surely drop if the law is enforced, and discontent will increase. The economic state of the nation will then be uniformly bad."

In October 1962, the consul in Tabriz, John M. Howison, discovered that landlord dissatisfaction with the shah had reached "an advanced stage" and was shared by the business and middle classes. He met with Ahmad Javadzadeh, a businessman and first secretary of the Tabriz Chamber of Commerce, and then filed a confidential report of their conversation (airgram A-27, dated 9 October 1962). Javadzadeh referred to the shah's land distribution as a "major blow" to Iran's economy because "in the view of the business community, agricultural production (the foundation of the national economy) will drop for an indefinite period as a result of land reform." Having ruined agriculture, Javadzadeh reportedly said, the shah was planning the same for industry by giving a 20 percent share to the workers. Unfortunately, "His Majesty's zeal to better the lot of the common man was not matched by a commensurate understanding of economic realities." Howison's comments are revealing. "Javadzadeh is a fairly conservative, eminently solid-citizen sort, and his expression of deep perturbation was of quite a different order from the usual poor-mouth talk of the Tabriz businessman. That he should have taken the initiative to state his views to the Consulate, and that he should have so forthrightly criticized the Shah (at a ceremonial occasion in the Shah's honor) are remarkable. If, as seems likely, his views are typical of the Tabriz Bazaar, the Shah may well have stirred up more opposition from the middle class than he intended or foresaw."

Reversal of American Policy

It is clear that with the 1960 election of President John F. Kennedy, embassy despatch 695 of 30 March 1959, which was to "serve as a basic reference for some years to come," was filed away in Washington and soon forgotten. It is also clear that Scotes's embassy despatch 524 of 20 February 1960 was ignored by Washington and forgotten by the embassy in Tehran. With Kennedy's election there was a complete "reassessment" of Iran's "land problem" in Washington and Tehran. The result of the reassessment was described in a confidential report (Foreign Service despatch 419, dated 1 February 1961), entitled "Status and Prospects of Land Reform and Distribution in Iran." Although the document was signed by Ambassador Edward T. Wailes, it was drafted by R. W. Dye, evidently a political officer at the embassy.

By early 1961, American policy had been completely reversed. Ignoring the reports by Consuls Franklin and Josif, Dye categorically declared that most of Iran's arable land was held by large absentee landowners. He indicated extreme dissatisfaction with what he considered to be a lack of progress on land reform and distribution. He expressed unhappiness at the Majlis and Senate dilution of the original land distribution measure, attacked the "loopholes" of that law, described the appointment of Ebrahim Mahdavi as minister of agriculture as a sell-out by the shah, and even questioned the shah's commitment to the land distribution program. On several occasions he stated that "the forceful intervention of the Shah" was called for. He called for "adequate counter-power" to be brought against the opponents of land distribution. He spoke of the "future decisive struggle between the Shah and these same vested interests" consisting of landowners and religious leaders. More ominously, he stated that only in an environment of crisis and revolutionary change could the opponents of reform and the traditional landed class be "neutralized."

Dye's report practically predicts the coming of Arsanjani, the "forceful" actions by the shah, and the "neutralization" of the opposition. It strongly suggests that what transpired under Arsanjani had been instigated by the United States. How could it be otherwise? Not surprisingly, there had been a parade of high government officials, including Lyndon Johnson, Chester Bowles, and Dean Rusk, declaring full support for the shah's land reform. Given the significance of this report, extensive excerpts are given:

> The purpose of this despatch is to bring reporting on the general subject of land reform and distribution up to date and provide a

reassessment of the problem.

The predominant pattern of land tenure in Iran is one in which absentee landlords, who, generally speaking, have little interest in agriculture other than for the status and income which they derive, own large tracts of land. A majority of the country's arable land is held in this manner. Under the circumstances, it is clear that the principal political and social aspects of land reform are associated with the problem of the large, private landholdings and the accompanying landlord-tenant relationships.

The distribution [of Crown lands] has been carried out in recent years by the Development Bank [Bank Omran], an organization of the Court. The Development Bank, in addition to establishing titles and distributing lands, was supposed to provide a wide range of facilities to the new small landholders. The services rendered so far have been far from optimum, however, and recently were sharply curtailed.

Ignoring all previous embassy and consular reports to the contrary, and in contradiction of its own statement in the above paragraph, the report leaped to the following conclusion: "While not uniformly successful, the Crown lands program has had initially beneficial effects in the areas concerned and has represented the principal concrete accomplishment of the Shah's well-publicized reform programs. As such, it has been a positive, though relatively minor, factor in maintaining the political stability of the Shah's regime." It continued:

> Despite the enactment of the Land Distribution Law in June 1960, up to the present time all proposals for private land reform have been effectively blocked in one way or another by the large landowners. Land ownership has traditionally been the principal source of wealth and prestige for the Iranian ruling class; and correspondingly the landlords dominate the Majlis, Senate, and upper levels of the bureaucracy, are influential in the top military ranks, and control the major newspapers. It is not difficult to see how in present-day Iran this group, united as it is in opposition to land reform, has been able to prevent any concrete steps from being taken. In the absence of the bringing to bear of adequate counter-power, land reform in the private sector so far has been limited largely to legal and ethical pronouncements.
>
> A case in point is the aforementioned Land Distribution Law. This Law was a serious effort by a small group of reform-minded Iranians, principally younger men in the Ministry of Agriculture, to

enact basic legislation which would contribute to a long-range solution of Iran's pressing rural problems. This group was led by Agriculture Minister Jamshid Amuzegar. The vision of the bill's supporters was to reduce the political and economic power of the large absentee landlords, create a class of small but competent free-hold farmers who would gain the incentive needed to make the required capital and technological improvements to raise agricultural production, reduce rural discontent and migration to the already overcrowded cities, and at the same time enhance the country's political strength and stability.

This law was passed largely because of the vigorous support and intervention of the Shah; and the process of the bill through the legislature provided a good picture of the relative strength of the regime's various supporters. In general, though the overriding power of the Shah was sustained by the passage of what was for the Majlis and the Senate a highly distasteful piece of legislation, the way in which the law was allowed to be amended after protests from conservative landlords and religious leaders showed clearly the present limitations on the Shah's power. (This view is tempered only by the feeling that the Shah was not too unhappy with the amendments, wanting for the time being mostly a law which he could offer as evidence of reform. Therefore, the probable outcome of a future decisive struggle between the Shah and these same vested interests is still uncertain. So long as the Shah continues displaying his penchant for compromise and withdrawal from leadership at times of crisis, however, such a struggle appears unlikely to materialize.)

Since the passage of the law, a period now of about eight months, virtually no progress has been made towards putting the law into effect. On the other hand, at least two actions which must be considered retrogressive have been taken.

Actions taken to date to implement the law include the formation of the High Land Reform Council (Art. 8); the naming of an Executive Director of the Council (Art. 8); the preparation by the Agriculture Ministry of a draft of the Landlord-Tenant Relations Regulations (Art. 33); and a decision by the Council that actual distribution, when it occurred, would begin in Kurdistan. This decision was released to the press and received fair publicity. (Reportedly, this action is based on the fact that the area has an exceptionally large number of absentee landlords, many of whom are not even in Iran. Also, the area has a background of political instability.) Reportedly, the

High Land Reform Council has been meeting regularly under the chairmanship of the Prime Minister. It is being assisted by a small staff under the designated Executive Director, Agriculture Parliamentary Undersecretary Abdol Hamid Hakimi. None of the staff is permanently assigned to the Council, and it has no separate budget.

The progress made in drafting landlord-tenant relations regulations unfortunately is more apparent than real. A draft has been prepared but reportedly is bogged down in the Ministry of Finance. That some such regulation may be approved and promulgated is seen by many as the principal hope for long-term benefit from the law. However, the law names the High Land Reform Council as executive body for carrying out the regulations, and as will be seen it is uncertain whether that body ever will develop the permanent staff and obtain the backing and funds needed to carry out administrative tasks of this nature.

In spite of the decision to begin in Kurdistan, no start has been made on detailed preparations for the actual land distribution or setting up facilities and organizations for replacing the vital services now being provided by the landlords. The first step, a complete cadastral survey, is under discussion for a Plan Organization project, but reportedly is being opposed by the Prime Minister. A proposal for training thirteen specialists in land distribution policies and procedures, however, is under discussion.

The lack of progress to date can be attributed to an apparent lack of a firm resolve to implement the law. As a matter of fact, the Shah has told the Ambassador that he does not plan to proceed with the law at this time, giving as his reason the fact that there are too many people on the land and too little cultivable land to allow the granting of adequate land to each new farmer. He said that he planned to wait until economic development had produced more arable land and reduced rural population.

Another indication of a lack of desire to proceed with the law is that reportedly a preliminary decision has been made that no funds are to be included in the upcoming (1340) budget to carry out the program. The argument is that the Council and its staff can continue to function using other agencies for support. Without money of its own, however, it is unlikely that the Council can do much of anything, either in the way of land distribution or enforcing agreed-upon reforms in landlord-tenant relationships.

More revealing than this, however, is that the Shah according to one report has decided that enough has been done for the time being and has given instructions that the program now be administered so as not to "hurt" people. On December 21, 1960, the Shah met the Agriculture Minister and other leading Ministry officials and remarked to the effect that there are not nearly as many large landholdings in the country as is popularly assumed. This remark, which was given normal publicity, has been cited by prominent landlords and Agriculture Ministry officials as indicating the Shah's desire to go slowly. It seems slim evidence on which to base such a conclusion, but presumably the speakers have more to go on in judging the Shah's intentions. Other than the Shah, of course, the law has no powerful Iranian supporters, and it is easy to imagine the result if he does let it be known that he is satisfied with just having the law on the books.

Another indication of retreat was the Shah's appointment of Engineer Ebrahim Mahdavi as Minister of Agriculture following the government changes in early September 1960. Prior to his appointment, Mahdavi, who is a large landowner himself, was an acknowledged opponent of the law and authored a pamphlet attacking it. There is a strong suspicion that he is still lukewarm to the idea and is dragging his feet whenever possible, though he has said that he respects and intends to enforce the law. His prior opinion on land reform, however, could not have been unknown to the Shah.

Still another indication is that reportedly the major stress now is being placed on the voluntary distribution of land. It will be remembered that the original bill was amended in the Majlis to allow the sale of excess lands to local farmers and peasants at the going price, or any other mutual arrangements, prior to the implementation of the law. Also, the prohibition against other transactions involving land in excess of the legal amounts was removed, though with the provision (short-lived) of a stiff 50 percent tax on all such transactions. These provisions ostensibly were to encourage the voluntary breakup and distribution of large estates. Further encouragement to voluntary sales of excess land was given recently when the 50 percent tax referred to above was rescinded. There is nothing, however, to prevent a large landlord from adding to rather than decreasing his holdings.

To summarize the facts, progress in preparing for implementation of the Land Distribution Law has been exceedingly slow. Actual accomplishments have been almost nil so far. Moreover, there are strong indications that from the Shah on down there is no present intention of proceeding to the stage of actual reform.

It seems clear that, given the present array of forces against the Land Distribution Law, only the forceful intervention of the Shah could give it effect. Contrariwise, if, as appears to be the case, the Shah for the time being intends to let events take their natural course, there is little hope that anything more than time-consuming preliminary maneuvers, interspersed with occasional optimistic press releases, will take place.

Even given the will to implement the present law, there would be very formidable difficulties to surmount. In the first place, the law provides a number of legal loopholes. Also, there is in addition to inadequate title and other land information, a conspicuous lack of trained and experienced personnel to carry out such a far-reaching program, though when the Crown lands distribution is completed some ten to fifteen months hence some experienced staff could be made available. Finally, there no doubt would be difficulty involved in finding enough funds to carry out an effective program on a wide scale.

Nevertheless, the fundamental problem is the apparent lack of the will to carry out meaningful land reform. Major land reform programs in other countries usually have resulted from and taken place in an environment of crisis. When a country is upset by military operations or is undergoing a revolution, the principal opponents of reform, i.e., the traditional landed class, are often neutralized. In Iran, however, the reformers are attempting to carry out land reform under peaceful, stable conditions.

The present regime in Iran, either of necessity or by choice, is still dependent to a considerable extent on the landlords, who it must be remembered include within their ranks top military, court, government, industrial, and commercial figures. If applied discriminatorily against some landlords and in favor of others, presumably the effect of the law on the regime's support could be minimized; but if it is effectively applied across the board, land reform could be expected to alienate a significant portion of the regime's traditional support.

It can be assumed that the Shah is aware of this dependence on the landlords. Viewed from his standpoint, the question perhaps is whether or not an alternative source of support exists or would be created by vigorous reform action. The gratitude of the peasants, presuming it would exist (a doubtful assumption), would not in present-day Iran mean much for the Shah's political position. The main opposition groups, while they probably would welcome a weakening of the power of the landlords, will not be placated by reform. Instead they have in mind the reduction of the Shah's powers. The benefits of the program, then, may to the Shah appear to be outweighed by the losses.

To summarize, land reform and distribution programs in Iran on the whole have made little progress. The major accomplishment has been the distribution of a large portion of the Shah's private estates and some land in the Public Domain. Land reform in the private sector so far has been effectively stymied by the landlords who still dominate the Majlis, the Senate, and the upper levels of the bureaucracy and the armed forces. A case in point is the 1960 Land Distribution Law, which has not been implemented as yet. Moreover, it appears that from the Shah on down, there is no present desire to proceed with actual reform and distribution of private lands. In the absence of forceful intervention by the Shah, of course, there would be little hope that significant progress can be achieved. In view of the Shah's dependence on the landlords and conservative classes in general, it may be that his reluctance to proceed stems from an unwillingness to antagonize some of his traditional supporters at a time when alternative sources of support appear not to be available in the short run.

Based on State Department records, the following summary can be given. Land distribution in Iran was strongly supported by the U.S. government between 1951 and 1955. Following extensive discussions with Iranian politicians, the U.S. embassy and the State Department became much more cautious between 1956 and 1960 and came to regard land distribution in Iran as politically and economically hazardous. Stung by continually unfavorable foreign media reports on land distribution in Iran, the shah pushed for a land distribution bill. The result was the bill that was submitted to the Majlis in December 1959. The bill encountered strong opposition from landowners and the ulama. The bill was amended by the Majlis, and the outcome was the Land Distribution Law of May 1960. Sensing strong opposition domestically and sensing unease and caution by the American embassy, the shah proceeded slowly and carefully. This was exemplified by the appointment of Ebrahim Mahdavi, a landowner, as minister of agriculture and in charge of land distribution. The evidence shows that there was a complete reversal in American policy in early 1961. Whereas previously the shah had been urged to exercise caution, he was now castigated for going far too slowly. He was advised of the need for "forceful intervention" and the need to "neutralize" the "vested interests" of landowners and ulama by wielding "adequate counter-power" and by creating revolutionary conditions.

R. W. Dye's embassy despatch practically describes the advent of Amini-Arsanjani three months later and clearly shows that the shah was forced to adopt policies that were ultimately disastrous to Iran as well as to the Pahlavi regime. The government of Ali Amini subsequently enjoyed the full political and financial backing of the American government. In a confidential report entitled "Progress of the Amini Reform Program" (Foreign Service despatch 353, dated 30 January 1962), Franklin J. Crawford, formerly the consul at Isfahan and now at the embassy in Tehran, discussed the "reforms" of the Amini government. He noted, "All this would not have been possible, of course, without the continuing support of the Shah, and substantial assistance from the United States. Through the end of 1961, the United States Government had made available to the Amini Government on a cash-flow basis a total of about $88 million, an amount of money which has made the difference between its survival and its downfall."

Phase Three of Land Distribution

With consular reports on the expropriation and plight of the huge class of small landowners coming in and the rising level of opposition as evidenced by the tribal uprisings and urban protests in the spring of 1963, the U.S. government moved to distance itself from the fiasco. By 1968, the embassy was highly critical of the shah and had no intention of sharing the blame for what had taken place. This critical attitude is illustrated by a confidential report by embassy officer C. W. McCaskill entitled "Third Phase of Land Reform Bill" (airgram A-926, dated 30 November 1968). During the Majlis opening on 6 October 1968, the shah surprised everyone by announcing that the government "would enact legislation under which approximately 1.1 million tenant farmers presently renting their lands would become landowners." On 11 December 1968 Abdol Azim Valian, minister of land reform, submitted a bill to the Majlis by which the small landowners who leased land to 1,121,473 tenants under Phase Two would be forced to "sell" to the tenants. Payment to the small landowners "would be made in twelve installments, each installment equivalent to one year's rent." This bill was called the Tenant Farmers Landownership Bill. The report also contained the following:

> Valian is said to have sold the new move to the Shah on the grounds that tenant farmers complained that they should have the same rights as those in the neighboring villages who had gotten

their land already. Government spokesmen took the line that the measure was necessary, that Iranian farmers, like farmers everywhere, have the right to own their own land.

In point of fact, the Shah may have announced the third phase of the land reform in his October 6 speech without sufficient prior planning or discussion. Bearing on this conclusion is the fact that the Ministry of Land Reform did not have a bill ready for presentation to the Majlis immediately and was forced to throw one together hurriedly. The Government party, Iran Novin, had not been consulted or informed prior to the Shah's speech. In short, this was not an impressive example of effective government.

Introduction of the bill in the Majlis created much concern among small holders and many complaints were registered with the Iran Novin Party, the Parliament, and Government and the press. (Ali Abtin, Administration Officer of the Senate, informed Embassy Officers that the Senate alone had received over two thousand letters protesting the measure.) In fact, the small holders seem to have had some ground for complaint. Many would not be able to live on the payments received for their land and would have to go to the cities or towns to look for work. Small holders also protested that payments spread over twelve years would prevent them from investing the money, since the sum received at one time would be so small. . . .

The regime seems guilty of bad faith with the landowners. Practically within months of having worked out long-term lease agreements, in accordance with the government's land reform program, they are now confronted with the proposal that their thirty-year leases are, in effect, to be terminated immediately by a new law which requires the sale of the leased property to the lessee. Some of the small holders will suffer real hardship; others will resent the Government's precipitate action. Some lingering small holder discontent seems likely.

It is difficult to believe that the embassy was unaware of the lingering chaos in rural Iran, the inability of landowners to collect their "legal" rent, and the resulting conflicts that could not be dealt with by the gendarmerie and the courts. The case studies given in chapter 11 describe the conditions in rural Iran in the late 1960s, and show why the government was forced to show "bad faith" with the small landowners. The legacy of Hasan Arsanjani had just begun.

Selected Publications and Bulletins of the Agricultural Union of Iran and Organizations of Small Landowners

The Agricultural Union of Iran attempted to influence public opinion by printing and distributing information bulletins. Some bulletins pointed out the constitutional violations that had been perpetrated by the government, and some described instances of peasant violence and lawlessness against landowners and their families. Telegrams were also sent to various political and religious personalities. Given the limitations of space, what follows is a sample of the material that was put out. It is noteworthy that for a brief period in 1961, the Agricultural Union of Iran could get a hearing in the national press. By the end of 1961, the censorship was complete, and the publications were distributed by any means possible.

Publications prior to the Cabinet Decree of 9 January 1962

In response to two speeches by Hasan Arsanjani on 19 and 20 September 1961 that were broadcast on the national radio, Majd's "open letter" to the prime minister and Council of Ministers was printed in the national daily *Etela-at* on 1 October 1961. Prophetically, Majd accused the government of having created conditions that were likely to result in one hundred years of turmoil:

> Open Letter to His Excellency, Mr. Dr. Amini, prime minister, and the respected Council of Ministers
>
> With the utmost respect, I submit,
> His Excellency, Mr. Arsanjani, the minister of agriculture, made some comments on Iran Radio on Thursday and Friday, 19 and 20 September, stating that the land reform law is insufficient to achieve the intended aims, because it will cover only a few villages. If one is to be satisfied with the present law, either the cultivators of the

neighboring villages must evict the landowners, or the owners of those lands must evict the cultivators of the distributed lands. Since the government lacks the ability to map the villages, one must abandon a reasonable and logical distribution, and distribute the land among the residents of the villages. For this purpose, a course has been established, and the trainees are instructed to examine the status of all the villages in Iran and prepare a list on the basis of which the villages will be distributed. The investigation and research in each province should not take more than a month and a half. The minister of agriculture also added that on the basis of a decree approved by the cabinet, treasury notes that are equivalent to money will be issued and given to landowners as payment for their land. The limit of ownership has also been reduced to 50–350 hectares of irrigated land and 600 hectares of nonirrigated land.

As the members of the Agricultural Union of Iran are Iranians and have a right to inform the government of what they consider to be in the national interest, we hereby wish to bring the following to the government's attention.

Since their occupation is agriculture, the members of this Union are strong believers in the need to improve the status of agriculture throughout Iran. For this reason we believe that the minister's plan for a blank division of land is not practical and will result in such disorder and chaos that will require one hundred years for normalcy to be restored. Distribution of free soup in front of a house always results in fighting among the recipients of the free soup. Moreover, how is it possible to change a law by a cabinet decree? Will the treasury notes issued without the necessary legal authorization be valid and valuable? It is the view of this Union that the only practical and logical way to proceed is to implement the law in all the villages subject to the law. In the future, as new experience is gained and administrative and technical personnel are trained, if the situation of the country permits, a new law that would expand the current one can be submitted to the legislative branch of government for its consideration. Undoubtedly, Iran will require additional reforms in the future. But where all the domestic and foreign observers concur is that in this turbulent world, domestic tranquillity and security are the most important requirements for the continued existence of the country. In this situation, the comments of the minister of agriculture on the need to evict the landowners or [whether] the landowner should evict the cultivators [serve] to instill fear and [issue] an open invitation to disorder and insecurity. You will agree that timing is the essence of states-

manship. The first of Mehr [22 September] is the day of annual agricultural rejuvenation in all of Iran. And in accordance with His
Majesty's order, it has been designated as the cultivator's day. In the
month of Mehr, the field outlays are established, young and old cultivators follow the oxen or the tractor to these fields, the landowners
open up the seed storage, and the necessary accords are concluded.
The result of this cooperation has been the provision of the essentials
of life to Iran's society since ancient times.

But when on the very eve of such day the minister of agriculture
makes these comments which advocate actions that are utterly illegal and against the interests of the country, the cultivator who hears
them from a responsible authority in the government will tell himself, "Now that I am the real owner of the land, why should I proceed
in the old fashion and share the produce with someone else?" The
owner also will certainly desist from actions on a land that he imag-
ines is on the verge of confiscation. A situation is created, the consequences of which are known only to God. The results of the
minister's remarks on the eve of 1 Mehr and the effects on cultivation and agricultural activity are clear.

But on the subject of confidence and economic security, which are
essential elements for continuity and prosperity in Iran, the people
of Iran will inevitably ask the following question. After the confiscation of all the agricultural lands, will it be the turn of factories and
mines to be confiscated by a cabinet decree and distributed among
the workers and the miners? Will it then be the turn of all the houses
and rented real estate to be confiscated from their owners and given
to the tenants and residents of the district?

We, the members of the Agricultural Union of Iran, on the basis of
faith and love for the continuity and stability of our country, in accordance with the provisions of the Constitution and the interest of
the country, request that you order that such publicity and unlawful
actions which will cost the country dearly be halted.

Mohammad Ali Majd

Agricultural Union of Iran

On 11 November 1961, the shah ordered Amini to implement, if necessary, a "modified" version of the 1960 Land Reform Law. In response to a
newspaper interview by Arsanjani, the following bulletin was issued by
the Agricultural Union of Iran on 27 December 1961:

Bulletin of the Agricultural Union of Iran

His Excellency the Prime Minister
Pursuant to the intrigues of the Tudeh Party for the purpose of sowing discord between the landowner and the cultivator, and the alien radio propaganda aimed at bringing ruin to the villages and poverty to the villagers, and to discourage landowners from undertaking steps that bring development, the minister of agriculture in your government has taken very long strides aimed at discouraging landowners from repairing and maintaining the ruined qanats and providing seed and credit to the cultivators. All of this at a time when a hostile nature has added to the sound of the danger bells concerning the state of cultivation next year.

In an interview that was published on 11 December 1961 in the newspaper *Etela-at*, number 10679, he openly declared that he was in the process of changing the land reform law of 16 May 1960 and that he had not the slightest fear of even one hundred lawsuits that might be brought against him.

Obviously, from someone who is totally ignorant of agricultural affairs, one cannot expect any concern for the provision of wheat and food for the people of Iran, because for such a person, passing time on the shores of Lake Geneva[1] is preferable to being in the midst of his compatriots at the time of famine and scarcity that have been brought about by the excesses of this individual. But for us in the Agricultural Union of Iran, the real farmers of this country, who have faced the aggressor during the dark days and by their actions have ensured the independence of this country, we deem it essential to let it be known in these critical days that the people of Iran will fight whoever rebels against the Constitution.

The country of Iran is a constitutional monarchy, and the guarantor of the continued existence of this proud 2,500-year-old monarchy is this same Constitution, which was gained with the blood of the martyrs who gave it on the way to freedom and constitutional government. Consequently, at no time and under no circumstances can a person tinker with the Constitution for the purpose of imposing his personal rule and will.

Principle 29 of the Constitution clearly states, "If a minister is unable to provide a satisfactory response on any of the measures that are part of a law bearing the royal signature, and it is established that he is in violation of the law or has exceeded his authority as prescribed by law, Parliament shall ask His Majesty for the dismissal of the minister. After the proof of guilt is established in a court of law, he will be barred forever from government service." When a minister is in violation of the law, the Constitution states that he is a traitor who is to be tried, convicted, and banned.

According to Principle 9 of the Constitution, "The people are secure in their life, property, home, and honor and safe from any transgression. No one can be disturbed except on the basis of law, and only in the manner prescribed by law."

According to Supplementary Principle 15 of the Constitution, "No property can be taken from the possession of its owner, except on the basis of religious ruling, and then only after the determination and payment of a just price."

According to Principle 16 of the Constitution, "Confiscation of people's property as punishment or for political purpose is forbidden, except on the basis of law."

According to Principle 17, "Dispossession of owners and holders of estates and property in their possession is forbidden under all circumstances, except on the basis of law. In that case, as long as this constitution is in force in our country, no one can interfere on his own will with people's property, and any authority or officeholder who contravenes this principle will be considered to be in a state of rebellion against the Constitution and will be prosecuted on the basis of Articles 82 and 83 of the Criminal Code."

It is in confirmation of the above important principle in the Constitution that regulations drawn up by governments, municipalities, provincial assemblies, and local councils that are in conflict with the law cannot be enforced by any court of law. Supplementary Principle 89 of the Constitution requires that "tribunals of justice and the courts of law will enforce the central, provincial, and local regulations and ordinances only if they are compatible with the law."

Thus, when the Constitution states that the courts and legal tribunals cannot enforce regulations and orders that are contrary to the law, how can a minister claim that he can change the law by his own will and expect that this unlawful action is binding and enforceable by the courts? He is fully aware that the members of the highest court of the country have ruled that, in the absence of the parliament, no regulation or order can be substituted for the existing laws.

In conclusion, we draw the attention of the prime minister, who has repeatedly declared that he cannot take any action that is contrary to the Constitution, the principles of constitutional monarchy, and the laws of the country, to the following two points:

First, Article 280 of the Civil Code clearly states, "Whenever a minister, or any public servant of any rank and state, unlawfully changes the law by issuing a decree, regulation, memorandum, or other written orders, or applies the law in a discriminatory manner, he shall be dismissed and banned from government service forever." Consequently, in addition to the fact that no unlawful regulation can be enforced in a court of law, those issuing the regulations are liable to prosecution.

Second, Supplementary Principle 69 of the Constitution states: "In addition to their responsibilities and tasks of their own ministries, all ministers, individually and collectively, are accountable for the actions of all the ministers and answerable to Parliament."

Assuredly, the words and the actions of a minister cannot escape the attention of the other ministers. Consequently, it is appropriate to bring the contents of this bulletin to the attention of the head of the government and to remind you that there is in place a land reform law that is not being implemented as required by law, and the government is in default of its legal duty. Instead, it resorts to actions that destroy the security and confidence of the farmers. We are reaching a point where "neither the vine nor its sign remain."
Agricultural Union of Iran

It appears that this bulletin struck a nerve in the government. The main response to this bulletin came two days later in the form of a front-page article in the *Setareh Tehran* (Tehran Star). It consisted of an attack on the Agricultural Union of Iran and a vicious personal attack on Mohammad Ali Majd.

Publications after the Decree of 9 January 1962

After the announcement of the contents of the decree of 9 January 1962, the following telegram was sent. Of course, given that the government prevented the publication of the statements and bulletins of the Agricultural Union of Iran in the media, their circulation was limited. The contents, however, throw light on the events and personalities of the time. The text of the telegram was as follows:

To Ayatollah Behbahani, Sardar Fakher Hekmat, Sadr ol Ashraaf, Keyhan *and* Etela-at *newspapers:*

In our system of constitutional monarchy, where the Constitution is the guarantor of the existence of the country and the rights of the people, at a point in time when Parliament and the Senate are both closed, how can a constitutional government annul a law that has been passed by both the Parliament and the Senate, and signed by the Sovereign, and then on its own, legislate a new law? Regretfully, the regulations that have been announced by the radio and the press under the guise of "land reform" are intended to deprive the landowners of their legal rights to ownership and security and forcibly confiscate their property by means of sham transactions. These regulations are in contravention of Principles 9, 15, 16, and 17 of the Constitution, but also in conflict with the laws of Islam.

Although, during the Ramadan of 1960, when the government at the time had drafted similar proposals and had submitted them to the Nineteenth Majlis under the guise of land reform, Mr. Borujerdi, leader of the Shiites, had issued his fatwa on this subject, and despite the absence of the houses of parliament, these same regulations have once again been included in the new decree.

On the basis of Principles 1 and 2 of the Constitution, which declare Islam to be the official religion of Iran and require that at no time are laws to be enacted that are in conflict with the holy laws of Islam, and given our adherence to Islam and as followers of our Religious Guide, we consider the new regulations known as land reform to be contrary to the laws of Holy Islam and in conflict with the Constitution. We also consider them to be impractical. We request that necessary measures be taken to prevent those individuals who, on the basis of this unlawful measure, attempt to transgress against the people, so that the laws of religion and the Constitution are upheld and people can once again set about their productive endeavors with security and under the protection of law.

Agricultural Union of Iran

The first region where the provisions of the cabinet decree of 9 January 1962 were implemented was Maragheh, East Azarbaijan. Shortly after the approval of the decree and its implementation, a long bulletin was issued by the Agricultural Union of Iran. This is an important historical document because it describes the many ways in which the government violated Iran's Constitution, civil laws, and religious laws. Again it stated that the Constitution was the guarantor of Iran's constitutional monarchy, and it warned that such government actions were sure to lead to a downfall of government and society. It had invited all those who were faithful to the principles of the Constitution and constitutional monarchy to join the Union in upholding the Constitution and the rule of law. My father filed a lawsuit in 1962 that challenged the legality of the 1962 cabinet decree. The lawsuit was supposed to serve as a test case. This bulletin contained many of the legal points that were used in Majd's lawsuit, and it was most likely prepared by Abol Hasan Amidi-Nuri and Arsalan Khalatbari, two seasoned attorneys who were members of the Agricultural Union of Iran. Some excepts are given here:

Bulletin of the Agricultural Union of Iran

In these days, regulations labeled "New Plan for Amending the Land Reform Law" have been announced by the radio and the media, and it is claimed that it is being implemented in Maragheh in the presence of the governor-general, the commander of the armed forces, the commander of the gendarmerie, chief of the security organization [Savak], and chief of the Azarbaijan police.

In the name of preserving the Constitution, which is the guarantor of our constitutional monarchy, the Agricultural Union of Iran deems it necessary to make its views known to the public.

The membership of this union who are all educated and well informed in the affairs of state have no doubt that there must be a land reform in this country for the purpose of improving both production and the life of the cultivator. But the requirements for these reforms are stability and security, measures that are hidden from the people of Iran. In this country there is neither stability nor legal security that is the guardian of our rights. Since the governments are responsible for providing stability and security, it is the governments that have to be reformed in the first place and thus refrain from aggression against the rights of the people so clearly recognized by the Constitution. Only after the reform of the government can one reap the benefits of reform that will come forth from the productive efforts of the people. Those government actions which more and more shake the foundations of society and more and more disturb the legal relationship between different people are rapidly leading us toward a certain downfall. We therefore consider it necessary to warn all those who seek the greatness and independence of our dear Iran. The people of Iran have been granted certain rights under the Constitution, and these rights cannot be assailed by anyone, especially by governments claiming to reform and preserve the country. For the benefit of some members of the government, some of the principles of the sacred Constitution are hereby stated, so that they can be followed."

The bulletin then gives numerous articles of the Constitution dealing with powers of legislation and the rights of the people. Under Iran's Constitution, the people were secure in their rights and property. All laws and amendments had to be approved by both houses of parliament and signed by the shah. Implementation of a law was contingent on its lack of conflict with the holy laws of Islam. The bulletin continues:

> Considering the above principles, which are binding on all the people of Iran, how can one reconcile the present situation with the Constitution? The religion of Iran is the Jaffari Faith of Islam, and the secular laws must not be in conflict with the laws of Islam, the determination of which is assigned to the ulama. It was for this reason that His Excellency Ayatollah Behbahani presented in the winter of 1960 the fatwa of His Holiness Mr. Borujerdi to the Nineteenth Majlis. The fatwa had declared the land reform law that had been submitted by the government of Dr. Eqbal to be in conflict with the laws of Islam. Thereafter, the deputies attempted to reconcile the law with the views cited, and the result was the law that was approved by the Majlis.
>
> Thus, how can the members of a government that claims to be a constitutional government draw up a set of regulations that are in far greater conflict with the Constitution and the laws of religion than were the ones that had been originally submitted to the Majlis, label them as a law, and then implement them by force of arms and bayonet? On the day when better regulations were discussed by the Majlis, they were met by the determined opposition of Ayatollah Behbahani. Today, when the head of the present government, accompanied by his former adviser, humbly goes to kiss the hands of the ulama, how can one expect that he orders the implementation of such regulations that are in stark conflict with religious laws?
>
> Now Mr. Arsanjani openly claims that he has not broken any constitutional or religious laws. He is implementing the same law that was approved by the Majlis but only with "improvements." Both a Moslem and an infidel can claim and declare adherence to the same God. But the infidel deletes the word *God* in his statement and then continues to insist that he also believes in the same God as the Moslem. No one is fooled.
>
> Mr. Arsanjani, who is devoid of the least information on the state of agriculture and on the landowner-cultivator relationship, has become the minister of agriculture. He can continue in his "analysis" and claim that he is only implementing the same law that was approved by the Majlis and signed by His Majesty, and he is duty-bound by the Constitution to implement it. We all know that during

the past eight months, he has been in a state of active rebellion against the Constitution, he has continuously attacked the authors of that law, he has spent all of his time in preparing the new measures, and up to now he has drawn and discarded numerous plans. The last one is the one that we have seen, and it is entirely contrary to the Constitution, the laws of religion, and the civil laws of the country. But he continues to insist that he is implementing the same law. According to Principle 15 of the Constitution, it is ordained that no owner may be deprived of his property, except for reasons of religion, and then only after the establishment and payment of a just price.

Religious laws require that a transaction be mutually consentual, that a just price be established to mutual satisfaction of both parties, and that the price be paid in cash or on mutually agreeable terms at the time of the transaction. But where the owner is dispossessed and the property is placed at the disposal of the buyer, the government signs the transfer deed on behalf of the owner, on its own determines a price to be paid in installments, each of which is a fraction of the annual rent from the property, and then takes over the land by sheer force, can anyone claim that these actions are compatible with Principle 15 of the Constitution and the important laws of religion? This is outright confiscation of people's property. Principle 16 of the Constitution has expressly forbidden the confiscation of property as punishment and as state policy. Yet Mr. Arsanjani has included provisions in the new regulations that allow the confiscation of private property by the government without compensation. In short, it is a crime to be a landowner in this country. According to Principle 17 of the Constitution, dispossessing the owner of his land is strictly forbidden. But Mr. Arsanjani intends to dispossess the owners by force and with the help of the bayonet and the gendarmes.

Can these actions be called enforcement of the Constitution? Are these the actions of someone who claims to be a follower of Mr. Borujerdi? According to Principle 17 of the Constitution, the three branches of government are separate, and legislation is in the power of the legislature and not the executive branch, and it is clearly stated, "The laws and regulations will be implemented by the ministers and other government agents in the name of His Majesty." How can Mr. Arsanjani, who admits he is not a legislator but a minister, take it upon himself to, in his words, "improve" an existing law? It is clearly stated in Principle 21 of the Constitution that whenever a law or a regulation pertaining to a ministry is to be altered, changed, or annulled, it can only be done with the approval of the Majlis.

According to Principle 49: "Concerning the financial affairs of the country that are under the sole discretion of the Majlis, if His Majesty requests a reconsideration of a matter, the reinvestigation must be done by the Majlis." This can only be done once. And then it states, "If the Majlis with a three-quarters majority of those present reconfirms its prior decision, His Majesty shall sign the law." Thus in view of the above, no minister is entitled to refuse to implement a law on the grounds that he wishes to improve the law. Changing or annulling a law, similar to new legislation, is the responsibility of the Majlis. How can the minister of agriculture, who claims to hold a doctorate in law, be unaware of this? Has Mr. Arsanjani not read Principle 33 of the Constitution, which states: "New laws that are deemed necessary will be drawn up by the appropriate ministry, and then submitted by the minister or the prime minister to the Majlis. After the approval by the Majlis, and the royal signature, it will be implemented in a timely manner"?

If Mr. Arsanjani had any respect for the Constitution, how could he put aside a law that bears the royal signature, and personally prepare new regulations without submitting them to the Majlis, and without Majlis approval and royal signature set about rapidly and forcibly implementing them? Is this the meaning and intent of the Constitution? Can one believe that Mr. Arsanjani, a former attorney and currently minister of agriculture, is unaware of Principle 89 of the Constitution, which clearly states: "Legal tribunals and the courts of law will only enforce those regulations issued by the central, provincial, and local governments, if they are compatible with the law"? Any attorney has repeatedly referred to this principle in the course of his legal work.

The truth of the matter is that Principle 7 of the Constitution, "The principles of the Constitution constitute a complete entity and are indivisible," has been forgotten. Whatever is desired by this government, it is labeled a law and then forcibly carried out on the basis of arbitrary force and bayonet. In any society where laws do not rule over its people and arbitrary force prevails, downfall is the inevitable outcome. The Agricultural Union of Iran, in the interest of preserving the independence and foundations of the country, is duty-bound to express its objection to this manner of government. We warn all those who are dedicated to preserving a constitutional monarchy and invite them to assist us on the path of return to constitutional rule in this country. Now that the memories of the Minor Tyranny have been revived, the principle of constitutional government is in danger and must be saved.

In conclusion it is added that in reference to the tragic event at the university, some government authorities have made totally baseless and ungentlemanly accusations that are trite and laughable. The prime minister and his minister of agriculture have alleged that one of the large landowners in Khorasan has given a check for 150,000 tomans and has undertaken to give 350,000 more. The Agricultural Union of Iran declares that it had neither a direct nor an indirect role in the tragic events at the university. Praying to God, and under the protection of the Constitution, the landowners of Iran have no need to resort to such actions, and hereby declare their distaste for such actions. We hereby ask the prime minister to give the check number, and name the payer and guarantor of the sums mentioned, so that he can be prosecuted and accordingly punished. If untrue, those who reported these falsehoods must be prosecuted and punished.

Agricultural Union of Iran

The "tragic events" referred to in the bulletin consisted of student protests at Tehran University on 21 January 1962. The protests were suppressed by the army, and several students were killed or injured. The landowners were accused of financing and instigating the protests. Subsequently, in an attempt to deny any involvement in the protests and to debate the issue of land distribution in public, Majd prepared a position paper on behalf of the Agricultural Union of Iran entitled "Some General Truths Concerning Agriculture in Iran in the Year 1962," and submitted it to the newspaper *Etela-at* for discussion in its "open forum." Not surprisingly, the government had denied permission to the Agricultural Union of Iran to appear on the open forum or to have its statement printed in the newspaper. The text of the letter to *Etela-at* and that of the position paper are given below. The paper contains many useful insights into Iran's agriculture and is given in full.

Agricultural Union of Iran
Date: 3 February 1962

His Excellency, Mr. Abbas Massoudi, respected editor of *Etela-at,*
The Agricultural Union of Iran hereby requests the use of the open forum for the purpose of discussing and analyzing the subject of agriculture in Iran. Please set the date and the time of the meeting and announce it accordingly. We also request that you invite the

prime minister and other ministers, well-known and prominent public figures, and also the American agricultural advisers to participate in the meeting. Apart from its own delegation, others will not be invited on behalf of the Agricultural Union of Iran.

Respectfully,
Mohammad Ali Majd
Agricultural Union of Iran

"Certain Truths Concerning Agriculture in Iran in the Year 1961"

The "position paper" that my father submitted to Etela-at is important because he accurately predicted some of the major consequences of the proposed land distribution. He discussed such matters as the structure of landownership, landlord-tenant relationship, previous experience with land distribution in Sistan during the 1930s, and the distribution of Pahlavi villages in the 1950s. He also addressed some of the political consequences of land distribution. With the removal of the landowner, he suggested, the qanats would dry up, the villages would be ruined, and the cultivators would be scattered in towns and cities where they would be susceptible to all forms of publicity and propaganda. Consequently, political instability would follow land distribution. Majd also noted that following land distribution in Sistan, the area had become dependent on wheat shipments from the neighboring Pakistan. He presented evidence that after the distribution of Pahlavi villages in Varamin and Qazvin, the qanats had been neglected and allowed to dry up. Subsequently, he also pointed out, following the distribution of khaliseh (government-owned) villages in Fars, many of the new land recipients migrated to Kuwait and Bahrain.

In reading the bulletin more than thirty-five years later, one is struck by how accurately Majd predicted the demise of Iran's system of qanats following land distribution and the rising levels of imports. In just over twenty years, the system of qanats was decimated (see chap. 13). It was replaced by an irrigation system that was entirely dependent on the provision of subsidized capital and energy, that is, one that is entirely dependent on oil revenue. An ancient and environmentally sound system was replaced by one that degraded the environment. Concerning food imports, Iran was basically self-sufficient in food in 1960. By 1995 it had become one of the largest agricultural importers in the world. While oil prices were high, agricultural imports did not constitute a heavy drain on the economy. But with the steep decline in oil prices and export revenues, agricultural imports have imposed a heavy burden. The paper is given in full:

Certain Truths Concerning Agriculture in Iran in the Year 1961

1. Under current conditions, out of the 164 million hectares that constitute Iran's area, only 5 million hectares are under cultivation each year. Of this, 4 million hectares are nonirrigated crops [*deimi*], and 1 million are irrigated [*abi*]. Potentially, with the provision of water and implements such as tractors and seed, some 35 million hectares can be brought under cultivation.

2. Of the country's 20 million people, 15 million are rural residents.

3. There are 50,000–55,000 villages, of which a third consist of endowed [*moqufeh*], *khaliseh*, and Pahlavi estates [*amlak-e Pahlavi*]. More than one-third of the villages are owned by the small landowners [*khorde-malekin*], and at the very most one-third of the villages are owned by one person or even one family.

4. The most developed villages in Iran are those that are owned by one person or one family. Then come the Pahlavi estates, which belong to one person. Then come the endowed and khaliseh villages. The least developed are the *khorde-malek* villages. Iran cannot be compared with Europe or even the neighboring countries because in Europe and in Turkey, Iraq, and Pakistan there is plenty of water. Only Afghanistan's water scarcity is somewhat similar to Iran's. In addition, the constant need to interact with government officials results in expenditure of much time and neglect of the agricultural duties, unless there is an intermediary between the cultivator and the government circles.

5. It is portrayed abroad that Iranian cultivators are similar to serfs in old Russia. The reality is completely different. The real owner of the land is the cultivator who holds and cultivates the land. He undertakes all kinds of transactions on this land, transferring and dividing the land with the other villagers, giving the land as dowry, and then dividing the same land among the cultivator's heirs. The cultivator is the real owner of the land and the orchards he holds. The only restriction is that because of geographical and natural conditions, for many centuries the produce of the land was divided on the basis of contractual agreements between the owner and the cultivator. No parts of Iran are similar in this respect. Even in neighboring villages, the relationship between owners and cultivators could vastly differ. In Azarbaijan, 80–90 percent of nonirri-

gated crop is the share of the cultivator, and 10–20 percent is that of the owner. In Gilan, the landowner's share is one-fifth and the cultivator's share is four-fifths of the crop. In Shahsavar, one-eighth is the owner's and seven-eighths belong to the cultivator. In another example, the village of Shal in Qazvin has a population of 12,000 inhabitants, and its sale of grapes comes to 2.4 million tomans per year. Of this, only 3,000 tomans are paid to the owner. In the conditions of nonirrigated cultivation in Iran, the owner's share is at most 20 percent of the crop, and 80 percent goes to the cultivator. Yet the provision of water, payment of taxes, the management of affairs, and dealings with government officials are all the responsibility of the landowner. It can be stated with certainty that the maximum rate of return on agricultural property in Iran is 3 percent per year, one of the lowest anywhere.

6. Land distribution in Iran was first contemplated and implemented in Sistan in 1933 by the late shah. All agricultural land in Sistan consisted of khaliseh land. In 1933, His Majesty, the late Reza Shah, visited Sistan and saw that the cultivators were impoverished. He thought that if the land were distributed among the cultivators, poverty would be alleviated. Subsequently, a law was drawn up and approved, and all land in Sistan was distributed. After the distribution, 90 percent of the land recipients sold their land and left Sistan. Subsequently, not even the domestic food requirements could be met, and each year 100,000 kharvars (1 kharvar = 300 kg) of wheat had to be brought in from the neighboring Pakistan.[2] With this experience, Reza Shah decided against a general land distribution, and instead a special law was passed by which government-owned villages were assigned to private individuals. Today, these privatized former khaliseh villages are the most productive and developed in Iran. Concerning the distribution of Pahlavi estates, the following results have been obtained. First, in the estates of Varamin, the majority of the cultivators have abandoned their villages and are now construction workers in Tehran. Second, before land distribution in Takestan, Qazvin, the qanats yielded forty stones of water. Today, the water flow has declined to a mere three stones, and agriculture has suffered accordingly. Third, before land distribution in Garmsar, cotton production stood at 7,000 kharvars. In 1961, it is only 100 kharvars.

In order to confirm the validity of the above, we request that investigators and researchers travel to these villages and stay for a few days. They should try to talk to the cultivators, despite the attempt by government agents to restrict all contacts between the villagers and outsiders. During the opening of a raisin factory in Takestan, His Majesty asked one of the cultivators if he was satisfied with the land distribution. The cultivator replied that the cultivators had been ruined after the land distribution. Thereafter, government agents have done all they can to prevent the expression of such views in front of His Majesty. In Bojnurd, Khorasan, and other places where land has been distributed, those who are lined up in front of His Majesty are told what to say to the shah. Those who do otherwise and speak freely are punished after His Majesty's departure.

7. As stated above, total land cultivated in Iran is 5 million hectares. In Iran's agriculture, one kharvar of seed is sown to four hectares of deimi land, and one kharvar of seed is sown in two hectares of abi land. This is the meaning of one pair of oxen; that is, each cultivator plants one kharvar of deimi seed and one kharvar of abi seed. Assuming each cultivator needs on average an additional two hectares of land for orchards and summer cash crops [seifi], as well as land for his residence, barns, and stables, then each cultivator will need eight hectares of land. If all the villages in Iran, including the Pahlavi estates, the khaliseh villages, and the villages owned by large and small landowners, are distributed among the cultivators, then only 630,000 cultivators will receive land, and the remaining 1.7 million will receive nothing. This will add to their dissatisfaction. Other impoverished rural residents will also demand land. The insistence on a land distribution by foreign governments as well as the Iranian government will only increase the level of dissatisfaction.

8. It is widely believed in foreign and domestic circles that when a cultivator becomes the owner of his land, his love of country and land will increase, he will be less susceptible to foreign propaganda, and God forbid, should the country be invaded by Russia, the cultivator will lay down his spade and take up arms in defense of the country. The reality will be the opposite. As described above, with the removal of the landowner, the villages will be ruined, and the villagers will be scattered in the

towns where they will be susceptible to all forms of alien publicity and communist propaganda.

9. Unfortunately, during the past nine months, ever since becoming the minister of agriculture, Mr. Arsanjani has spent all of his time in spreading lies and false publicity for the purpose of ruining the relationship between the cultivators and landowners. In order to discredit Iran's true patriots, he has resorted to shameless lies and falsehoods. Last week, Arsanjani and Dr. Amini announced that one of the large landowners in Khorasan had given a check for 150,000 tomans for the purpose of fomenting disorder and that he had promised to provide an additional 300,000 tomans. Last week, the Agricultural Union of Iran published a long bulletin in which it described at length the manner in which the recent government actions had violated Iran's laws and, in particular, its Constitution. In the same bulletin, we categorically denied these baseless accusations, and we asked the government to announce the identities of the donor, the guarantor, and the recipients of these alleged sums so that they can be prosecuted. If it is established that the allegations are lies, then the individual responsible should be punished. Unfortunately, under complete government censorship, we have not been able to distribute our bulletin.
Agricultural Union of Iran

Statement to the Foreign Press

The Agricultural Union of Iran also prepared a statement for the foreign press. In response to hostile foreign reporting, the following (with minor editorial correction by this author) was sent to the foreign press bureaus in Tehran.

Agricultural Union of Iran

A Response to the Reporters of United Press International, Associated Press, Reuters, German News Service, and Agence France Press

1. That which concerns us and our government, we will discuss in the domestic press and is of no concern to you. We only wish to remind you that like the other free countries of the world, we too have a democratic regime, and if the government behaves contrary to the laws of the country, we have a right to resist.

2. But concerning that which is of concern to you gentlemen of the foreign press and foreign publications, not only in the name of the

class of landowners but also in the name of the nation of Iran, we have the right to point out that part of the news you have conveyed to the world is insulting to the ancient people of Iran, and we wish to correct it.

First, neither feudalism nor serfdom has ever existed in Iran. In contrast to the periods when feudalism was prevalent in important parts of Europe and Asia, our Iran was one of the most advanced and highly civilized countries that existed, ruling over a continent (from the Nile to the heart of India), a system of rule known as the united states, similar to the system existing in America and parts of Europe. Consequently, this report was very insulting and has to be rectified.

Second, contrary to the published allegations that the implementing of the land reform decree will block communist penetration in Iran, the truth is that it will do the opposite. Removing the landowner, who is a dedicated supervisor of ignorant peasants and a staunch anticommunist, and replacing him with semicommunists under the guise of cooperatives is a clever plan to guide Iran toward communism. Essentially, these harmful actions such as the confiscation of people's land and property, violations of and disrespect for the constitutional laws of the country that are inextricably tied to the laws of religion, are Bolshevik in nature, designed to incite the ignorant people against the principles of capitalism and democracy and to promote communal ownership. In addition, the poisonous propaganda against the landowners and the phony sympathy for the cultivators has resulted in rebellion and lawlessness, results which are desired and awaited by the powerful neighbor with sharp claws.

1. The sound agricultural foundation of Iran during the past several thousand years has been the close cooperation between the landowner and the cultivator. In much of the agricultural lands, the cultivator has a right of possession known as tabar tarashi [ax clearance] or karafe in the Caspian coastal regions, and nasaq, haq-e risheh [root rights], and dast-range [reward] in the south and other regions. This right is so strong and respected that it was even observed during the distribution of the Crown lands. That is, each cultivator in Mazandaran received the amount of land that he held and cultivated. Thus some cultivators received one-half hectare and others received five hectares of land. The reason was that the cultivators' right of possession was far more weighty than the owner's owner-

ship right in the land they held. Thus, the cultivator holds direct possession of the land he cultivates, and his share of the crop in nonirrigated land is no less than 80 percent, while his share in irrigated land is no less than 60 percent. In Gilan and Mazandaran, the cultivator's share is in excess of 90 percent of the crop. There is no doubt that the Iranian cultivator is dedicated to his land, home, and cultivation. In return for paying the owner's dues, the cultivators are provided with water from qanats that are established by the landowners, they are furnished with seed and loans, and their rights are defended and upheld in their dealings with government officials and gendarmes. It was this cooperation between landowner and the cultivator which has enabled Iran to often export its surplus grain to Russia and even Germany (for example, in 1935).

2. Thanks to Islam, feudalism and serfdom, that is, treatment of cultivators like slaves, has never existed in the past, let alone in the present era. With the establishment of the Constitution and constitutional government, there have been notable cultural, educational, and institutional advancements. Before the Constitution, there were several large landowners such as the late Mohammad Vali Khan, Sepahsalar Azam, and the late Asad-Dowleh Zanjani, who each owned several hundred villages. But their descendants and heirs who now number in the hundreds have all been reduced to the status of simple, small landowners through the process of inheritance and subdivision.

3. The holy religion of Islam is the best guarantee that large ownerships will be broken up and social justice maintained. In practice, many landowners have endowed one-third of their property to be used for religious and charitable purposes. The rest is divided among the heirs. In contrast, in such European countries as England and Germany, everything is inherited by the eldest male heir for the purpose of preserving large estates.

4. The reason the rural residents, and the urban population, are dissatisfied with their condition is not because they feel they are exploited by the landowner and treated as slaves. It is because of the tyranny of some government agents and agencies and the expenditure of all government revenues in urban areas. Not even a small portion of the oil revenue and foreign loans is used to assist rural areas and agriculture. Fifteen million rural residents of Iran have to sell their produce at a low

price, while they have to pay dearly for such items as sugar, cigarettes, and tobacco, which are government monopolies.

5. The friendly cooperation between landowner and cultivator has been the tradition for several thousand years. Tearing the landowner apart will not serve as a barrier to communism. On the contrary, deprived of water, seed, and assistance, the cultivators will be forced to abandon their land and leave for the cities, and the production that exists will be lost. Past experience with land distribution shows that far from improving the cultivator's lot, the result has been economic and social ruin. The khaliseh lands that were distributed in Sistan were ruined, and some of the cultivators even migrated to Afghanistan. In Fars, the new recipients of khaliseh land have migrated to Bahrain and Kuwait. The level of water flow from the qanats in the distributed Pahlavi villages such as Takestan in Qazvin and Davood Abad in Varamin has fallen drastically.

6. To resist communism and improve the cultivator's lot, instead of destroying the landlord-tenant relations, the government should spend a significant part of its income and oil revenue on improving conditions in rural Iran and helping the landowner and the cultivator to improve the agricultural condition of the country. Such is the meaning of His Majesty's "positive nationalism." The other path will constitute "negative nationalism," which led to the bitter experience of the days before 19 August 1953.

Agricultural Reform Instead of Land Distribution

In their communication with the foreign press agencies, the Agricultural Union of Iran had advocated agricultural reform instead of the proposed land distribution. This was further elaborated upon in the correspondence with Ali Amini. Faced with a strong resistance by landowners (as well as the ulama, described below), Amini had made some appeasing gestures toward the Agricultural Union of Iran. In response to a conciliatory speech by Amini, Majd sent the following letter, dated 26 November 1961:

His Excellency Dr. Amini, Prime Minister

Your comments to the Association of Newspaper Writers concerning land reform, and the request and invitation to landowners to cooperate with the government in reforming and expanding agriculture, have been very encouraging to the membership of the Agricultural Union of Iran in both Tehran and the provinces. While thanking you greatly for your accurate comments, we wish to bring these points to your attention.

As shown by the articles of association and the aims of this union, our main purpose is to bring an improvement to the backward and sorry state of agriculture, adopt technical, social, and economic solutions for land reform, and bring economic improvement to farmers (owner and cultivator). The steps taken in the furtherance of your comments to the Association of Newspaper Writers are as follows:

1. Since the first and most important reason for agricultural decline is the shortage and scarcity of water, the Agricultural Union of Iran has appointed a commission, consisting of five members with expertise in this field, to investigate this essential problem and, in consultation with authorities in the Plan Organization, to find practical ways to encourage investment in establishing qanats, deep wells, and large and small dams and to prepare and submit a report to the Union.

2. The next step for agricultural reform is mechanization of agriculture. Unfortunately, in the current state of affairs, this is under the control of a group of importers and middlemen. This has resulted in exorbitant prices, scarcity of parts, lack of repair facilities, scarcity of fuel, and proliferation of makes. The Agricultural Union of Iran has appointed a commission to investigate this matter and suggest ways to take it out of the control of importers and middlemen, so that millions of hectares can be brought under cultivation.

3. In addition to low yields, the abundance of pests such as locusts, bugs, vine-borers, and others has resulted in the loss of much of the meager produce to these pests. Consequently, neither the cultivator nor the owner can earn a satisfactory return to his labor and capital. This Union has appointed another commission to investigate this problem and, in consultation with government authorities, suggest ways to increase investment in fertilizer production and use and pest control.

4. More than anyone else, the landowners are acutely aware of the lack of social services such as health services, education, and adequate housing in the villages. These shortages have contributed to a labor shortage in agriculture. On the other hand, the scarcity of irrigated land in relation to population growth has expanded the landless population, which has become an additional burden on the active cultivators.

In the villages owned by small landowners, many social and agricultural problems have grown more complex and have imposed an additional burden on the government. But in villages owned by large landowners, most of these problems can be handled with government help. For this reason, the Agricultural Union of Iran has appointed a commission to study social issues in rural areas. We hope to have useful suggestions for the government.

After the submission of the reports of the above four commissions, we beg you to establish a commission that includes representatives of the Agricultural Union of Iran so that, subject to the approval of the commission, the recommendations are implemented.

In conclusion, we wish to remind you that all of the above are conditional on the existence of legal rights and security of ownership for the owners, as well as peace of mind for the cultivators. In the absence of confidence and security, no one will undertake a step to improve the agricultural and economic condition of Iran.

Respectfully,

Mohammad Ali Majd

Agricultural Union of Iran

Amini followed his conciliatory remarks with a letter to the Agricultural Union of Iran seeking ways to promote reform. Majd reports that the Union received a letter from the prime minister, number 35047, dated 26 November 1961, the same date as the Union's letter to Amini. In his letter, Amini had solicited the Union's views. After many meetings and consultations, the Union prepared a report entitled "Proposals for Agricultural Reform in Iran." The suggested reforms consisted of a series of measures that aimed to increase agricultural production, yield, productivity, and income of the agricultural population. It included suggestions for increasing investment in irrigation facilities, promoting mechanization, using chemicals, improving marketing and storage, supporting prices for farm commodities, reducing imports of agricultural goods, and subsidizing the agricultural sector. It was a relatively complete agricultural development package that substituted agricultural reform for land distribution. By increasing production, it increased agricultural income of the peasant and thereby eliminated the need to improve the peasant's lot by confiscating the landowner's property and giving it to the cultivator.

In reality, what the landowners in Iran were advocating was identical to the measures that were subsequently adopted in Turkey. As discussed in the literature, despite heavy pressure by the United States to undertake a landownership redistribution similar to that of Iran, the Turkish polity adopted the very same measures that the landowners in Iran were advocating: large-scale mechanization, increased chemical inputs, heavy subsidies, and guaranteed pricing of agricultural products. The resulting rural prosperity eliminated the need for a land redistribution in Turkey.[3]

The report was delivered to the prime minister's office on 3 February 1962, some three weeks after the approval of the cabinet decree of 9 January 1962. In its haste, the government had not waited for the reform views of the Agricultural Union of Iran. In any event, the activities of Arsanjani and his provocative speeches, which were broadcast on the national radio, ensured that the "honeymoon" was very brief. Thus, Amini's conciliatory gesture to landowners was simply a political maneuver to buy time and to try to reduce landowner opposition activity for a brief period.

Lawlessness and Violence against Landowners: Documentary Evidence

As noted above, the first district where the land distribution decree was implemented was in the Maragheh region in East Azarbaijan. With rising lawlessness and violence against landowners, a bulletin in Persian and English entitled "Some Instances of Insecurity and Lawlessness in Maragheh Region" was put out by the Agricultural Union of Iran. A copy was sent to the U.S. embassy and given to the foreign press agencies. It described and documented twenty-one instances of violence against landowners and their property in Maragheh during March 1962. The exact text of the English bulletin (with no editorial correction by this author) is given here.

Agricultural Union of Iran
Date: 11 April 1962, Number 910/3

Some Instances of Insecurity and Lawlessness in the Maragheh Region

1. In the village of Chaldan-e Sofla, Rural District of Saraju, Township of Maragheh, a group of adventurers who had fled the region after the Pishevari disturbances have recently returned to the village and have forcibly seized the landowner's land, plundered much of his machinery, and have prevented the landowner from carrying out his tasks.
2. In the village of Yanbolaghi, Township of Hashtrud, the cultivators have seized the owner's land, which had been ploughed by a tractor, and have prevented him from cultivating his fields.

3. In the village of Omran Kondi, Township of Hashtrud, the cultivators have prevented the owner's tractor from ploughing his personal field, cut the trees belonging to the owner, and have prevented him from coming to the village.

4. In the village of Amir Ghayeb, Rural District of Gavdol, Township of Maragheh, the cultivators have seized the owner's sheep.

5. In the village of Gharakh Bolagh, Rural District of Charadeimagh, Township of Hashtrud, the inhabitants have plundered the owner's storage bins containing twenty tons of grain.

6. In the village of Goli Bolagh, Rural District of Charadeimagh, Township of Hashtrud, the local inhabitants have plundered some of the owner's grain.

7. In the village of Hezaran, Township of Hashtrud, the inhabitants have plundered the owner's grain.

8. In the village of Jalil Abad, Township of Hashtrud, the inhabitants have plundered the owner's property and animal feed, insulted and beaten him.

9. In the village of Pareh Lor, Township of Hashtrud, incited by a few adventurers, the cultivators have seized the owner's private mechanized land, prevented him from ploughing his land, and have destroyed an apple orchard.

10. In the village of Qazal Dagh, Township of Hashtrud, the cultivators and other inhabitants surrounded the owner's house during the night and plundered his household furniture and money. Without the intervention of the gendarmerie, the lives of those in the house would have been in danger.

11. In the village of Tazeh Kand, the inhabitants slaughtered the owner's horse, insulted him, and have prevented him from watering his fields.

12. In the village of Gol Lav, Rural District of Chardimagh, Township of Hashtrud, the cultivators have beaten the owner, insulted him, and prevented his entry into the village.

13. In the village of Payk, Township of Hashtrud, the cultivators have seized the owner's orchards and have built walls to partition the orchard.

14. In the rural district of Diz Jarud, the inhabitants have seized the orchards belonging to Engineer Akbar Akbarian and have divided them among themselves.

15. In the village of Aghcheh Rish, Township of Hashtrud, the inhabitants have plundered part of the owner's grain and have

insulted him and his family. A hooligan by the name of Esmail Imani, who had migrated from the village the year before, has returned and is now the source of insecurity.

16. In the village of Hajesh, Hashtrud, the inhabitants have prevented the owner from transporting his grain.

17. In the village of Hosseinabad, Hashtrud, the inhabitants have prevented the owner from planting the spring crop on his mechanized land and have prevented his entry into the village.

18. In Shahin Dej, a large village where the land is bought and sold by the meter, the inhabitants have enclosed and seized the owner's cultivated land.

19. In the village of Pasha Beyk of Hashtrud, the inhabitants have cut down the owner's poplar trees.

20. In the village of Keshavar, Township of Miandoab, they have prevented the owner from carrying out his mechanized cultivation.

21. In the village of Dashatan of Maragheh, and in the other villages of Mr. Ahmadi, the inhabitants have cut the trees and seized his land and alfalfa fields, as well as the inn belonging to the owner. Some leaders of the cultivators who had migrated have returned and are causing trouble.

The above incidents are only a few examples of what has taken place since March in Maragheh, the first area where land reform has been implemented. The situation is such that all landowners, both large and small, are completely unable to enter their own village.

Publications by Organizations of Small Landowners

On 17 January 1963, the cabinet of Assadollah Alam issued a decree that came to be known as the Additional Articles to the Land Reform Law. Three weeks later, on 10 February 1963, it issued another decree, the "Implementation Regulations" of the Additional Articles. These actions resulted in a flurry of activity and publications by the opposition. In his private papers, Mohammad Ali Majd kept several pamphlets published by organizations that represented small landowners. Some of these pamphlets are quoted in his memoirs. It turns out that these publications are of enormous historical significance. They reveal a crucial aspect of the land distributions that has been neglected by scholars, a side that the Pahlavi regime did its utmost to conceal. And the cover-up succeeded for nearly thirty-five years. What these pamphlets show is that the population of Iran's petty landowners was far greater than has been reported in the official data on land distribution. They also point to an entirely new avenue for research on the subject, some of which is developed and pursued in chapter 12 of this book. That the population of Iran's small landowners was so vast was the inevitable result of the Islamic practices of matrimony and inheritance. Moreover, a reexamination of the available evidence shows that the figures given in these pamphlets are essentially correct. In examining the fate of the small landowners, one begins to understand the political damage that was inflicted and why the shah's regime was not able to strengthen its base through land distribution. One also begins to understand the depth and strength of the opposition that was seen during the protests of 5 June 1963. What these numerous pamphlets reveal is that grassroots opposition had come into existence, and it consisted of separate organizations that had sprung up. The opposition was not yet organized into a united front. That is why the Pahlavi regime was so anxious to suppress the opposition and implement its program at full speed. As noted by Lambton, it wanted to complete the job before the opposition could organize. In an open and democratic system, the opposition could have organized and prevented the measures through the established political channels. By suspending the Constitution, suppressing the opposition, and driving it underground, the government provoked a violent revolution.

Fig. 7.1. *Front row, left to right:* Jaffar Sharif-Emami, Mohammad Reza Shah, Amir Assadollah Alam, and Amir Abbas Hoveida. Tehran, circa 1972.

It is noteworthy that several organizations of small landowners were politically active during this time. One such organization was the Central Agricultural Council, whose Tehran address was Baharestan Square, opposite Sepahsalar Mosque (see endnote 2). Based on documentary evidence in Majd's papers, the Central Agricultural Council was in touch with the Agricultural Union of Iran, and the liaison was Hosein Khakbaz. Another organization was called the Society of Farmers (Kanoun-e Keshavarzan), which represented a group that called itself the Small Landowners of the Province of Tehran. It submitted a paper to the economics conference held on 10 March 1963 entitled "The Reform Views of the Small Landowners of the Province of Tehran." The date of the conference was a few weeks after two key events. The first consisted of the two cabinet decrees of 17 January 1963. The other event was the referendum of 26 January 1963, which supposedly had approved these measures (see chap. 10). The paper was written in response to the Additional Articles. It is not known whether the paper was actually presented in the conference or was similar to Majd's position paper; it was not permitted to be discussed in the "Open Forum" or published. It ended as follows:

> In conclusion, we deem it necessary to stress the following. The class of small landowners, which *consists of several million individuals* [emphasis added], has rendered so many useful and productive services, and has paid so much indirect and direct taxes. . . . In short, this valuable and effective part of Iran's society begs the executive and judicial branches of the government, and the centers of publicity and information, that it be provided with security and judicial protection, and be permitted to pursue its lawful economic goals with security and dignity, and be able to contribute to the development of dear Iran.

The paper had noted that it would be a terrible pity and a huge loss to Iran if so much managerial talent and technical expertise were allowed to go to waste.

Another publication a few months later was entitled "To the Attention of the Joint Commission of the Senate and the Majlis Empowered to Investigate the Regulations of the Second Phase of Land Reform: A Discussion of the Regulations, Objections, and Suggestions." This twenty-page pamphlet was published "on behalf of small landowners of different provinces." It was obviously prepared by lawyers, and it discussed the various provisions of the regulations and the adverse impact on the small landowners. In referring to the thirty-year lease option of Phase Two, it contained the following:

Having lost access to his property, and entirely dependent on the timely payment of the rent, what guarantee is there that the rent will be paid on time, or if at all? Does the small landowner not have a right to life? Is ownership of these few hectares a crime? In addition, the next day the Bureau of Taxes will come to demand taxes on income that exist only on paper. Who will respond to the Bureau of Taxes?

The pamphlet accurately predicted that, without legal guarantees or sanction, the cultivators would not pay the owners' rent and the hapless landowner would have to spend all of his time and energy chasing the peasants for the pitiful amounts that were "legally" his.

Another pamphlet, entitled "His Excellency, the Prime Minister of Iran," was published by an organization that called itself "The Population of Small Landowners." From the various dates in the pamphlet, it can be concluded that it was published in March or April 1963, shortly before the protests of 5 June 1963, and the "open letter" was addressed to Assadollah Alam. It describes some of the injustices that were inflicted on the small landowners, and it portrays a desperate government that was raging out of control and seemingly answerable to no one. It describes how the cabinet would issue a set of "laws," and then a week later it would issue another set of regulations that were in conflict with the earlier measures and that completely negated the very measures that had been "approved" by the national referendum a week earlier. Its tone is bitter and angry. It warns the government of the day when the people will rise in anger, and it advises the regime that it should at least have pity on itself. Reading the pamphlet more than thirty-five years later, and given the vast numbers that are cited therein, it becomes very clear that the Pahlavi regime embarked on a path of self-destruction. This is an important, powerful, and revealing document. A few excerpts are given:

His Excellency the Prime Minister of Iran
In the midst of the vicious storm and assault on the rights of small landowners that followed the cabinet decree of 17 January 1963, the aggressions and injustices that have been committed against small landowners in the villages and hamlets were such that they even caught the attention of the regime. Even you yourself declared in your news conference of Tuesday, 23 February 1963, that the government was willing to listen to suggestions for improving the decree. Although the vast majority of the small landowners have been forced to abandon their homes and property and have been driven and scattered in the towns, and are awaiting measures to heal this

192 / Resistance to the Shah

grave and profound injury and injustice, it is not clear why the new
set of regulations that have been labeled the Implementation Regulation (ayin-nameh ejraii) that were issued by the same cabinet on 10
February 1963, not only did not solve any of the problems but created many new ones and greatly worsened matters. Although we
have no hope that things will improve, and we know that under the
pretense of "reform" new damages will be inflicted, for the record
we wish to register our objections. . . .

Up until now, based on the cabinet decree of 9 January 1962,
government policy has been based on restricting ownership to six
dangs. During the past year, the government's propaganda machinery has loudly claimed that the unit of a "hectare" was not appropriate for Iran, and the practical measure consisted of "six dangs." But
now suddenly during the past two months, first the thirty-hectare
rule appeared in the cabinet decree of 17 January 1963, and in the
decree of 10 February 1963, hectares have become the unit of measure in all parts of the country. What benefits do the authors of the
regulations gain from such vacillations and personal arbitrary measures that only bring ruin to a population of 5 million small landowners and their dependents? These are matters that determine the
fate of 7 million cultivators and their kin and 5 million small landowners and their kin. They need to be discussed within the framework of Iran's Constitution and all other relevant laws, and not dealt
with by mere "cabinet decrees" masquerading as laws. Unfortunately, the meaning of *constitution* and *law* has been forgotten in this
country. . . .

From the above, we can derive the following conclusions. First,
the cabinet decree of 10 February 1963, the so-called Implementation Regulations, is an entirely new "law." Second, it is in conflict
with the cabinet decrees of 9 January 1962 and 17 January 1963,
which the government itself claims were approved by a national
referendum and thus on the basis of "national will" have the force of
law. This government can approve what it wishes, label it a law, and
then implement it by force of arms. Third, the more the small landowners point to the illogical nature of these measures and complain
of the injustices, the response of the government is to write measures
that are the exact opposite of the measures desired by small landowners and that are clearly intended to punish the small landowners for complaining. Consequently, we the undersigners only expect
things to get worse. Our only source of hope is that this ruling establishment, which on the basis of naked force approves and enforces

all sorts of regulations that are totally unjust and contrary to the laws of the country, should at least take pity on itself. By these measures, the country is assuredly placed in danger of famine. Second, the very existence of this regime is placed in jeopardy by the anger of a desperate people who have lost all hope of improvement. Once again, we warn and appeal to the government that these regulations should be changed immediately, and that it should at least listen to the suggestions of the undersigners so that a way can be found to restore the relationship between the owner and the cultivator, improve production, and improve the lot of the cultivator and the small landowner.

8

Landowners' Appeal to the Ulama and the Response

It has been suggested that the ulama were opposed to the shah's land distribution primarily because they themselves owned land. There was some truth to this. Ayatollah Khomeini came from a family of clerics and landowners in Arak.[1] The leaders of the Agricultural Union of Iran, Mohammad Ali Majd, Hosein Khakbaz, and Ayatollah Nasrollah Bani Sadr (father of Abol Hasan, the first president of the Islamic Republic), had clerical backgrounds or were members of the ulama. My father, Majd, was the son of a Hojat ol Eslam and a descendant of a long line of mojtaheds. Khakbaz was an Arak landowner and a son of the Shia Mojtahed Haj Mohsen Araki. The clerical component was even more pronounced in the Union's Azarbaijan branch, where four of the eight leaders were descendants of the ulama: Haj Mirza Javad Mojtahedi, Seyed Reza Sheikholeslami, Seyed Taqi Khan, and Haj Seyed Lotf Ali Khan Tabatabaii. In a list of landowners for Isfahan given by Akhavi, several are clerics.[2] The ulama and their kin were well represented in the ranks of large and small landowners. So the shah's land distribution was a veritable assault on traditional Persia and thus a real revolution.

Initial Appeal to and Fatwa by Grand Ayatollah Borujerdi

The ulama's stance on the shah's land distribution has sparked controversy. In surveying the literature on this subject, it becomes clear that many statements have been made and conclusions reached without any factual evidence.[3] As implied by Floor, most often the stated positions are based on wishful thinking and ideological bias.

In his memoirs and private papers, Majd kept several of the original fatwas that were issued by the senior ulama against land distribution, including the fatwa of Ayatollah Khomeini. These documents bear the signature and the seal of the ulama, and they establish the close relation-

Fig. 8.1. Amir Entesar *(center)* and a group of landowners and ulama in Tonekabon, circa 1890. The cleric to Entesar's right is his brother-in-law, the father of Gholam Hosein Akbarpour Sheikholeslami, Eqtedar Soltan.

ship between landowners and the ulama. They also establish the expressed opposition to the proposed land distribution by the ulama, including some who were alleged to have favored such a measure, including Ayatollahs Hakim, Golpayegani, and Shariatmadari. Using my father's memoirs, I can construct a chronological account of the growing resistance by the ulama.

The Agricultural Union of Iran and the senior ulama worked together from the very beginning. One of their first actions came in response to the land distribution bill that Prime Minister Manucher Eqbal submitted to the Majlis in December 1959. Majd provides the following account:

> The law that had been drawn up by the government of Eqbal and submitted to the Majlis under the name of land reform was against the laws of Islam and violated the constitution and civil laws. The first step was to draw the attention of Ayatollah Borujerdi, who was considered to be one of the most eminent sources of emulation during this century. Mr. Bani Sadr and Mr. Khakbaz went to see Mr. Ayatollah Borujerdi, and after much coming and going, this handwritten letter addressed to Ayatollah Seyed Mohammad Behbahani, a most eminent cleric [rouhani], was issued.

Majd kept a copy of Ayatollah Borujerdi's letter in his private papers (fig. 8.2):

> In the Name of the Almighty, the Compassionate and Merciful, Your Excellency, Hojat-ol Islam va al-Moslemin, Mr. Behbahani, May the Blessings Continue,
>
> This is to inform your excellency that following the widespread rumors of threat to private ownership, I was duty-bound to advise the prime minister and His Majesty, may His Greatness continue, in writing, of the conflict with the laws of the Holy Islam. The replies received have not been satisfactory. Currently, we receive a large amount of correspondence from individuals and groups from all parts of the country seeking my humble opinion. Given that reticence concerning the laws of God is not possible, I am obliged to reply to the people's questions. Although it has been known from the beginning that the admonition given by this humble to the authorities has been for the sole purpose of observing religious laws and serving the interests of the country, I am astonished that there is so much haste to approve this measure without sufficient consideration and debate and in the absence of His Majesty.
>
> I beg Your Excellency to instruct both houses of parliament, in an appropriate manner, to desist from the approval of this law. I pray for the glory of God and improvement in the affairs of Moslems. Salutations to you, and may the blessings of God be upon you. 23 February 1960, Hosein El-Tabatabaii El-Borujerdi

Ayatollah Borujerdi declared his unequivocal opposition to land distribution. Any such measure, he declared, was contrary to the sacred laws of Islam and thus invalid. This was a clear rebuke to the shah. In response, Ayatollah Behbahani wrote the following open letter to Hekmat Sardar Fakher, the speaker of parliament. A copy of the original of this letter was also found in Majd's private papers. He reminded Hekmat that the proposed measure was contrary not only to the Constitution but also to the laws of Islam. To stress the conflict, Behbahani quoted Principles 2 and 15 of the Constitution:

> Respected Leadership of the National Consultative Assembly, His Excellency Mr. Hekmat Sardar Fakher, May Good Fortune Be Upon You,
>
> A law under the name of land reform that has been rumored for some time has caused anxiety for Moslems and disturbed public feelings, for the above-mentioned law contains material that is con-

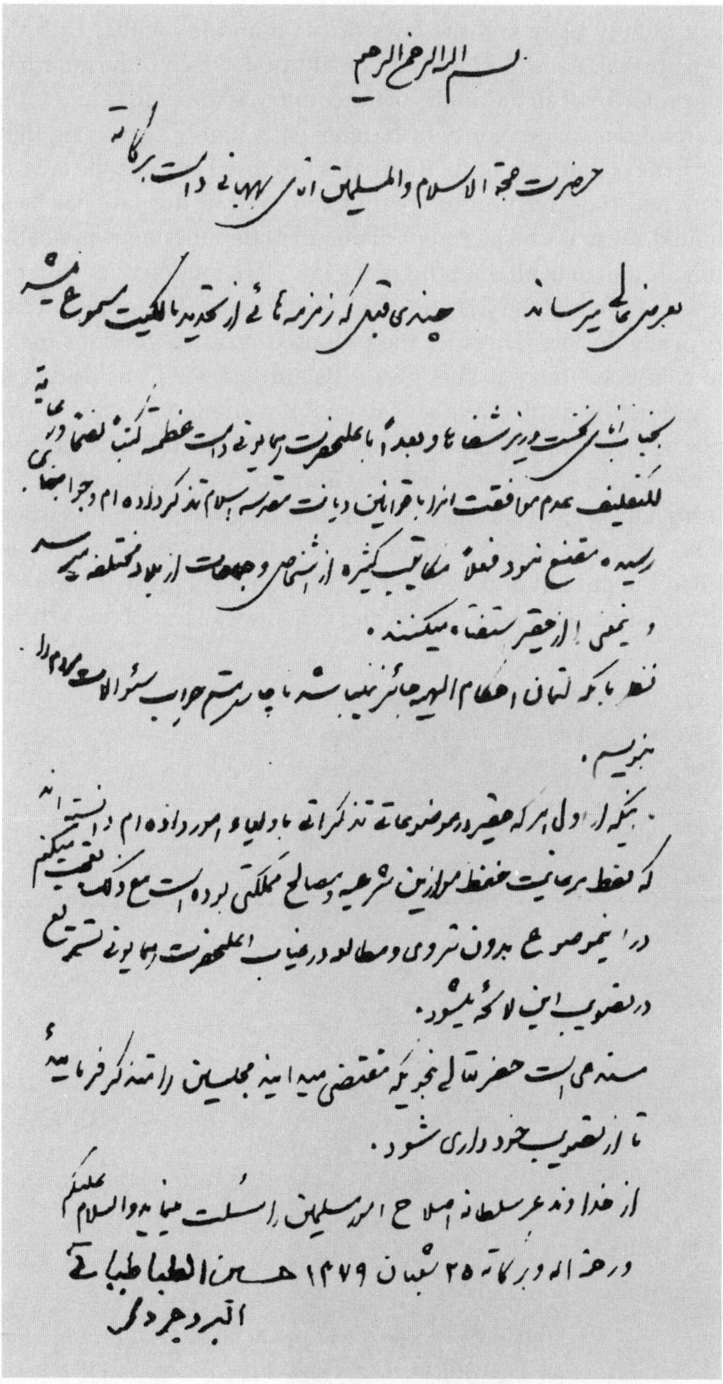
بسم الله الرحمن الرحیم

حضرت حجة الاسلام والمسلمین آقای بهبهانی دامت برکاته

بعرض عالی میرساند چندی قبل که زمزمه‌هائی از تحدید مالکیت مسموع میشد بجناب آقای نخست وزیر شفاهاً و بعداً با اعلیحضرت همایونی دامت عظمته کتباً نصحاً و از لحاظ تکلیف عدم موافقت آنرا با قوانین دیانت مقدسه اسلام تذکر داده‌ام و جواب نهائی رسیده و مقنع نبود فعلاً مکاتیب کثیره از اشخاص و جماعات از بلاد مختلفه میرسد و بعضی از حقیر استفتاء میکنند.

نظر باینکه کتمان احکام الهیه جائز نیست باید با چند سطر جواب سئوالات مردم را بنویسم.

بعلاوه اول هرکه حقیر در موضوع مانحن فیه تذکراتی با اولیاء امور داده‌ام دانسته‌اند که فقط در رعایت حفظ موازین شرعیه و مصالح مملکتی بوده است مع ذلک تعجب میکنم در این موضوع بدون تروی و مطالعه در غیاب اعلیحضرت همایونی تسریع در تصویب این لایحه میشود.

مستدعی است حضرتعالی بنحویکه مقتضی میدانید مجلسین را متذکر فرمائید تا از تصویب خودداری شود.

از خداوند متعال صلاح امور مسلمین را مسئلت مینمایم والسلام علیکم ورحمة الله وبرکاته ۲۵ شعبان ۱۳۷۹ حسین الطباطبائی البروجردی

Fig. 8.2. Fatwa of Ayatollah Borujerdi against land distribution

trary to holy piety and the laws of Islam and in conflict with the Constitution. As respect for the Constitution, which is the guardian and protector of all the affairs of the country, is imperative and is the desire of the vast majority of Iranians, it is highly surprising that, given the blatant conflict between this proposed law and the laws of Islam and the Constitution, permission to draft this law has been granted. Were the respected parliamentary deputies unaware of the Constitution or at all doubtful of the law's obvious conflict with the laws of Islam and the Constitution? In any event, I humbly and categorically declare that since the proposed measure contains material that is contrary to the laws of Islam and the Constitution, it should not be drafted as a law. Even if it is drafted as a law, it will have no legal validity. Since the declaration of this ruling is the duty of the learned ulama, and since His Excellency Ayatollah Borujerdi, the highest learned authority and the sole religious guide, and based on his religious duty, has given the necessary instructions and assigned the pursuit of the matter to this humble, I present herewith the exact text of his holy decree, and I enclose the text of two articles

Fig. 8.3. Ayatollah Haj Seyed Hosein Borujerdi, circa 1960.

of the Constitution. All the interested Moslems and this humble expect you, well known for your dedication to the protection and the upholding of law, not to permit the drafting and debating of laws that are contrary to the laws of the Holy Islam, and in conflict with the Constitution, and not to permit the destruction of the historic bravery that our great predecessors took in this path. Humblest, Mohammad El-Moussavi Behbahani.

Principle 2. The holy Consultative Assembly that has been established with the consideration by and approval of the Blessed Hidden Imam, and granted by the generosity of His Majesty, the Shahanshah of Islam, May God perpetuate his reign, and under the guardianship of the learned men of Islam, whose numbers be preserved by God, and all of the nation of Iran, must at no time, until the end of time, legislate laws that are contrary to the holy laws of Islam, be it clear that the determination of the conflict with the laws of Islam being and will be the duty of the learned ulama. This article is not subject to change until the Coming of the Messiah, the Hidden Imam, may the Lord hasten his coming.

Principle 15. No owner may be deprived of his property, except by religious decree.

The Embassy's View of Ayatollah Borujerdi's Fatwa

It is noteworthy that the account given by the American embassy is greatly at variance with the one given by Majd. The American embassy completely missed the religious and political significance of Ayatollah Borujerdi's fatwa and portrayed it as a minor political intrigue that had strengthened the shah. In a confidential report (Foreign Service despatch 593, dated 17 March 1960), Robert R. Schott, second secretary of embassy, described the affair as an attempt by Ayatollah Mohammad Behbahani to "blackmail the Shah with religious opposition to the bill in return for the Majlis and Senate seats of his son and brother, respectively."

> According to rumors in the city, Behbahani had been approached on several occasions by important landowners to oppose the bill. Among these landowners were Senator Hosein Dadgar, former Deputy Mohammad Ghoreishi, former Deputy Mehdi Batmanqelij, former Deputy Mahmud Afshar, Abdul Hosein Tavakoli, and Lotfollah Taraqi. At first Behbahani was not willing to commit himself against the government. It was only when Behbahani was informed that his brother, Mir Seyed Mohammad Behbahani, and son, Seyed Jafar Behbahani, would not be returned to their seats in the

new Senate and Majlis, respectively, that he decided to listen to the landowner group which reportedly was also ready to make it financially worth his while. (Seyed Jafar Behbahani is a well-known critic of the regime.) Ayatollah Behbahani, therefore, was said to be primarily moved by the fate of his family and was using religious opposition to land reform to blackmail the Shah so that his brother and son would not be removed from the parliament.

Despite the fact that the letter came from Borujerdi, most sources agreed that old and senile man is too simple to have thought up this particular "ploy" by himself. They point to Behbahani, who is considered a Machiavelli type in priest's garb, as the real inspiration of the letter. One Majlis Deputy told an Embassy officer that Behbahani tricked Borujerdi, adding that the latter is too naive to be aware of the consequences. . . . At the same time, the British were being conjured up as the evil originators of this move by Behbahani, who has always been considered a British stooge. The British, according to these rumors, want to torpedo the "American-inspired" land reform bill. The belief that the bill is American-inspired has been reinforced by a report prevalent at the moment that the Shah promised President Eisenhower that he would vigorously push the legislation. While little credence can be given to the tales about the British, it is a political fact that many Iranians believe them. At the same time, it would not be surprising if Behbahani and the others were capitalizing on these supposed British affiliations to trick their more gullible compatriots.

This particular letter from Borujerdi was not a formal *fatwa,* or religious proclamation, against land distribution. It might, however, have been a forerunner of such a document if the bill had been passed by the Majlis without making changes in it to make it more consonant with the principles of Islam. . . . The Embassy cannot predict what would have happened if Borujerdi had eventually issued a *fatwa.* Much fanaticism exists among the lower classes of Iran. . . . In any event, a serious impasse might have developed. When the powerful landlords ally themselves with the still influential clergy, this is a danger signal. The emasculation of the land bill, as it is considered to be American-inspired, would also have adversely affected the American prestige in Iran, as well as the Shah's prestige abroad.

Several points about this report are noteworthy. First, despite the alleged villainy of Ayatollah Behbahani, the author at one point confuses him with his brother, calling both by the same name. Second, the author is unaware of Ayatollah Behbahani's open letter to Hekmat, the speaker of parliament. Third, the American embassy had been misinformed about the origin of Ayatollah Borujerdi's letter. It is not surprising, because Schott's sources were firm believers of the "British" theory. How could they supply him with meaningful information? Instead, the writer consoled himself that the letter was not quite a fatwa. On such an important matter, that is, a fatwa by the Supreme Source of Emulation of the Shia Faith, the American embassy was misinformed and misled. No wonder the Islamic Revolution surprised the U.S. government. The report also described the response of the shah and analyzed his position.

> When Majlis speaker Reza (Sardar Fakher) Hekmat brought to the Shah in Khuzistan the news of further religious opposition to the land reform bill, he was reportedly very angry and ordered that the Deputies accompanying him return immediately and finish work on the bill. He also allegedly stated that, if the mullahs opposed this action, he would deal with them as his father used to do.[4] The Shah told Ambassador Wailes that he was, in fact, annoyed at the mullahs. He commented that Borujerdi was an innocent old man, but characterized the Tehran clerics as scoundrels, indicating that they were being paid by someone. He did not say by whom, but said that for their pains in opposing the law several Senators and Deputies would not be re-elected to the next Parliament. Most observers feel that Behbahani and the landlords have made a serious political blunder and that the Shah has emerged much stronger. . . . [The large landowners] may rue the day when they opened up Pandora's box of religious opposition.

Reading the report nearly forty years later, one cannot avoid astonishment at the embassy's wishful thinking that the shah had somehow been strengthened by a letter from the Supreme Source of Emulation declaring that the shah's cherished land distribution bill violated the laws of Holy Islam.

A Second Appeal to the Ulama

The impact of Ayatollah Borujerdi's fatwa on Majlis deputies was decisive, and it resulted in the enactment of the land reform law of May 1960. One year later, the government of Amini and Arsanjani was appointed, and the Majlis and Senate were dismissed. Ayatollah Borujerdi died on 30 March 1961, and no clear successor had emerged. In this desperate situation, Majd records that the Agricultural Union of Iran once again appealed to the ulama:

Rulings from the Sources of Emulation

Arsanjani was inciting and ordering the peasants to assault or kill the landowners or chase them out of the village. Any landowner who complained to the authorities was turned away and treated like a leper. In short, the pressure placed on the landowners was far worse than at the time of the Mongol invasions, Genghis Khan, Tamerlane, and Holaku Khan. In those times, if someone resisted and fought, he was killed. Otherwise, he would be left alone. Presently, the landowners' unforgivable sin was ownership of land, and they had no right to life and liberty. It became clear that the government was not going to put an end to the plunder, extortion, dishonor, and insult by peasants. We thought that with an appeal to the highest religious authorities and religion, we might be able to lessen the pressure by the cultivators. We thus approached the Sources of Emulation in Qom and Najaf, and they issued several rulings. These rulings were printed and by any means available distributed in some villages. But everywhere the government stopped us and fueled the incitement against landowners.

On 4 November 1961, the Agricultural Union wrote to the senior ulama in Najaf and Qom. At this time, the shah was about to instruct Amini to "improve" the existing land reform law.

In the Name of the Almighty, The Merciful and Compassionate
Your Excellency, Grand Ayatollah ———

In the course of last year, under pressure from the government at the time, the Iranian Majlis and Senate passed what it called a land reform law, a copy of which is tendered for Your Holiness's review. Since three-quarters of Iran's citizens are village dwellers, and all are Moslems and are subject to the location necessities of religious cleansing, bathing, and prayer, after reading and consideration of this law, we beg you to pronounce your opinion on this law's compatibility with the laws of Holy Islam. So that Your Holiness can become fully cognizant of the law's contents, we outline some of its articles and clauses.

1. Under article 2 of the law, maximum ownership has been limited to four hundred hectares of irrigated land and eight hundred hectares of nonirrigated land. No one is permitted to own more land.
2. Under article 3 of this law, the owner can transfer to his descen-

dants or inheritors only one and a half times the above areas. If, for example, he gives more than six hundred hectares of irrigated land, or one thousand two hundred hectares of nonirrigated land to his descendant, according to article 6 of the law, the government can confiscate the excess land without any compensation.

3. In the case of endowments, both totally public and private—with the exception of the endowments of the holy shrines of the blessed Imams, that of Hazrat Massoumeh, and two or three other instances, all are subject to this law.

4. Under article 6 of this law, it is stated that whoever comes into ownership of land in excess of the above limits, be it by means of purchase, inheritance, settlement of dispute, exchange, or any other means, the permitted maximum area will remain in his possession, and the excess will be confiscated without compensation by the government.

5. Under articles 11 and 12, the government can undertake the distribution of a jointly owned property between several persons or the termination of a lease without the consent or input of the owners.

6. Under article 13, the consent or the input of the owner in the determination of the price of the property is not required. As the buyer, the government appoints a commission, and the commission determines the price.

7. Under article 15, please consider the issue of mortgage on the land and determine its compatibility with religious law.

8. Under article 17 of this law, it is written that if the owner fails to present himself within two months of the invitation for the signature and transfer of deed, he will be fined. That is, for each hectare of irrigated land, the fine is 150 tomans per year, and for each hectare of nonirrigated land, he has to pay 75 tomans per year (of course, this is over and above the taxes normally paid). The sum of 150 tomans exceeds the price of land, especially since it has to be paid every year, and most of the irrigated land in the colder mountainous regions is not worth more than 150 tomans per hectare. In short, the owner is forced either to sell to the government or to pay a sum equivalent to the price of the land to the government under the guise of development tax.

9. Other components of the law are also noteworthy. For ex-

ample, the owner is obliged to transfer the house and the land that house stands on to the cultivator, without any compensation.

It is noteworthy that the letter does not contain any reference to the plight of the landowners and the lawlessness that prevailed in rural Iran. Instead, each alem was asked to express his opinion on the main clauses of the 1960 land reform law and to determine the law's compatibility with the sacred laws of Islam. This was despite the fact that the law had supposedly been shorn of its anti-Islamic clauses. It was evident that with the appointment of Arsanjani and the impending "amendment" of the law by cabinet decree, as well as his onslaught on landowners, the actual implementation would be radically different from the intent of those who had designed and passed the 1960 law. In their desperation, landowners were following the same strategy that had succeeded in 1960.

Ayatollah Khomeini's Fatwa

The response of the Sources of Emulation to this appeal must have been disappointing to landowners and highly encouraging to the government. The disarray and silence in the ranks of the ulama had several reasons. First, there was the well-founded fear of violence and retaliation by the government against the ulama in Qom and Mashhad. Second, Ayatollah Borujerdi had no clear successor. Ayatollah Hakim was to succeed him, but he resided in Najaf, and at first he chose to remain silent. Third, some of the ulama may have been waiting to see what would happen. The evidence shows that of the ulama in Qom, only Ayatollah Ruhollah Khomeini responded to this initial appeal by landowners and issued a fatwa. His remarkable courage and sense of political judgment established him as the leader of the religious opposition and then as the leader of the Islamic Revolution. It should also be added that Ayatollah Khomeini had been a close disciple and associate of Grand Ayatollah Borujerdi.[5] By issuing a fatwa, he was following the precedent set by Borujerdi. Of the ulama in Najaf, only Ayatollah Shirazi and Ayatollah Khoii had responded to this appeal, and each had issued a brief fatwa. Both clerics resided in Najaf and could issue fatwas in relative safety. In contrast, Ayatollah Khomeini resided in Qom and thus was vulnerable to retribution by the regime. In his fatwa, Ayatollah Khomeini did not mince words:

In the Name of God, the Compassionate and Merciful
That which is being contemplated for implementation under the label of land reform law is contrary to reason, religion, and the interests of the country and in conflict with Islamic justice and jurispru-

dence. Although the practice of many large landowners who do not obey the laws of Islam concerning the rights of the poor is contrary to reason, religion, and the interests of the country and in conflict with Islamic justice and jurisprudence, Islam respects the principle of private ownership, and no authority has the right to confiscate someone's property, or transfer the property to another, without the consent and free will of the owner. Confiscation of property contrary to the desire of the owner is sinful, and no prayer on property confiscated in such a manner is valid or permitted. The principle of preserving and giving the rights of the poor is sacred in Islam, and no owner can usurp such rights. It is a capital sin to usurp the rights of the poor prescribed by religious laws and to deprive the poor of their lawful dues. If the proceeds are used to purchase property, the ownership is void, and no prayer on property that rightfully belongs to the poor is valid. Society's supreme religious jurist [faqih] with powers of fatwa can take possession of that which rightfully belongs to the poor and use it for the purpose prescribed by religion.

Ruhollah El-Moussavi El-Khomeini

Khomeini sought to protect private property and landowners as well as to preserve the rights of the poor. The faqih is the only rightful authority vested with the powers of confiscation, and only property that has been illegally acquired is subject to seizure. It is also noteworthy that Khomeini attacked the shah's land distribution on both religious and secular grounds. He declared it to be contrary to Islam as well as to national interests. In contrast, the other two Grand Ayatollahs who issued opinions condemned land distribution only on religious grounds. Thus, from the beginning, Ayatollah Khomeini portrayed the Pahlavi regime as traitorous as well as irreligious. He saw the shah's land distribution as a foreign plot to destroy Iran's agriculture and independence, make the country dependent on imports, and enable the imperialist powers to plunder Iran's wealth. He continued to expound this same line for the next fifteen years with devastating effect.[6]

Of all the charges that were leveled at the Pahlavi regime by its opponents, none was more damaging and widely believed than the accusation that the shah had destroyed Iran's agriculture. In the eyes of the people, the evidence was the transformation of Iran from a self-sufficient country in agricultural products into a major agricultural importer. Having predicted Iran's rising dependence on imports, Ayatollah Khomeini was vindicated. Of course, this was the very argument that had been advocated by the Agricultural Union of Iran.

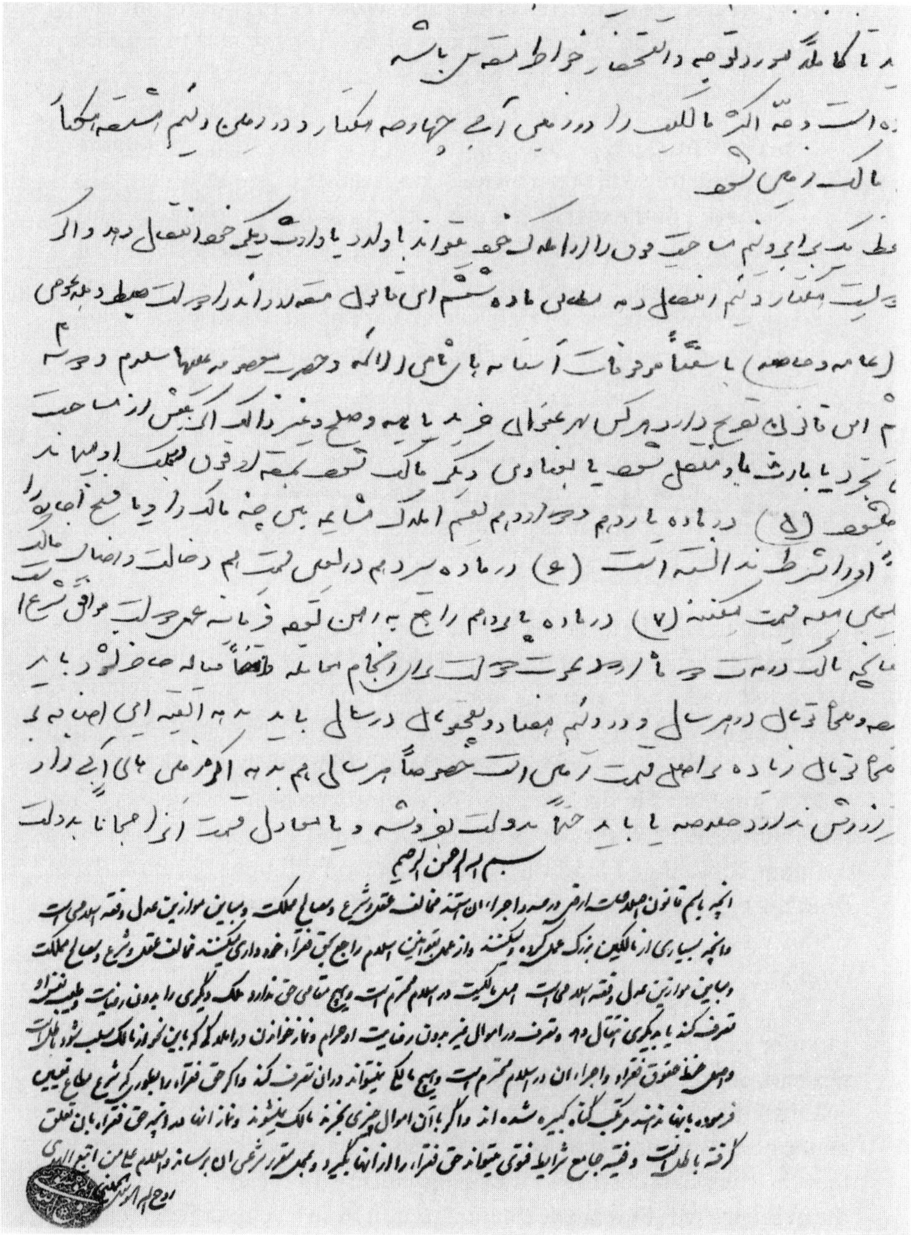

بسم الله الرحمن الرحیم

آنچه باسم قانون اصلاحات ارضی در صدد اجرای آن هستند مخالف عقل و شرع و مصالح مملکت و منافی موازین عدل و فقه اسلامی است
و آنچه بسیاری از مالکین بزرگ عمل کرده و میکنند و از عمل بقوانین اسلام راجع بحق فقراء خودداری میکنند مخالف عقل و شرع و مصالح مملکت
و منافی موازین عدل و فقه اسلامی است اصل مالکیت در اسلام محترم است و هیچ مقامی حق ندارد ملک دیگری را بدون رضایت و طیب نفس او
تصرف کند یا بدیگری انتقال دهد و تصرف در اموال غیر بدون رضایت او حرام و نماز خواندن در املاکی که باین نحو از مالک سلب شود باطل است
و همچنین حفظ حقوق فقراء و اجرای آن در اسلام محترم است و هیچ مالکی نمیتواند در آن تصرف کند و اگر حق فقراء را بطوری که شرع مطاع تعیین
فرموده بآنها ندهند مرتکب گناه کبیره شده اند و اگر با آن اموال چیزی بخرند مالک نمیشوند و نماز انها در آنچه حق فقراء بآن تعلق
گرفته باطل است و فقیه جامع شرایط فتوی میتواند حق فقراء را از آنها بگیرد و بمصرف شرعی آن برساند والسلام علی من اتبع الهدی
روح الله الموسوی الخمینی

Fig. 8.4. Fatwa of Ayatollah Khomeini against land distribution

The fatwas of Ayatollah Shirazi and Ayatollah Khoii were terse declarations that the confiscation of private property was contrary to the laws of Islam:

In the Name of the Almighty

The content of the above-mentioned material is contrary to the holy laws of Islam. If, on the basis of the above material, a person takes possession of a property, he is condemned as a usurper, and the property is deemed to be illegally acquired. Abdol-Hadi El-Hosseini Shirazi

In the Name of the Almighty, the Merciful and Compassionate

. . . Based on the above saying of the Holy Koran, acquiring ownership of another's property or seizure of the same without the owner's consent is forbidden. All prayer on such land is forbidden and null and void. It is hoped that Moslems do not disobey the laws of the Koran, so that they are bestowed with happiness in this world and the next. Abol-Qasem El-Moussavi El-Khoii

I discovered the original fatwas (bearing the signature and seal of each alem) in my father's private papers. It appears that the rest of the ulama chose not to respond or get involved at this time.[7]

Fig. 8.5. Ayatollah Haj Seyed Ruhollah Khomeini, circa 1963.

Ulama's Response to the 1962 Cabinet Decree

The meager response of the ulama to the landowners' appeal may have convinced the government that the clergy was divided on the issue of land distribution and emboldened the regime to proceed with its plans to "amend" the existing land distribution law and undertake a far more radical land redistribution. The blatant violation of the laws of Islam and Iran's Constitution and other laws by the 1962 land distribution decree, the grievous tyranny and inequities, the rapid implementation of the decree, and the cries for help and urgent appeals from the landowners who had nowhere else to turn, had prompted the ulama to make a more united stand against the Pahlavi regime. Moreover, subsequent actions by Arsanjani appear to have provoked and further embittered the religious establishment. Floor has noted the opposition of Ayatollahs Behbahani (Tehran), Khonsari (Tehran), Golpayegani (Qom), Hakim (Najaf), Mar'ashi-Najafi (Mashhad), and Shaikh Baha ud-Din (Shiraz). Floor also reports that Ayatollah Milani (Mashhad) spoke to the shah concerning the adverse effects of the decree and government policy on Iran's large population of small landowners. Faced with the implacable opposition of the ulama, the Pahlavi regime had attempted to create the impression that its land confiscation and distribution policy had the support and blessing of the ulama. It was a risky and desperate policy that was also intended to humiliate the ulama. In this policy, the government had an eager collaborator in the person of Arsanjani, even though Arsanjani's own father was a cleric and a member of the religious classes. He repeatedly declared during his news conferences that the ulama approved of the land takeover and distribution, and many newspapers and magazines repeated this claim. Arsanjani also sent open telegrams to members of the ulama, thanking them for their support. This maneuver appears to have misfired, and it forced some members of the ulama to state their positions. A revealing case in point is the open telegram from Hasan Arsanjani dated 9 March 1962, addressed to Grand Ayatollah Golpayegani on the occasion of the Islamic feast of Eid Fetr:

> Your Excellency, Grand Ayatollah Mr. Seyed Mohammad Reza Golpayegani,
>
> On the occasion of the Eid Fetr, I convey my most sincere greetings to you. My most sincere thanks to their holiness the ulama of religion for the interest they have shown in preserving the rights of all the Moslems in the implementation of Islamic justice and in the granting of land to the cultivators. I pray for your continued efforts in upholding and de-

fending the holy principles of Islam, and I hope that you will not deprive me of your prayers.

    Dr. Arsanjani, minister of agriculture

In response, a clearly angered and embarrassed Ayatollah Golpay-egani wrote an open letter addressed to Qods-Nakhaii, deputy prime minister, and refuted the "baseless accusations" leveled at a senior member of the ulama by the minister of agriculture. He reiterated the clergy's opposition to land confiscation because it violated the laws of Islam. He also warned the minister to refrain from such "provocative" actions:

His Excellency, Mr. Qods-Nakhaii, Deputy Prime Minister

    Mr. Dr. Arsanjani, Minister of Agriculture, has conveyed to this humble what he terms a greetings telegram, and in it he has thanked the ulama for their interest in and support for giving land to cultivators. In addition to the fact that there has been no endorsement of the land reform law by the senior ulama, any law that is contrary to the sacred laws of the holy religion of Islam is void and without effect. Since such baseless accusations levied at religious authorities from

Fig. 8.6. Ayatollah Haj Seyed Mohammad Reza Golpayegani.

one who calls himself the minister of agriculture are reprehensible and provocative, and are only designed to force the ulama to declare their opposition, I hereby request that the adverse consequences of such actions, especially in the absence of the prime minister, be brought to his attention, and that actions be taken to absolve the ulama of such accusations. Seyed Mohammad Golpayegani

Arsanjani sent a similar open telegram to Ayatollah Shariatmadari:

To Your Excellency, Hojat ol Eslam va al Moslemin, Mr. Seyed Kazem Shariatmadari

It is to inform Your Exalted Holiness that the minister of agriculture has in his news conferences and other declarations portrayed the supreme learned ulama [ulama-e elam] *and the sources of emulation* [mara-je taqlid] *to be in agreement with the land reform law. And according to reports, in a greeting telegram to Your Holiness on the occasion of the blessed Eid Fetr, the minister had thanked the ulama for their support. We beg you to declare your views on this issue.*

Edda-aleina baraka-takam, *on behalf of a group of faithful,*
Abdollah Ebadi

On the same sheet of paper, Ayatollah Shariatmadari responded:

In the Name of the Almighty God the Merciful and Compassionate,
On the written matter mentioned above, their holiness the supreme ulama, and myself, have not declared any support. Confiscation of people's property without the consent of the owner is forbidden and invalid. Whatever is against the laws of religion is without force and must be abolished. The humblest, Seyed Kazem Shariatmadari, 24 April 1962.[8]

The fatwas and declarations from Ayatollahs Borujerdi, Behbahani, Khomeini, Shirazi, Khoii, Golpayegani, and Shariatmadari were printed as a pamphlet by the Agricultural Union of Iran in the spring of 1962. This pamphlet, *For the Information of All Moslems,* was signed "Union of Moslem People," a pseudonym designed to protect the Agricultural Union. Its introduction read:

At the time of the submission of the land reform law to the Majlis, His Excellency the late Grand Ayatollah Borujerdi declared in writing on 23 February 1960 that the measure was contrary to the laws of religion. While informing the Majlis of Ayatollah Borujerdi's fatwa, His Excellency Mir Seyed Mohammad Behbahani declared the law to be in conflict with the laws of Islam and the Constitution. After the

Fig. 8.7. Ayatollah
Haj Seyed Kazem
Shariatmadari.

passage of this law in the houses of parliament, under circumstances that are known to all the Moslems, to learn of their religious duties and obligations concerning such estates that are forcibly confiscated by the government, or with government encouragement are taken from their owners by cultivators and farmers, devout Moslems wrote to all the Shia Sources of Emulation, both in Najaf and in Qom. The replies received are chronologically printed in this pamphlet. Be it known to all the Moslems and Shia of the world that on such confiscated lands, or endowed lands so acquired, no prayer, ablution, fasting, or burial of the dead is permitted or acceptable. Even a fetus conceived on such a land is deemed to be a bastard. And such group of persons, farmers and cultivators who with government encouragement confiscate the owners' land and dispossess them of their property, are driven from the sight of the Almighty God and are in a state of war against the Blessed Holy Hidden Imam. Any person or any reader who doubts these rulings, or claims that such rulings were not issued by the Sources of Emulation, is requested to come to the office of His Excellency Ayatollah Behbahani and view the original letter of the late Ayatollah Borujerdi. Or they can consult the biography of the late Ayatollah Borujerdi written by Hojat ol Eslam,

Mr. Mohammad Hossein Alavi Tabatabaii, which was also read and inspected by His Excellency the Late Ayatollah, and in which all the fatwas and religious rulings are chronologically given.
Union of Moslem People

The introduction was followed by Ayatollah Borujerdi's fatwa and Ayatollah Behbahani's letter to Sardar Fakher Hekmat, the speaker of the Majlis. Then came the text of a letter to the Shia Sources of Emulation in Najaf and in Qom, dated 4 November 1961. The replies and communications received by the Agricultural Union of Iran were printed. The subsequent fatwas and letters of Ayatollah Hakim, Ayatollah Khonsari, and Ayatollah Behbahani were received later and printed separately. According to Majd, attempts were made to distribute the pamphlets and printed material in the villages, but the government interfered. Judging by the large amount of printed material I found in Majd's papers, very little of this had been distributed.

In June 1962, Ayatollah Hakim decided to make his position public. He had succeeded Ayatollah Borujerdi and was considered the supreme Source of Emulation. In a letter dated 9 June 1962, the Agricultural Union of Iran informed Hakim:

Of course, Your Exalted Holiness is fully aware of the decision of the current authority in Iran, that is, the government of Mr. Amini, concerning the confiscation of people's property on the basis of a decree. Since Mr. Arsanjani, this government's minister of agriculture, has repeatedly declared that such action is undertaken with the support of their holiness, the ulama, we beg you to declare your views on this matter so that the faithful can be informed.

Ayatollah Hakim responded in the form of a fatwa:

In the Name of the Almighty the Merciful and Compassionate
There is no doubt of the illegality of the confiscation of people's property. And if they desire to portray my consent and agreement, the very opposite is the truth, for we have made our views known to the authorities on numerous occasions. 27 June 1962, Mohsen el-Tabatabaii el-Hakim

On the same day, he responded to a letter from a friend, most likely Ayatollah Nasrollah Bani Sadr, since the letter was subsequently published by the Agricultural Union of Iran. Hakim's letter to his friend is a revealing historical document. It shows that the shah's regime was fully cognizant of the ulama's opposition and had offered some conciliatory gestures. It also indicates that the shah attempted to promote the ulama in Najaf as a counter to the ulama in Qom:

Fig. 8.8. Ayatollah Haj
Seyed Mohsen Hakim.

In the Name of the Almighty, the Compassionate and Merciful

I respectfully submit. After conveying my salutation, and inquiring of Your Excellency's health, we were informed of the contents of your written communication. You had written that Mr. Arsanjani, minister of agriculture, has repeatedly stated that the seizure of property has been undertaken with the support of the ulama. If they refer to me, it is all falsehood, libels, and lies. If they refer to others, I do not believe it is true. Repeatedly, I made my opposition known to the powers that be. Mr. Kani informed me that he had come to see me on behalf of the prime minister, Dr. Amini. I made my opposition known to him, and he informed me that he would convey my opposition to the authorities. He gave me hope that the implementation of this law would be prevented. Mr. Abbas Aram, Iran's ambassador and currently foreign minister, also gave me reason to hope. After him, Mr. Ardeshir Zahedi, who came to Najaf for a pilgrimage, also came to see me. I gave him a full account of my views. He told me that he will warn the authorities, and afterwards he promised to fight to get rid of this law. And at the end of the month of Ramadan, and on the occasion of Eid Fetr, His Majesty sent a greetings message to me, and in my response I reminded him of my position. I have made my position known at every possible occasion. Not long ago,

His Holiness Hojat-ol Eslam, Mr. Sheik Mehdi Najafi wrote to me from Isfahan, informing me that the press in Iran writes that the implementation of the land reform law in Iran has the blessing and support of the ulama. In my response to His Holiness, I gave a detailed account of the above, and I requested that my opposition be made known to the believers. Of course, Your Excellency too will inform our faithful brothers of our opposition.

Va alsalam aleikom va rahmatollah va barakatah,
from Najaf Ashraf, 27 June 1962, Mohsen El-Tabatabaii El-Hakim

In the attempt to promote the Najaf ulama as a counter to the ulama in Qom and Tehran, the shah contacted Ayatollah Khoii. He responded in the form of an open telegram that must have displeased the shah and that was subsequently printed by the Agricultural Union of Iran. Additional evidence is provided by a telegram from Ayatollah Khoii to the shah, the text of which was found in Majd's papers and is given in Majd's memoirs. In his telegram, Ayatollah Khoii gave the shah a lesson in Islamic history and rule:

Tehran—Your Imperial Majesty

Your telegram declaring your support for the sacred laws and declarations of Islam was received, and it caused us much joy. Proclamation of certain laws that clearly show emulation of foreigners, and are contrary to the laws of Islam and the Constitution, is entirely invalid in the eyes of the vast majority of Iranians. As Your Majesty had stated, the upheavals in certain parts of the globe are undeniable. But we draw Your Majesty's attention to the consequences of these upheavals on the people. I beg Your Majesty, who is widely informed, to observe and learn from the history of Islam. Under the guidance of Holy Islam, considering the conditions of time and location, every reform can be undertaken because Islam supports justice and opposes corruption. Based on these same laws, the great Islamic rule was created. The lessons of world history clearly show that the progress and greatness of a country depend on high morality and social justice. We can observe from recent history that certain strong countries that strayed and pursued immorality followed the path of downfall and are paralyzed. It is hoped that the premier person of the country who is entrusted with an Islamic country and all that is holy therein will guard it with the utmost effort and will bring tranquillity to the hearts and minds of the Moslems.

Abol Qasem El-Moussavi El-Khoii

By the fall of 1962, the confiscation of the large landowners was completed. It appears that two issues forced the remaining senior ulama who had remained silent to take a stand. The first was the plight of the petty landowners who were being forcibly driven from the villages and who could no longer collect rent. The second was the issue of electoral participation by women and the proposal to "reform" the electoral laws by a cabinet decree. Floor reports that Ayatollah Milani had spoken with the shah about the situation of the small landowners and the effect of government policy on them. Ayatollah Ahmad Khonsari issued a fatwa and declaration, which were read before a congregation of thousands at the Mosque of Seyed Azizollah in Tehran on 1 November 1962:

In the Name of the Almighty the Compassionate,
The purpose of this blessed gathering on the occasion of the passing of Hazrat-e Sediqeh Tahereh, blessing upon her, is the expression of devotion to [deity], and prayer for the betterment of the affairs of religion and the world of Islam. To perform my religious duty, I feel bound to bring certain matters to the attention of the Blessed Ulama, to all the faithful and devoted people, and to address the respected leadership of the government. Recently, representatives of the different classes of the people of Tehran and many letters and telegrams from the provinces have asked me to draw the attention of the members of the government and those in authority to the need to respect and protect the pious laws of religion and orders of the Holy Islam and to warn them of the dangers of transgressions. Currently, that which is of concern to the blessed religious authorities and all of the Moslem people, and as a humble religious servant, I also stress that in the holy religion of Islam no minor detail is neglected, and no important matter is left unaddressed. Consequently, it is to my deep regret that those who in the name of Islam and in the name of responsibility hold power, and whose obligation is to enforce and protect the laws and the honor of God, have instead altered the laws of God and Islam by means of cabinet decrees [tasvib-nameh], and in the name of land reform they have weakened the principle of private property which is sacred and essential in Islam, and as the result of these usurpation rulings they have placed the Moslem people in grave difficulties. Or, contrary to the laws of religion, they have permitted the participation of women in social affairs. Strange that they believe they can alter the blessed laws of the Almighty and of the Holy Koran by means of cabinet decrees. Woe unto him who trans-

gresses or aggresses against the laws of Islam. Obviously, the laws of Islam are unalterable.

I trust that these warnings and reminders, which are given in a spirit of goodwill and purity, will be accepted and heeded. In conclusion, I wish to inform the people of my views concerning two issues.

First, seizure of the property of the people within the framework of the laws and regulations of Islam is permitted. Forceful confiscation of property by means of various decrees is unlawful and subject to the laws of usurpation. And it is among those sins that not only individual dimension but also its consequences will be the responsibility of society. Therefore, ablution and washing and prayer on such land is null and void, and the possession of such land is sinful.

Second, since the participation of women in social affairs involves private matters and the potential for much corruption and immorality, it is contrary to God's will and the laws of the Holy Islam. It is forbidden and must be stopped. May God help everyone to respect and follow the laws of Islam.

Va-al salam-o aleikom va rahmatollah-e va barakatah, 1 November 1962.
The Humblest,
Ahmad El-Moussavi El-Khonsari

Fig. 8.9. Ayatollah Haj Seyed Ahmad Khonsari.

The Ambassador's Conversations with the Shah and Alam

By late November 1962, the rising opposition of the ulama had alarmed both Prime Minister Alam and the shah. To deflect criticism, they decided to announce plans to hold parliamentary elections in June or July 1963. On 20 November 1962, the American ambassador, Julius Holmes, held his regular weekly meeting with Alam. A report of the meeting was given in a secret State Department airgram (A-318, dated 26 November 1962). The ambassador's report included the following:

> Mr. Alam then gave me an explanation of the decision to make the announcement that national elections would be held in June or July of the coming year. He said that his decision had been brought about by continued agitation on the part of the Mullahs openly criticizing the Government for a provision in the law governing municipal and provincial elections which would permit women to vote. Although this was the specific criticism offered by the Mullahs, in fact their opposition was directed at land reform and was inspired by an un-holy alliance with certain landlords. It was felt that the next move on the part of all of the opposition to the partition of land, by the Mullahs and by the landlords, would be an attack on the govern-ment on the grounds of unconstitutionality in the absence of a Majlis. Considering the fact that the distribution of land to the peas-antry will be completed before June and that this would largely eliminate the landlords' control over the peasants and in the light of the peasants' new position, a Majlis of a different character could be elected.

The next day, 21 November 1962, Ambassador Holmes had a two-hour meeting with the shah, and the meeting was described in a secret State Department airgram (A-319, dated 26 November 1962). The report in-cluded the following:

> In much the same manner as the Prime Minister had done in a conversation the day before, the Shah explained why a decision had been made to announce that elections would be held in June or July. He was even more vehement in his criticism of the Clergy than Alam had been. He felt that seeing their source of personal income disap-pearing with the elimination of the great landlords, the Mullahs were desperately trying to maintain a position of power in the coun-try which he would not permit.

Thus, by late November 1962, the shah and Alam did not plan to hold a referendum. If they had, the American ambassador would have been the first to know and report. Instead, the shah and Alam were considering how to deal with the thorny issue of the "Constitution" and the potential legal challenge, by electing a suitably appropriate Majlis. Thus, the decision to hold a referendum in January 1963 was a spontaneous one.

Ayatollah Khomeini's Declaration on the Referendum of 26 January 1963

The cabinet of Assadollah Alam issued two new decrees on 17 January 1963. One was the so-called Additional Articles, and the other nationalized Iran's forests and pastures. To obtain "national approval" of these and previous decrees, the shah held a referendum on 26 January 1963. Two issues concerning the referendum further enraged the opposition. First, in Iran's Constitution and other laws, there was no provision for a referendum. For this reason, a 1953 referendum by Mossadeq (see chap. 10) was declared to be illegal by the Pahlavi regime. Second, the entire matter was announced and hastily carried out all in nine days. In response, the Agricultural Union of Iran wrote to Ayatollah Khomeini and elicited his views on the subject of the referendum. His responses were then printed as a two-page leaflet and distributed. The leaflet is classic Khomeini:

> In the Name of the Almighty
>
> Although I did not wish to make a public statement, nevertheless, through Mr. Behboudi I informed His Majesty of the state of affairs and of the evils, and I thus did my duty. Since my views were not accepted, I must now undertake my solemn religious obligation.
>
> In my opinion, this referendum, which for the purpose of dealing with some difficulties has been termed national approval, can express the views of the Islamic religious bodies and the will of the decisive majority of the people, on the condition that there is no intimidation and corruption and bribery and that the nation is fully aware of its actions. I will not address here some of the religious issues regarding a referendum or a national approval. Such a measure, in principle, has no worth in Islam. I also will not deal with some of the legal difficulties associated with such a measure. I will only address a few general issues.
>
> 1. In Iran's laws, there is no provision for a referendum. With one exception, such a measure has no precedent.[9] Even then, it was declared to be illegal by some authorities, and some people got into difficulty and were deprived of their freedom and social

rights, on charges of having taken part in the referendum. Why was such an act declared illegal then, but it is considered legal now?

2. It is unclear which authority has the right to undertake a referendum. The law must rule on this.

3. In countries where a referendum is legal, people must be given sufficient time to examine and discuss every item, and the views of the opponents and supporters must be openly given in the press and the media. It must not be undertaken within a short notice of a few days with vague declarations and no knowledge of the people.

4. The voters must be sufficiently well informed so that they know what they are voting for. Consequently, the vast majority of the people do not have the right to vote on such matters. Only some of the inhabitants of the towns and districts who have the power to reason are qualified to vote on the Six Principles. And they are without exception opposed to the measures.

5. Voting must take place in an atmosphere that is free of all pressure, intimidation, violence, and bribery. In Iran this is not possible. Many have been bribed, and the rest of the people have been intimidated by government agencies in all parts of the country and placed under extreme pressure and difficulty.

In general, the undertaking of a referendum is for the purpose of mitigating the illegal acts of those authorities who will inevitably be held accountable and punished. It is for the benefit of those who are responsible to the people and who have misled and deceived His Majesty.

If they wish to do something for the people, why do they not adopt Islam's way and approach Islamic experts, so that with Islamic plans all the classes will be provided a comfort and happiness on earth and the everafter?

Why have they created these cooperative funds? It is to plunder the product of the cultivator. With these cooperative funds, Iran's market will be totally lost and the farmers and merchants ruined. Subsequently, the remaining classes will also be ruined.

The religious authorities sense that the Koran and religion are threatened. It appears that this tyrannical referendum is a prelude to destroy the contents of religion. On the basis of the government's past actions concerning the election of the regional and provincial

associations, the ulama of Islam feel that Islam, the Koran, and the country are in danger. It appears that the enemies of Islam want to carry out the same tricks using a group of deceived simpletons. Whenever they feel that Islam and the Koran are in danger, the ulama of Islam are duty-bound to warn the people, so that they will have done their duty in front of God. I pray for the preservation of the Great Koran and for the independence of the country.
Ruhollah El-Moussavi El-Khomeini

After such a declaration, no reconciliation was possible between the Pahlavi regime and Ayatollah Khomeini. Moreover, this episode provided a vivid illustration of the manner in which the active alliance and cooperation between landowners and the ulama, including Ayatollah Khomeini, was gradually but assuredly destroying the foundation of the Pahlavi regime.

Gathering at the House of Ayatollah Qomi in Mashhad, 20 January 1963

In a confidential report (airgram A-15, dated 24 January 1963), the American consul in Mashhad, J. P. Mulligan, reported that just three days after the promulgation of the decree of 17 January 1963, also known as the Additional Articles, about 1,000 representatives of Khorasan's small landowners had gathered at the house of Ayatollah Hasan Qomi in Mashhad, joined by Ayatollah Hadi Milani. The next day, while the wives of the petitioners went to the house of Ayatollah Milani, a paid announcement addressed to the shah appeared in the daily newspaper *Khorasan*. The American consul in Mashhad, J. P. Mulligan, submitted a confidential report (airgram A-15, dated 24 January 1963) on the rising level of unrest in Khorasan:

> According to their declarations, approximately 1,000 representatives of 10,000 small landowners in Khorasan assembled in the presence of Ayatollah Hasan Qomi and Ayatollah Hadi Milani, who are considered to be the most deeply religious and at the same time the most independent clerical leaders in Meshed [Mashhad]. These petitioners apparently hoped with good reason to obtain sympathy and support for their cause from these influential leaders. Ayatollah Qomi, the more conservative of the two, is said to have advised these petitioners to select several representatives and send them to Tehran to plead their case. Acting on this advice, two persons, Mahmoud Bahrabadi and Ali Akbar Mo' Aven, departed for Tehran

on January 22nd, with the intention of seeking an audience with the Shah. Subsequent to their departure, wives of the petitioners who signed the appeal to the Shah, as well as widows and others, have called on the more liberal minded Ayatollah Milani to request his support and advice.

Apart from the justice of the matter as they see it, many of those who are now active in appealing the Government's decision are deeply concerned that the application of this new decree will seriously deprive themselves and their dependents of adequate income on which to live. There is also a feeling that the Shah has betrayed his trust and his promise of the past that small landowners in the true sense would not be affected by the land distribution program.

It has become apparent that considerable unrest and dissatisfaction over the new amendment and strong criticism over the haste and arbitrariness with which it was prepared and announced is being voiced privately. In view of the uncertainty associated with its actual application and the pressure being applied to insure a favorable response to the "package deal" referendum, it appears doubtful that the dissatisfaction which is building up here will affect the voting which takes place several days hence.

The following is Mulligan's translation of the small landowners' appeal to the shah:

The honorable office of *Khorasan* newspaper:
It is requested that the following news be printed in your newspaper:
On January 20, 1963, about 1,000 of us, representatives of approximately 10,000 small landowners of Khorasan, have assembled in the house of His Eminence Ayatollah Qomi and in the presence of His Eminence Ayatollah Milani. While we betake ourselves to the religious authorities, it is agreed, after much talk and consultation, that all of us should unanimously request the just Shahinshah to issue orders to the Cabinet Council to revise its recent decree of January 17, because its enforcement will destroy us. Revision of said decree will make it possible for agricultural activities to be carried on, and the right of ownership to be respected. Thus, the toilers of Khorasan, as well as those in the rest of Iran, can be assured that they may feel secure to continue in their work and vocation.

Your Majesty: We, the small landowners of Khorasan, do not have any other industry or profession except farming. If, as required by the recent decree, we rent or sell our small holdings and remain unemployed ourselves, our income from rent will not be sufficient to support us and our families.

Your Majesty: Our crowned Father knows best that we, the farmers of Khorasan, have been engaged in farming all our lives; and the result of our activities and savings is only the land which we have bought with various terms and installments. Now by issuance of this decree they want to take our holdings from us. We, the distressed or the small landowners, do not know what to do.

Your Majesty: After the completion of land reform, which is a useful and benevolent action on the part of our crowned Father, we are no longer members of the upper class to be subject to the Government's love or rancor. We have, due to the years of experience and practice, become experts in farming. It is not possible for a real farmer to rent or sell his land under force. We request that the just Shahinshah issue orders that, with regard to conditions in Khorasan, a limit be established for our landholdings so that we, Your Majesty's devotees, may be engaged in farming personally.

Moreover there are hundreds, if not thousands, of very old or invalid men and women among the small landowners who earn their living merely by farming. With the enforcement of the Amendment Decree of January 17, the rights of ownership of small landowners of Iran will be terminated and their rights will be suppressed, and this is far from justice. [Signatures: 35 names printed, others not listed]

Following the protests in Tabriz and Qom on 21 March 1963, the government responded with force and even attacked the Faizieh School in Qom on 21–22 March 1963.[10] In response to this outrage and the brutal suppression of the protests, Ayatollah Khonsari and Ayatollah Behbahani issued a joint declaration:

For the Information of the People

Recent events and unexpected incidents that have taken place and are contemplated have attracted public attention and have created immense anxiety among the clergy and the Moslem people. Based on their religious duty, the ulama and the respected Sources of Emulation have searched for a solution, and in the spirit of friendly advice, they have given the necessary counsel. They are now awaiting their well-wished suggestions to be quickly heeded by the authorities. They shall keep the people informed, and the public should rest assured that the religious authorities will perform their religious duties.

The Humblest, Ahmad El-Moussavi El-Khonsari

The Servant, Mohammad El-Moussavi El-Behbahani

Some Concluding Observations

By its land distribution policies, the Pahlavi regime alienated a large and influential part of Iran's population. Not only were large, medium, and petty landowners living in the villages expropriated and driven from the villages by peasant violence. A sizable portion of the urban middle class was also adversely affected. With very limited industrial and commercial investment possibilities, purchase of agricultural land had been the investment of choice by the middle classes, including bazaar merchants,

Fig. 8.10. Ayatollah Haj Seyed Mohammad Behbahani.

traders, shopkeepers, army officers, bureaucrats, university professors, and teachers. The loss of their savings was a bitter blow to these people. Many had put their meager savings into purchasing part of a village. It was a source of income and a retirement nest. For others, this tiny income from land was all they had. As shown in chapter 12, Iran's small landowners and their dependents constituted at least 20 percent of the population. While many were ruined and lost everything, others were forced to watch as their life savings, retirement nest, and inheritance disappeared.

This situation of profound unease and turmoil had in turn greatly strengthened the position and role of the ulama. Having been totally alienated from the Pahlavi regime, and seemingly powerless to do anything about it, a large section of Iran's politically active and influential population now looked to the ulama for leadership and guidance. This was perhaps best illustrated by the appeals of the Agricultural Union of Iran to the ulama and the gathering at the house of Ayatollah Qomi in Mashhad on 20 January 1963. With the closure of parliament and the imposition of total censorship, the pulpit in the mosque and street protests became the only means available to the opposition. Perhaps never in Iran's history were the politically active people and large sections of the population so united in their opposition to what they rightly saw as grievous tyranny and injustice by the shah. In short, thanks to the misguided policies of the United States and the shah's complete obedience to these policies, a historical opportunity was created for the ulama. The genius of Ayatollah Khomeini and his historical contribution was to seize the leadership of this opposition from the very beginning.

America's Role As Seen by the Opposition

Conspiracy and Betrayal

I noted in my introduction that the U.S. government actively promoted land distribution in several countries where it yielded influence. My father, Mohammad Ali Majd, was convinced that land distribution in Iran, particularly the manner in which it was enforced and implemented, was all instigated by the U.S. government. He repeatedly stresses in his memoirs that the 1960 land distribution law approved by Iran's parliament was never implemented because the Kennedy administration did not feel it would serve long-term U.S. plans in Iran. While the avowed intention of the Americans was to avert communism through land distribution, the opposition saw it as a conspiracy to destroy Iran's agriculture and its independence. Majd claims that the destruction of Iran's landowning class and its agriculture was a carefully designed American plan begun in the early 1950s that culminated in the 1962 land distribution cabinet decree. The intention was to destroy Iran's agriculture and make the country dependent on food imports, and thus force it to sell oil in exchange for food. Another aim was the destruction of Iran's political elite and leadership. Thus, the violation of Iran's Constitution, the religious and civil laws perpetrated by the Iranian government, the rural lawlessness and violence directed at landowners, the confiscation and disenfranchisement of Iran's landowners, including the huge class of petty landowners—all were done at the urging of the U.S. government. Inevitably, Mohammad Reza Shah, Ali Amini, Hasan Arsanjani, Assadollah Alam, and others who served the shah were seen by the opposition as traitors and willing collaborators with the foreign oppressors. The same view was expounded by Ayatollah Khomeini with devastating effect in the 1960s and 1970s. In this devilish design, Iran's landowning population and their dependents, conservatively estimated at 5 million, were readily sacrificed.

According to Majd, the Iranian government adopted a policy of "cheap food" in 1955, or after the dismissal of Zahedi, who was a landowner. The avowed aim of the policy was to benefit the urban residents and prevent a rise in food prices in the cities. Given that 75 percent of Iran's population resided in rural areas and thus depended on agricultural income, this policy was highly regressive. It also hampered agricultural growth and economic development. In an entry he wrote 17 May 1968 in the village of Pelet Kaleh in Zavar, Majd gives the following account:

Rare was a landowner who was not heavily in debt. Everything had increased in price except wheat and barley. In order to keep bread cheap in the cities, the government prevented a rise in wheat prices. In 1955, during the government of the late Hosein Ala, the Americans signed a deal with Iran whereby on the pretext of financial assistance to the army, 200,000 tons of wheat were to be given to Iran on two conditions. First, the price at which this wheat was to be sold was to be determined by the Americans. Second, 30 percent of the revenue accrued to the American embassy and 70 percent to the government as assistance to the army. The quantities of wheat imported increased over the years. From that day, wheat and barley production did not see a happy day.

From that year on, and based on carefully crafted American plans, the situation of landowners and landownership deteriorated. The villages were either not profitable or only slightly profitable. The cultivators also were in great difficulty due to the fall in the price of wheat and barley. This added to the burden of the landowners, who had to support their cultivators as well. In short, from this date on, 90 percent of the landowners were forced to borrow. Even with land as collateral, landowners had to borrow at 24 percent interest per year. If a landowner borrowed 100,000 tomans in 1955, by 1959, he owed 200,000 tomans. By 1963, the debt had grown to 400,000 tomans. By 1967, this unfortunate individual owed a staggering 800,000 tomans. What I write is not a story but the reality that befell 5 million of Iran's inhabitants. Following the land distribution cabinet decree, a red line was drawn around 55,000 privately owned villages. First, under the decree, the landowners could no longer sell the property. Even if they could, no one would come forward to buy, and the land was worthless. Second, no one would lend to the landowners and accept land as collateral. Third, the government seized everything except one village and would pay whatever it wished over fifteen years. The one village that was left to the landowner provided no benefit because the peasants would not pay any rent. Under the provisions of the Phase Two decree, even that one village was to be sold to the cultivators, leased for thirty years to the cultivators, or divided with the cultivators. Only under the sale option have the interests of a few landowners been satisfied somewhat. The thirty-year lease provision is a joke. The division option has not been practical because landowners often do not reside in the village, and there is a continuous conflict and dispute over water and land boundaries. Most often, out of envy and anger, the villagers destroy the landowners' summer and winter crops. Under Article 33 of the regulations, the Land Reform Organization is empowered to act as the complainant, prosecutor, and judge, and it always rules in favor of the cultivators. The landowners' only recourse is to appeal to the Almighty.

Conspiracy versus Ignorance

The reality was more complex because the attack on landowners and traditional landownership had actually begun under Reza Shah. The same policy was continued by his son and successor. It is difficult to subscribe to a conspiracy theory in matters of foreign policy.[1] For instance, the wheat aid that Majd refers to was part of the PL 480 program, which gave surplus American grain to many countries in exchange for domestic currency. It could hardly be construed as conspiracy. It is, however, evident that the U.S. policy was flawed with respect to land and agriculture in Iran because it was, at least initially, based on ignorance and assumptions that were entirely wrong. Concerning the ownership of land, it appears that, despite excellent consular reports (see chap. 12), American policymakers continued to believe that nearly all of Iran's land was owned by a small number of individuals. For example, there were articles in the American press in 1961 stating that of the 45,000 villages in Iran, 42,000 were owned by 1,000 families. This was utterly false. One source of such a grossly inaccurate figure appears to have been a landownership "survey" undertaken by the U.S. army in the 1950s, which reported that 57 percent of all villages were owned by 400–500 landowners.[2] Such "studies" simply reinforced Lambton's erroneous conclusions. Based on the 1960 census of agriculture, less than 20 percent of the land was actually owned by large landowners, and half was actually owned by a huge number of petty landowners. This was the inevitable outcome of the Islamic practice of matrimony and inheritance.

Another issue about which American policymakers appear to have been at least initially ill-informed is that of rural landlessness. By giving land to the landless tenants, it was believed, communism would be averted and greater political stability achieved. As it was repeatedly stated in the publications and bulletins of the Agricultural Union of Iran and in letters to visiting American officials, Iran did not have a problem of landlessness. The situation in Iran was totally different from such densely populated countries as South Korea, Taiwan, the Philippines, and Egypt, where the limit of cultivation had been reached long ago, and where there was an acute shortage of land. Given the land shortage and the high labor to land ratio, landowners were in a strong bargaining position and could easily evict a tenant and have him replaced by someone else. Under these conditions, tenants held the land for a fixed term, and annual contracts were widespread. In Egypt, land was often leased to a tenant for a period of one year.[3]

In contrast to these countries, the thinly populated Iran was a country with much uncultivated land and a shortage of labor and capital. I pointed out above that total cultivated land in Iran in 1960 was 5 million hectares, and potentially an additional 20–30 million hectares could have been brought under cultivation with appropriate investment in mechanization and irrigation. During the 1950s and 1960s, Iran possessed large areas of uncultivated land even in the fertile Caspian region.[4] In this condition of land abundance, agricultural tenants and sharecroppers held secure rights of tenure to the land and could not easily be evicted by the landowners, nor was there an incentive to evict them. These rights of tenure were known variously (depending on the region) as *nasaq*, root rights, *karafe*, ax clearing, etc. These rights were so important that they are even mentioned in the contracts between Reza Shah and the peasants of Zavar (see appendix A). These tenure rights were inherited by the tenant's heirs, and the so-called tenants gave land as dowry and often "traded" land among themselves. Contrary to American misconceptions, the sharecroppers and tenants were not "landless." Since the tenants were in possession of the land and could not be evicted, they were the real owners. This situation was a reflection of, and indeed possible because of land abundance. Another important indicator was the relatively low levels of rent paid by tenants even in the Caspian region (see chap. 11). The low rents and secure rights of tenure that extended to the tenant's offspring could not have existed in a situation of land shortage and high population density. The real "landless" and vulnerable population of Iran was the huge class of petty landowners, who often owned a small fraction of a dang. The situation in Iran was radically different from what American policymakers and officials had experienced in Southeast Asia.

These intricacies and complexities of landownership and tenure had been explained to American officials residing in Iran and to the visiting senior officials, such as Vice President Lyndon B. Johnson and presidential adviser Chester Bowles. It had also been pointed out that the landowner fulfilled an essential role in Iran's agriculture. In conditions of semi-arid cultivation, the landowners established qanats and new villages and ensured the maintenance of the irrigation infrastructure. Moreover, some of the most productive and developed villages of Iran in 1960 were the ones that had been "privatized" during the 1930s, when the ownership of some government-owned (khaliseh) villages had been transferred to private individuals. In the case study given in chapters 3 and 11, a group of highly neglected and "ruined" villages had been privatized in 1935 (the Zavar exchange). By 1960, these privatized villages were among the most productive in Iran. The landowner invested large sums in these villages and established several qanats. In addition, the outcome of land distribution was very unfavorable in Sistan during the 1930s and in Pahlavi estates in Takestan, Garmsar, and Varamin during the 1950s. According to Majd, all had experienced large declines in agricultural output. The land recipients in Varamin and Garmsar had become mostly migrant wage earners in Tehran. Cotton production had ceased in Garmsar. The qanats in Takestan had all but dried up, and Sistan had become dependent on wheat imports from Pakistan. Distribution of khaliseh land in Fars had fared no better, and many of the cultivators had migrated to the other side of the Persian Gulf. All of this had been explained repeatedly to the American officials, as well as to the Iranian government, but to no avail. It is not surprising that the opposition had reached the conclusion that land distribution was a plot to "destroy" Iran's agriculture and force it to sell oil in exchange for food.

Majd's Relationship with American Officials

The political activities of Mohammad Ali Majd following his forced departure from the Senate, the founding of the Agricultural Union of Iran, and its activities as an independent political body caught the attention of the American and British missions in Iran. My father's emergence as a serious politician not linked to the shah elicited the keen interest of the American embassy, which initiated contact with him in 1959. Hoping to be able to influence U.S. policy, Majd welcomed the overture. Between 1959 and 1961, he had extensive contacts with two members of the American mission: General John C. Hayden, chief of the U.S. military mission in Iran, and senior diplomat James C. O'Neil. In time Majd came to regard these Americans as friends.

Majd's account indicates that the U.S. government wielded enormous power and influence in Iran during the 1950s and 1960s. Through the control of the military and security apparatus, Hayden and O'Neil believed they could appoint and dismiss governments, and to Majd's astonishment and consternation, they even discussed removing the shah himself. Majd's account points to real divisions within the American government in regard to its policy in Iran. Despite Eisenhower's 1959 visit, some American foreign policymakers were unhappy with the shah and were evidently contemplating a new coup. In preparation, they wished to establish working relationships with other politicians, including my father. Such relationships ended, however, with the 1960 presidential election. In 1961, the Kennedy administration confirmed its support for the shah. O'Neil left Iran in August 1961. A few months later, Majd wrote to the American embassy but did not receive a reply. Instead, his letter was forwarded to Arsanjani and published in a British newspaper. Arsanjani then called a press conference to accuse the landowners of treason. For Majd and his associates, this was further proof that land distribution was instigated by the U.S. government and was thus a plot to destroy Iran's agriculture. The letter's publication in the British newspaper also "proved" to landowners that Arsanjani was a British agent who had been recruited by Ann Lambton of the British embassy. To preserve accuracy, Majd's account of his conversations with Hayden and O'Neil is given:

From 1959, American personnel assigned to the army, police, and gendarmerie, as well as agents of the CIA, became very friendly with me. Of the Americans that I dealt with, an amicable relationship was established with General Hayden, who was chief of the U.S. military mission in Iran, a man of considerable and attractive personality who subsequently after leaving Iran became chief of the American army in New York, and Mr. O'Neil, a very clever person who at first introduced himself as General Hayden's deputy, but then it became evident that he was a senior official who had long served in South Korea. I was frequently invited to their homes and to the American Club for lunch, dinner, and afternoon tea. Both my wife and I were very warmly greeted and treated at these gatherings by our American hosts.

O'Neil came to see me at least three times a week in the morning and afternoon and discussed the situation in Iran. The gist of his conversation was that America harbored no territorial ambitions in Iran, but desired only the progress and independence of the country. He stressed that Iran had a strategic importance for the United

States, and if Iran was attacked by Russia, the United States would go to war. The aims of American policy that were portrayed by O'Neil, that is, progress and independence of Iran, were also shared by me. In this way, I developed a solid friendship with General Hayden and O'Neil. They both asked me to cooperate and assist them in their efforts. I accepted, and then I asked General Hayden why I had been selected and if there were many other politicians like me with whom the U.S. government had established secret relations. He assured me that of the many friends in Iran, I was the most trusted, respected, and valued friend. He said that they had found a book that a Swiss writer had written about Iran between 1932 and 1948. Fully twenty-eight pages of the book were devoted to my services and in particular my resistance to the communists. The writer had said that in his opinion, I was the only patriotic politician he had seen in Iran. General Hayden said that they had made extensive inquiries about me and found that I was anticommunist, honest, well informed, and had no links to foreign governments. That is why they had pursued my friendship. At the time of President Eisenhower's visit to Iran, a group of Secret Service agents had come to Iran to guard him. At the suggestion of General Hayden, I invited all thirty-three of them to a dinner reception at my house one evening. Before becoming prime minister, Dr. Amini came to see me one day, and he asked me to put in a good word for him with my friends. He had heard of my close relationship and influence with the Americans.

The Americans often sought information on political figures and asked many questions. I would tell them frankly all I knew, and ten or fifteen days later, during a meeting O'Neil would declare that he had made his own inquiries, and what I had said about a particular individual was correct. Since I do not wish to sully reputations, I will not name any names.

My relationship with General Hayden was very warm. One day he suggested that in order to converse more freely and without pressure, he and I should take a trip. I suggested that we should go to Pelet Kaleh in Zavar. I invited General Hayden, his wife, daughter, and son, and in the summer of 1960, they were my guests for one week in Pelet Kaleh. During their stay, my house was closely guarded by the police and the gendarmerie. In order to show them that the cultivators in Iran are not really poor and show them the conditions in which the peasants lived, for several days I took them to lunch on several occasions to the houses of farmers in the villages of Kotra and Talusarak. They saw firsthand the conditions of the farmers and were greatly surprised at the comfort and cleanliness of their houses.

Unspeakable Secrets

Our conversations continued for a considerable time. My suggestion for the best way to reform in Iran was through the Majlis and the Senate and the election of honest and patriotic people. This will result in good government because the prime minister must receive a vote of confidence and be confirmed by the Majlis. Similar to the Fourteenth Majlis, this will result in the appointment of such individuals as Saed, Qavam Saltaneh, and Sadr ol Ashraaf. Second, the government will be responsible to the Majlis and under its supervision. For its own survival, such a government will desist from actions that are contrary to the interests of the country, bad laws will not pass, and those that exist will be reformed.

O'Neil invited me one day to lunch at the Club Tehran [the British club]. As I spoke little English, and O'Neil's French was poor, I took along Dr. Asad Behrouzan to act as interpreter. During the conversation at lunch, I suggested that the United States should reach an

Fig. 9.1. *From left:* Amirzadeh Razieh Majd, Touran Akbar, General John C. and Mrs. Hayden, Amir Banou Majd, Miss Hayden, Narges Mehre Monir Majd, and Brigadier Zia ad Din Khalatbari, deputy chief of the Tehran police. Pelet Kaleh, Zavar, August 1960.

accommodation with the shah, because His Majesty was greatly interested in reform and development of the country. Astonishingly, O'Neil said that the United States would get rid of the shah. Greatly upset and angered that Iran had sunk to a position whereby foreigners could so easily entertain such designs, I responded that the shah could not be overthrown because the people of Iran were monarchists and loved their king. He said, "Where were the people of Iran when Reza Shah was so unceremoniously thrown out?" I said, "That was during the war, when the country was under foreign occupation. Besides, Reza Shah abdicated in favor of his son, the current shah." He said that the United States had total control of the army, the police, and the gendarmerie, and could do as it pleased. I said, "Suppose you control the army and can depose the shah? Who will you put in his place? The only way is for a republic to be declared." He agreed. Who will be president? Mossadeq? If Mossadeq, then you will have brought your own enemy to power. If not Mossadeq, then given the strength of the Tudeh Party and its activities, the president will be a friend of Russia and not America. He said, "We will carry out a coup d'état." I said, "By whom?" He said the coup will be by one of these four: 1. General Alavi Moqadam, chief of police; 2. General Kia, army chief of staff; 3. General Bakhtiar, chief of security organization; 4. General Azizi, chief of gendarmerie.

He was most interested in Azizi. I asked if these people had been contacted and informed of the plan. He said, "Absolutely not. We are only in the exploration stage, and we wish to consult with you." I said, "Please do not even contemplate such raw and dangerous action. First, these officers are loyal to the shah and will not betray him. Even if you succeed in the coup, it will be the beginning of endless trouble for Iran and America, and Iran will eventually fall to the communists." He said that he would convey my response to the appropriate individuals, and the meeting came to an end. For nine months the conversation concerning this matter continued, and I pointed out to both General Hayden and Mr. O'Neil the consequences of such a raw and dangerous action. I pressed them until they both assured me that I had convinced them and they were no longer considering a coup.

Several times I went to the Court and requested an audience with His Majesty. Each time I was told by Mr. Behbudi that His Majesty was too busy to see anyone. Unable to get an audience, I informed Mr. Alam of the outlines of my conversations, and he undertook to inform His Majesty.

My contacts with the Americans were interrupted from 2 January 1961 until the end of April 1961 because of my trip to Europe. After my return, our social interactions and conversations resumed. At the suggestion of the Americans, Dr. Amini was appointed prime minister in May 1961. Because of the appointment of Arsanjani, I had terminated all contacts with Amini. Although only a few months had elapsed since the appointment of Amini, rumors of American dissatisfaction with Amini became rife. General Hayden and O'Neil came to see me and stated that Dr. Amini lacked experience and talked too much. Someone else was needed. I suggested Mr. Mansur ol Molk (Ali Mansur) and Mr. (Mehdi) Farrokh. It was decided that they should come to my house one night and meet Mr. Mansur ol Molk and Mr. Farrokh. The meeting was held at my house, and General Hayden, Mr. O'Neil, Mr. Mansur ol Molk, and Mr. Farrokh all came to my house. The next day Hayden and O'Neil came to see me and said, "Mr. Mansur ol Molk is highly experienced and wise, but according to our investigation, he is very close to the British government, and he will never sacrifice British interests for the sake of the Americans. Mr. Farrokh is very impatient and prone to rash decisions. In the end we decided that you should become prime minister, and we request that you accept the post." I thanked them and declined the offer. They asked for reasons. I said that I had recently undergone surgery in London and had been forbidden by my physicians to work excessively. They insisted, and I persisted in my refusal. The real reasons for my refusal were as follows:

1. Since the source of my appointment to the post of prime minister was the Americans, I would have been completely in their service, and this was contrary to the principles of patriotism by which I had lived.
2. I lack the characteristics that are dear to the shah. I do not flatter, and I am outspoken and will do whatever is in the interest of the country. These characteristics have resulted in the shah's dislike of me. Although I personally like the shah and wish him well in serving the country, if I were imposed on him, his hostility would increase.
3. I was surrounded by debt. With two years of drought in Qazvin since 1959, I had been obliged to borrow for my living expenses, to borrow just to pay the interest and the investment needs of my villages. Even my cultivators, especially those of Jamjerd and Khoznein where the drought was most severe,

had become a burden on me. If I had become prime minister, I could not have possibly settled my debts.

In any event, for the above reasons, right or wrong, I turned down the suggestion of General Hayden and Mr. O'Neil. Again I advised them that instead of going to this and that person, they should come to terms with the shah, and the shah would meet their demands.

British Ambassador in Pelet Kaleh

In the summer of 1961, Brigadier General Zia ad Din Khalatbari, deputy chief of police, came to see me one day. He informed me that since the British ambassador, Sir Geoffrey Harrison, wished to spend a few days as my guest on the Caspian Sea, I should extend an invitation. I invited the British ambassador and his wife, who happened to be the daughter of Sir Reader Bullard, the British ambassador during the events of August 1941, and they were my guests in my humble house in Pelet Kaleh. Our conversation centered mostly on land reform. I tried to convince them that the actions by the government and the American insistence on land reform were against Iran's interest and to the benefit of the communists. They never expressed an opinion, and from time to time, they asked a few questions and sought clarification. To show them that, contrary to Miss Lambton's writings, Iranian cultivators were not poor, I invited them one day for lunch in the house of Hosein Aqai in the village of Kotra, then for lunch to the house of Ehsani in the village of Talusarak, and then to lunch in the House of Haj Qorban in the village of Habib Abad. They could not believe that the villages of northern Iran were so prosperous, and the cultivators lived in such comfort. After his return to Tehran, the ambassador wrote the following letter to me:

British Embassy
Tehran
18 July 1961

Dear Mr. Majd,

I write to you to convey our warmest and very sincere thanks for the generous hospitality that you extended to us during our visit to Shahsavar. We greatly appreciated the wonderful arrangements you made for our reception and entertainment, and we particularly enjoyed the opportunity you gave us of seeing some of your villages. The few days we were privileged to spend as your guests will be amongst our happiest memories of Iran.

With warmest regards to yourself and your family, and with
our renewed thanks,

I am,

Yours very sincerely,

G. W. Harrison

Letter to the American Embassy and Its Publication
in the *Manchester Evening News*

Early in 1962, with land distribution in progress in the Maragheh district
of Azarbaijan, presidential adviser Chester Bowles visited Iran and expressed satisfaction with the implementation of land distribution. On 14
February 1962, Majd sent the following letter to Bowles on behalf of the
Agricultural Union of Iran.

It has been reported in the Tehran newspapers that in a news conference you held at Tehran Airport, you stated that the distribution of
land and the implementation of land reform have been met with a
very positive response in Washington. You also said that you had
come to Iran on a fact-finding mission. In welcoming you to Iran, in
the name of the people of Iran, we are duty-bound to bring the following to your attention:

1. Land cultivated each year in Iran is about 5–6 million hectares.
   To provide for his family's needs and subsistence, each farmer
   needs at least 10 hectares of land. One-third of the land consists
   of Crown lands, government lands, or endowments and are
   not subject to this law. One-third of land is the property of small
   landowners, which is also exempt from this law. Thus, only
   one-third of the land is subject to division. Consequently, only
   200,000 cultivators will receive land. The remainder of the rural population, said to be 15 million by the minister of agriculture, will not receive land. This in itself will result in conflict
   between land recipients and those without land. Much to the
   satisfaction of the communists, the domestic conflict, and the
   breakdown of law and order that results from land distribution, will surely propel the country toward communism.
2. The Crown lands and government-owned villages that have
   been distributed in recent years are in a state of ruin, with the
   cultivators impoverished and scattered as migrants to Tehran
   and other towns. The villages that have been distributed in
   Varamin and Garmsar in Tehran, Takestan in Qazvin, and

Fig. 9.2. *From right:* General Atapour, Haj Qahreman, Lady Harrison, Narges Mehre Monir Majd, son of Sir and Lady Harrison (wife of the British ambassador), Zahra Ghazavi Majd, Brigadier Zia ad Din Khalatbari, and an unidentified police officer. At the house of Haj Qorban, village of Habib Abad in Zavar, summer 1961.

Fariman in Khorasan are now all in a state of ruin, and the cultivators are impoverished.

3. Sadly, if these types of actions and propaganda continue, the seeds of communism will have been planted in all the villages, and soon Iran will become communist, thanks to our own actions. During the past year, as the result of the propaganda by the current minister of agriculture, who is a well-known communist, agricultural production has declined by at least 50 percent all over Iran, resulting in scarcity, poverty, famine, and distress for the cultivators, well-known causes of communism.

4. There is no feudal lord or serf in Iran. Everywhere, the cultivators are the real owners of the land, and excellent relations between the cultivator and owner existed. We have brought all of the above to the attention of the authorities, but it is claimed

that the purpose of the above law is to satisfy the American government, and it is undertaken by the Iranian government even though it is fully aware that it is totally contrary to the interests of Iran and America.

We shall be very happy to give additional verbal explanations. In order to give additional clarification, please let us know when representatives of the Agricultural Union of Iran can meet with you, or we will be happy to meet with experts who are designated by you.

Failing to elicit a response from Mr. Bowles, and based on his friendly relations with O'Neil and General Hayden, my father and the Agricultural Union of Iran wrote a letter to the American embassy in Tehran. The letter was accompanied by the two-page bulletin entitled "Some Instances of Insecurity and Lawlessness in Maragheh Region" (see chap. 7). The exact text of the letter, dated 16 April 1962 (with no editorial correction by this author), is given in appendix C. Here, only excerpts will be given. The letter stated:

That which takes place in Maragheh now, coincides with that which Lenin in the beginning of his rule carried out in the vast country of Russia. Lenin allowed the peasants, backed by the Red Army soldiers, to confiscate lands and to drive away the owners from their home. Today, this actually takes place in Maragheh, supervised by communist leaders whose names are recorded in the archives of the Security Organization. . . . Now, under the leadership of well-known communists, our simple-minded peasants are led to tread upon their religion and to overthrow their country's laws and rules, and these communists then attribute these actions to the persistent demands of American policy in the Middle East. . . . Thus you are compelling our country to neglect her religion and to forego the rights of her people. Strange and mysterious policies are very ably creating a general hatred against the American government. . . . The nation of Iran is that very same nation which assimilated within herself the attacks of Alexander and Changhiz, and is yet alive and proud; this very nation will sooner or later repel this present danger which threatens us and which is unfortunately strengthened by your financial aid and the leadership of communists.

This letter was leaked by the American embassy to Arsanjani and parts were printed in the *Manchester Evening News* on 15 May 1962. In a press conference on May 31, Arsanjani accused the landowners of treason and threatened them with prosecution. Arsanjani's news conference received prominent coverage in the national daily *Keyhan* on 1 June 1962.

At 1:30 P.M. yesterday, the minister of agriculture, Dr. Arsanjani, held a news conference. At first he stated, "The implementation of land reform in the announced areas is rapidly progressing. In addition to the six townships where the implementation announcements have been published, in the very near future the announcements will be published for the rest of the country. During the past few days, patriotic landowners from all parts of Iran have announced their readiness to place their estates at the disposal of the government for distribution to the cultivators. These actions have considerably eased our tasks, and this is contrary to the pessimistic views by some who have held that resistance by landowners will hinder the implementation of the law. These pessimistic individuals must desist from their intrigues. Most of the landowners in Fars, Kerman, Sanandaj, and Kermanshahan have suggested to me their willingness to transfer their lands to the government. I thank them for their goodwill, and I hope land reform can soon be implemented in the whole of Iran."

Trip to Europe

On the subject of his trip to Europe, the minister of agriculture said, "I have been invited by the government of Yugoslavia to go there and closely inspect the system of agriculture there. Afterwards, I will go to several other European countries for the purpose of medical treatment. The duration of my trip to Europe will be up to four weeks. In my absence, Mr. Engineer Qaragouzlou, head of the Irrigation Bureau, will be in charge of the Land Reform Council, and other responsible members of the Ministry will continue in their tasks, and the regional heads of the Land Reform Organization will be fully watchful so that the implementation of the law in the announced regions proceeds accordingly. I am hopeful that the implementation of the law will be completed in three provinces and the necessary announcements issued in the remaining provinces and the law implemented."

Referring to comments made by foreign radios, the minister of agriculture said, "I do not wish to respond to their comments, because they are free to make any comments they like. But for the information of the Iranian people, I must address this issue. In the villages of Esfarain, when the land was distributed among the cultivators, the cultivators of the neighboring villages were willing to pay in cash three times the price of the land assessed on the land recipients. In Gilan, the best land has been distributed among the cultivators. The annual installment paid for the land by the cultivators is one-third of the rent they previously paid to the landowners. To those who criticize us, they should go to the scene and talk to the farmers and then assess the validity of our claims. During this time, foreign ambassadors, members of the foreign press, and other groups of people have gone to the villages that have been divided and observed the situation firsthand. If they wished to criticize us, it would have been more helpful if they offered constructive criticism."

Referring to the participation of the people, the cultivators and all landowners in the development projects, the minister of agriculture added, "If we rely on government revenues for development projects, the amount of government revenue is clear. It is either from taxes or the sale of oil. Oil revenues belong to all the people. I do not believe that the 10 percent that we obtain from the cultivators for the development of the villages is contrary to social justice. If it is unjust, then I do not know what social justice is. Such statements are broadcast by radio stations that are against all reform."

The Minister of Agriculture had this to say on the intrigues of a few landowners: "The *Manchester Evening News* in its issue of 15 May 1962 has printed an article" (At this time the introduction of the article was handed out to the reporters.) "It stated: 'The wealthy and powerful Iranian landowners claim that America is helping communism in Iran. The group of landowners are resisting the new land reform program in Iran, and have written letters to Washington, stating America is forcing Iran to undertake a revolutionary project that will ultimately benefit communism. In a letter to the American embassy in Tehran, the Agricultural Union of Iran has stated that surprising and mysterious policies are creating hatred toward the American government. The members of the Union, some of whom own countless villages, claim that the distribution of their land, and the eradication of feudalism in favor of small landowners, will deliver part of the Iranian soil to Khruschev.'"

The Minister of Agriculture then said, "If these reports are true, then it must be said that it brings shame and dishonor to those who perpetrated it. According to the newspaper, a group of landowners under the name of the Agricultural Union, whose existence is probably unknown to the vast majority of landowners, have written to foreign governments requesting that they put a stop to land reform. These gentlemen believe that if land distribution is implemented, patriotism will disappear, and the people will become communist. To maintain their own interests, they have appealed to foreign governments and have thus sacrificed their own national honor. To benefit the millions of Iranian people, we shall sacrifice these traitors who appeal to foreign governments. If this published document is correct, then each and every one of its authors must be put on trial on charges of treason. I am certain that the vast majority of landowners detest and are ashamed of such actions. I saw in Gilan and elsewhere that landowners voluntarily came forward to transfer their property. As His Majesty has said, land belongs to the cultivator who works it.

"I warn these traitors and troublemakers with evil pasts, who as landowners have been the source of misery and oppression of millions of people, that they will be tried on charges of treason and appeal to foreigners and brought to justice. What form does appeal to foreigners take? It was these same people who placed Iran in danger every day. They would appease the aggressor and surrender their country. These will be terminated forever."

At the end, the minister of agriculture said, "This year's crop rightfully belongs to the cultivators. In other areas where the implementation of the law has not been announced, the cultivators must give the owners their share of the crop until their turn comes. Cultivators must not become instruments in the hands of those who appeal to foreigners and believe that foreigners can stop or help a reform measure. Shame on these lowdown landowners who for the sake of their unlawful interests are willing to sacrifice their national honor."

Finally, it appears that the Agricultural Union of Iran made one last attempt to sway American policy. During Vice President Johnson's visit in August 1962, they sent him a five-page letter describing the government policy and predicting some of the consequences. I found this letter, dated 25 August 1962, among my father's papers. Prophetically, the letter warned Johnson that U.S. policy was misguided and dangerous for both Iran and the United States. It stated that neither the government nor society in Iran could long survive the consequences of the actions taken by the government of Iran. Johnson apparently never responded.

Letter from a Visiting American Professor to Dean Rusk, Secretary of State

In 1963, Dr. George A. Meyer, professor emeritus at Utah State University, visited a former student in Mashhad, Khorasan. Meyer spent six weeks in Iran. Upon his return home, he wrote to Dean Rusk about the plight of Iranian landowners. Meyer's letter, dated 2 June 1963, is revealing and is given in full:

Dear Mr. Secretary,

At the time of your recent visit to Iran, there appeared in Keyhan a statement from you that the United States will give full support to the Land Reform Program in Iran. The announcement was received with some misgivings by numerous persons, American as well as Iranian, who feel that injustices have been and are being done to certain landholders under the program as it has been administered by Mr. Arsanjani and sub-officials charged with carrying out the plan.

I wish to tell you briefly about two of the persons affected. I attempted to reassure them that our government would certainly not want to sponsor injustices perpetrated under the law, and that every effort should be made by those affected to bring their cases before competent authorities, perhaps the American Agricultural Attaché, or some official of the Iranian government who would take cognizance of their situation. While visiting one of my former students in Meshed, I made the acquaintance of his five uncles who are all farmers who inherited 2,000 hectares of undeveloped land that had never been cultivated because of lack of water. One uncle, Hassan Shayegi-Neek, seems to have been the driving force. He has installed six diesel driven pumping stations and developed an irrigation system that enables them to crop most of the land. He uses all types of modern equipment: tractors, ploughs, disks, etc., and employs chemical fertilizers with expert care. I saw lush stands of wheat and barley nearing harvest, beets ready for thinning and huge areas being planted to melons.

In an area where there were no inhabitants ten years ago, there are now twenty villages and a population of 2,000. His tenants are making 40,000 rials annually, seven times the average of villages under many other landlords. He is trying to see that they all increase their take. At the age of 53, he is still a hard-working farmer, with ulcers, who never travels to Europe, doesn't put his profits in the bank, but always re-invests in improvements and in the villages, which are models of their kind. Under the Land Reform Law he has been told that he will receive a total of 120,000 tomans, payable in 15 yearly installments. The land now brings him 200,000 tomans annually. He feels terribly let down with the prospect of having his "baby" to which he has given his whole life, taken from him. Telegrams and written appeals to the government have gone un-answered. He sees no future other than to migrate to the States, where some of his children are in school.

I told him that I was going to have dinner with Dr. Ali Pasha Saleh in Teheran in a few days, and that I would put his case before Dr. Saleh, to see whether there was any recourse for him, either at the American Embassy or with the Department of Agriculture. I urged that he go to Teheran and talk to Dr. Saleh and possibly to Mr. Engelretson. He felt that he was not smart enough with talk to make any impression.

When I dined with Dr. Saleh, he listened with a quizzical smile to the story, and then said, "You are talking to a man who is in the same situation as Mr. Shayegi-Neek." He then told me that he and his wife had put all their savings in a relatively small piece of land to which they wanted to retire after his service at Teheran University ceased. But the Land Reform Program was taking it from them at a ridiculously low figure, and none of his appeals had received any response.

Knowing of his long and honorable service to the U.S. Embassy, as well as to Teheran University, I decided that I would bring his case to the attention of the Department of State, and suggest that our government may have some obligation to the people of Iran to ensure that Land Reform does not blindly, with meat-ax techniques, play havoc with the lives and efforts of persons who have given their own intelligence and energies unstintingly to building a better future for Iran.

On 17 June 1963, M. Gordon Tiger, the officer in charge of Iranian affairs, responded:

Your letter of June 2 to the Secretary has been referred to this office for reply.

You may be interested to learn that since you were in Iran General Esmail Riahi has replaced Hassan Arsanjani as Minister of Agriculture. General Riahi is known as an able administrator and has stated his intention to carry out the Land Reform Law with due regard for the interests and legal rights of both landlords and peasants.

The Secretary did indeed state that land reform in Iran enjoyed the full support of the United States. While this is primarily an internal Iranian problem, I am certain that Americans everywhere wish to see this policy of social reform carried out in a manner that is fair and just to all.

Please do not hesitate to write to me, whenever you feel I may be of further assistance.

Suppressing the Opposition and Silencing the Agricultural Union of Iran

With all other forms of political activity closed, the opposition resorted to street protests. The governments of Ali Amini and Assadollah Alam responded violently. On the front page of the national daily *Etela-at* on 20 July 1961 (no. 10559), Hasan Arsanjani, spokesman for the government of Ali Amini and minister of agriculture, announced that any demonstrations planned for the next day "would be crushed by the government with the utmost force." These demonstrations would commemorate the 21 July 1952 protests that had toppled the government of Ahmad Qavam, Arsanjani's late boss, and had returned Mossadeq to power. The next day, protesters were attacked by police and the army, and many were arrested.[1]

The next major confrontation came on 21 January 1962, shortly after the issuing of the land distribution cabinet decree. Paratroopers attacked a large protest rally at Tehran University, killing or injuring many students. This attack was compared at the time to a second "Mongol invasion." Amini claimed that the protests were financed by landowners, and he charged that Mohammad Ghoreishi had contributed 150,000 tomans and had pledged 350,000 more. Student protests clearly showed the unhappiness of the urban middle classes.

Protests of 5–8 June 1963

In September 1962, a large protest rally was held in Qom. After the approval of the Additional Articles and the nationalization of forests and pastures in January 1963, large-scale demonstrations resumed. On 21 March 1963, paratroopers attacked the Faizieh School in Qom. In response to this outrage, there were protests in Qom, Mashhad, and Tabriz in April 1963. Few people were prepared for the events of June 1963.

A day after the arrest of Ayatollah Khomeini, on 5 June 1963, which corresponded to the most somber Shia day of mourning commemorating the martyrdom of Imam Hosein in Karbala (Ashura), riots erupted in Tehran and several other cities. They continued for three days and were brutally suppressed by the army, with a large number of protesters killed or injured. It was a defining event for both sides. It is now seen as the beginning of the Islamic Revolution, and as such it is a hallowed date in the history of the anti-Pahlavi resistance. It was the beginning of the end for the Pahlavi regime. As this study has shown, the timing and the force of the uprising cannot be understood without considering the plight of the small landowners, who had been driven from the villages and had lost everything, and the opposition of the middle class, who had lost their life savings.

Assadollah Alam had much to say about the uprising. When he was appointed prime minister in July 1962, he believed that his main task was to suppress opposition to land distribution.[2] Mounting opposition culminated in the protests of 5 June 1963. In his diaries, Alam repeatedly blamed the "disturbances" on the alliance between the ulama and the landowners. He displayed much pride at having suppressed the alliance of *akhnd-ha* (pejorative term for the ulama) and *feodal-ha va khavanin* (the terms used to portray landowners and tribal leaders). It was Alam who ordered the troops to open fire on demonstrators. In his diaries, Alam compared the killing of demonstrators on 5 June to the 1935 bloody incident in the holy shrine of Imam Reza in Mashhad, in which two hundred protesters and opponents of Reza Shah's unveiling of women were killed by machine-gun fire. Alam claimed that the Mashhad incident had been "forgiven and forgotten" because it had served the interest of the country. He expressed confidence that since the killing of demonstrators on 5 June was also "in the interest" of the country, in time it would be "forgiven and forgotten." Events proved him wrong.

Finally, no account of the 1963 resistance to the land policies of the Pahlavis is complete without recognition of the brave resistance of the tribes in southern Iran. As described in chapter 12, there were villages that were jointly owned by an entire tribe. With the expropriation of their villages, and the nationalization of pastures, the tribes faced the loss of the little that they had and an obliteration of their way of life. In desperation, they waged several brave but futile uprisings against the Pahlavi regime. The rebellions were crushed, the tribal leaders were captured, and many were executed by the government of Assadollah Alam.[3]

Retaliation

The government was bound to retaliate. As an opposition leader, my father was libeled in the newspapers, slandered on the radio, and harassed and detained by Savak, the secret police. My family's property was confiscated, including land that was supposedly "exempt" under the land distribution regulations. My parents filed a lawsuit against the government, challenging the legality and the constitutionality of the land decree. The lawsuit was significant for three reasons. First, it was partly in response to this legal challenge that the shah decided to hold a national referendum. The referendum further enraged the opposition and the religious establishment and strengthened the ties between the landowners and the ulama. Second, the lawsuit's outcome contrasted sharply with that of a similar lawsuit filed in Turkey a decade later. Third, the legal briefs and the government response provide a lucid statement of the ways the land distribution decree had violated Iran's Constitution and its other laws. Majd accused the government of waging rebellion against God and Iran's Constitution. For his opposition to the Pahlavi regime, Majd paid a heavy price.

Personal Vilification

Government spokesman Hasan Arsanjani often singled out Majd as the "arch feudal traitor" from Qazvin who had illegally amassed land. In speeches vilifying landowners, he accused Majd of greedily gaining the original and the exchanged villages. Such newspapers as *Setareh Tehran* portrayed the Agricultural Union of Iran as a reactionary movement and accused Majd of illegally amassing land and oppressing the helpless cultivators. On 27 December 1961, the Agricultural Union of Iran put out a bulletin entitled "His Excellency the Prime Minister of Iran" (see chap. 7). Two days later, the government responded in *Setareh Tehran*. Although the article was signed by Nasser Khodayar, a close associate of Arsanjani, there is no doubt that the actual author was Arsanjani himself. This article is interesting not only because of the numerous falsehoods, outright lies about alleged oppression of cultivators in Qazvin, and scurrilous attacks. It also clearly illustrates Arsanjani's reasoning and ideology. The vocabulary is unquestionably that of a Marxist. Under the headline "Let Us Crush Feudal Oppressors and Feudalism," Arsanjani states:

> Our era is not that of feudalism. Hundreds of large landowners must be sacrificed for the existence of the homeland. This is a histori-

cal necessity. The bulletins of such reactionary organizations as the Agricultural Union of Iran cannot alter or throw stones in the natural path of history and social change. We shall persist until the White Revolution of the Monarchy is all-encompassing. On this path, let there be violation of all laws that protect the feudal oppressors!

In yesterday's issue, I analyzed some of the contents of the bulletin by the so-called Agricultural Union of Iran. This bulletin, which was addressed to His Excellency, the Prime Minister, was in reality against all modernization in Iranian agriculture. I promised yesterday to continue to investigate some other points in the bulletin. Since yesterday, I have had a chance to make inquiries about this Agricultural Union of Iran and its leadership. All the respectable individuals whom I asked had not heard of this union nor did they know its leadership. This in itself was a source of comfort to me. It showed me that people did not want to waste their time to find out about this mysterious union whose purpose, origin, and leadership are unknown. I asked one of my friends who owns a village near Tehran and who has done a great deal for the cultivators . . . if he knew who had established this union. In response to my question, he reflected and said, "I have heard of this union. Its founders are a group of large landowners who only think of their own interests. If I recall correctly, one of the directors of this union is a large landowner by the name of Fatn ol Saltaneh Majd."

By hearing the name of this large landowner, I gained complete insight into the nature of this and similar unions. I am not a stranger to the name of Fatn ol Saltaneh Majd. If I wanted to name one large landowner in the twentieth century who was so disliked by the cultivator class, I have to mention him. I believe that if there is an encyclopedia established in our country, to explain such words as *large landowner, oppressor, despot,* and *selfish,* all that is needed is a picture of him next to the words. This Fatn ol Saltaneh, who was even a senator, and his partners and cobelievers should be placed under a microscope and explained as a social phenomenon to the deprived and toiling people of Iran.

The likes of Mr. Fatn ol Saltaneh Majd, who is one of the major landowners in Khoramdareh and Qazvin, could not even be found in the Middle Ages. Just last year, there were many complaints against his oppression of the cultivators that were reported in the respectable newspaper *Keyhan.* They recounted incidents that were related to Mr. Majd. I am truly ashamed to describe these complaints. It is painful to see that during the twentieth century an individual permits himself to aggress against and oppress another class.

If my memory serves me right, he owned some estates in Mazandaran that became government property and in exchange he was given some hamlets in Khoramdareh. After August 1941, and ignoring all of the 2,500-year-old achievements, Mr. Majd set about reacquiring the estates of Mazandaran. Of course, in this endeavor he was aided by the prevailing laws. Similarly, once again he intends to use current laws to prevent land reform in Iran. In any event, he reacquired the estates of Mazandaran, and most interestingly, he also kept the other land that had been given in exchange for the estates of Mazandaran. Of course, the governments at the time allowed him to regain this land, and Mr. Majd's colonies, similar to the British Empire, continued to grow. And according to him, for a while the Constitution and the blood of the martyrs was safeguarded. I also recall that he was to be impeached in the Senate. But since the wealthy classes did not wish to see one of their own impeached, it did not happen.

For a while, there was no news of Mr. Fatn ol Saltaneh Majd, who is said to be one of the main movers of this so-called Agricultural Union of Iran. The reason was that neither the Constitution, the blood of the martyrs of freedom, nor the 2,500-year-old achievements had been threatened in the estates of Mazandaran, Qazvin, and Khoramdareh. But now the situation is different, and a real danger threatens these fertile estates which rightfully belong to the cultivators. This threat is equated with the abrogation of the Constitution, wastage of the blood of the heroes of the Constitution, anxiety by the ghosts of Sattar Khan and Baqer Khan . . . , and the establishment of dictatorship and tyranny, and the imposition of the personal will of Dr. Arsanjani, members of the Tudeh Party and other communist elements. It is to "save" the country that the Agricultural Union of Iran has seen the need to issue this bulletin. It is a futile and pathetic effort by Mr. Fatn ol Saltaneh Majd and his accomplices. As Mr. Dr. Arsanjani himself has stated, if the government's land reform policy is termed communist, I myself am a staunch communist!

The Agricultural Union of Iran must learn that the people of Iran are fed up with this reactionary movement and inhuman oppression and tyranny. The people want to tear these chains of bondage and to sacrifice themselves to save the cultivating class from feudalism. If Mr. Fatn ol Saltaneh Majd and the other leaders of this so-called Agricultural Union of Iran call this communism, then the entire nation of Iran under the leadership of our dear beloved Shahanshah is communist! It is truly shameful that along the very borders of the Soviet Union, even in the neighborhood of Turkey, Iraq, and Pakistan, there are such people in our midst holding such reactionary and selfish views. They have been blinded by their selfishness and do not wish to open their eyes and ears to the dangers that threaten us. Today, with this White Revolution of the shah, we can stop this danger of communism. By giving land to the cultivators, we can create a patriotic class of small landowners who will rise to defend this land in the hour of crisis. Patriotism, duty, and defense of the country that the same Fatn ol Saltaneh Majd never showed in the hour of crisis [in August 1941].

The era of feudalism is now past. Hundreds of large landowners must be sacrificed for the country. Thousands of selfish oppressors who have unjustly usurped land must be sacrificed for the benefit of the toiling and deprived masses. This path is dictated by history. Everywhere in the world a group of selfish parasites have been sacrificed for the benefit of the many. This will have to take place. The screams and cries of such reactionary organizations and shameful unions as the Agricultural Union of Iran cannot change the path of history or throw stones in the path of social progress. This path will be followed despite the conspiracies, the selfishness, the futile and poisonous efforts of these feudal oppressors.

Please permit me to analyze some other contents of the bulletin of this so-called Agricultural Union of Iran. On the basis of Article 28 of the Constitution, these large landowners have declared that any minister who violates the Articles of the Constitution is a traitor and must be tried and condemned. In another place, they conclude from Article 9 that the people are secure in their homes. From Supplementary Article 15 they claim that no owner may be deprived of his property. Then they seek the help of Article 16 and claim that the confiscation of the people's property is forbidden.

Such knowledge, adherence, and love of laws by those who are the very source of illegality, and whose very existence is illegal, are most interesting! These people who carefully page through the Constitution and continuously find and cite laws are the same people who have chosen to ignore the laws of justice, nature, and of the Almighty. These same people, who claim that on the basis of the Constitution the people are secure in their homes, have without pity forced out the cultivators from their homes and have shown no respect for the rights of the toiling masses. You who use Article 15 of the Constitution as your instrument to claim that no one can be deprived of his property, have you ever considered that this land which you have so unjustly usurped rightfully belongs to the cultivator? . . . If respect and adherence to such laws means a continuation of tyrannical and oppressive feudalism, then I have no doubt that all the people of Iran will shout loudly, "Let these laws be ignored and violated!" When a land reform law was submitted to parliament, and it was possible to enact an equitable law, the likes of the leadership of the Agricultural Union of Iran and the likes of Fatn ol Saltaneh Majd succeeded in turning the law into a meaningless document. By such actions, the spirit of the Constitution and its martyrs was violated. At that time such conspiracies and aggressions against a proposed law were possible. But now that it has been decided that such transgression against laws and feudal oppression should be terminated, there is a loud cry that the Constitution is in danger, and the Tudeh Party and alien radios have entered the scene. Do you think that with these childish plays you can stop the path of history? . . .

Elsewhere in this notorious and shameful bulletin by this so-called Agricultural Union of Iran, there is a reference to Article 61 of the Constitution, and the council of ministers is reminded that all ministers are collectively responsible for all the affairs. What do they think? Do they think the past can be restored? Can we force our intellectual youth to be blind and deaf so that the feudal likes of Fatn ol Saltaneh Majd can maintain their unjust hegemony? Is it possible to maintain millions of Iran's toiling and deprived masses in chains solely for the benefit of the Agricultural Union of Iran, which has launched a pathetic attempt to maintain a feudal regime? Not only do all the ministers proudly accept responsibility in this important and holy matter, but millions of the oppressed and exploited people of Iran are willing to rise against the oppressive feudals and destroy the unholy consequences of feudalism. In this holy path, we shall not abandon our beloved shah. We shall continue until this White Revolution of the shah is all-encompassing. Let there be transgression and violation of all the laws that protect feudal oppressors and feudalism!

At the end of its bulletin, the so-called Agricultural Union of Iran writes, "There is in place in this country a special land reform law. Instead of implementing this law, the government is in dereliction of its legal duty, and instead has resorted to actions that destroy the confidence of the farmers." This law, which is so beloved by the feudals, is not a law. It is an inedible mixed salad that was carefully prepared by their skilled parliamentary cooks so that it is neither swallowable nor digestible. A law that is approved by feudals is not a law that benefits the millions of the toiling and deprived masses. It is a law that the wolves pass to swallow the lambs. Strange that the feudals pretend to be farmers and try to speak on behalf of the farmers. These same feudals who decimated a law that could have benefited the farmers now pretend to speak on their behalf. This is similar to the story of a man who killed his own father and mother, but then at his trial he claimed to be an orphan!

The bulletin concludes with this statement: "Things have reached a state whereby neither the vine nor the vineyard remains." The respected members of the Agricultural Union of Iran have forgotten that the vine and the vineyard disappeared long ago. If anything remains, it is only felt by the greedy feudal oppressors. The progressive people of Iran will uproot and extirpate that vine which only serves the feudal oppressors. They will deal with the vine owners whose vineyards have brought ruin and misery to millions of toiling masses. You do not believe it? Study the fate of feudalism in all the countries of the world. Learn from the fate of all such vineyards and their owners. It is my ardent desire and that of every progressive and reform loving person that no sign of these vineyards and their owners remains even in the pages of history.
Nasser Khodayar

Ironically, the Pahlavi regime later attempted to make Arsanjani himself disappear from the pages of history. There was practically no mention of Arsanjani in the official and semiofficial accounts of the shah's "White Revolution" that were published in the 1970s. It was as though he had never existed. By making him disappear, it was evidently hoped that some of his legacy, too, would disappear.

False Press Reports and Confiscation of Property

Just as the government had planted false reports in the press concerning the ulama's alleged support for land distribution, the government planted false reports that the program enjoyed the support of the landowners as well. A case in point is the article on the front page of the national daily *Keyhan*, dated 6 June 1962, claiming in large print that Mohammad Ali Majd had transferred all of his villages to the government for distribution to peasants. Several other landowners were said to have done the same. Of course, this was utterly false. The government's aim was to discredit Majd in the eyes of his fellow landowners, portray him as a turncoat, and thus weaken the opposition. Majd reports that many landowners in Azarbaijan and elsewhere had been greatly disheartened by the report, and their opposition had been weakened. By the time the falsity of the claim was made known, considerable damage had been inflicted.

Summary seizure of the property of the opponents was a highly effective way of silencing them. Since most landowners were heavily in debt and their land had been mortgaged, the loss of their land resulted in financial ruin. Their debts and liabilities remained, while the assets were lost. A case in point was the confiscation of Majd's property. In order to humiliate Majd and weaken the opposition, the confiscation of his property and that of his spouse received national press and radio coverage. The confiscation of the village of Khoznein by Khosrow Mehdizadeh, head of the Land Reform Organization in Qazvin, was headline news in the *Keyhan* issue of 6 September 1962. The same newspaper had claimed three months earlier that Majd had "voluntarily" surrendered Khoznein and that he had submitted the necessary declaration forms (*ezhar nameh*). But now *Keyhan* was claiming that they had not been submitted in a "timely" fashion. Majd states that the required forms were submitted on time and the newspaper was wrong. The village was confiscated under Article 14 of the land decree simply on the basis of "notification" of the prosecutor general and the signature of the head of the Land Reform Organization. There was no judicial recourse or process. The transfer papers had been signed by Mehdizadeh, who was acting as the owner's "representative" and had signed "on behalf" of the owner. It was a revealing case of the application of Article 14 of the land decree. Khoznein, the reader will recall, was one of the "exchanged" villages in the 1935 Zavar exchange. As if to underscore the lawlessness of the action, the confiscation proceedings were held at 10 P.M., long after regular office hours. Majd reports that two days after this article, the confiscation of the village of Shal in Qazvin (the birthplace of Majd's father) was broadcast with much fanfare on the national radio and was reported in the national dailies. This confiscation of Shal violated the 1962 land distribution decree. Next, the government moved to confiscate Majd's property in Khoramdareh, Zanjan, another major violation. The government then distributed Majd's property among its supporters and high government and military officials (see chap. 11). Heavily in debt and facing financial ruin, Majd lost much of his effectiveness as an opposition leader.

Detention and Intimidation

It is clear from Majd's account that the membership of the Agricultural Union of Iran expanded rapidly after 1961. The reason was simple. Following intense government propaganda, all landowners, including those who owned a few dangs or even a few hectares, were being driven from the countryside by the peasants. These disenfranchised landowners were joining the resistance. Greatly alarmed, the government sought to break up the Agricultural Union of Iran or at least silence it. Majd gives the following account.

> We were trying to prevent the confiscation of people's property. As I have described in these memoirs, we gave many reasons. We appealed to the country's laws and interests. But the government would not listen to us. With government protection and encouragement, the peasants forcefully seized the owners' land. If an owner objected and refused to transfer his land for a pittance, the Ministry of Agriculture would quickly confiscate the land under Article 14 and would leave one village for the owner. Even in the village that was supposedly "retained," the cultivators refused to pay rent, or even permit the owner to enter the village. Eventually, after much discussion, we landowners decided to stage a sit-in at the court or at the Senate or the Majlis. It was decided that we should gather at the house of Mr. Hosein Khakbaz that day. Until then, the gatherings had been at my house in Shemiran, and the government had not harassed us. The reason was that I was known to the American officers who worked in Savak, the army, and the police. Consequently, Savak officers only kept my house under surveillance and kept a record of the visitors. But they did not bother us. That day when we had gathered at the house of Mr. Khakbaz on Khiaban Fardis off Villa, suddenly Savak officers entered the house and asked why there was this gathering. We responded that we were not rebels. The government wanted to confiscate our property, and nobody was paying any attention to our cries for help. Now we had gathered for a march and a sit-in at the royal court. The officers consulted with their headquarters and ordered us to disperse. They took four of us to be interrogated by General Pakravan, chief of Savak, on the pretext that we could ask him to convey our message to His Majesty. The four individuals were Mr. Amir-Teimur-Kalali, Mr. Hosein Khakbaz, Mr. Abu Taleb Shirvani, and myself. They took us and we went and talked with General Pakravan, and he promised to convey our complaints to His Majesty. I would like to add that the night

before at 1 A.M., Mr. Mohammad Ghoreishi, a highly active member of the Agricultural Union of Iran, had been arrested at his home and taken to Qaleh Morghi Prison in Amir Abad. This was supposed to serve as a warning to the rest of us. Heavily in debt, and with our property gone, we saw that we were about to lose the little respectability that remained us. We were thus forced to discontinue the open meetings of the Agricultural Union of Iran."[4]

The Legal Challenge, 1962

Majd had also waged his opposition to the land confiscation/distribution program through the judicial system.

What the government did with landowners on the basis of a mere cabinet decree had no precedent anywhere under normal circumstances. Under the French Revolution, the revolutionaries first confiscated the property of the aristocracy and distributed it to peasants. But after Napoleon and the restoration of the Bourbon dynasty, this land was gradually restored to the owners. After the Russian Revolution, the property of landowners was confiscated by the government. But at the same time, all debts owed by landowners were also nullified, health care and education were made free, and most of the former landowners were given work and paid a living wage. But in Iran, the property of the landowners was confiscated while all debts previously incurred and other expenses remained the obligation of the former landowners. How were they to pay their debts? With this background, I filed a series of lawsuits against the Land Reform Organization and the Ministry of Agriculture and a criminal suit against Dr. Khosrow Mehdizadeh, head of the Qazvin Land Reform Organization.

Majd reports that the initial challenge to the land distribution decree came from members of the Office of Registration and from Notary Office 7 in Maragheh, the first area where land distribution was implemented. Some members of the Office of Registration had refused to ratify the confiscation of land under Article 14, and they were all summarily dismissed. The Maragheh notary office also refused to record and register the confiscation on the grounds that the owners held valid ownership deeds and were unwilling to sign the transfer documents. In response, the head of the Central Office of Registration, Mr. Amin, issued a directive that ordered all notary offices to promptly record and register the government "acquisition" of land. Majd's legal challenge was more serious. In August

1962, my parents each filed a lawsuit against the government that challenged the legality of the land decree. They also filed a criminal complaint against Khosrow Mehdizadeh, head of the Qazvin Land Reform Organization, for illegally confiscating private property. The lawsuit was considered to be a test case of the land distribution program. In theory, if the court had ruled against the government and had declared the decree to be illegal, that would have been the end of land distribution. Moreover, if the court had ruled against the government, Khosrow Mehdizadeh and his immediate supervisors, Abbas Salour and Hasan Arsanjani, would also have faced criminal prosecution under Iranian law. Majd's legal brief describes the manner in which the 1962 cabinet decree violated the 1960 Land Reform Law and how it violated Iran's Constitution and its other laws.

Initially, the government did not take the lawsuit seriously. Khosrow Mehdizadeh issued a very brief statement: "Office of Justice, Township of Qazvin, In response to notice numbers 2013–7/8/41 and 2011–7/8/41 concerning the complaint by Mr. Ali Oveissi as attorney for Mr. Mohammad Ali Majd and Mrs. Shams ol Moluk Entesar Khalatbari, I submit that my actions as Head of the Land Reform Organization in Qazvin were in accordance with Article 14 of the Land Reform Law and other relevant clauses. Head of Land Reform Organization, Qazvin Region, Dr. Mehdizadeh, 9 November 1962, Branch 2, Civil 41 2/20." In its carelessness, the government had alluded to Article 14 of the Land Reform Law as the basis for confiscation of private property. Technically, this was a bad mistake. Legally, the Land Reform Law of 1960 had been approved by the Majlis and duly signed by the shah. Article 14 of that law did not empower the government to confiscate private property. One month later, on 6 December 1962, Majd filed his response. The legal brief is lengthy, and only extracts can be given here. The brief starts by saying that according to his own admission, Mr. Mehdizadeh had gone to Notary Office 1 in Qazvin and had declared himself the "legal representative" of the landowners. He had then signed the transfer papers "on behalf" of the landowners and had transferred the property to himself as a representative of the Ministry of Agriculture. He had then transferred the ownership of the property to the Ministry of Agriculture. These actions were described as illegal and fraudulent. The perpetrator was to be prosecuted and the property restored to its rightful owner. The brief then claimed that Mr. Mehdizadeh's allegation that his actions were in compliance with Article 14 of the Land Reform Law was also fraudulent, because Article 14 contained no such provision. The provisions of Articles 13 and 14 are then given:

Article 13. In each region where land distribution is to be implemented, an Appraisal Commission will be set up by the Provincial Land Reform Commission. The Appraisal Commission will then determine a just price for the land.

Article 14. The price so established under Article 13 will be paid in ten yearly installments. The government is required to provide the necessary funds."

The suit then points out that a just price is to be paid for the land, and nowhere is there a provision that enables government employees to confiscate land. Then Articles 16 and 17 of the Land Reform Law are given:

Article 16. After determining the land to be divided in a region and the price of the land, the Provincial Land Reform Commission will inform the landowners at the address cited in the declaration form, and will also announce and publish its decision in the local newspapers and will post its decision in appropriate spots. If the landowners have an objection to the land to be distributed or to the price established by the Commission, they must notify the Commission within two months of the announcement. The Commission must then respond within six months, and its decision can be appealed in the provincial court. The provincial court will then investigate and rule, and its ruling is not subject to appeal.

Article 17. After all final rulings, the Land Reform Commission will invite the landowner in writing and by announcement to come and sign the transfer to the government and receive the price (as determined by this law). If the owner does not present himself or his representative within two months to sign the transfer, then he will be liable to a yearly development levy of (a) 1,500 rials per hectare of irrigated land (cultivated or not cultivated), orchards and vineyards, and nurseries, (b) 750 rials per hectare of nonirrigated land (cultivated or not cultivated), (c) 500 rials per hectare of waste land.

Nowhere in the law is a government employee empowered to confiscate land by acting as the owner's "representative." Consequently, Mr. Mehdizadeh's claim that he acted according to law was fraudulent. The legal brief continues:

If Mr. Mehdizadeh's claim is on the basis of Article 14 of what has been labeled a cabinet decree of the government of Dr. Amini that was announced in the issues of *Etela-at* and *Keyhan* newspapers of Monday, 16 January 1962, the content of Article 14 is as follows. Article 14. After the final decisions of the relevant authorities, the

Land Reform Organization will invite the landowner in writing and by announcement to come forward and transfer the land to the government and receive the price (as determined by this law). If within fifteen days of the date of the announcement, the landowner or a designated representative does not come forward and draw up and sign the transfer papers, the representative of the Land Reform Organization will sign the transfer documents on behalf of the landowner within one week, and notify the public prosecutor. There is no doubt that the above signature is devoid of any legal basis.

The brief then states that under Iran's Constitution, all new laws or amendment of existing laws must be approved by the Majlis. Specifically, the cabinet and His Majesty cannot issue and implement laws on their own without approval of parliament. Consequently, the cabinet decree which had "amended" an existing law was illegal and unconstitutional. Under Iran's constitution, the people's rights, freedom, and property were secure. The Constitution specifically prohibited the confiscation of the people's property. In conclusion, the plaintiffs had asked that the transfer of their property to the government be nullified and that the property be restored to the rightful owners. They had also requested compensation for damages and the criminal prosecution of the perpetrators.

On 24 January 1963, the government responded to Majd's legal arguments. This two-page response by Khosrow Mehdizadeh must occupy a special place in the annals of Iran's judiciary. Reading the file thirty-five years later, it is difficult to avoid astonishment. The response began with the declaration that land reform was the most important national program, and that by raising such matters as legality and the Constitution, Majd was trying to maintain his "unjust" ownership of the properties and to justify his continued rebellion against the measures and the legal authority. Displaying its open contempt for the judiciary, the government then declared that since matters pertaining to the Constitution and the manner in which laws had been drafted and implemented were beyond the competence and jurisdiction of Iran's judiciary, "for this reason no additional response was needed" to Majd's complaint that the 1962 cabinet decree was in violation of the Constitution. Second, the government was now describing the 1962 cabinet decree as the "implementation regulations" (*moqara-rat-e ejra-i*). Mehdizadeh had declared that "since the initial land reform law had been approved by the Majlis and the implementation regulations (approved on 9 January 1962) had received royal signature, and His Majesty had ordered that it be implemented, consequently, there is no conflict with the Constitution and it is entirely consistent with the Constitution." Third, Mehdizadeh had quoted from Article 27 of the Constitution, which stated, "Legislative power consists of the power to draw up and approve laws. This branch consists of His Majesty, the Majlis, and the Senate. Each branch has the right to initiate legislation." Therefore, His Majesty had the right to "initiate" legislation. Finally, Mehdizadeh stated that the plaintiffs had failed to demonstrate that they were the "real" owners of the property that had been seized by the government.

In his final brief, Majd pointed out that Mehdizadeh had selectively and misleadingly quoted from Article 27 of the Constitution, which states, "Legislative power consists of the power to draw up and approve laws. This branch consists of His Majesty, the National Consultative Assembly, and the Senate. Each has the right to initiate legislation. But implementation of a law is contingent on its lack of conflict with religious laws [sharia], and approval of both houses of parliament and royal signature." The last sentence had been omitted by Mehdizadeh. The new "law" had not even been submitted to parliament. Laws could not be changed by measures masquerading as "implementation regulations." The plaintiffs also pointed out that this "law" had been declared by the Blessed Ulama to be in conflict with the laws of the Holy Islam. It was not the complainants who were in rebellion against the Constitution. It was the government which was in active rebellion against God and the Constitution. It had at first refused to implement the law, which had been duly approved by parliament and signed by the shah, on the grounds that the law was "impractical." It had then usurped the powers of legislation by approving a decree and calling the decree the "amended law," and implemented the decree by force of arms and in contravention of the fatwas that had been issued by the highest religious authorities. The plaintiffs had again requested the nullification of the transfers, compensation for damages, and criminal prosecution of those involved.

Legal Challenge and the Referendum of 26 January 1963

Majd reports on public reaction to his lawsuits:

> Iran's landowners and all those who believed in the Constitution and all those faithful to the laws of Islam were greatly heartened by my lawsuits. On the other hand, the government was greatly angered because if the court had ruled in my favor, other landowners would have similarly filed suit and could cite my ruling as a precedent, and in short, that would have been the end of the decree of 9 January 1962. His Majesty had summoned Mr. Nured-din Alamuti,

the minster of justice in the cabinet of Ali Amini, and had asked his opinion concerning my lawsuit, and had inquired which way the court was likely to rule. Mr. Alamuti had responded that since he was not personally familiar with the case, he could not tell. Instead, he had suggested that his deputy, Mr. Shahab Ferdows, should be contacted. During the audience, Mr. Ferdows informed His Majesty that the judges had no choice but to rule in my favor because the land reform law had been approved by both houses of parliament and had received the royal signature. A law could not be changed or annulled by a cabinet decree. Informed of this, His Majesty decided to hold a referendum. In the manner in which the readers are aware, the approval of the six principles was announced by the media on 26 January 1963. The six points were the following: 1. Abolition of the system of landowner-tenant by land reform. 2. Nationalization of forests and pastures. 3. Sale of government factories for the purpose of financing land reform. 4. Making workers shareholders of factories they worked in. 5. Reform of electoral laws. 6. Creation of a literacy corps. These six points came to be known as the "White Revolution of Shah and People." A new and ubiquitous expression had entered the vocabulary. I would like to add that in Iran's Constitution and its civil laws, there is no provision for a referendum.

Since these "six principles" were based on cabinet decrees and thus had no legal basis, the shah decided to hold a referendum. The "national approval" was to be substituted for parliamentary debate and approval. In this, the shah was following the precedent that had been set by Mossadeq in 1953 when a referendum was held giving Mossadeq the power to dismiss the sitting parliament, which was no longer complying with his wishes. A fundamental problem in both instances was that there was no provision for a referendum in Iran's Constitution. Subsequently, the Pahlavi apologists attempted to provide legal justification on the grounds that Article 26 of the Supplement to the Constitution had stated that "the powers of the realm are all derived from the people." Thus, the shah's referendum was "legal" because it was an appeal to the people.[5] If that is the case, then Mossadeq's referendum was also legal. Why had it been termed "illegal" all these years, and as Ayatollah Khomeini pointed out in his declaration, why had people been prosecuted for partaking? The shah himself saw fit to describe the referendum as a defining event in his rule. He had even referred to 26 January 1963 as a date "which must be considered as the starting point of Iran's modern history."[6] It was claimed that 6 million voters (90 percent of the electorate) took part in the referendum, and fully 99 percent voted to ratify the "sacred" six principles of the White Revolution of Shah and People. The similarities with Mossadeq's 1953 referendum were striking. In 1953, 99 percent of the voters had voted to grant Mossadeq the power to dissolve the Majlis. In 1953, there were two separate voting booths: one for the supporters and one for the opponents. No sane man would enter the opposition booth. Consequently, the results were not in doubt. Similarly, under the shah's 1963 referendum, there were two separate voting booths. Again, the results were not in doubt.

Evidently, by 1963 the shah had forgotten what he had written in his book about Mossadeq's referendum. The shah had stated the following:

> And for the referendum Mossadegh, the great champion of free elections, arranged that those in favour of dissolution and those against it should vote in separate plainly marked booths! Everyone understood that if a man had the courage to vote against dissolution he would probably be beaten up by Mossadegh's toughs or by those of the Tudeh—actually the two groups were by this time almost indistinguishable. The results were all that Mossadegh—or Hitler before him—could have desired. Dissolution won by over 99 percent of all votes cast.

Eleven years later, the shah was emulating Mossadeq, whom he had condemned in no uncertain terms. On the same page, the shah had said the following about Mossadeq:

> During all his years in Parliament, Mossadegh had posed as a champion of constitutional principles, representative government, and due process of law. He had railed against the idea of martial law and had eulogized free elections and freedom of the Press. But now Mossadegh had in a few months abolished the Senate, dissolved the highest court of the land, and claimed a mandate from the people to eliminate the National Assembly [Majlis]. He had stifled the Press, in effect abolished free elections, extended martial law, and tried his best to weaken my constitutional position. What had become of our hard-won Constitution of 1906?[7]

By 1961, the shah himself had chosen to openly violate and disregard the Constitution.

Scene in a Courtroom in Qazvin, 20 August 1964

Fourteen months after the violent events of 5 June 1963, Mohammad Ali Majd had gone to the courthouse in Qazvin. On that day, the court was to render a verdict on his lawsuit against the government. The atmosphere of terror and intimidation was such that even Majd's new attorney in the case, Abdollah Khavari (Ali Oveissi, the first attorney, had resigned), had chosen not to be present in the court on that day. As if to underscore the loneliness of the struggle, given that this was supposedly an important test case, nevertheless, the courtroom was empty and there were no spectators. Apart from the court clerk and the recorder, there were only three men in the courtroom: Majd, the attorney for the government, and a stranger. Majd gives the following account:

> On 20 August 1964, I went in person to the courthouse in Qazvin. Apart from the secretary, there was seated at the desk to the right of Mr. Golchin an individual whom I did not know. The attorney for the government, Mr. Hosein Tonekaboni, a capable and respected attorney in Qazvin, was seated facing me. He stared at me and made signs by raising his eyebrows. I did not understand, but realized that something was afoot. At this time, this unknown third person was called out of the courtroom. He got up from behind the desk and left the room. Hurriedly, Mr. Tonekaboni approached me and whispered in my ear that this person was a Savak agent who had come to arrest me. If I was to say anything against land reform or the government, the gentleman would arrest me on the spot on trumped-up charges. He then returned to his seat. Sensing the futility of the exercise, right on the spot I wrote a letter and, following His Majesty's desires, withdrew my complaints against the government.

By then, Majd was in no position to continue his active opposition. First, the events of 5 June 1963 had completely terrorized the opposition. Majd was seventy-three, he had recently undergone a major operation, and he had had an encounter with Savak the previous year. It is doubtful that he could have survived Savak interrogation and imprisonment. Moreover, by then much of his property had been confiscated, and since he was heavily in debt, he now faced financial ruin. His house in Vali Abad and my childhood home in Tehran had been seized by the creditors. On that day, the government had won and the opposition had been silenced temporarily. But its "victory" was short-lived. A few years later, when the people's anger and the upheavals of revolution began to shatter the foundations of the Pahlavi regime, such individuals as Mohammad Ali Majd who had rebelled against the lawless tyranny of Mohammad Reza Shah, and who had paid dearly for their resistance, were assuredly vindicated and exonerated by history.

Finally, this course of events and the outcome of Majd's lawsuit were in sharp contrast to the experience of Turkey, where a land reform measure nearly identical to the one just implemented in Iran was pushed through a reluctant parliament by the Turkish military in 1971. Just as in Iran, Turkey's land distribution was to be implemented in three phases. Moreover, the compensation for expropriated land was to be on the basis of the land tax, which was much below the market value of land. The measure was challenged in court, and the Turkish Constitutional Court ruled in 1976 that the key provision of the law, that is, the compensation of landowners on the basis of the land tax, was unconstitutional. It also ruled that the manner in which the law had been legislated was unconstitutional. That was the end of land distribution in Turkey.[8]

The Views of the Turkish and American Consuls in Tabriz

There are other revealing comparisons between Turkey and Iran. During the 1940s and 1950s, government lands were distributed in Turkey among the small cultivators.[9] In March 1962, American consular officials discussed the land distribution program with Recep Yazgan, the Turkish consul in Tabriz since 1959. Yazgan informed his American counterpart that a similar land distribution of government lands undertaken in Turkey had turned out to be a disappointing failure. Moreover, the Turkish consul said that because conditions in Azarbaijan were very similar to those in eastern Turkey, "the greater the extent of Iranian effort in this field, the greater will be the failure."

The conversation was reported in a confidential report (Foreign Service despatch 67, dated 14 March 1962). Yazgan's views were quickly dismissed by U.S. Consul John M. Howison, who remarked, "Both of these premises are faulty. Yazgan apparently has few reporting responsibilities, and he does not trouble to keep himself informed regarding Iranian affairs. His totally pessimistic view is probably based largely on general comments he has heard from Turkish-speaking landlords."

11

Theory and Practice of Land Reform

Case Studies in Landownership, Taxation, and Land Distribution

Theoretical arguments for agrarian reform are to be found in the writings of nineteenth-century American economist Henry George. In his 1879 classic, *Progress and Poverty,* George advocated a single tax on land in lieu of all other taxes, thereby eliminating the advantages of private landownership. Leo Tolstoy demanded a "solution to the land problem" in Russia by dividing up the large estates among the serfs. German writer Adolph Damaschke (1865–1935) suggested severe limits on private landownership and distribution to the farmers. In England, such writers as John Stuart Mill, Thomas Carlyle, and Herbert Spencer denounced landowners for the high rents levied on tenants. Significant contributions on the subject during the early twentieth century are to be found in the writings of Zionist thinkers who were involved in establishing Jewish agricultural settlements in Palestine. Convinced of the evils of private landownership and the resulting land speculation and exploitation of workers, the Zionist writers advocated state ownership of land, subdividing land into small plots, and leasing the land to settler families for long periods. The leases were inheritable and practically irrevocable, although formal ownership remained with the state. The farms were to be managed with family labor and with no outside wage labor. This became the basis of agricultural settlement in Israel. In this way, the exploitation of labor would be avoided and families would be provided with a livelihood. The sale of products, purchase of needed inputs, and the capital requirements were all handled through a system of cooperatives. It was considered an ideal agrarian reform by the Israeli writers. It is noteworthy that prior to land distribution in Iran, officials in the Ministry of Agriculture in Iran were sent to Israel to be trained in matters of land and rural cooperatives.[1]

Modern Theory of Land Reform

A more recent theoretical basis for land reform can be found in the writings of Marxist scholars such as Alain de Janvry, non-Marxist writers such as Albert Berry and William Cline, and World Bank economists Hans Binswanger and Miranda Elgin.[2] The Marxist writers have stressed the economic and political aspects of limited "antifeudal" reforms. Such reforms are said to strengthen capitalism, increase agricultural production, and promote political stability. How the seizure of private property was supposed to "strengthen" capitalism was never explained. Others have stressed the efficiency of land distribution. Berry and Cline demonstrated that when in a labor-surplus underdeveloped "dual" economy the landholding is bimodal (that is, small farms with excess labor exist side by side with large farms with little labor), resources are misallocated. The marginal product of land on small farms exceeds the marginal product of land on large farms. Total output will increase with a reallocation of land from large to small farms. However, this reallocation cannot be brought about through the real estate market. Land will be overpriced, and the small farmers may lack the purchasing power to buy land. Consequently, a redistribution of land by the state, consisting of the breakup of the large farms and distribution to those with little or no land, would result in more efficient allocation of resources, greater level of output, and also greater economic growth. Such a land redistribution implicitly assumes some form of confiscation and coercion.

It is important to note that Berry and Cline's result applies only to large and small farms (operational units) and not ownerships. In theory, the land could be owned by an individual, and as long as the land was divided into small equal parcels, and each piece was rented to a tenant, the distribution would be efficient in the sense that no additional output could be achieved. Moreover, the authors concluded that a simple transfer of land from the owners to the cultivating tenants was unlikely to result in greater output and efficiency. That is, while no adverse consequences (output and growth decline) could be expected, few gains were likely from such a land transfer. This result presented the proponents of land reform with a dilemma. Since nearly all of the land reforms consisted of a simple transfer of ownership of land to the tenants, arguments had to be developed that tenancy and sharecropping were inherently inefficient. A long and complicated debate took place on the supposed inefficiency of sharecropping.[3] Empirical studies, however, did not demonstrate serious inefficiency. All of this led Berry and Cline to conclude that "the efficiency aspect of sharecropping remains, to put it mildly, ambiguous."[4] Binswanger and Elgin maintained that the transfer of landownership to the tenant was still beneficial, but in recognition of the results of Berry and Cline, they declared that the gains were less than previously believed. Binswanger and Elgin were pessimistic about the prospects for land reform during the 1990s and beyond, because it was no longer politically feasible to confiscate landowners by such measures as pricing land on the basis of tax payments. Since neither the governments nor the tenants had the necessary funds, few reforms were expected. Instead, they advocated agricultural reform in lieu of land reform (see chap. 7). It should be stressed that nowhere in the theoretical writings was the possibility or desirability of expropriating a large number of small landowners advocated. At most, land was to be taken from a small number of those who constituted the rural elite and given to the poor farmers and tenants.

Binswanger and Elgin implicitly assumed that the "hated absentee" landlord did not perform any useful economic task, or at least none that could not be performed by the small owner-farmer. While this assumption may have been valid for agricultural conditions prevailing in East Asia, parts of India, much of Africa, and South America, it was clearly invalid for the conditions that prevailed in much of the semi-arid Middle East and Iran. On much of the Iranian plateau, landowners performed essential investment and maintenance tasks: digging new qanats (underground irrigation source), and constructing and establishing new agricultural villages in the vicinity of new qanats. Landowners also maintained and repaired the qanats. Investment in new qanats, establishment of new villages, and provision of working capital to the new farmers were essential for agricultural growth and had long been the main source of expanded cultivation. These essential tasks were beyond the capability of the small owner-farmers. It was for this reason that most of Iran's villages had been named after their original founders, that is, the person who had established the qanat and built the settlement (e.g., Hasan Abad, Ahmad Abad, Vali Abad, etc.)

A main condition assumed in the theory of land reform was that of land shortage and surplus labor. As noted in chapter 7, with over 30 million hectares of potential farm land, and a population of 20 million, Iran could not be considered a labor surplus country. The relative land abundance and shortage of labor are demonstrated by the low level of rent that was paid by tenants even in the fertile Caspian region.[5] These figures indicate a low marginal product of land and, by implication, a high marginal product of labor. Conditions in Iran were the opposite of those envisaged in the theory. In any event, given that land distribution in Iran consisted of giving land to the tenants, little additional efficiency could be expected on theoretical grounds. On the contrary, given the historical investment role of landowners and given the Islamic practices of matrimony and inheritance, tenancy and sharecropping fulfilled vital economic and social functions. It is for this reason that sharecropping is approved in Islam. The sudden abolition of landlord-tenant relations was bound to be highly disruptive and costly. It is perhaps not a coincidence that following land distribution, Iran became heavily dependent on food imports.

The First Phase of Land Distribution: Khoznein, Qazvin

Under the 1962 cabinet decree, also known as Phase One, maximum ownership was reduced to one village, and the excess was transferred to the government. Compensation was on the basis of the land tax. The case studies of landownership and the implementation of Phase One include the villages of Khoznein, Shal, Khoramdareh, and villages in Mazandaran and Arak.

Located southwest of Qazvin, Khoznein was part of the 1935 exchange between my maternal grandfather, Amir Entesar, and the government, in which the estate of Zavar was exchanged for a group of villages in Qazvin, Zanjan, and Arak. Upon Amir Entesar's death, it became the property of my mother, Shams ol Moluk, Amir Banou. My father reports that Khoznein had 2,000 hectares of fertile land, and a population of 3,000 in 1960, some 500–600 households, many of whom were resourceful farmers. Despite its proximity to the Khar Rud River, Khoznein suffered from extreme water shortage. Majd reports that his numerous attempts to establish a viable qanat had failed. He also explored the possibility of deep wells, but the project had been deemed very risky and uneconomical. Even a small mechanical failure during the irrigation season was likely to require lengthy delays and to result in crop failure. Instead, Majd reports that each year he would purchase part of the water flow of Khar Rud for twenty days and divert the water to the fields in Khoznein. Each year, the farmers planted the fields with the expectation that this system would continue. Majd reports that in 1935, as a government-owned village, Khoznein had been contracted out for a mere 16,000 rials, and its annual tax was 1,600 rials. By the time of land distribution in 1962, its wheat crop alone was 1,800 kharvar (600 tons). Majd also reports that he had established extensive vineyards in the southwestern part of Khoznein, and they had been rented out to the sharecroppers. He named the development Mohammad Abad. By 1960, the annual grape harvest had reached 600 kharvars (200 tons). He had also built a large two-story house and garden (arbabi) in the center of the village. Reliance on the waters of Khar Rud and precipitation inevitably resulted in frequent crop failure. Majd records severe drought in 1941 and 1942 and again in 1960 and 1961. In both instances, Majd came to the aid of his sharecroppers. During the 1941–42 drought, hunger in Khoznein was averted by delivery of several truckloads of rice. This was made possible because Majd was the governor of the rice-producing regions of Gilan and Mazandaran. In 1960–61, Majd sent several trucks of wheat from Ebrahim Abad and Khoramdareh. In return, the grateful residents of Khoznein grew to respect and admire their landlord, and they demonstrated their gratitude to Majd during one of Arsanjani's visits to the village in 1962.

The real value of Khoznein can be seen from three revealing episodes. Majd reports that in 1944, the prime minister, Mohammad Saed, informed him that an Assyrian by the name of Avaz-Zadeh was willing to purchase Khoznein for $300,000, payable in the United States. Majd told the prime minister that he and his ancestors had lived in this country and that he hoped the same for his children; consequently, he had no need for dollars. In 1954, when both Saed and Majd were senators, Saed recounted this episode to his colleagues in a speech on the Senate floor. Majd reports that in May 1961, a government commission went to Khoznein for the purpose of evaluating the village prior to land distribution on the basis of the original 1960 land reform law. The government commission had set a price of 21 million rials ($300,000). However, on 15 September 1962, Khoznein was seized by the Land Reform Organization in Qazvin under Article 14 of the cabinet decree for 2,560,000 rials ($30,000) in land reform bonds, bearing 6 percent interest and redeemable over fifteen years. With an actual market interest rate of at least 20–24 percent (this was the borrowing rate with land as collateral), the market value of the bonds (the present value of a stream of fifteen payments of $2,000 each) was about $10,000, or about 3 percent of the value of the property as determined by a government commission the previous year. Moreover, as shown here, the real land reform "price" for Khoznein was less than one year's net income from the property. The text of a legal certificate of clearance and settlement of accounts drawn up between Majd and Haj Dr. Rais-Dana, the person to whom Khoznein had been leased during the crop years 1958 and 1959, testifying that Rais-Dana had met all the obligations for the two years, shows that the rent for Khoznein during 1959 was 700 kharvar of wheat and 320 kharvar of barley, and 160,000 rials in cash. That is, the net rent for 1959 was 1,020 kharvars of grain (340 tons). Even assuming a ridiculously low price of $50 per ton of grain, the total is $17,000 for grain. Add the cash rent, and the sum approaches $20,000 per year. Thus a village with net income of $20,000 per year was "purchased" for $10,000 under land reform. It is noteworthy that this is nearly identical to practices under Reza Shah.

That the entire process was a charade can be seen from the text of the announcement by the Land Reform Organization that appeared on 27 August 1962 in the newspaper *Voice of Qazvin*. The announcement, signed by Dr. Khosrow Mehdizadeh, head of the Land Reform Organization in Qazvin and Zanjan, is directed at eighteen Qazvin landowners who were being "notified and invited" to come forward and sign the transfer papers and receive the price as determined by the Land Reform Organization. Failure to come forward and sign the transfer papers within fifteen days resulted in seizure by the government with the "notification" of the public prosecutor. The first two on the list were my parents, who were being "informed and invited" to come and sign the transfer papers for Khoznein and Shal. Khoznein belonged wholly to my mother, and as an indication of the haste and carelessness with which the announcement had been prepared, all eighteen landowners cited were said to have partial ownership of Khoznein. As noted in chapter 10, the confiscation of Khoznein received prominent coverage in the national daily newspaper *Keyhan* on 6 September 1962. The same newspaper had claimed earlier that Majd "voluntarily" surrendered Khoznein. It should also be noted that only nine days had elapsed between the publication of the announcement and the actual seizure of the village. Under the 1962 cabinet decree, landowners had fifteen days to appear and sign the transfer papers.

Majd also recounts a revealing episode concerning Arsanjani's 1962 visits to Khoznein following its confiscation. On the night of 1 September 1962, an earthquake shook the Qazvin area, wounding or killing large numbers. Khoznein suffered heavy casualty and damage. Majd reports that 400 of its residents were killed and all the houses, including the arbabi, were reduced to rubble. Following the tragedy, a group of Tehran merchants, headed by philanthropist Abu Hosseini, granted 3 million rials to the residents of Khoznein, to assist them in rebuilding their houses. Majd reports that following the confiscation, the merchants withdrew their offer. The government then spent 30 million rials to build an entirely new village and dig three deep wells, all at its own expense. In short, Khoznein had become a showcase for government help to the rural residents, and Arsanjani frequently accompanied visitors and government guests. On a visit to Khoznein, Arsanjani gave a speech that vilified my parents. Some of the former sharecroppers were offended by the insults heaped on the very person who had come to their assistance during the drought of 1960–61, and they spoke favorably of my father. Angered, Arsanjani ordered their arrest. They were taken to Qazvin and released.

In addition, knowing that this was confiscated land on which no prayer was valid or permitted by religious law, Majd also reports that each year after the confiscation, a delegation of devout Moslems from Khoznein, headed by the former headman, Khadkhoda Haj Mahdavi, would visit Majd and ask for his absolution and permission to pray on that land. In Majd's private papers he kept numerous letters from farmers of Khoznein who had written to ask for absolution and forgiveness.[6] These are remarkable documents. They demonstrate a profound adherence to Islam by the simple farmers. They also show that some farmers were deeply uneasy with what had taken place. The letter about construction of a mosque and water storage on "usurped land" and the imperative to obtain Majd's permission is very informative. Evidently, by its land policies, the Pahlavi regime had not even gained the uniform support of Iran's peasant farmers to whom it had given land.

Shal, Qazvin: A Case Study in Landownership and Land Distribution

Shal is west of Qazvin and three kilometers from Khoznein. It sits on the banks of Khar Rud River. Majd's father, Sheik Mohammad Majd-ol Kottab (also known as Shali), was born in Shal. Majd had a close relationship with the residents of the village of Shal, who regarded him as one of their own.[7] It is clear that he could command substantial influence over the electoral and political affairs in Qazvin.[8]

Shal became the property of my great-grandfather, Mohammad Vali Khan Tonekaboni, Sepahsalar Azam, in 1900. According to Majd, Sepahsalar had owned 143 villages in Astarabad (Gorgan). Because he also owned land in Gilan and Mazandaran, the government grew apprehensive of Sepahsalar's influence in northern Iran, and acquired his property in Gorgan in exchange for Shal. Eventually, it was inherited by his heirs. Following my grandmother's death in 1933, her property was inherited by my mother. My parents owned 233 shares out of 585 shares of Shal, of which 197 shares belonged to my father and 36 shares to my mother. Shal produced prize-winning sheep, grain, and raisins. Its population in 1960 was 12,000 inhabitants, about 2,000 households, of whom 1,200 were engaged in agriculture. Majd reports that Shal annually produced 10,000 kharvars (3,000 tons) of grain and 20,000 kharvars (6,000 tons) of grapes. The raisins from Shal commanded a premium of 2,000 rials per kharvar in the Qazvin market. Most residents were wealthy. In 1957, Majd counted 72 individuals whose wealth exceeded 1 million rials, a large sum by the standards of the time. Some owned as many as 1,500 heads of sheep, which were valued at 5,000 rials per head. That is, they owned 7.5 million rials in sheep alone ($100,000 at 1957 prices, or about $1 million at today's prices). Majd reports that 3,000 hectares of land in Shal were vineyards, and the rent consisted of a negligible 10 rials per 100 vines, while the rent in the surrounding villages consisted of one-quarter of the grape crop. No doubt for political reasons, Majd decided not to raise the rent. In May 1961, a government commission visited Shal and placed a value of 84 million rials ($1.2 million) on the vineyards.

My parents owned 233 shares out of 585 shares in Shal. Since the extent of the ownership was less than the total, under the provisions of the land decree, it was defined as scattered partial ownership (*amlak-e dangi-e parakandeh*). Under Addendum 3 of Article 2 of the 9 January 1962 decree (see appendix B), such ownerships could be sold directly by the owners to the cultivators before the announcement of land distribution in a region. My parents decided to sell their shares in Shal in accordance with the said provision. In August 1962, at the height of Arsanjani's campaign against landowners, Majd visited Shal and met the notables and head farmers (*sarbonehs*). They offered to purchase Majd's share in the vineyards for 1 rial per square meter in cash, or 1.5 rials per square meter, payable in five annual installments. Majd selected the latter option, and an agreement was drawn up for a sum of 45 million rials and signed by all the parties. The registration office in Qazvin was notified and was asked to measure and map the vineyards.

Majd reports that following the announcement of the impending sale, Arsanjani sent a delegation from the Ministry of Agriculture to Shal, headed by his own brother, to find "incriminating" evidence and thereby prevent the sale. The delegation returned empty-handed. The 1 September earthquake had inflicted minor damage in Shal, and the work of the registration office in mapping the vineyards had not been seriously disrupted. Majd records that on 17 September 1962, just eleven days after the confiscation of Khoznein, the national radio and newspapers announced with much fanfare that my parents' entire ownership in Shal had been "acquired" by the government under Article 14 of the land decree for 5.3 million rials. That is, Majd's vineyards and cropland had been seized. Once again, the confiscation proceedings had been held in the dead of night (at 11 p.m.), and Khosrow Mehdizadeh had signed the transfer papers "on behalf" of my parents. Thus, when Arsanjani failed to nullify the impending sale to the cultivators, he simply seized the village under Article 14. This was a violation of Article 2, Addendum 3, which specifically permitted the direct sale of scattered ownerships of less than six dangs.

Moreover, the government's allegation that Majd had not been willing to transfer his ownership was false. Majd points out that an agreement had been drawn up with the cultivators, and the registration office had been duly advised. The registration office itself was in the process of preparing the groundwork for an impending transfer. Under the conditions of the decree, the Land Reform Organization's decision to confiscate was final and without judicial appeal. The government could do and say whatever it wished. In his memoirs, Majd reports that as a reward for his deeds, Khosrow Mehdizadeh was "elected" (or more appropriately, appointed) to the 21st Majles.

Shal: A Case Study in Land Taxation

When Majd agreed to sell Shal to the farmers in August 1962, they set a price of 45 million rials ($590,000), payable over five years. Of course, given that a government commission itself had assessed the value of the vineyards at 84 million rials, and given the prevailing conditions at the time, the ever-present threat of confiscation facing the owner, and the awareness on the part of the farmers, this was nothing but a "distress" price. Nevertheless, in September 1962, Shal was seized by the Land Reform Organization under Article 14 of the land reform decree for 5.3 million rials in land reform bonds (not money), redeemable over fifteen years and yielding an interest rate of 6 percent. Given the actual market rate of interest of at least 20 percent, the market value of these bonds, hence the real compensation was $25,000–30,000. A property for which farmers were willing to pay $590,000 in five equal installments (present value at least $400,000) for its vineyards alone was "purchased" by the government for a sum equal to 7 percent of the distress price of the vineyards. The price set by the Land Reform Organization for Shal and Khoznein was based primarily on the annual tax for the two villages. Majd's account of the manner in which the tax rates on these properties were established in 1933 and 1955 and the use of "land reform bonds" in place of money is informative. It also demonstrates that the use of the tax rate to establish the price of a property under the 1962 land reform decree and payment in land reform bonds constituted de facto confiscation.

It is now readily acknowledged in the professional literature on land reform that the past practice of pricing land on the basis of tax rates, and the use of bonds in lieu of money as the mode of compensation to the expropriated owner, constituted thinly disguised outright confiscation. Binswanger and Elgin note that in practically no country in the world are land taxes an accurate indicator of the land's value, nor is farm income subject to any real taxation. In fact, in most countries, farm incomes are subsidized. Land taxes are low everywhere because it is recognized that heavy taxes discourage agricultural development and reduce land values. In addition, in the case of Iran, there were other reasons that had historically resulted in low taxes on land. There was the high level of risk associated with semi-arid agriculture and the frequency of crop failures and drought years. High taxes in bad years could have caused financial ruin. Majd states that a common form of rural taxation consisted of a lump sum payment to the government by the landowners in exchange for reducing tax payments in future years. The system was advantageous to both sides. For the landowner, the reduction in future tax payments increased the value of the property and reduced the risk of insolvency and debt in the years of crop failure and drought. It was also advantageous to the government in the short run because it gave the government access to a sum that was equivalent to several years of future tax revenues.

The system is illustrated by the history of taxation of Shal and Khoznein. Majd reports that in 1933 the annual tax for Shal was reassessed at 1,170 kharvar of grain (351 tons) and 120,000 rials in cash. To reduce future tax payments, Shal's owners (the heirs of Mohammad Vali Khan Tonekaboni) paid the government a lump sum of 430,000 rials ($26,000) in 1933. This was a large amount by the standards of the time (the reader should recall that the entire estate of Kojour was "purchased" for 175,000 rials by Reza Shah). The new annual tax was henceforth to be 150 kharvar (45 tons) of grain and 30,000 rials in cash. Thus the tax payment for Shal in 1962 was low because its tax had been "prepurchased" in 1933 and converted to the "fractional" rate. Majd reports that the process of tax assessment was a cumbersome and time-consuming task. Between 1924 and 1955, most of Iran's villages underwent tax reassessment. However, as it became evident during the land distribution, many villages still lacked tax records and had never been assessed. Majd also points out that since Khoznein and Ebrahim Abad were owned by the government before the 1935 exchange for Zavar, they bore a nominal tax of 1,600 rials (1,200 rials for Ebrahim Abad), because the government had little interest in taxing itself. This tax remained unchanged until 1955, when it rose to 60,000 rials for Khoznein and 50,000 rials for Ebrahim Abad. Majd protested this fortyfold increase in taxes, and the tax for Khoznein was reduced to 20,000 rials on the grounds that Khoznein did not possess a working qanat. The point is that rural taxes were low in 1962 for complicated historical and economic reasons. Thus, the use of tax payments by the government to establish "price" for a property and the use of land reform bonds whose value would plummet on the market were a disguised form of confiscation.

Estates of Kojour, Mazandaran, and Arak

The estates of Kojour comprised 212 items, including villages, hamlets, pastures, and forests. The property stretched 48 kilometers from Chalous in the west to Alamdeh in the east. Of these, 69 items were farm villages and hamlets, and the remaining 143 items were forests and pastures. Baharein Forest was said to contain three million chestnut trees, and each tree was conservatively priced at 10,000 rials ($140). These estates were the property of Mohammad Vali Khan Tonekaboni, Sepahsalar Azam, and as outlined in chapter 3, they were acquired by Reza Shah after Sepahsalar's suicide. With the downfall of Reza Shah, the heirs of Sepahsalar filed suit for the return. As Amir Zadeh's sole survivor, my mother stood to inherit one-ninth of the estates of Kojour. As part of the litigation against the government, she transferred her ownership to Mehdi Batmanqelij in 1944. After the victory against the government, Batmanqelij transferred a 6 percent share of the estates to Majd and retained the rest as his fee.

In 1963, the 143 forests and pastures were summarily nationalized by a cabinet decree, and as Majd records, not a single rial of compensation was paid to the owners, who had spent a great deal of money and effort in litigation for the recovery of the Pahlavi estates. The owners fared no better in the case of agricultural land seized by the government. The implementation of land reform in Kojour and Arak represents interesting cases of paper and phantom compensation to the landowners. Majd reports that under Phase One of land reform, his 6 percent ownership in 23 of the 69 villages was seized by the Land Reform Organization under Article 14 for 280,237.68 rials ($3,600). Three more villages were also seized but not "purchased," because the tax payments on these villages were high and, therefore, the corresponding price would have been high. For example, Majd's share in the village of Shekar Lakal would have been 128,720.15 rials ($1,700). Thus, to avoid payment on these villages, the Land Reform Organization simply seized them. As to the remaining 43 villages, since the land was already in the farmers' possession, and since they had stopped paying rent, the Land Reform Organization refused to formally purchase the land or to provide compensation. Some of the prices established by the Land Reform Organization for the 23 villages that were supposedly "purchased" were ridiculous. For instance, Majd's 6 percent share in the hamlet of Aja Kol was "valued" at 55.08 rials ($0.70), implying that the entire hamlet had been "priced" for $8. At 68.34 rials ($0.80), the village of Chamar Kuh did a little better. The chicanery is extended to such levels that some of the prices (the villages of Khajak and Kangar) are

Table 11.1. Land Reform Valuation of Majd's 6 Percent Share in Twenty-three Villages in Kojour, Mazandaran

Village	Amount (rials)
Nirang	50,422.90
Ashkar Dasht	15,518.55
Gard-e Kol	35,471.05
Sham-e Jaberan	22,578.45
Molla Kol	17,502.15
Halak	33,087.40
Kohneh Sara	24,336.35
Bazyar Kola	12,666.15
Dozdak	34,441.75
Farash Kala Sofla	6,704.00
Joladeh	5,239.50
Azad Bareh	5,239.50
Sang-e Now	1,251.54
Vazyvar	5,009.30
Sang Sara	4,389.40
Nil	1,043.256
Khajak	1,913.3568
Kangar	2,119.3662
Kateh Kosh	333.35
Nafchal	354.45
Khorshid Abad	492.50
Chamar Kuh	68.34
Aja Kol	55.08
Total	280,237.68

Source: Memoirs of Mohammad Ali Majd.

given to the nearest 1/10,000th of a rial, a totally meaningless measure intended to add digits after the decimal.

Not even these paltry sums were paid to the expropriated owners because the Land Reform Organization claimed that the land had not been properly registered. In the brief interlude since the restoration to the heirs of Sepahsalar and the 1962 land decree, it had not been possible to register the property of the large number of individuals and complete the requirements for obtaining title deeds. Thus, although in the document of transfer to the government it was stated that the specified payment had been made to the owners, the actual checks and the land reform bonds had been issued to the registration office in Nowshahr for safekeeping until the registration formalities had been completed. In the event of objection by third parties, the money would remain with the registration office, pending the outcome of the ultimate court ruling, which could take many years. Interestingly, although no compensation had been received, the owners were deemed responsible for any known liens or mortgages on the land and any as yet unknown claims for the next fifty years. In reality, the only difference between the confiscation of Kojour by Reza Shah in 1930 (see chap. 3) and its confiscation by the Land Reform Organization in 1962 was the matter of the diamond ring that had belonged to Amir Zadeh.

Majd also hints at a similar outcome concerning the estates of Arak. As part of her inheritance from her father, my mother had an ownership share in 25 villages in Arak. After some sale and transfers, by 1962 she held a one-eighth ownership in 25 villages in Arak. According to two separate announcements by the Land Reform Organization of Arak, her share was valued at 880,000 rials ($11,000) in land reform bonds. However, as of 1968, six years after acquisition by the government, Majd had only received 350,000 rials of the bonds, and in his words, "There was no sign of the rest."

Khoramdareh, Zanjan

Located along the banks of Abhar Rud River and on the Qazvin-Zanjan highway, Khoramdareh is six kilometers west of the town of Abhar. Its 1960 population of 12,000 was concentrated mostly in the area of Khoramdareh-ya-veisi. Majd states that Khoramdareh was first owned by my great-grandfather, who sold it for 330,000 rials in about 1900 to the heir to the throne, Prince Mohammad Ali Mirza, who resided in Azarbaijan. When the prince lost his throne in 1909, the government confiscated his estates, including Khoramdareh. In 1935, seven of the fifteen hamlets that constituted Khoramdareh were included in the Zavar exchange with Amir Entesar. Majd became owner of the following hamlets in Khoramdareh: Dareh-akhund, Shina-kabir, Rudkhaneh-bala, Chehel-mir, Khoramdareh-ya-veisi, Jamal-ahmad, and Soltanabad. Majd reports that in 1935, all of Khoramdareh had been leased out by the government for a mere 20,000 rials. With much investment and effort by Majd, the income from the six remaining hamlets at the time of land distribution reached 2 million rials. By 1959 Khoramdareh had become one of the most productive villages in Iran. The following is a detailed list of Majd's rent in kind and in cash from the seven hamlets in Khoramdareh for the year 1959.

The development of Khoramdareh was to a great extent the result of Majd's efforts and expenditure of funds. He established a diesel-powered

Table 11.2. Revenues in Kind and in Cash for 1959, Khoramdareh, Zanjan (in kharvars and rials)

	Wheat	Barley	Beans	Grapes	Alfalfa	Straw	Cash (rials)
Dareh-akhund	35	12	32	941	54	45	71,100
Chehel-mir	27	11	69	242	91	40	216,000
Soltanabad	618	156	—	23	417	765	12,300
Rudkhaneh-bala	2	—	8	4	14	2	184,000
Jamal-ahmad	9	2	41	124	21	11	197,000
Shina-kabir	—	—	8	47	—	—	5,200
Khoramdareh-yv	—	—	—	142	—	—	4,300
Total	691	181	158	1,523	597	863	689,900

Source: Registry Office 118, Tehran, items 7964–7968, 14/9/38 [5 December 1959], reproduced in the memoirs of Mohammad Ali Majd.

electric generating station in Khoramdareh in 1954. This made Khoramdareh one of the first villages in Iran to receive electricity, and it received far better service than the city of Qazvin. Majd also installed a diesel-powered flour mill in Khoramdareh. In 1954, he purchased one spiked-wheel Case tractor and three Massey-Harris tractors (which frequently broke down and required expensive repairs), and thus introduced mechanization in Khoramdareh. In 1957, he bought a Case tractor-drawn combine harvester for 900,000 rials ($12,000), a large sum at the time; it was also very costly to maintain.

The distribution of land to peasants in Khoramdareh was actually begun by Majd in 1952. An examination of the Khoramdareh file in Majd's private papers shows that in 1952, the hamlet of Khoramdareh-ya-veisi was divided into plots and distributed to peasants. The process continued in 1959 when parts of the two hamlets of Chehel-mir and Dareh-akhund were distributed. They were divided into 1,200 lots each with registration tag and identity (pelak-e sabti), of which about 700 had been distributed by the advent of land reform. Thus, Majd was not opposed to land distribution per se. He was clearly one of the first landowners who had distributed land. His opposition was to the proposed land reform as "legislated" and implemented by the shah and Hasan Arsanjani. The balance of Majd's ownership at the time of land distribution consisted of the following:

1. The remaining parts of Chehel-mir and Dareh-akhund, consisting of both orchards and croplands.
2. Shina-kabir, a small but highly productive area.
3. Rudkhaneh-bala, a large and well watered area with more than 1 million poplar trees.
4. Jamal-ahmad, which also contained 600,000 poplars as well as cropland.
5. Soltanabad, located north of Khoramdareh, consisting of some 3,500 hectares of land.

Majd reports that Mohammad Reza Shah had established some vineyards in Soltanabad, but with the advent of government ownership, the qanat dried up and the vineyards withered. By 1935, Soltanabad was a ghost town.

Majd states that he spent a great deal of money and energy on the development of Soltanabad. He repaired the qanat, which had a flow of nine stones, built a mosque and a series of rural houses, and brought in settlers from Khoramdareh as well as other parts. He also planted vineyards and poplar nurseries. In short, he established a viable agricultural community. In addition, Majd reports that with the purchase of the tractors and combine harvester, he began mechanized cultivation in Soltanabad in 1954. By 1960, with the use of machines and wage labor, the area had expanded to some 500–1,000 hectares.

To summarize the situation in 1962, the land in the hamlet of Khoramdareh-ya-veisi had been entirely distributed to the cultivators; the hamlets of Dareh-akhund and Chehel-mir had been partially distributed. Soltanabad, Shina-kabir, Jamal-ahmad, and Rudkhaneh-bala remained. Jamal-ahmad, Shina-kabir, and Rudkhaneh-bala consisted of orchards, vineyards, and land cultivated by peasant sharecroppers. Soltanabad consisted of two parts, irrigated crop (*abi*) and nonirrigated crop (*deimi*). The irrigated portion had a qanat and was cultivated by tenants. The nonirrigated part of Soltanabad, however, was free of sitting tenants and had been cultivated by tractors and wage labor since 1954 and was thus exempt from distribution. Under the 1962 cabinet decree, there were two important exceptions to the land to be distributed. The first consisted of orchards, vineyards, and gardens. The second consisted of "mechanized" land, that is, land cultivated by machinery and wage labor and not by tenants. These two categories were to remain the property of the landowner. Specifically, Article 3 of Part 2 of the decree exempted the following categories of land. First, the owner retained orchards, gardens, nurseries, tea plantations, and vineyards where he owned both the plants and the land, along with water allocation. Second, the owner retained up to 500 hectares of the land that had been cultivated by wage labor and machinery (not by tenants or sharecroppers).

In 1962, land distribution was implemented in Khoramdareh. As in the case of Shal and Khoznein, all peasant-cultivated land in the four hamlets and the remaining parts of Chel-mir and Dareh-akhund were summarily seized by the Land Reform Organization. In addition, the mechanized part of Soltanabad, which was "legally" exempt, was also confiscated. This was a blatant violation of the land reform decree, which had specifically exempted up to 500 hectares of mechanized land. Moreover, since the determination made by the Land Reform Organization was final and without any judicial appeal or process, there was nothing to be done. Majd also reports in his memoirs that as a reward for his deeds, the head of the Land Reform Organization in Zanjan, Taghi Zand, was appointed to the 21st Majles.

Some other aspects of the affair are worth noting. Majd reports that in 1960 he turned down a purchase offer of 63.6 million rials ($848,000) for Khoramdareh. Based on the annual tax payments, the same property was "purchased" by the government in 1962 for 2,270,000 rials ($30,000) in land reform bonds. Of this sum, 750,000 rials ($10,000) was for Jamal-ahmad, 650,000 rials ($8,700) was for Rudkhaneh-bala, 270,000 rials ($3,500) was for Soltanabad, and 38,000 rials ($507) was for Shina-kabir. Given that the overall figures were similar to those of Khoznein, the real "compensation" for Khoramdareh was $10,000, or 1 percent of a purchase offer in 1960. As noted above, the reason that tax payment was low in Khoramdareh was similar to the case of Ebrahim Abad and Khoznein. Khoramdareh had been owned by the government until 1935, and the only tax assessment had been in 1955.

Majd also reports in his memoirs that he turned down a purchase offer of 18 million rials ($250,000) for Soltanabad in 1960. In 1961, Soltanabad had been used as collateral for a loan of 3 million rials, and Shina-kabir, which went for a mere 38,000 rials, was collateral for another loan of 3 million rials. Both obligations remained outstanding after the confiscation. That is, two hamlets that were collateral for a loan of nearly $100,000 were seized by the government for $4,000 in land reform bonds whose market value was $1,500. Under the provisions of the decree, in the event the assessed value by the Land Reform Organization was less than the amount of the loan or mortgage, while the land would be taken, the balance of the loan would remain the obligation of the ex-landowner, and the creditor could recover the balance through "normal legal channels," which meant the creditor could seize other properties. Concerning the ownership of the orchards and vineyards, legally, both the land and the plants belonged to Majd because he not only owned the land but he also paid for and established the trees and vineyards. Thus, under the provisions of the various land decrees, the orchards and vineyards were supposedly "exempt." But since they remained in the peasants' possession, and since there was no legal provision to enforce the owner's right, the orchards and vineyards became the de facto property of the peasants. With an interest rate of 24 percent, and unable to service the debt, Majd writes that by 1964, the 6 million rial debt on Soltanabad and Shina-kabir had grown to 13 million rials. Subsequently, Majd's house in the Valiabad district of Tehran, where I spent my childhood, was seized by the creditors in 1964.

It is also clear that, given the widespread incidence of indebtedness among landowners, the case of Khoramdareh and Majd was by no means unusual. Majd states that what the Pahlavi regime did to landowners in Iran was far worse than what the communists did to landowners in Russia, China, and Eastern Europe. In the communist countries, not only land but all other forms of wealth (factories, mines, urban real estate) were expropriated. The government annulled all debts when it confiscated property. In contrast, in Iran, only one group of people was singled out for vilification. Their property was confiscated, but all of their obligations, debts, and expenses remained. What the Pahlavi regime did to Iranian landowners was worse than what Nasser did to Egyptian landowners. In Egypt, after the expropriation of the large landed property (unlike Iran, small Egyptian landowners had been exempted from expropriation), Nasser moved to confiscate nearly all of Egypt's industry, commercial and trading enterprises, and much real estate. In Iran, only the landowners were expropriated, and the newly emerging industrial elite, and those with liquid assets, often those with ties to the Pahlavi regime, could then purchase the land reform bonds at a small fraction of their face value and exchange them for shares in the government factories and other assets. The misfortune of one group became a source of profit for another group.

To recap, it was stated by Majd that, since 1954, the landowning class had fallen into debt. The reason was a drastic decline in the relative price of the agricultural products. For this Majd blames the government for maintaining a cheap food policy for the benefit of the urban population and the foreign aid policy of the American government. In 1955, under the government of Hosein Ala, the U.S. government's assistance to the Iranian army had included 200,000 tons of wheat, which was about 10–15 percent of the domestic annual production. Its quantity had expanded over the years. According to Majd, this amount of wheat had been dumped on the market, depressing grain prices and causing severe difficulty for the land-owners as well as the peasants. This, Majd believes, was part of a plan by the U.S. government to weaken the landowning class. With declining real incomes and the landowners' need to assist the sharecroppers, who were similarly affected by the low agricultural prices, the landowning class as a whole had gone into debt, and their land had been heavily mortgaged. The annual interest rate for debt to landowners, with land as collateral, was 24 percent per year. If the debt was not serviced, then it would double every three years. With the advent of Arsanjani and the impending threat of land confiscation, agricultural land lost its value (no one would buy land under those circumstances), and the landowners could no longer borrow to service or reschedule their debt. In addition, with Arsanjani's incessant and open encouragement to peasants to seize the land and drive out the landowners, peasants stopped paying rent. That is, even small landowners who were not subject to the land distribution decree of 1962, because they owned less than or equal to six dangs of rural property, also lost their income and were driven from the villages. Thereafter, the government moved to confiscate land at a fraction of its value and pay the landowners over fifteen years. Under these circumstances, the landowners were unable to service their debt. This resulted in the doubling of the obligation every three years. Last but not least, the land distribution decree contained the inequitable and pernicious provision that if the value of the land, as established by the land decree regulations, was less than the amount of the loan, while the land would be taken, the balance of the loan would remain the obligation of the ex-landowner. The creditor could then recover the balance by seizing other property of the unfortunate land-owner, including his place of residence. This is what happened to Majd and countless others.

Ownership of Soltanabad, Khoramdareh, after 1962

In the course of implementation, land distribution regulations were violated in many ways. The egregious cases of Shal and Soltanabad were described above in detail. Lambton also describes in her 1969 book several instances where land was given to individuals, such as farm workers and water pump operators, who were not eligible to receive land under the 1962 decree. What transpired in Soltanabad in 1968 was different from the episodes described by Lambton. Land that had been seized by the government in violation of the 1962 decree was sold to persons close to the court or to Abdol Azim Valian, the minister for land reform, at prices well below market value. At the time of confiscation by the government in 1962, Soltanabad had no sitting tenants to receive the land and thus remained the property of the government. In 1968, Soltanabad was "sold" to individuals close to the royal court or high government circles for 520 rials ($6.90) per hectare. In fairness, it should be added that what transpired in Khoramdareh between 1962 and 1968 had many precedents in Persian history.

The identities of those who received land in Soltanabad are public record and available from the Revolutionary Court of Zanjan. They included men who were closely connected to the royal court, as well as several Majlis deputies and high-ranking officers and officials. Some of the land was subsequently acquired by a member of Iran's industrial elite, who built a Minoo biscuit factory in Soltanabad. After the Islamic revolution, some of these men were arrested and promptly executed. Others fled the country. Nearly all of Soltanabad, including the Minoo factory, was confiscated in favor of the Bonyad-e Mostazafan (Foundation for the Deprived), and remains in the possession of the Bonyad. It was the fifth time since 1911 that the Iranian state had intervened to determine landownership in Khoramdareh. The ownership of Soltanabad had not brought lasting happiness to any of its owners. It is also noteworthy that despite much talk of "Islamic justice," and similar to the practices under its two predecessors, the Office of Royal Estates under Reza Shah and the Pahlavi Foundation under Mohammad Reza Shah, the Bonayd under the Islamic Republic made no attempt to return such properties to their previous owners.

Ebrahim Abad, Qazvin: A Case Study in Landownership

Ebrahim Abad is located south of Qazvin and a short distance east of Khoznein. Its population in 1960 was 2,000–3,000 and its total area consisted of 7,000 hectares of highly fertile land. At one time, the village had possessed four qanats. According to Majd, the qanats were neglected and gradually stopped flowing when the village became government property. Its last operational qanat went dry following the floods of 1921. Majd reports that when he became the owner in 1935, Ebrahim Abad lacked even drinking water, which had to be brought from the neighboring village of Nowdeh. Majd began digging new qanats. For many years and after much expenditure, he failed. At last in the late 1940s, a highly productive qanat was established, yielding a flow of eighteen stones. Named Qanat-e Elahieh after my sister, Elahe, it became the best qanat in the Qazvin region, and the village became one of the most productive in all of Iran. Majd reports that in 1963 a report on Qazvin region had been prepared by the Israeli consulting firm, Tahal, which had received a fee of $2 million. In its report, Tahal had described the qanat in Ebrahim Abad as

Fig. 11.1. Dignitaries of Ebrahim Abad, circa 1955. Mohammad Ayati Ghaffari, accountant and chief inspector of Majd's estates *(fourth from right)*, Mohammad Shams, head supervisor of Ebrahim Abad *(center, wearing dark glasses)*, and Mousa Najafi, supervisor of Ebrahim Abad *(third from left)*.

the premier qanat in the entire Qazvin region. Majd also built an arbabi house and garden in Ebrahim Abad in 1950. He also bought a Case tractor and began cultivating sugarbeets.

The last tax assessment in Ebrahim Abad occurred in 1955. The assessment booklet contains some interesting information on the village. First, there was no problem of "landlessness" in the village. According to the tax assessors, the 1955 population was 1,500 persons. There were 130 farmers *(rayat)*. Only fifty people were described as *khoshneshin* (without land or cultivation rights); most landless residents were shopkeepers, professionals, artisans, and their families. That landlessness could not be a problem is established by the fact that of the 7,000 hectares of land, only 4,200 hectares were designated as "cultivated," of which 2,100 hectares were left fallow each year. Thus, average annual cultivation per farmer was 16 hectares. Records also reveal that at the time of land distribution in 1965, the number of farmers in Ebrahim Abad had declined to 104, despite this land abundance. There clearly had been some rural–urban migration. Whatever its causes, land shortage was not one of them.

Table 11.3. Winter and Summer Crop Production in Ebrahim Abad, Qazvin, 1955

	Seed Cultivated (kg)	Production (tons)	Owner's Share (tons)
Wheat	24,000	144	40
Barley	12,000	84	24
Sugarbeets	—	400	120
Melon	—	100	30
Potato	—	36	12
Cotton (American seed)	3,000	12	4
Peas	1,200	10	3
Oil seed	—	1.8	0.6

Source: Ministry of Finance, tax assessment booklet, 1955, village of Ebrahim Abad, district of Zahra, Qazvin.

Table 11.3 lists the amount of seed planted and the production of various crops for the year 1955. The village also contained 180 hectares of orchards, vineyards, and alfalfa fields. The production of grapes, alfalfa, cucumbers, and tree crops is reported in table 11.4.

Establishment of Majd Abad, 1957

Between 1955 and 1960, there was major development in Ebrahim Abad. First, with ample water supply from the qanat, an entire new village, named Majd Abad, was established to the east in 1957. Majd built twenty-six houses, a water storage, and a mosque, and settled nomadic members

Table 11.4. Production of Grapes, Alfalfa, and Tree Crops in Ebrahim Abad, Qazvin, 1955

	Production (kharvars)	Owner's Share (kharvars)
Grapes	400	100
Alfalfa	240	60
Pears, plums, and apples	24	6
Almonds	8	2
Cucumbers	4	1
Poplar trees (rials)	60,000	15,000

Source: Ministry of Finance, tax assessment booklet, 1955, village of Ebrahim Abad, district of Zahra, Qazvin.

of the Shahsavan tribes in the new village. The new settlers all had the same last name of Inanloo Shamloo. The new village's allocation of water from the qanat in Ebrahim Abad was 72 hours out of each 252 hours. Many vineyards, orchards, and poplar trees were planted. Within a short time, the farmers of Ebrahim Abad and Majd Abad were delivering 1,000 tons of sugarbeets per year to the sugar factory in Karaj, making Majd its largest supplier. In the absence of paved roads, the transportation of 1,000 tons of sugarbeets in a short period represented a major task. As an indication of the rapid pace of development in Ebrahim Abad and Majd Abad, the two villages had been leased out for 2 million rials for the year 1959 to Haj Rais Dana. The details are contained in a formal lease contract found in Majd's papers. Two clauses in the lease are most significant. First, the owner was obligated to maintain and repair the qanat. Second, as part of the lease agreement, Rais Dana was to spend 100,000 rials building a new qanat.

The twin cases of Ebrahim Abad and Majd Abad are important because they illustrate three key points. First, Iran was a country with surplus land and a relative scarcity of labor. Clearly, it would have been much cheaper and more efficient to settle the new village with experienced farmers. However, Majd Abad was not settled with farmers because they were not available. Instead, the village had to be settled with nomads of the Shahsavan tribe with no previous agricultural experience. They required several years of education. There was no "surplus" population or "land hunger" in the villages of Ebrahim Abad, Khoznein, Shal, or any of the many villages in the vicinity of Majd Abad. Second, the establishment of Majd Abad illustrates the role of landowners in establishing new villages. Third, some of the most productive and developed villages in Iran had been privatized in the 1930s. In 1935, Ebrahim Abad was a government-owned village with no operational qanat. Its last qanat had been dry since 1921. In 1935, it was "exchanged" for Zavar. By 1960, it was among the most developed villages in Iran and the one that was selected for purchase by the Aga Khan. Majd reports that in 1960, he was contacted by the chief of Tehran Police, Brigadier General Shah Khalili, who informed him that the Aga Khan, who was on a visit to Iran, had shown a desire to purchase a village in Iran. Of the 55,000 privately owned villages in Iran, he had selected Ebrahim Abad. Was Majd interested in selling? Heavily in debt, Majd had consented. An Irish agronomist and a Pakistani financial adviser of the Aga Khan came to Iran and accompanied Majd to Ebrahim Abad. Impressed by the state of agriculture in the village, they also decided to purchase the neighboring Khoznein. The parties agreed on a price of £500,000 for Ebrahim Abad and £150,000 for Khoznein. But, hearing rumors of land confiscation and distribution, the Aga Khan quickly withdrew his offer.

Concerning his relationship with the farmers of his villages, and as an example of the landlord-tenant relationship, Majd gives the following account:

> Whenever I visited Shal and Khoznein, a large group of individuals, including the elders and the head farmers, assembled outside the village to welcome me. In Shal, nearly everyone came, and often a sacrifice was made, and poetry was recited in my praise. But nothing like this took place in Ebrahim Abad, Jamjerd, and Khoramdareh. Usually, a day after my arrival, the headman and the head farmers would come to pay their respects. Subsequently, individuals would come to make requests. In the summer of 1961, at the height of Arsanjani's power and vilification of landowners, I decided to visit Ebrahim Abad. I notified the villagers of the time and day of my arrival. As I approached the village outskirts, I noticed a large gathering in front of the gates of the arbabi garden. Fearing that the same treatment that had been given to the other landowners following Arsanjani's incitement awaited me, I grew apprehensive. I told the driver to slow down so that I could decide whether or not to proceed. I decided to go on, and the car stopped in front of the arbabi. To my surprise, I saw that the farmers stood in several rows and had made a sacrifice. One of them came forward and addressed me with the utmost respect. He said that it was not customary for the farmers to welcome me and make a sacrifice. "But in these days, following much publicity against landowners in general, and the specific attacks on you by the minister of agriculture, we have come to welcome you and prove that we are not influenced by these actions. We wish to declare in a loud voice that we are satisfied with our landlord, and grateful for all he has done for us."

Land Distribution in Ebrahim Abad and Majd Abad:
A Case Study in Inequity and Injustice

Under the Additional Articles issued in the cabinet decree of 17 January 1963, landowners were given the following options on land not formally seized under Phase One: sale of land to the farmers, division of land with the farmers, leasing the land to the farmers for thirty years, purchase of cultivation rights, and joint cultivation. The last two options were impractical and, in practice, insignificant. What follows is a case study of the sale option in the case of Ebrahim Abad, division option in the case of Jamjerd, and the lease option in the cases of Zavar and Nashta.

The implementation of land distribution in Ebrahim Abad and Majd Abad provides an excellent example of some of the inequities and absurdities of the land decrees that were so rapidly approved and implemented. It is a spectacular case that will be examined in detail. It shows why the shah's land distribution had been declared to be against reason, religion, justice, and the fundamental interests of the country. Under the provisions of Phase One, each owner was permitted to retain one village. Majd had retained Ebrahim Abad. The village was collateral for a debt of 12 million rials, some of which had been incurred during the establishment of Majd Abad, and the creditor was threatening Majd with foreclosure, which would have meant sale by public auction. On the basis of the sale option under Phase Two, and under the pressure of debt, and having recently lost our house in Vali Abad to creditors, Majd reached a quick agreement with the farmers of the village for the sale of the land to the farmers. The agreed price for Ebrahim Abad was 19.2 million rials in cash. A similar agreement was reached with the farmers of Majd Abad, and the price agreed was 10 million rials in cash. On 11 April 1965, the appropriate land reform forms (Forms 10 and 11) were completed and signed by Majd, the 104 farmers of Ebrahim Abad, and the 26 farmers of Majd Abad, and the agreements had been duly certified and ratified by the representative of the Land Reform Organization. The total agreed price was 29.2 million rials ($384,000), of which 19.2 million rials was for Ebrahim Abad, and 10 million was for Majd Abad. Clearly, the farmers thought they had obtained a good deal, and they had no difficulty in raising an average of $3,000 per farmer. Although Majd had been offered over $1 million for the same property five years earlier, given the pressure of debt and his difficult situation, he had no choice but to accept whatever he could get. However, if Majd and, as it turned out, the hapless farmers of Majd Abad believed that this was the end of the matter, they were sadly mistaken.

Upon inspection, the Land Reform Organization in Tehran objected on the grounds that the property consisted of two separate villages, one of which, Majd Abad, should have been included under Phase One. This was decided despite the fact that Majd had personally established the village of Majd Abad from scratch and brought in the settlers during the previous decade, and the village of Majd Abad had no separate registration or tax identity. The reason Majd Abad did not have a separate tax identity was simple. The last tax assessment before land distribution in this region had taken place in 1955, when Majd Abad had not yet been established. In any case, not having a separate tax and registration identity, how was the village to be "appraised"? If treated as a separate village and legal entity from Ebrahim Abad, Majd Abad could lose its share of qanat water from Ebrahim Abad. Where were the hapless farmers of Majd Abad to obtain irrigation water? In short, what should have been a simple sale to the farmers was turned into a nightmare for Majd and the farmers of Majd Abad. Moreover, as Lambton's account shows, this was by no means an isolated case. As discussed in chapter 5, a special cabinet decree had been issued in 1962 concerning the villages that did not have a separate tax record. In reviewing this case almost forty years later, one cannot help but feel that there were inside elements sabotaging the Pahlavi regime from within. Otherwise, it is impossible to come up with a rational explanation for such acts.

Although Majd was extremely anxious to complete the transaction and pay off the creditor, the matter could not be completed until the problem of Majd Abad had been sorted out. It required establishing the boundaries of the new village and determining its "price" under the provisions of Phase One. There began a trail of correspondence between Majd and the Land Reform Organization in Qazvin and Tehran that could be of great interest to students of Iran's land distribution and agrarian history. A chronological account of the correspondence and appropriate documentation is provided. Seven months after the conclusion of the sale agreements with the farmers of Ebrahim Abad and Majd Abad, Majd received the following letter from the Land Reform Organization:

> Lion and Sun
> Ministry of Agriculture
> Land Reform Organization
> Number 11924
> Date: 14 November 1965
>
> His Excellency Mr. Mohammad Ali Majd,
> According to the contents of letters numbers 22932–11/8/44 and 24822–11/8/44 of the Head Bureau of Agriculture, Development and Land Reform of the Province of Tehran concerning the villages of Ebrahim Abad and Majd Abad, and in consideration of the cultivation situation in the above villages, and Article One of the 37th Ruling by the [Land Reform] Council, the original registration tag number 11 is determined to consist of two separate six-dang villages. Consequently, your total ownership amounts to twelve dangs, and in accordance with Article Two of the land reform law you should have only kept six dangs. It is hereby requested that in less than twenty days you should select your chosen village, contact this office, render the necessary cooperation with the registration

officials for the purpose of determining the boundaries of the two villages, and sign the necessary certificates under the supervision of representatives of this bureau. Naturally, in the event of failure to contact this office, and in accordance with the appropriate laws and regulations, this office will take the necessary action concerning selection of your village and the purchase of the excess amount. In such a case, subsequent objection will not be forbidden.

Chief of Land Reform, Qazvin Region,
Engineer Soltanzadeh

Under pressure to get the transaction moving, Majd sent the following letter, dated 22 November 1965, to the Land Reform Organization in Qazvin.

Respected Leadership of Land Reform Organization, Qazvin Region,

In response to letter number 11924, dated 14 November 1965, on the subject of the village of Ebrahim Abad, registration tag 11, District of Ramand, Qazvin, I bring the following to your attention.

1. Ebrahim Abad is my chosen village, and Majd Abad is part of Ebrahim Abad. But since the Land Reform Bureau in Tehran insists that there are two villages, matters have come to a halt. Based on my rights and without endangering my legal rights, I declare that Ebrahim Abad is my chosen village, and if Majd Abad is considered a separate village and in excess of the maximum permitted, then its tax should be determined.
2. In your letter number 2972 dated 28 July 1965 to Notary Office 1 in Qazvin, you had acknowledged that form number 10 had been completed and signed by myself as landowner and all the cultivators, and the sale of Ebrahim Abad and Majd Abad finalized for a price of 19.2 million rials for Ebrahim Abad and 10 million rials for Majd Abad. Although the real value of Majd Abad is considerably more than 10 million rials, I expect that its assessed tax should at least reflect this amount.
3. On the subject of determining the border of the two villages, I have to arrange it in such a way that conflict between the inhabitants is minimized.
Respectfully,
Mohammad Ali Majd

Three days later, Majd traveled to Ebrahim Abad and met with the head farmers and the elders, and they signed the following statements:

In the year 1955 when the village of Ebrahim Abad underwent a tax assessment by the Ministry of Finance, the hamlet of Majd Abad did not exist. Its establishment and cultivation began in the year 1957. I hereby request those who are knowledgeable about the above to certify the above. With thanks, 25 November 1965, Mohammad Ali Majd (signature).

We, the sarbonehs and motamedin [respected persons] and cultivators of the village of Ebrahim Abad hereby certify that in the year 1955 when the village of Ebrahim Abad was assessed for taxation, the current hamlet of Majd Abad did not exist. The hamlet of Majd Abad was established and settled in 1957, and cultivation was begun at that time. (Signatures or fingerprints belonging to twenty-six individuals)

A few days later, the following letter arrived:

Lion and Sun
Ministry of Agriculture
Land Reform Organization
Number 13146
Date: 2 December 1965

His Excellency Mr. Mohammad Ali Majd,

In reference to your letter of 22 November 1965, it is declared.

First, based on legal determination, the villages of Ebrahim Abad and Majd Abad have been recognized as two separate and independent villages.

Second, as you are aware, the determination of price of the estates that are in excess of the limit set by law under Phase One is subject to special regulations and cabinet decrees. Tax assessment and valuation of such properties is not under the control or jurisdiction of a specific bureau.

Third, concerning the establishment of the borders of the two villages of Ebrahim Abad and Majd Abad, you have to personally go to the Bureau of Registration of Documents and Estates, Township of Qazvin. Consequently, in order to expedite and finalize matters concerning your estates, contact the registration bureau in Qazvin as soon as possible, and notify this office of the outcome. Of course at the time of establishing the borders of the above villages, the officials of this office will provide the necessary cooperation.

Chief of Land Reform, Qazvin Region
Engineer Soltanzadeh

And so the correspondence continued. On 7 December 1965, Majd wrote to the Land Reform Organization and enclosed several documents, including a copy of the original 1935 ownership deed to Ebrahim Abad and a copy of the tax assessment in 1955 in which the owner's revenues are listed. In neither document was there any mention of Majd Abad. How could there be? He also enclosed a copy of the signed affidavit and certificate by the twenty-six individuals certifying that Majd Abad had been established by Majd in 1957. Finally, he enclosed a copy of the lease agreement for the year 1959 in which the two villages had been leased out for 2 million rials, and showed that in the years following the establishment of Majd Abad, revenues had doubled. Not having received a response, with rising frustration, on 4 January 1966, he wrote to Arsanjani's successor, General Esmail Riahi:

General Riahi, Respected Minister of Agriculture

Pursuant to my letter of 11 April 1965, I trouble you with the following.

1. As you are aware, on 11 April 1965, and in the presence of the officials of the Qazvin Land Reform Organization, an agreement was concluded between me and the cultivators of the village of Ebrahim Abad and those of the hamlet of Majd Abad, which is one of the hamlets and part of Ebrahim Abad. By this agreement, the village of Ebrahim Abad was to be transferred to the cultivators for 19.2 million rials, and the hamlet of Majd Abad was to be transferred for 10 million rials. At that time, Form 10 was completed, signed by all, and certified by officials of the Land Reform Organization.
2. Officials of the Tehran Agriculture Bureau traveled to Ebrahim Abad on inspection. On their return they declared that there were two villages.
3. Although their reasons were illegal, I had no choice but to surrender. I asked that the Majd Abad file be examined and its tax determined. The reason was Ebrahim Abad was assessed in 1955. In 1957, I established Majd Abad and developed part of the uncultivated land. Thus, at the time of tax assessment in 1955, Majd Abad did not exist to be assessed. In the enclosed copy of ownership deed to Ebrahim Abad and the tax assessment form, there is no mention of Majd Abad. In addition, a

     copy of the signed certificate by the head cultivators is ten-
dered.

4. I beg you to order that the enclosed documents be closely examined and, if they confirm what I have said, the annual revenue and tax for Majd Abad be determined.

5. In conclusion, since the agreement between me and the cultivators of Majd Abad had set a price of 10 million rials and
Form 10 signed by all in the presence of Land Reform Organization representatives, any appraisal of less than 10 million
rials is subject to my objection on the basis of Article 13 of the
law.

Respectfully,
Mohammad Ali Majd
Copy sent to Land Reform Organization, Qazvin District.

Four weeks after he wrote to the minister, and nearly a year after his
agreement with the farmers, he received the following letter from the
Land Reform Organization:

Lion and Sun
Ministry of Agriculture
Land Reform Organization
Number 16491
Date: 2 February 1966

Mr. Mohammad Ali Majd,
In response to letter number 10–98–13/10/44 addressed to the highest authority of the Ministry, a copy of which was sent to this bureau, as you were informed in person and from your contact with
the registration bureau, arrangements have been made for separating and establishing the boundaries of the villages of Ebrahim Abad
and Majd Abad, and a surveyor has been selected. Unfortunately,
matters have been delayed because of rainfall, but as soon as the
weather permits, separation and purchase of Majd Abad in accordance with the provisions of Phase One of the land reform law will
be undertaken. Concerning Ebrahim Abad, it will be subject to the
provisions of Phase Two of the land reform law. Concerning item 4
of your letter, pursuant to the correspondence with Tehran, this
office sees no need to reexamine the revenues of Majd Abad. Concerning item 5 of your letter, after the determination of the purchase price of Majd Abad and notification, you should submit your

objection and documents so that it can be dealt with in accordance with Article 13 of the law.

Chief of Land Reform, Qazvin Region
Engineer Soltanzadeh

Five weeks later, Majd received an announcement and notification dated 13 March 1966, number 18220–1014, concerning the purchase price of Majd Abad. Although Majd Abad had no tax record, the announcement claimed that on the basis of "certificate number 15688–24/7/41" from the Bureau of Finance in Qazvin, the tax in Majd Abad was determined to be 10,052.23 rials. How this tax had been determined is not clear. With a "coefficient" of 130, the "price" of Majd Abad was determined to be 1,306,789.90 rials ($18,500) in land reform bonds with a rate of interest of 6 percent. The cash value of the bonds was about $7,000. The announcement also reminded Majd that unless he came and signed the transfer papers within fifteen days, on the basis of Article 14 of the Amended Land Reform Law, the Land Reform Organization would act as his "representative," sign the papers on "his behalf," and notify the public prosecutor. Majd immediately lodged a protest. In response, the Land Reform Organization wrote to Majd that his protest had been "received and registered." Shortly thereafter, Majd Abad, similar to Khoznein, Shal, and the seven hamlets in Khoramdareh, was seized by the Land Reform Organization under Article 14 of the land decree.

Several points about Majd Abad are noteworthy. In a case where the farmers themselves were willing to pay $150,000 in cash, the village was seized by the government for an amount that was barely 5 percent of the distress price. In addition, the injustice was compounded by the fact that those who had been enterprising and had created new qanats and villages were so heavily penalized. In this case, Majd would have been much better off if he had not built Majd Abad. First, the $7,000 "compensation" was less than what he had spent on building the houses, a mosque, a water storage, and an irrigation canal that brought water to the fields of Majd Abad from the qanat in Ebrahim Abad. Second, the price for Ebrahim Abad would have been higher if Majd Abad had not existed. In his memoirs, with great bitterness, Majd notes that his "reward" for building Majd Abad, expanding production, and establishing a viable community was a heavy penalty and a pile of unpaid debts. Ebrahim Abad was sold to the farmers for 19.2 million rials ($260,000), most of which went for the repayment of the debt on the property. In 1960, Majd had been offered £500,000 for the same village. It was not just the likes of Majd who were ruined. The same fate was dealt to those who owned a few hectares or a fraction of a dang.

Jamjerd and Fatn Abad, Qazvin

Located in Qaqazan District of Qazvin, in the foothills of the Elburz
Mountains, and three kilometers south of Qazvin-Zanjan highway, Jam-
jerd enjoys cool summer temperatures. It was once owned by my great-
grandfather, Mohammad Vali Khan Tonekaboni. The government seized
it in 1923, then released it around 1930, and my grandmother, Amir
Zadeh, inherited 5.5 dangs. After her death, my mother inherited her
property. The remaining half dang eventually went my mother's cousin,
Anis Dowleh, daughter of Amir Asad and wife of Abol Hasan Amidi-
Nuri. In the years Jamjerd was under government seizure, it was neglected.
There had been two qanats, called Jamjerd Qanat and Einestan Qanat.
Einestan had fallen into disrepair and had dried up. Majd reports that in
1933, when he took control of Jamjerd, most of its seventy-two families
had scattered and were employed in construction and other activities in
Tehran and Qazvin. Majd had brought them back, paid their debts, and
provided them with working capital. By the 1950s, his tenants were planting 214 kharvars of seed, and my father's share reached 800 kharvars of
grain. He also constructed a new arbabi building in 1954. As in Majd
Abad, Majd established a new village in the land of Jamjerd, where he dug
a new qanat and built thirty-two homes. This village he named Fatn
Abad.

Fig. 11.2. Qanat Einestan, Jamjerd, circa 1955.

Since Jamjerd and Fatn Abad had been transferred to the nine children of Majd and the three sons of Amidi-Nuri before the 1962 land decree, they were exempted from Phase One of land distribution. Under Phase Two, Jamjerd and Fatn Abad were divided between the farmers and the owners on the basis of the respective crop shares. A formal agreement was drawn up and signed, and the boundaries were delineated and confirmed by the head of the Land Reform Organization in Qazvin. I was in Jamjerd when the agreement was signed in August 1967. Under the division, 4,000 hectares were given to some 120 farmers of Jamjerd and Fatn Abad, and 1,000 hectares (800 hectares in Jamjerd and 200 hectares in Fatn Abad) remained the property of the twelve children of Majd and Amidi-Nuri. Einestan Qanat and all vineyards and alfalfa fields irrigated by Einestan became the property of the farmers. The owners retained one-fourth ownership in the Jamjerd and Fatn Abad Qanats. However, it soon became clear that some of the farmers of Jamjerd were unhappy with the division, and they openly coveted the land that remained with the owners. The decade following land distribution was one of continuous conflict and friction between the owners and the former sharecroppers, who repeatedly attempted to encroach and seize the land of the owners, resulting in several complaints to the gendarmerie and the judiciary. In retrospect, the unhappiness of the Jamjerd farmers is understandable. Having been told for several years that the land "belonged" to them, they felt cheated because they had only become part owners of Jamjerd. Under the prevailing conditions in Iran, formal and "legal" agreements and private property rights had little meaning and commanded no respect.

The number of qanats declined drastically in the years following land distribution. Jamjerd provides an excellent illustration. First, the Einestan Qanat, which had been entirely transferred to the farmers, was not maintained, and by 1980 its flow had slowed to a trickle. This was a clear example of the farmers' inability to perform tasks that had been undertaken by the landowners. Cooperation and coordination among some 120 farmers was not possible. The other qanat in Jamjerd fared only slightly better. At first, the landowners tried to maintain the qanat and the irrigation canals. But the farmers were unwilling to contribute their share of the costs. With deterioration in relations and continuous conflict between the two sides, the owners no longer commissioned repairs, and the lower part of the qanat collapsed in 1980.

With the advent of revolution and the temporary breakdown of law and order in the early days of the revolution, my family's land in Jamjerd was seized by the villagers as well as by outsiders. It is noteworthy that some of the squatters were actually residents of the city of Qazvin. That is, they had migrated from Jamjerd and had sold or rented out their land. Now they had returned and were in the process of acquiring more land. In the anarchy, the arbabi, which had been repeatedly burglarized and vandalized by the local villagers before the revolution, was demolished by vandals, and its brick and lumber were carted away. The squatters continued to retain the land, and in 1986 the Islamic Majlis passed a law that formally gave them this land. Two years later, the squatters were authorized to obtain formal title deeds to the land they held. The law also contained a provision for giving a "just" compensation to the expropriated owners. However, as of 1999, we have received nothing. The implications of this case with respect to the land policy of the Islamic Republic will be addressed in the concluding chapter of this book.[9]

Lia, Qazvin

The disturbances in Lia after land distribution were more serious. The village of Lia is located in Dashtabi District south of Qazvin. It is close to a sugarbeet processing plant. Five and one-half dangs (5.5 shares out of 6 shares) of Lia had been owned by Abol Hasan Amidi-Nuri, whose three sons owned one-half dang in Jamjerd. Long a Majles deputy, he had served as deputy prime minister under Zahedi and he was one of the most accomplished and skillful attorneys in Iran. He was also one of the active leaders of the Agricultural Union of Iran. Under Phase Two, Lia had been divided between the landowners and farmers on the basis of crop shares. However, similar to Jamjerd, the farmers in Lia were unhappy, and there was much friction between the two sides. After the division, in order to strengthen his ownership, Amidi-Nuri began mechanized cultivation, and in 1968 he planted 200 hectares of wheat and barley, 30 hectares of sugarbeets, and some cotton. One night in May 1968, the residents of the village destroyed Amidi-Nuri's crop. Several gendarmes to the village came to investigate and were attacked by the villagers. Several villagers were then imprisoned.

Transfer of Zavar, Tonekabon, January 1962

Nikki Keddie, among others, claims that many landowners were able to avoid loss of property by transferring it to their kin. Some of this undoubtedly took place, but the attempt to keep land was ultimately futile. Sensing an imminent confiscation of private estates, early in 1962, my parents transferred ownership of their Zavar estates to their nine children. My father recounts:

> Under the original land reform law of 1960, which had been approved by the Majles, the owners had two years to transfer to their

children an amount of land that was 1.5 times their personal limit of ownership. Although more than a year remained to the law's deadline, with the chaos and unpredictability that had been created under Arsanjani, I decided to take advantage of the provision. It was decided with Amir Banou Khanum that 3.5 dangs of Zavar would be transferred to her seven children (two shares for each son, and one share for each daughter). Thereafter, in the interest of justice, two shares out of twelve would be transferred to my other children, Zahra and Mehri. This was accomplished in the notary office of Mr. Abol Fazl Alameh on 2 and 3 January 1962. Thereafter, I went to Qazvin, and the village of Jamjerd was similarly transferred to my nine children. Seven days after this transfer, the cabinet decree of 9 January 1962 was issued. Under the decree all land transfers and transactions were prohibited from the date of the decree's issue.

Arsanjani's first step after the decree was to dispatch about thirty land reform officials to the estates of Zavar that had been transferred to my children. They made a list of all the farmers and declared to the tenants that the land was theirs. Arsanjani came personally to Zavar and incited the farmers to seize all seaside land so that nothing should remain for the landowners. Fortunately, he was met with the brave resistance of such individuals as Mr. Abol Fazl Alameh, head of Notary Office 1, Mr. Eslami, governor of Shahsavar, Mr. Azodi Deilami, head of the judiciary, Mr. Foroutan Jafari, the prosecutor general of Shahsavar, Mr. Salar Goudarzi, head of the local registration office, and Mr. Jafari, head of the land reform office in Shahsavar. Although, apart from Mr. Alameh, I did not even know the other gentlemen, based on their duty and conscience, they strongly confirmed the date and the transfers of 2 and 3 January. Arsanjani had subsequently claimed that the transfer and the date were forgeries, and the transaction had taken place after 9 January. He even sent the Inspector General of the Registry Office to inspect the transfer and have it nullified. By the will of God, he failed in his attempts.

Land Distribution in Zavar, 1963–1971

Just as in 1934 when Amir Entesar had vainly attempted to save Zavar from the clutches of Reza Shah, the 1962 transfer was similarly and ultimately futile. It saved Zavar from immediate confiscation by the government. However, the government gradually but systematically moved to confiscate Zavar. The implementation of the various land decrees in

Zavar reveals the various phases of land distribution, the manner in which the owners were deprived of their property, and the token compensation paid for the land. A detailed account will be given below. Here, suffice it to point out that between 1935 and 1965, Zavar was confiscated twice by the Pahlavi regime.

The 1954 settlement agreement with the Pahlavi estates, described in chapter 4, gave my mother 3.5-dang ownership (3.5 shares out of 6 shares) in the following villages and hamlets: Kotra (consisting of three hamlets, Kotra-ye Olia, Kotra-ye Sofla, and Lot-e Kotra), Zavar, Habib Abad, Babulat, Rud Posht (consisting of Rud Posht-e Bala and Rud Posht-e Sofla), Ashraf Abad, Kat Kaleh, Al-e Kaleh, Pelet Kaleh, and Mohammad Hosein Abad. The settlement also gave 3.5-dang ownership in the following pastures: Hosein Abad, Tamesh Kot, and Chal Sara. In addition, six dangs of the village of Til Borde-sar and six dangs of the pasture of Talusarak were my mother's property from an earlier ruling. The villages and hamlets were transferred, but she retained ownership of the pastures.

These pastures were taken from her under the 1963 nationalization cabinet decree. Then the Land Reform Organization determined that the property transferred to me and my brothers exceeded the maximum of six dangs permitted under the 1962 land distribution decree. It had somehow decided that each of us actually owned the equivalent of seven dangs. How this arbitrary determination had been made remains a mystery. Since the Land Reform Organization's ruling was final, it apparently did not have to provide an explanation. Thus, after much negotiation with the Land Reform Organization of Mazandaran, the village of Mohammad Hosein Abad and the valuable hamlet of Lot-e Kotra were transferred to the government for a mere 170,000 rials ($2,200) in land reform bonds, redeemable over fifteen years. Majd states that Lot-e Kotra alone was worth 12 million rials ($170,000).

Phase One had not been completed in Zavar. Two years later, right in the middle of Phase Two, we received a letter dated 25 September 1965 from the Land Reform Organization. It stated that the previous communication was in error and that the male owners still owned "excess" land and were thus still liable to the provisions of Phase One. The Land Reform Organization does not explain how it had arrived at the first or the subsequent computation of ownership. It arbitrarily decided that a landowner was "still" subject to the provisions of Phase One. In response to this ruling, Majd reports that the shares of his three sons in the villages of Rude Posh-te Sofla, Rude Poshte-e Olia, and Babulot were transferred to the government for a sum equal to 1 percent of the value, payable over fifteen years. That was the nominal end of Phase One.

Meanwhile, Phase Two was in progress. What came to be known as the Additional Articles to the Amendment Law of the Land Reform Law, subsequently called Phase Two of land reform, was the cabinet decree of 17 January 1963, which "supplemented" the earlier "amended law." Addendum 6 of Article 1 of the Additional Articles stated the following: "Concerning the rice fields, the owners can retain up to 30 hectares, and then select Alternative A or B. Land in excess of 30 hectares will be distributed between the farmers. The price of each hectare of rice field sold to the farmers will be based on the last tax payment before January 1962 and the land reform coefficient and will be determined by the Land Reform Organization." The Addendum defined the alternatives:

> Alternative A—The owners can rent their land to the farmers at a cash rent equal to the average revenue of the previous three years. The Land Reform Organization is required to establish a regional rent coefficient. The duration of the lease will be thirty years, and the rent will be subject to revision every five years.
>
> Alternative B—The owners can sell their land to the farmers by mutual consent. Winter and summer crops that are planted prior to the sale of the land will be divided according to the usual customary manner.

In short, the owners of rice fields with more than 30 hectares were required to sell the "excess" to the farmers on terms identical to those of Phase One. With the remaining 30 hectares, they could choose either to sell the remaining land to the farmers or lease it for thirty years. Rents were to be based on the average of the previous three years when tenants had withheld rent.

Shortly after the transfer of the above three villages, the Land Reform Organization informed us that the rice fields were to be leased out to the farmers for thirty years. Initially, the Land Reform Organization had said nothing about the 30-hectare limit. Evidently, it decided on its own that only selective clauses of the decree were to be applied. Concerning the rent to be paid to the landowners, Majd records that it was arbitrarily fixed at 260 rials ($3.30) per jarib (1,000 square meters), or $33 per hectare. This contrasted with a rent of 550 kilograms of rice per hectare before land reform. Only after the leases had been made, the Land Reform Organization had stipulated that under the provisions of Article 1 of the Additional Articles, the maximum amount of ownership of rice fields was to be 30 hectares. The excess was to be transferred to the government for distribution to the farmers. Once again, failure to respond within the prescribed period would result in the application of the notorious Article 14. Majd reports that after the transfer of the "excess" land at a "price" that barely amounted to 5 percent of the real worth of the land (payable over fifteen years), each person was left with a nominal ownership of 30 hectares and a nominal rent income of 78,000 rials ($1,000) per year. However, in practice, even this paltry rent could not be collected, because many farmers refused to pay this "legal" rent.

Under Phase Three, all leased lands were to be sold to the farmers or divided with them. Given that the owners could not even collect rent, the division option was not a realistic alternative. In 1969, the Land Reform Organization informed my family that under the provisions of Phase Three, the 30 hectares that had remained for each owner were to be sold to the farmers who leased the land. The price to be paid was twelve times the annual rent, payable over ten years. It came to 936,000 rials ($12,000) in land reform bonds per owner. With the normal discount on these bonds, the real compensation was about $6,000 per owner, less than the price of an Iranian-assembled Peykan automobile. Phase Three of land distribution completed the systematic and nearly total confiscation of all of the landowners in Zavar. With the three phases of land reform and the nationalization of forests and pastures, *all* agricultural land belonging to the landowners had been seized.

Land Distribution in Moalem Kala, Mazandaran: A Comparison with Zavar

The village of Moalem Kala sits in Mazandaran between Amol and Mahmoud Abad. Before land distribution, it had been owned by Princess Fatemeh Pahlavi, a sister of the shah. Like Zavar, its land consisted of rice fields, forests, and pastures. After the implementation of land distribution and the nationalization of forests and pastures, the princess continued to own much land in Moalem Kala. As demonstrated above in the case of Zavar, the landowners were not permitted to maintain agricultural land in the rice-growing region of Mazandaran. Nor were they allowed to maintain forest and pasture lands that had been nationalized in 1963. That the princess continued to own land indicates that there had been a violation of the regulations. Another possibility is that the forests and pastures in Moalem Kala had been "exempted" from the 1963 nationalization cabinet decree. Whatever the situation, the farmers in Moalem Kala felt cheated. The situation exploded in 1968. The following account is given by Majd.

The princess had assigned the management of her land in Moalem Kala to a retired army colonel. In 1965, the colonel reached an agreement with the farmers of Moalem Kala concerning previously uncultivated land belonging to the princess. The farmers were to clear the land of trees and bushes and plant rice. Thus, it was similar to the agreements between the farmers and the Office of Royal Estates under Reza Shah (see appendix A). In return for developing the land, the farmers could plant and harvest rice for three years without paying rent. In 1968 they were to vacate the land, and the colonel would take over on behalf of the princess. In 1968, the farmers refused to turn over the land to the colonel. In response to the colonel's complaint, the gendarmerie in Amol was beefed up with twenty gendarmes from Sari, and the officers were dispatched to Moalem Kala. Armed with clubs and scythes, the villagers resisted, and several gendarmes were wounded. The gendarmes then opened fire, killing four and wounding nine, and forced the villagers to flee. Although the gendarmerie quickly cleared the land belonging to the shah's sister, it ignored the cries for help from small landowners who were unable to collect the supposedly "legal" rent.

A Case Study of a Small Landowner in Nashta, Tonekabon

The estates of Nashta were located along the Caspian shore, east of the township of Tonekabon in the province of Mazandaran. A neighbor of Zavar, Nashta consisted of eighteen villages and hamlets and about twenty pastures and forests. Most of Nashta had been the property of one Hedayatollah Khan Massoudi Tonekaboni, Massoud ol Molk (died ca. 1925). The exact amount of his property is undetermined because some of Nashta was long held by small landowners. Hedayatollah Khan had three wives and was survived by six sons and eight daughters. One of his daughters and inheritors was Soghra Khanum Massoudi Tonekaboni (1900–1975). According to the Islamic inheritance practices, each son's share was one-tenth and each daughter's share was one-twentieth of the inheritance. Thus, upon her father's death, Soghra Khanum inherited one-twentieth of her father's land in Nashta. In 1925, she married my uncle, Hosein Qoli Tonekaboni, Amir Nasri (1905–1932), whose parents owned the neighboring estates of Zavar. Amir Nasri and Soghra Khanum had two children who died in infancy. Reza Shah confiscated Nashta in 1932, and the owners were arrested and exiled. Amir Nasri perished in prison, and Soghra Khanum came to live with my parents. Given the mores of the time, it would have been unthinkable for a young widow to live on her own. She never remarried and did not own a home.

In 1944, the court returned her land.[10] Although she was the daughter of a prominent family, she was not wealthy. I am amazed at how little income she derived from her land.[11] Her meager resources should come as no surprise, however. Her property was the equivalent of 57 hectares of

Fig. 11.3. Soghra Khanum Massoudi Tonekaboni, Tighestan house and garden, Shemiran, circa 1950.

rice fields. Assuming a rent of 300 kilograms per hectare, her gross rent would have been 17 tons of rice before tax. A good portion would have consisted of collection costs as well as legitimate expenses, leaving her with perhaps 10–12 tons. Her income would have been no greater than that of a medium peasant cultivating 3 hectares of rice.

An account of how Soghra Khanum fared under the land distribution of 1962–71 can be drawn from her private papers and her land reform file. By the time land distribution came, she was in her mid-sixties and had long been addicted to opium. If she had expected comfort and security in her old age, she was sadly mistaken. Under Phase One of land distribution, maximum ownership was set at one entire village, or its equivalent of six dangs in scattered villages. Since the extent of her property appeared to be below the maximum allowed, Soghra Khanum was not initially included under Phase One. Nevertheless, her income ceased abruptly. First, following intense government propaganda against landowners, tenants stopped paying rent. Second, following the January 1963 decree that nationalized forests and pastures, her income from grazing and sale of wood for charcoal and timber ended. None of this deterred the Ministry of Finance from demanding the usual agricultural and land taxes. In 1964, the Ministry informed Soghra Khanum that unless she immediately paid some 38,000 rials ($550) in back taxes and penalty for the previous three years, it would seize and auction her property, including her home. In vain she pleaded that she had received no income for three years. But the Ministry was adamant. Under Phase Two, her land was formally leased to the cultivating tenants. But the tenants frequently refused to pay rent. Yet the Ministry of Finance continued its harassment and tried to collect taxes on income that existed only on paper. Third, emboldened by government propaganda and state-sponsored lawlessness, a group of peasants seized some of her land by the sea. Numerous letters record her complaints to the prosecutor general, Fereydoon Foroutan, as well as to the gendarmerie in the village of Nashtarud. It appears that after the squatters were evicted, she had to have the land enclosed by a wall.

Another matter that put her to considerable trouble and expense was that of property registration. In compliance with the 1962 cabinet decree, subsequently known as Phase One, she completed the mandatory form, declaring her ownership in the villages of Nashta. Convinced that she was exempt from Phase One, she volunteered to sell her land to the Ministry of Agriculture for distribution to peasants, if a mutually agreeable price could be arrived at. However, the Land Reform Organization of Mazandaran notified her in 1963 that no record of her ownership existed in the Bureau of Registration and Deeds, even though she was recognized as one of the owners of the estates of Nashta and had paid the agricultural tax. She was instructed to contact the bureau to clear up the situation. It was then learned that although the ownership of 26 shares out of 480 shares in each of the villages of Nashta had been bestowed on her by a court order in 1944, the matter had not been formally registered. She began the long process of recording and registering her ownership. This was an expensive process, and it was not completed until 1967–68. Given her meager finances, she could ill afford the registration and legal fees. It is very clear that this process was undertaken in response to the orders of the Land Reform Organization.[12]

From the announcements in the official publication of the Ministry of Justice, Central Bureau of Registration of Documents, it is learned that Soghra Massoudi Tonekaboni, daughter of Hedayatollah Khan, was owner of 26 shares musha (jointly owned) out of 480 shares in each of the eighteen villages of the estates of Nashta, not including the parts held by the small landowners. In aggregate, her ownership consisted of 468 shares (18 x 26) out of 8,640 shares (18 x 480). (Each dang consisted of 80 shares, and a whole village was equal to 480 shares, 80 x 6). After this information was established, it was determined that Soghra Khanum *was* subject to Phase One of land distribution after all. The reason was that as an inheritor of the share of a sister, Om-Mol Khaqan, who died in 1955, Soghra Khanum had inherited one-twelfth of her sister's share of one-twentieth of the estates of Nashta (1/12 x 1/20 x 8,640 = 36). When these 36 shares were added to her own 468 shares, the result was 504 shares. This exceeded the permissible level of 480 by 24 shares. She was thus liable to Phase One and had to divest herself of 24 shares. An examination of the land distribution file shows that her actual nominal ownership in terms of area, and not just shares, was at most 57 hectares musha (jointly owned) of rice fields. Despite the small amount of land owned, Soghra Khanum was included in all three phases of land distribution.

According to an announcement by the Land Reform Organization, District of Shahsavar (Tonekabon), notice number 1447, dated 6 July 1968, her 26 shares out of 480 shares in the village of Khoshke-bur (excluding the land belonging to the small landowners) was to be purchased for 67,881 rials ($960), based on an annual tax of 332.75 rials. This sale reduced her ownership to 478 shares, just below the permitted 480. The announcement informed her that on the basis of Article 13 of the Amended Law to the Land Reform Law, her property was to be purchased, and she was notified of the price. If she objected to the proposed price, she had ten days to register her objection. She also had ten days to present herself at the specified notary office and sign the transfer papers. Based on Article 14 of the Amended Law, if she failed to present herself within the prescribed ten days, the Land Reform Organization was empowered to act as "her representative" and sign the transfer papers "on her behalf," then transfer her property to the government and notify the public prosecutor.[13] After receiving this notice, Soghra Khanum went to the notary office within ten days and signed the transfer papers. However, because the registration process had not been completed, she received no money, since in such cases the money was placed at the registration office until the completion of the process. Two months later, she received a letter and a new notice from the Ministry of Agriculture, informing her that an error had been made in computing the price of her property in the village of Khoshke-bur. In the "corrected notice," the price was halved to 33,940.50 rials ($480) (see table 11.6). She was instructed to go immediately to Notary Office 47 in Shahsavar (Tonekabon) and sign the corrected transfer papers.

The provisions of Part 6 of Article 1 of the Additional Articles that con-

Table 11.5. Ownership of Soghra Khanum Massoudi Tonekaboni's Property in Seven Villages and Its Appraisal and Purchase by the Land Reform Organization under the Provisions of Phase Two

Village	Ownership Share*	Ownership in Hectares	Annual Tax (Rials)	Purchase Price (Rials)
Luleh Deh	26/480	4.097	548.75	55,972.50
Pol Sara	26/480	1.776	221.40	22,582.80
Tubon	26/480	3.861	923.00	94,146.00
Palang Abad Sofla	26/480	2.321	361.40	36,862.80
Palang Abad Olia	26/480	1.281	240.20	24,500.40
Pasandeh Olia	26/480	5.576	516.25	52,657.50
Pasandeh Sofla	26/480	8.067	617.10	62,944.20
Total	182/3360	26.979	3,428.10	349,666.20

Source: Ministry of Agriculture, Land Reform Organization of Shahsavar, Announcement 3757, 22/6/49 [11 September 1970].
* The announcement stated that Soghra Khanum's ownership was "exclusive of the property of the small landowners," whatever that was.

cerned the ownership of rice fields were given above. Not surprisingly, Soghra Khanum had selected Alternative A. That is, she had selected to "retain" 30 hectares, and this land was to be leased to the farmers for thirty years. The "excess" was to be sold to the farmers on terms equal to that of Phase One. According to a mandatory declaration form dated 24 May 1969 submitted to the Ministry of Land Reform, she had selected to

Table 11.6. Appraisal and Purchase of Soghra Khanum Massoudi Tonekaboni's Property by the Land Reform Organization under the Provisions of Phase One

Village	Ownership Share*	Annual Tax (Rials)	Purchase Price (Rials)
Khoshk-e Bur	26.00/480	332.75	33,940.50
Moalem Kuh	17.33/480	845.25	81,868.00
Rudgar Mahaleh	17.33/480	510.95	50,142.00
Luleh Deh	17.33/480	473.65	48,312.00
Pol Sara	17.33/480	519.00	52,938.00
Total	95.32/2,400	2,681.60	267,200.50

Source: Ministry of Agriculture, Land Reform Organization of Shahsavar, Announcement 3834, 26/6/47 [17 September 1968]. Ministry of Cooperatives and Rural Affairs, Office of Rural Cooperatives, Shahsavar, announcement 3643, 25 July 1972.
*Both announcements stated that Soghra Khanum's ownership was "exclusive of the property of the small landowners."

retain her ownership share in eight villages where the sum of her ownerships was equivalent to 30 hectares. The villages were Hangu (1.7 hectares), Mak Rud (2 hectares), Rudgar Mahaleh (2 hectares), Tamesh Gol (3.5 hectares), Faqih Abad (8.2 hectares), Marzeh (3.8 hectares), Moalem Kuh (5.2 hectares), and Nashta Rud (3.6 hectares). These 30 hectares had then been leased to the sitting farmers according to Alternative A. The annual rent from 30 hectares of rice fields was a mere 70,882 rials ($1,005), the tax on which was 7,980 rials ($113).[14] Her net income was $75 per month. That this was a ridiculously low rent can be seen from the following. Assuming the price of rice was $150 per ton (it was imported at that price), her rent was equivalent to 7 tons of rice. Total rice production on 30 hectares would have been 100–110 tons. That is, her rent was less than one-fifteenth of the output. Even then, she had difficulty in collecting this negligible rent. The evidence in the file is compelling. Despite the fact that the rent contracts had been drawn up by the government as part of land reform and were "legally" binding, the landowner could not collect the rent, because the tenants refused to pay and there was no meaningful enforcement mechanism. Repeated complaints to the government by Soghra Khanum were exercises in futility.[15] Considering that her ownership in these villages was 15 hectares, or half of the land she had "retained," the rent she had collected for the year 1970 was $500, a fraction of the average per capita income of the country.

The remainder of her property, which amounted to 27 hectares, was "purchased" by the government and transferred to the tenants. The relevant information is given in announcement number 3758, dated 14 August 1970, and the accompanying letter from the Ministry of Land Reform. She was notified that on the basis of part 6 of Article 1 of the Additional Articles to the Amended Law of the Land Reform Law, her property was to be purchased, and she was hereby given notice of the price. She was reminded that unless she signed the transfer papers within ten days, the Land Reform Organization would sign the papers "on her behalf" and notify the public prosecutor. Soghra Khanum's ownership in excess of 30 hectares was 27 hectares. That is, her average ownership of 26 shares in a village was equivalent to 3.8 hectares per village, the range being 1–8 hectares. The 27 hectares were purchased by the Land Reform Organization for 349,666 rials ($4,990), which was $185 per hectare. That is, the "price" of a hectare of rice field was a little more than the price of a ton of rice. Alternatively, the owner's "compensation" for the land was half of the annual produce of the same land. It is worth noting that her "compensation" for land taken by Reza Shah was also less than the annual revenue of the land.

The third and final phase of land reform was called the Law for the Sale and Division of the Rented Estates. Under this 1968 law, the owners were given the option of selling the 30 hectares to which they retained nominal ownership or dividing the land with the tenants on the basis of the traditional crop shares. Soghra Khanum opted for the division option, and the Land Reform Organization was so notified. This law should have permitted her to retain ownership of some 5–10 hectares of land in the seven villages in which she retained nominal ownership, and in theory, the land retained would have been free of tenants. However, the law also specified that the division option required the "notification" of the tenants of the owner's intent at division. Only after the tenants had affixed their signatures to the required notification form would the land be divided. But the tenants were not about to consent to a division of the land and sign the green notification form. Reading the file thirty years later, it is difficult to avoid outrage at this charade. For nearly two years, this elderly woman, who had had no income for a decade, tried to get the peasants to sign the green division forms. Whenever she or her representative went to the village, the farmers refused to come forward. Who can blame the peasants? Since there was no sanction in not signing, there was no incentive to sign. Moreover, my aunt's rights seemingly counted for naught. In desperation, she wrote to the Land Reform Organization in 1970 announcing her "willingness and readiness" to sell her land to the government. The price under Phase Three was set at twelve times the annual rent, payable in ten annual installments. It came to 850,000 rials ($11,000), and the annual installment was $1,100. This was $90 per month before tax.

Meanwhile, in 1970, her brother Esfandiar Massoudi died, and his only survivors were the few remaining siblings who inherited his estate. Amazingly, the Land Reform Organization ruled that with her inheritance, Soghra Khanum was again holding "excess" property and was thus again liable to the provisions of Phase One. According to the announcement by the Ministry of Land Reform, now duly renamed the Ministry of Cooperatives and Rural Affairs, announcement number 3643, dated 25 July 1972, Soghra Khanum's "excess" ownership consisted of 17.33 shares out of 480 in each of the following four villages: Moalem Kuh, Rudgar Mahaleh, Luleh Deh, and Pol Sara. They were to be "purchased" for 267,200 rials ($3,400) (see table 11.6). At a time when the rising oil prices had resulted in a boom in land values, the "price" offered for Soghra Khanum's land was a fraction of the land's market value. In a letter to the Ministry of Cooperatives and Rural Affairs dated 3 August 1972, she protested the proposed "price" for her shares in the four villages and requested a reconsideration. There is no record of a reply to her protest.

Moreover, since the registration of the property was subject to several objections, none of the money was payable. The money and the land reform bonds were retained by the registration bureau until the registration process had been completed. On 19 August 1973, which happened to be the twentieth anniversary of the coup that had restored Mohammad Reza Shah to power, she wrote to the Ministry of Cooperatives and Rural Affairs, appealing for the release of some of her money. Sadly, this was the last letter contained in her file. She died in January 1975.

In contemplating the fate of this unfortunate woman, one begins to appreciate the cruel tyranny and lawlessness that was all too often a characteristic of the Pahlavi rule. In her youth, Soghra Khanum Massoudi Tonekaboni had been deprived of her husband and her property and she had been exiled from Mazandaran. In her old age, her property was again confiscated and she was reduced to poverty. Yet she was among the "lucky" ones. She had no dependents, and she did not have direct living expenses because she lived with my parents. She was never faced with homelessness and hunger. What would have happened to her if she had been forced to provide for herself? Some answers can be obtained by examining the fate of some of Soghra Khanum's siblings. When her brother Parviz Khan Massoudi died in 1964, his property in Nashta was confiscated under the three phases of land distribution. The compensation given to his widow and three young daughters was similar to that given to Soghra Khanum. Another landowner in Nashta, Jahanshah Massoudi Tonekaboni, was arrested and exiled in 1932. Three years later he was one of the signatories to the Zavar document of exchange. He was imprisoned as an insolvent debtor in the 1970s. Seventy-four years old and in poor health, he fell ill, and he died in 1976 shortly after his release. When Majd wrote in his memoirs that many landowners had been reduced to poverty and faced imprisonment as insolvent debtors, he spoke from firsthand experience.

Beneficiaries of Land Distribution: Case Studies

An examination of land distribution will not be complete without a look at how it affected the tenants and sharecroppers. Since the land distribution file on Ebrahim Abad and Majd Abad contains detailed data, a summary is given here. As reported above, 7,000 hectares of fertile land and the premier qanat in Qazvin region were transferred to 104 farmers of Ebrahim Abad and 26 farmers of Majd Abad. The measurement of the ownership and land given to each farmer is recorded in *fards* (literally persons but in this case shares) rather than hectares. It appears that this was done to facilitate and expedite the transfer of ownership. The total

Fig. 11.4. Jahanshah Massoudi Tonekaboni, Nashtarud, 1957.

land area and water was defined to consist of 130 fards, which corresponded to the 130 farmers. While the average per farmer consisted of one share, there was a wide range in the amount received by each farmer. Under the provisions of land distribution, the amount of land given to each farmer depended on the amount the farmer already cultivated. In this case, the amount ranged from two-fifths of a share to three shares. In terms of hectares, each share was equivalent to 54 hectares of land. The smallest farmers received 21.5 hectares of land and water, while the largest farmers received 161 hectares of land and water. Thus, as in Zavar and Nashta, the large farmers did very well. But it was hardly social justice. Whereas the farmers gained, the landowner lost his house to creditors.

Another case study will demonstrate how land distribution impacted one tenant in the village of Habib Abad, Zavar. It concerns a farmer, Haj Qorban Mohammadpour (see fig. 9.2). Although formally a "sharecropping tenant," Haj Qorban and his four wives lived very comfortably, and with the title of "Haj," he had already made his pilgrimage to Mecca. He was clearly much wealthier than such "landowners" as Soghra Khanum, who did not even own a house. He cultivated some 20 hectares of rice fields and some 20 hectares of orange groves. By the standards of the Caspian region, this was a large amount of land. How had Haj Qorban acquired so much land? The answer is to be found in the case study of establishing orange groves under Reza Shah given in appendix A. The land had been assigned to him by the Office of Royal Estates for development and had remained with him. Qorban's name appears in table A in appendix A.

Under Phase Two and Phase Three, rice fields were transferred to the farmers at a price that was barely 5 percent of the value of the land, payable over fifteen years. Since there was no mechanism to enforce the owner's rights, citrus groves became de facto the property of the tenant farmers. Thus, under land distribution, Haj Qorban received 20 hectares of rice fields and 20 hectares of citrus groves at practically no cost. Already wealthy by the standards of rural Iran, he became very wealthy during the 1960s and 1970s. He sent several of his sons to the United States to pursue advanced studies. The case of Haj Qorban was by no means unusual. There were numerous cases in each village in Zavar and Nashta. For example, Haj Qahreman and Hosein Aqaii were wealthy cultivators in the village of Kotra and in Zavar who became wealthier after land distribution. It is noteworthy that Qahreman's name is also cited in the table in appendix A. Others examples included Haj Ehsani in Talusarak, Karbelaii Hadi Asri in Pelet Kaleh, and the Bahrami brothers in Nashta and Zavar (Seyed Abol Fazl Bahrami, a prominent name in the table in appendix A, was assigned 49 jaribs of land in 1940.) Under land distribution, they received property at no cost. These instances fully demonstrate some of the regressive aspects of land distribution in Iran. While such individuals as my aunt, while not wealthy to begin with, were ruined because of land distribution and faced hardship in their old age, while the orphaned children and widow of Parviz Khan Massoudi had faced hardships, and while Jahanshah Massoudi Tonekaboni was imprisoned for debt and insolvency, the prosperous cultivators whom land distribution favored became even wealthier. Such social engineering destroyed one class as it created another. It was hardly social justice. As illustrated in the next chapter, there were at least some 1.3 million small landowners whose property was methodologically confiscated, and they were reduced to poverty.

The Structure of Landownership on the Eve of Land Distribution

Expropriation and Plight of the Small Landowners

After a long debate on the nature and extent of land distribution in Iran, it is now generally accepted that land reform resulted in an extensive transfer of ownership of land to the sitting tenants. Data published by the Islamic Republic during the 1980s show that 1.8–1.9 million individuals received land under the three phases of land distribution: private, government-owned, and endowed land.[1] Because land reform in Iran gave land to so many peasants, it has been cited by Binswanger and Elgin as "an outstanding example of a successful land reform."[2] However, nothing has been written about those who lost. It needs to be remembered that for every peasant who received land, a landowner was expropriated. Without this information, it is not possible to assess the political, social, and redistributive consequences of land reform. Nor is it possible to investigate its immense social and political consequences. The history and assessment of this event, which Lambton called the most important since Iran's Constitutional Revolution of 1906, is incomplete because only one side of the issue has been examined. This one-sided approach must now be rectified. This chapter first provides a statistical summary of the number of peasant beneficiaries under the three phases of land distribution between 1962 and 1971. When the results are compared with the findings of the 1960 census of agriculture, they indicate that land distribution gave land to nearly all of Iran's sharecroppers and tenant farmers. I then investigate the number of landowners expropriated by examining the available evidence on landownership before the 1962 land reform. Again I rely on the 1960 census.[3] Based on the distribution of landownership in 1,787 villages contained in the census, as well as micro- and village-level studies, it is possible to obtain a relatively accurate picture of the situation and of the numbers expropriated.

The 1960 Census of Agriculture and the Land Distribution Statistics

Unlike Egypt, where the first agricultural census took place in 1929 and where detailed information on landownership has been available since 1900, Iran's first agricultural census was not performed until October 1960, and even then reliable information on landownership was not made available.[4] It can be speculated that data collection was delayed in Iran because a census would have revealed the extent of land confiscation by Reza Shah and subsequently by his son. Over 6,000 villages, hamlets, and pastures were seized by Reza Shah between 1926 and 1941. As discussed in chapter 4, these lands were sold in the 1950s. Only after the bulk of this land had been sold was an agricultural census undertaken. It is also clear that publication of the 1960 census was delayed by almost ten years because the census findings were at odds with the government's line on land reform. It is to mask this belated publication that Iran's first official agricultural census does not even have a publication date. This cannot be explained by a simple bureaucratic oversight.

Just as incredibly, while the census contains much information on landholding, it contains very little on landownership in 1960. This is in marked contrast to the agricultural censuses of 1950 and 1961 in Egypt, which contain detailed information on both ownership and holding of land. The 1960 census in Iran presents only the landownership data in the 1,787 sampled villages, and unlike landholding, it does not extend the sample results to establish the overall ownership pattern and structure in the country. This is indeed astonishing, since all of the data in the 1960 census, including the structure of landholding, are based on the same sample. Clearly, if the data on landownership were even remotely supportive of the government line at the time of land distribution, it would have resulted in prompt publication and substantial exposure. It is most revealing that while the census allocated prominent space and tables to such mundane matters as the farm distribution of mules and horses, the critical matter of landownership is relegated to the very end. Buried on the very last two pages of the last volume (volume 15), there are three tables in small print that offer some data on landownership in the 1,787 sampled villages and without any extension of the findings. This dearth of data on landownership contrasts sharply with the contents of the guidelines issued to the data collectors at the time. In the instruction manual on data collection for the 1960 census, which I recently found in the library of the Ministry of Agriculture in Tehran, there is a detailed description of the types of landownership the investigators were likely to encounter and instructions for recording and tabulating the information.

It is clear that detailed information was collected but not published. This information must be somewhere in the archives of the Ministry of Interior.

There is also some inconsistency between the material in volume 15 and the information obtained from the specific regional data. Volume 15 has greatly overstated the number of multiple ownerships. Whether this was an error or deliberate misrepresentation it is difficult to say.

Given that the most common measure of landownership consisted of ownership of a "village," or fraction thereof, it is necessary to establish the number of villages at the time of land distribution. Under the population census definition, a village or rural settlement is one with less than 5,000 inhabitants. The 1966 population census enumerated 60,520 rural settlements, a figure that is entirely consistent with land reform statistics. Under Phase One, 3,992 privately owned villages and 1,535 government-owned (*khaliseh*) villages were transferred in total to the cultivators. Under Phase Two, all the remaining villages were affected. This included the villages that were partially affected by Phase One, those that were entirely owned by peasant cultivators whose ownership status was confirmed by the Land Reform Organization, and those that were endowed for public charitable (*vaqf-e amm*) and private charitable (*vaqf-e khass*) purposes. The number of villages subject to Phase Two was declared to have been 54,994.[5] When added to the 3,992 privately owned villages and 1,535 khaliseh villages that had been transferred under Phase One, the resulting total is 60,520, the same as reported by the 1966 population census. Moreover, it is clear that Lambton's reported figure of 52,533 villages affected by Phase Two refers to the number of privately owned villages that were subject to the second stage of land distribution. It then follows that the remaining 2,461 villages were entirely endowed for religious and charitable purposes.

The ownership status of 1,787 sampled villages in the 1960 census is reported in tables 12.1 and 12.2. The last column in table 12.1 gives the overall ownership estimated from the sample and the total of 60,520 villages. The consistency of the estimated figures with the overall results of the first phase of land distribution indicates the sample results accurately reflect the actual state of landownership. First, under Phase One, all khaliseh villages, reported to include 1,535 six-dang (entire) villages, or 2.5 percent of 60,520 villages, were sold to the peasants. The 44 khaliseh villages in the sample also corresponds to 2.5 percent of the 1,787 villages, and the estimated figure based on the sample is 1,490 villages, which is 97 percent of the actual figure. Next, the number of endowed villages from land distribution data was estimated to be 2,461 villages. Based on the sample figure of 74 endowed villages, the estimate of 2,506 villages is again identical to the land distribution figures. Next, the census results are fully consistent with land distribution results concerning large land-owners (six-dang and above, one or more villages). Esmail Ajami reported that 2,250 landowners fell into this category. Each was permitted to retain a "chosen village," and the remainder of the land was confiscated and transferred to peasants.[6] Land distribution data reported that 3,992 entire villages were transferred to the peasants under Phase One. When added to 2,250 villages that owners were allowed to retain under Phase One, the resulting 6,242 villages is nearly identical to the estimate of 6,265 derived from the census findings. In addition, the 11,043 partially affected villages of Phase One are completely accounted for by the 11,650 villages in the three to under six-dang category estimated from the sample. As indicated below, most of the villages in this category were also owned by the 2,250 large landowners and were thus included in Phase One of land distribution. These limited results show that large landowners had full ownership of at most 10 percent of the villages and partial ownership in another 19 percent. (In 19 percent of the villages, one owner held half or more, but less than the total, three to less than six-dang.) Thus, large land-ownership was considerably less prevalent than it was made out to be. Moreover, the data also show that the frequent argument that there was large-scale evasion because landowners transferred property to kin has no foundation in fact. The most striking finding is that 64 percent of the villages were owned by medium and small owners (less than three-dang), and fully 31 percent were entirely owned by the petty landowners (less than half-dang).

The 1960 census of agriculture, undertaken on the eve of land distribution, reported 3,218,000 rural households. Of these, 2,442,000 were am-

Table 12.1. Ownership Status of 1,787 Sampled Villages, 1960

	Sample Villages	%	Overall Country
Entirely owned by government	44	2.5	1,490
Entirely endowed	74	4.1	2,506
Entirely owned by one landlord (6 dangs)	185	10.4	6,265
Largest landlord owns from 3 to <6 dangs	344	19.2	11,650
Largest landlord owns from .5 to <3 dangs	594	33.2	20,117
All landlords own <.5 dang	546	30.6	18,492
Total	1,787	100.0	60,520

Source: *First National Census of Agriculture, October 1960*, vol. 15 (Tehran: Ministry of the Interior, n.d.), p. 84 and table 1.

Table 12.2. Ownership of 1,787 Sampled Villages by Region, 1960

Region	Entirely Owned by One Landlord	One Landlord Owns 3 to <6-dang	One Landlord Owns .5 to <3-dang	All Landlords Own <.5-dang	Entirely Endowed	Entirely Govt. Owned	Total
Tehran	16	24	48	48	4	3	143
Gilan and Mazandaran	38	72	112	80	31	—	333
Azarbaijan	53	79	93	40	8	4	277
Khorasan	15	29	74	116	18	—	252
Kermanshah and Kurdistan	26	63	75	24	3	3	194
Fars and Chahar Mahal	12	22	53	64	6	9	166
Esfahan and Yazd	6	4	32	69	2	—	113
Khuzestan	9	33	43	39	1	24	149
Kerman, Sistan, and Baluchestan	10	18	64	66	1	1	160
Total	185	344	594	546	74	44	1,787

Source: *First National Census of Agriculture, October 1960*, vols. 1–14 (Tehran: Ministry of the Interior, n.d.).

biguously described as khanevar-e bahreh-bardar (cultivating or beneficiary households), and 776,700 were described as khanevar-e gheir-e
bahreh-bardar (noncultivating or nonbeneficiary households). The census does not contain a description of the various classifications or the
basis on which the households were classified. Astonishingly, in the introduction to the data in the census, it is stated that a description of the
household categories and the basis for the classification of the households
"will be given at a later date." Of course, a description was never provided. All of this leads to the inevitable conclusion that the aim of the
government was to hide and minimize meaningful information on the
agricultural sector at the time of land distribution. Clearly, there was information that the government wished to hide. As shown in this study,
despite the government's attempt to cover up its activities, the census
contains extremely valuable data.

Land distribution sought to transfer the ownership of land to the sharecroppers and tenants. The census had enumerated 624,283 owner-operated holdings (*bahrebardari melki*) and 203,538 mixed holdings (part-owned
and part-rented). Assuming that each owner-operated holding was operated by one household, then of the 2,441,760 "cultivator households"
(*khanevar-e bahrebardar*), 1,817,477 households (2,441,760 – 624,283) were
eligible to receive land. Of these, 1,613,939 were sharecroppers and tenants, and 203,538 were part-tenant/part-owner cultivators. Analysis of
the data on land distribution indicates that 1.8–1.9 million tenants received land. Specifically, 800,000 were given land under Phase One, 214,000
under Phase Two, and 1,200,000 under Phase Three. However, it has been
shown that of the 1,200,000 beneficiaries of Phase Three, 400,000 had also
received land under Phase One. Adding the 800,000 first-time land recipients of Phase Three to the recipients of Phases One and Two totals
1,814,000. This indicates that all those eligible to receive land did so.[7]
These results were also confirmed by data published during the 1980s. In
the nine provinces for which the data were published, 1,074,217 households received land.[8] By any measure, it was a major land distribution
program.

Distribution Data on Landowners

While much is written on the number of beneficiaries, in contrast the fate
of the losers has attracted practically no attention. To start with, while
there is a good deal of information on the peasants included in Phase One,
no information was published on landowners affected. The official statistics on the number of landowners expropriated by the subsequent phases
of land distribution are incomplete, vague, contradictory, and conse-

quently unreliable. Moreover, the data on the villages affected by Phase One are deliberately vague. The preliminary aggregate data on Phase Two found in Lambton are also vague and unhelpful. While the land recipients are peasant households, there is no indication of the number of landowners expropriated, only of the "estates" transferred to the peasants. No definition of the term is provided. The subsequent data on landowners affected by Phases Two and Three that were published by the Ministry of Land Reform are not only inconsistent but also greatly at odds with the available micro-level evidence. Under Phase Two (1964–67), *all* of the country's landowners were subjected to at least one of the five provisions of the regulation.[9] The Ministry of Land Reform reported that 311,531 noncultivating landowners and 784,882 owner-cultivators had been affected by Phase Two.[10] The implication is that before land reform, there were 1.1 million landowners in the country. While the data on owner-cultivators are mostly substantiated by the 1960 census (the census figure was 728,000), there are at least three sources of difficulty with the 311,531 figure. First, it is inconsistent with landownership data subsequently published by the same Ministry of Land Reform. Second, it was wildly different from landownership figures published by other organs of the government, notably the Ministry of Agriculture. Third, it is inconsistent with the micro-level evidence found in the works of Lambton and of Salmanzadeh and Jones, as well as the 1960 census of agriculture.

Concerning the inconsistency with other land distribution statistics, data on Phase Two reported that of the 311,531 landowners affected by Phase Two, 37,550 were involved in the sale of land, division of land, or purchase of peasant cultivation rights. That is, their status was finalized and most would not be involved in Phase Three. The remaining 273,981 landowners were involved in tenancy agreements. Thus, in compliance with the regulations of Phases Two and Three and according to official data on Phase Two, at most 273,981 landowners would be affected by Phase Three. However, the official data on Phase Three reported that 357,724 landowners were "included" in Phase Three, which is inconsistent with Phase Two data. No explanation was provided for the 84,000 discrepancy. These inconsistencies concerning landowners indicate that the statistics were unreliable and possibly deliberately misleading. They were also wildly different from earlier published statistics.

Contemporary Data on Landownership

Reliable and authoritative information on the broad outlines of landownership was given by Hushang Ram, the person in charge of the distribution and sale of the shah's estates. The information is contained in a verbal report given in the shah's presence on the occasion of the distribution of the land deeds to cultivators in Mazandaran. The report was given in the national daily *Etela-at* on 12 June 1961. In the presence of the shah, Ram stated the following:

> Last week, one of the well-known weekly magazines in America referred to the agricultural reform in Iran, and in this context, it stated some falsehoods that are cause for dismay. For example, the magazine stated that of the 45,000 villages in Iran, fully 42,000 were in the possession of the large landowners. It had also stated that 16 million cultivators in Iran were under the yoke of a mere 1,000 families. The same article contained some other errors. It stated that under the new law, maximum ownership had been set at 2,500 acres or 1,200 hectares. According to the data gathered by us at the Bank Omran, half of Iran's agricultural land is owned by small landowners. Apart from the royal estates, the endowments, and government-owned land, the amount of privately owned land subject to the land law does not exceed 300,000–400,000 hectares. I beg Your Majesty that my remarks should be taken note of. It is regretful that foreign reporters, acting from ignorance, publish such erroneous material about our country.

This report is immensely important because it is fully substantiated by the findings of the 1960 census of agriculture. Moreover, it establishes the fact that the shah and the Pahlavi regime were fully cognizant of the landownership situation in Iran. They knew that half of Iran's agricultural land was owned by small landowners.

Some information on small landowners is found in the literature that was put out in the early 1960s by organizations that opposed the proposed land redistribution program. It was shown that resistance by landowners to land confiscation-distribution measures grew during the early 1960s. At first, it was mostly the opposition by large landowners. But following intense propaganda by the government and incitement against landowners in general, including Arsanjani's open encouragement of peasants to seize the land by force, the small landowners were either driven from the villages or no longer able to collect rent from peasants. It is also clear that by 1962 many small landowners had joined the large landowners and were politically active. An organization calling itself Society of Cultivators (Kanoun-e Keshavarzan) had published a pamphlet entitled "The Progressive Views of the Small Landowners of the Province of Tehran, Submitted to the Economics Conference of 1 March 1963." The conference occurred shortly after the cabinet decree of January 1963, known as the Additional Articles, which had initiated the de jure confiscation of the small landowners. The pamphlet was written in response to the Articles. It concluded:

"We deem it necessary to stress the following. The class of small landowners, which *consists of several million individuals* [emphasis added], has rendered so many useful and productive services, and has paid so much indirect and direct taxes. . . . In short, this valuable and effective part of Iran's society begs the executive and judicial branches of the government, and the centers of publicity and information, that it be provided with security and judicial protection.

Another organization calling itself the Population of Small Landowners published numerous pamphlets outlining the adverse effects of government propaganda against small landowners and criticizing the regulations of Phase Two. One such pamphlet, "His Excellency the Prime Minister of Iran," also printed in early 1963, bitterly complained of the injustices inflicted on the small landowners and warned the government that its policies would lead to disaster (see chap. 7). The pamphlet stated that the number of small landowners and their immediate dependents, that is, landowners who rented land to peasants, was in excess of 5 million persons. Assuming an average household size of five members, it follows that the organization estimated the number of small landowners to be more than 1 million. As demonstrated below, such owners numbered in excess of 1.3 million.

Equally important, an article on land distribution on the front page of the *Etela-at* on 9 May 1964 stated that 2 million *khorde-malekin* (small landowners) would be affected by the implementation of the Additional Articles. The landowners were required to "clarify their situations with the cultivators." Although the article does not provide information on the composition of these landowners, the figure of 2 million landowners is significant. Moreover, the 2 million figure is consistent with data subsequently published by the Ministry of Agriculture and the findings of the 1960 census. With the Majlis approval of the provisions of Phase Three (the final transfer to peasants of land subject to the tenancies of Phase Two), the Ministry of Agriculture published data indicating that 1.2 million small landowners were liable to expropriation under Phase Three of land distribution.[11] What is noteworthy about the 1.2 million figure is that it is consistent with the figure given by the Population of Small Landowners, the results of the 1960 census of agriculture, and the data published in *Etela-at*. The census reported 728,000 owner-operated holdings (entirely owned or part-owned and part-rented). These owners were not subject to expropriation under land distribution. This figure was also confirmed by the data from Phase Two of land distribution, which reported 784,000 such landowners who held onto their property under land distribution.[12] Subtracting this from 2 million results in 1.2 million landowners subject to expropriation under Phase Three, which is the figure given by the Ministry of Agriculture. However, despite the fact that the 1.2 million estimate was at least consistent with previously published data, it was quickly "revised" by the Land Reform Ministry. The new figure stated that only 274,000 landowners were subject to expropriation under Phase Three. No reason was given for the discrepancy between the two figures.[13] As above noted, the 274,000 figure was also inconsistent with published Phase Three data. Of the 56,525 privately owned villages, at least 50,000 (83%) were owned by more than one owner and were thus technically khorde-malek villages.

Some Descriptions of Landownership in Iran

Any study of modern landownership in Iran must consider Lambton's 1953 work. The value of her work is found in its qualitative, not in its quantitative, insights. It is easy to see that Lambton's main conclusions concerning the structure of landownership are inaccurate. For example, she repeatedly states that peasant proprietorship was rare and confined to remote areas. However, the 1960 census of agriculture revealed that of the 2.442 million cultivating households, fully 728,000 (30%) were owner-operators with an average size of 5 hectares, which indicates that the vast majority were peasant owners. Peasant ownership accounted for one-third of the land. While cognizant of the role of the Islamic law of inheritance in breaking up large ownerships in a few generations, she nevertheless concluded that much of the land was owned by "large landed proprietors."[14] However, land reform data showed that at least 90 percent of the privately owned villages had more than one owner and were thus khorde-malek villages. In addition, an early indication that the actual structure of landownership was very different from the prevailing view in the literature as well as government propaganda is found in the results of the first phase of land reform. Phase One aimed at eliminating large landownership by setting the maximum ownership at one entire village and confiscating the "excess" villages. However, of the 56,525 privately owned villages, only 3,992 villages were expropriated in their entirety and transferred to peasants, and another 11,043 were transferred in part. Thus only 27 percent of the private villages were directly affected by Phase One, and the amount of land transferred to peasants was considerably lower. It is frequently claimed that the reason "only" 15,000 villages were included in Phase One was that landowners were able to transfer their villages to kin and thus avoid the reform. The proponents of this view need to explain why the other 15,000 villages were not similarly transferred. Moreover, the findings on landownership in 1,787 villages found in the 1960 census of agriculture and given in this chapter show that the argument is without merit. In addition, that large ownerships were limited both in number and in the amount of land was readily acknowledged by the minister for land distribution. Hasan Arsanjani stated in a radio interview that current legislation was insufficient because it covered a small minority of the villages (those consisting of large ownerships). He said that to include the other villages, additional "legislation" was necessary.[15]

Lambton provides data on a few khorde-malek villages in her 1969 book. The village of Khosrowjerd in the Neishabur district of Khorasan had 190 absentee owners, and the land was cultivated by 50 sharecroppers. Lambton reports that the village of Goud Asia in the Sabzavar district of Khorasan had 150 small owners, while the village of Bahman Abad in Ilam was owned by 150 peasant cultivators. Salavatabad, Khaleh Kah, and Ghaleh Cheh, all in the Firuzabad district in Fars, were owned by seventy individuals in the case of the first village and by "several" in the case of the latter two. Rezab and Nigil in the Marivan district of Kurdistan were owned by seven and eighteen owners, respectively.[16] These numbers notwithstanding, it is difficult not to criticize Lambton for her failure to provide more useful information on landownership in the hundreds of villages she had occasion to study in the preparation of her 1969 book on land reform. While she offers much data on the number of peasants who received land in the villages she studied, the information on landownership is surprisingly incomplete and unsatisfactory. In only rare instances are actual numbers of landowners in a village given. Usually, the terms *numerous* or *several landowners* are substituted in lieu of numbers. Given that Lambton was the author of *Landlord and Peasant in Persia*, I'm surprised by this one-sided emphasis and glaring omission.

Salmanzadeh and Jones's detailed micro-level study of land distribution in southwestern Iran provides some real insights into the structure of landownership on the eve of land distribution. The study reported that of the 159 private villages, 56 were affected by Phase One, and of the 6,927 peasants with land rights, 2,404 received land under Phase One. That is, 35 percent of the private villages and 34.7 percent of the peasants were included in Phase One. Overall results of Phase One show that 15,000 villages (27 percent of 56,000 privately owned villages) and 709,000 peasants (37 percent of the 1,877,000 holdings with land) were included in

Phase One. Given these similar proportions, it is reasonable to conclude that the landownership characteristics in southwestern Iran were representative of the situation in the rest of the country. Salmanzadeh and Jones found that the amount of land transferred to peasants in Phase One was 11 percent of the total privately owned land. Moreover, they found that the landownership pattern that had evolved from the Islamic matrimonial and inheritance practices was extremely complex and that much of the land was owned by a large number of individuals. It is well worth quoting from this study. They give the following description of landownership:

> In rural Dezful, as in other parts of Iran, the common unit of rural land ownership was, until very recently, the "village." Traditionally, in rural Iran, a village could be divided into six arbitrary parts; ownership of a village or any piece of landed estate in its entirety was referred to as shish-dang, literally meaning ownership of six parts. However, in rural Dezful it was more common to divide a village or part of a village into 24 equal parts. Each part was referred to as a nokhud, literally a pea, and ownership of a village or part of a village (in its entirety) was referred to as bist-o-char nokhud, literally meaning ownership of 24 parts (peas) or ownership of an entire estate. Thus there was no term to describe the area of land owned, since in the rural context it was the produce of the land and not the area of land owned that interested the traditional landlords. Each nokhud could be subdivided into 24 jow or sheir (barley), and each jow could be further subdivided into 24 kunjed (sesame). Thus, according to this system, a village or any part of it could be divided into 24 x 24 x 24 (= 13,284) parts and each part or even a portion of a part could have a different malik (owner or title holder). In fact, this system could allow the ownership of a village to be divided into an almost unlimited number of shares without affecting the peasant sharecroppers, for the system did not involve any physical boundaries or division, and each landowner's share of the harvest would be calculated in accordance with the number of shares held.
>
> Furthermore, this system of land ownership was compatible with the Islamic law of inheritance, since it would accommodate the innumerable division of land among all the heirs of the deceased landowner without disturbing the exploitation of the land by the peasant sharecroppers. Second, this abstract or imaginary form of ownership of an undefined area of land had become more complex by the practice of musha, which involved joint ownership of undivided shares (three brothers and a sister, for example, might own between

them two nokhuds of one village and one nokhud, three jows, and five kunjed of a second village).[17]

Summing up the landownership pattern, they state:

Before the land reform program started in the DIP area, 159 villages (out of 169 studied) were held privately in whole and a further 5 in part. The size of an individual holding (ownership) could not be easily established because of the prevailing pattern of joint and undivided ownership. A village might be commonly "known" to be in the possession of a single individual, but in most cases such a village was owned in the name of a large number of individuals (including women and minors), or even a clan but with only one person acting as the authorized representative (i.e., the head of the family or clan). In the entire DIP area, only two villages were entirely owned by one person (i.e., individual estates); the remaining privately owned villages were in the form of undivided estates and owned by more than one person. The number of "shareholders" (owners) of a certain unit of land, that is, a village, might vary from two to fifty or more. Moreover, the numbers of village owners and the sizes of their holding were continually changing through property transactions and through inheritance.[18]

These passages indicate a possible reason why Lambton misjudged the structure of landownership. As noted by Salmanzadeh and Jones, villages that "appeared" to be owned by "large landed proprietors" were frequently owned by many individuals. Of course, Lambton on several occasions showed an awareness that a village which gave the appearance of belonging to a "large landed proprietor" was in fact technically a khorde-malek village owned by many individuals, but she concluded that they were not numerous. What also emerges from the Salmanzadeh and Jones study is that the number of petty landowners in some villages could equal or exceed the number of peasant sharecroppers. For example, prior to land distribution, the village of Bonvar Hosein in the Dezful area of Khuzestan was owned by thirty-three small owners and was cultivated by thirty-eight peasants with land rights.[19] These owners of Bonvar Hosein had been formally expropriated under Phase Three. Evidence on landownership in Mazandaran also points to a complex pattern. Two other illustrative cases consist of the ownership of the estates of Nashta and Golsefid in Mazandaran. As described elsewhere in this study, both Nashta and Golsefid were acquired by Reza Shah in the 1930s and restored to the owners in the 1940s. Through a process of inheritance and

324 / Resistance to the Shah

subdivision, by the advent of land distribution in 1962, Nashta was owned by some sixty individuals, including numerous widows and or-phaned minors.[20] Golsefid was owned by forty-six individuals. They were all expropriated during the three phases of land distribution.

In addition to the study by Salmanzadeh and Jones, our understanding of landownership in central and southern Iran is greatly enhanced by a description of landownership in Isfahan by Franklin J. Crawford, U.S. Consul in Isfahan. Crawford's report was included in a long, confidential report on land reform that was discussed at length in chapter 6 (Foreign Service despatch 695, dated 30 March 1959). Crawford's report is given in appendix C. As described by Crawford, landownership in Isfahan was dominated by small ownerships, often not exceeding a few square meters. The largest landowner in the entire Province of Isfahan controlled four villages, two of which were owned by his son and wife.

Distribution of Private Landownership, 1960

The data on the village ownership (tables 12.1 and 12.2) show that the sample results are consistent with the results of Phase One. Data also throw light on the nature and extent of large landownership in 1960. The distribution of private landownership by size provides a more useful and accurate indicator of landownership. It also provides an indication of the number of landowners affected by land reform. The 1960 census sample provides the distribution of ownership in the 1,669 privately owned villages. An ownership-estate (melk) is defined to consist of the extent of the ownership of one owner (malek) in one village measured in dang or frac-tion thereof. The range of an ownership is from six-dang to a fraction of a dang. Thus, the 185 villages each having one malek results in 185 owner-ships with an average size of six-dang. On the other hand, if 185 villages are each owned by 150 small owners, this would result in 27,750 owner-ships (185 x 150), with an average of 0.04-dang per ownership. The num-ber of ownerships indicates the upper limit of the number of owners. To the extent that one owner owns parts of different villages, the ownership count would exceed the number of owners.

One owner may own two dangs in each of three different villages. He thus owns six dangs in total, which is equivalent to an entire village. Table 12.3 provides the distribution of ownership by size of ownership con-verted into six-dang village equivalents. For instance, the 1,669 privately owned villages in the sample consisted of 10,014-dang (1,669 x 6) and were owned by 130,190 ownerships, of which 127,276 (97.8%) were under half-dang. These very small ownerships covered 4,960.5-dang out of 10,014-dang (49.5%), which is the equivalent of 826.75 full six-dang vil-

Table 12.3. Distribution of Private Property in 1,669 Villages

Property Size	Ownerships	Village Equivalent	Multiple Ownerships	Single Ownerships
6 dangs	185	185.00	134	51
3 to <6 dangs	414	242.74	255	159
.5 to <3 dangs	2,315	414.51	1,251	1,046
<.5 dang	127,276	826.75	*	*
Total	130,190	1,669.00		

Source: *First National Census of Agriculture, October 1960*, vols. 1–14 (Tehran: Ministry of the Interior, n.d.).
* Not listed in census.

lages. At the other extreme, there were 185 six-dang ownerships, implying that each of the 185 villages had no more than one owner. The landownership pattern was one of enormous complexity with medium and minute ownerships existing in the same village. The census also contains data on the extent of single and multiple ownerships in the categories of landownership. A multiple ownership is one in which the proprietor owns land outside of that village. A single ownership is one whose owner owns no other land, in which case the ownerships are equal to owners. For example, in the category of six-dang and above, 51 owners (out of 185, or 27.6%) did not own other land. The remaining 72.4 percent owned other land. In the three to under six-dang category, 38.4 percent were single ownerships. Out of 2,315 ownerships in the half to under three-dang range, 1,046 (45.2%) were single ownerships. There is thus an increasing proportion of single ownerships with the decline in the size of ownership. Thus, it appears that at least half of the 127,276 ownerships of under half-dang were single ownerships.

Based on 56,525 privately owned villages and the results of table 12.3, the overall private property distribution is provided in table 12.4. The most startling and previously unsuspected information revealed is the extent of ownerships of less than three-dang in terms of numbers and the amount of land covered. Ownerships of under three-dang constituted 99.5 percent of the total and accounted for the equivalent of 75 percent of the villages. Remarkably, half of the villages were owned by the petty khorde-malekin (under half-dang), with an average ownership size of under 1/25th of one-dang, indicating an average of 150 owners per village, a figure that Lambton notes on several occasions. Combining the ownership figures with those of holdings (operational units), the following results can be established. The 56,525 privately owned villages (out of

Table 12.4. Distribution of Private Property Based on 1,669 Sample Villages

Property Size	Ownerships	Ownership Equivalent	Average in Dangs	Single Ownerships	Multiple Ownerships
6 dangs	6,265	6,265	6.00	1,727	4,538
3 to <6 dangs	14,021	8,221	3.52	5,389	8,632
.5 to <3 dangs	78,403	14,038	1.07	35,425	42,978
<.5 dang	4,310,529	28,001	0.04	*	*
Total	4,409,218	56,525			

Source: Tables 12.2 and 12.3.
* Not listed in census.

60,520 villages) consisted of 4.4 million ownerships and 1.76 million hold-ings (out of 1.88 million), that is, 2.5 ownerships per holding. The signifi-cance of this result is that just as in the case of Egypt, a crucial purpose of sharecropping and tenancy was to combine small and uneconomic own-erships that resulted from the Islamic inheritance laws into viable eco-nomic holdings. A comparison with landownership in an Islamic country such as pre-1952 Egypt is illustrative.

The 1950 census of agriculture in Egypt, undertaken on the eve of Nasser's 1952 land distribution, had enumerated 2.8 million ownerships and 1 million holdings. Mahmoud Abdel-Fadil drew this inescapable conclusion:

> A simple comparison of the size-distribution of *landholdings* with the distribution pattern of *landownerships* brings out quite clearly that one of the basic features of the land tenure system in Egypt is the *tendency to concentrate the land into larger holdings than the freeholds.* In this respect, the economic function of tenancy is to break up large ownerships and consolidate very small parcels into holdings of op-erational size.
>
> As can be seen, recourse to tenancy was widespread among both large landlords and the small absentee owners who could not draw a living from their minute plots. The large discrepancy between fig-ures for *landownerships* and those for *holdings* in the size class of "less than five feddans" illustrates the fact that these small landowners tend to be the net *out-leasers* in the system. This is mainly attributable to the fact that there are more absentee ownerships among the very small proprietors (in particular owners of less than one feddan) than among the medium and large-scale proprietors.[21]

The main economic role of tenancy under a system of Islamic inheritance laws was the consolidation of small uneconomic ownerships into viable economic landholdings. The similar results for Iran and Egypt indicate than in an Islamic society the number of ownerships is considerably greater than the number of landholdings. Moreover, the number of ownerships could grow ad infinitum without affecting the number of holdings. Thus Abdel-Fadil's description of landownership and the crucial role of tenancy in Egypt is identical to the description given by Lambton. Lambton also stressed the point that "if a holding is broken up by inheritance into units too small to afford a livelihood to a family, the usual practice is for the holding to be sold, or for the joint heirs to lease their shares to one of their number and themselves to emigrate elsewhere in search of permanent or casual employment."[22] Moreover, the inevitable conclusion to be drawn is that sharecropping served to combine the minute ownerships that had evolved from the Islamic inheritance system into viable economic holdings.

Large and Medium Landowners

Combining the landownership statistics with the data from Phase One, one can obtain a measure of the extent of large landownership defined as an ownership of six-dang and above, or one or more villages. As stated above, Ajami had reported that 2,250 landowners owned one or more villages. The census results had revealed 6,265 six-dang ownerships of which 1,727 were single ownerships. It then follows that 523 landowners (2,250 − 1,727) owned 4,538 villages (table 12.5). Under the provisions of the 1962 land distribution decree, maximum ownership was limited to one village, that is, each of the 523 landowners subject to the provisions of

Table 12.5. Landowners and Privately Owned Villages on the Eve of Land Distribution

Property in Dang	Number of Landlords	Equivalent Villages	% Villages	% Avg. Ownership (No. Villages)
>6-dang	523	9,598	17.00	18.4
6-dang	1,727	1,727	3.00	1.0
3 to <6-dang	5,389	3,161	5.60	0.6
.5 to <3-dang	44,020	14,038	24.80	0.3
<.5-dang	2,065,781	28,001	49.50	
Total	2,117,440	56,525	100.00	

Source: Tables 12.3 and 12.4.

the decree were permitted to retain one village, and the remainder was expropriated. Subtracting 523 from 4,538 yields 4,015 villages subject to expropriation. Interestingly, land reform figures report that 3,992 entire villages were included in Phase One.

Concerning the three to under six-dang category with an average ownership of 3.52-dang (six-tenths of a village), 5,389 (38.4%) constituted single ownerships. The remaining 8,632 were multiple ownerships, and given the large average size of ownership, most would have been included in Phase One. In terms of villages, and using the average size of ownership, the single owners in this category owned the equivalent of 3,161 villages, and the remaining 5,060 equivalent villages were owned by the multiple ownerships. Conservatively assuming that these villages were also owned by the large landowners included in Phase One, we can draw some conclusions on the amount of land transferred to the cultivators under the first phase of land distribution. Adding 5,060 to 3,992 villages gives 9,052 full village equivalents that were transferred to tenants under Phase One,[23] or some 16 percent of the privately owned land was included under Phase One. That this figure is on the excessive side and thus overstates the amount of land under Phase One is indicated by the fact that the corresponding figure for the Dezful area reported by Salmanzadeh and Jones was 11 percent of the land. The sample findings indicate that the half-dang to under three-dang ownerships contain 35,425 single ownerships and 42,978 multiple ownerships (tables 12.3 and 12.4). The results point to 44,020 landowners who owned the equivalent of 14,038 villages.[24]

Summing up, the results indicate that 2,250 large landowners (with six-dang and above) possessed the equivalent of some 11,325 villages (4,538 + 5,060 + 1,727 or, alternatively, 6,265 + 5,060). This was 18.7 percent of the total and 20 percent of the privately owned villages, a result that is nearly identical to the situation in Egypt and is in stark contrast to the material in some of the literature that claims large owners owned 50–60 percent of the villages.[25] Considering medium landowners as those with half to under six-dang, the following results are indicated. There were about 49,400 medium landowners (5,389 with three to under six-dang and 44,020 with half to under three-dang) who owned the equivalent of 17,200 villages. Medium landownership accounted for 28 percent of total and 30 percent of private land. Adding 2,250 large landowners shows that some 52,000 large and medium landowners owned the equivalent of 28,524 villages, which was 47 percent of total villages and 50 percent of privately owned villages. The rest were owned by the small landowners.

Small Landowners

The data indicate that half of the villages were owned by 4.3 million ownerships of under half-dang (tables 12.3 and 12.4). These owners constituted the petty khorde-malekin with an average of under 1/25-dang. This implies an average of about 150 owners per village. This is identical to the situation in the hill country of Jordan, where the eleven villages studied had 1,663 owners.[26] Unfortunately, the sample does not contain information on single and multiple ownerships in this category. Consequently, it is not possible to establish an independent estimate of the number of petty landowners. However, assuming that the proportion of single ownerships in this category remains the same as the one-and-a-half to under three-dang category, it would indicate 1.94 million single ownerships. Again, this is an underestimate because we know that the proportion of single ownerships increased with declining size of ownership. Next, even assuming twenty ownerships per owner in the multiple ownership category (that is, each owner owned shares in twenty villages) results in 117,500 owners. Added to 1.94 million owners derived from single ownerships, the result is 2.06 million small landowners (table 12.5). Thus, the figure of 2 million khorde-malek reported in the semiofficial daily *Etela-at* is consistent with the findings of the 1960 census of agriculture. In all, 2.1 million individuals owned land, of whom 52,000 were medium and large landowners. It is known that some 800,000 holdings were owner-operated, with an average of 5.4 hectares, an indication that the vast majority were owned and operated by peasants. These were not subject to confiscation under land distribution. Subtracting from 2.1 million owners results in 1.3 million owners subject to expropriation under Phase Two and Phase Three of land distribution. Once again, the data published by the Ministry of Agriculture stating that 1.2 million small landowners were subject to the provisions of Phase Three appear to have been accurate. In short, under the three phases of land distribution, some 1.3 million persons were expropriated, and their ownership was distributed to 1.6 million tenants.

The enormous number of petty ownerships was an outcome of Islamic matrimonial and inheritance practice as well as the laws of population growth. The widespread practice of polygamy among the privileged classes (which continued up to the 1940s, since the "modernizing" Reza Shah himself had numerous wives) resulted in large numbers of heirs. Under the Islamic inheritance practice, all the descendants shared in the land. The process resulted in a geometric growth in the number of landowners and corresponding decline in the size of ownership. Although Lambton underestimated the importance of peasant proprietors and of khorde-malekin, she identified three distinct categories of small land-owners.[27] First, urban residents (mostly small merchants) who buy land in the neighboring villages as an investment. Lambton states that most of the villages near the urban areas were purchased as investments. The second type of absentee small landownership "is found in different parts of Persia and not just in the neighbourhood of towns." With inheritance, the ownerships of these landowners had grown too small to be economical, forcing them to migrate and rent the land to a sharecropper. According to Lambton, "Many of these owners return in summer to their villages to collect their dues from the harvest." The third category included owners who resided in the villages. Lambton gives the following description:

> The small-holder who is not mainly an absentee, but lives in the village, differs from the peasant proprietor in that he does not work on the land himself. In most cases he derives his property from hereditary right, subdivision by inheritance having reduced his own status or that of his forebears to a position of a small-holder. In other cases he may be a comparative newcomer, or a peasant proprietor who, by greater industry or greater fortune, has succeeded in increasing his own holding. Where small-holders of this type are found in peasant-proprietor villages, it frequently happens that they own small areas of land in neighbouring villages also. Thus, in Abianeh, near Kashan, which is mainly owned by peasant proprietors, some of the more prosperous people own land in the neighbouring villages; in a similar way part of the land of Abianeh is owned by the people of the neighbouring village of Hanjan, which is also mainly owned by peasant proprietors. In most peasant proprietor-villages there are in any case usually one or two families who own rather more land than their fellows, which they work either on a crop-sharing basis or by employing paid labour. This type of landowner, so far as he does not work the land himself but employs labour usually on a crop-sharing basis, resembles the large landed proprietor, but his social, political, and economic position is vastly different from that of the large landed proprietor.[28]

Data in the 1960 census of agriculture give an indication of the number of rural-based small landowners described by Lambton (see appendix C).

Landowners' Plight

Commenting on the plight of the small landowners, Lambton stated:

> By the summer of 1962, the peasants in many areas, especially in Azarbayjan, were withholding the payment of the landowner's share of the crop from land which had not yet been transferred or was not subject to transfer. Some of the large landowners, if their share of the crop was withheld, turned to the local governor and the gendarmerie for help in collecting their dues. The small landowner, on the other hand, had little opportunity for redress. There were in many parts of the country considerable numbers of small people who had put their savings into land to supplement their income by an often tiny (but to them important) sum; and it appeared likely that this class, if not dispossessed, would be at least driven into a lower rank of society.[29]

As demonstrated in this study, their numbers were far greater than has been realized by analysts or reported by the Pahlavi regime.

In an entry dated 5 March 1968, written in the village of Pelet Kaleh in Zavar, Majd makes the following observation concerning the confiscation of the property:

> Landowners and their dependents who are said to number 5 million persons have been reduced to poverty. This includes a group of re-spected individuals who had served this country. They have lost everything and are unable to earn a living. Those who were elderly and unable to work live in abject poverty and are now destitute. These conditions encompass 99 percent of the former landowners. Unable to pay their debts, many are involved with the courts or have tasted prison as insolvent debtors. Their lives have been destroyed. Most laughably, at this time the government is holding a human rights convention in Tehran.

He then gives an example of a family that lost everything:

> The Sufi family was a respected landowning family in Gilan, and their estates were located in Amlash, in the eastern part of Gilan. They had been followers of the founder of the Safavi Dynasty, Shah Esmail I, and ever since had faithfully served the country. In 1945–46, when the landowners in Gilan rebelled against the Tudeh Party and the agents of the Russians, the Sufis were in the forefront of the fighters. In 1950, when I was governor-general of Gilan, I was invited by the Sufis, and I visited Amlash and saw firsthand the com-

fort in which they lived. Those in charge of land distribution often consisted of veteran members of the Tudeh Party, and they took this opportunity to extract a terrible vengeance from the Sufis. They lost everything and were reduced to dire poverty.

Majd describes the fate of another landowner, Jaffar Khan Rashvand of Qazvin, who in 1945 took up arms against the Tudeh Party and the Russian sympathizers. Majd had delivered arms to him in 1945. His property in Rudbar was confiscated in 1962, and he was left with one village. However, the tenants refused to pay rent. Jaffar Khan complained to the Qazvin Land Reform Organization, and a land reform official was assigned to accompany him to the village. Once in Rudbar, Jaffar Khan was insulted and the official was beaten by the villagers. Majd gives other instances of landowners who lost everything and could no longer earn a living.

Small Landowners and the Diaries of Alam

The implementation of Phases Two and Three of land distribution resulted in the de facto and de jure confiscation of the small landowners. It appears that the confiscation of the petty landowners caused concern at the highest levels of government. The matter is discussed in the diaries of Assadollah Alam, minister of court, the shah's most trusted aide and by far the second most powerful personality. Referring to the provisions of Phase Three of land distribution, Alam points out that the proposed compensation of the khorde-malekin was a thinly disguised way of outright confiscation. He appears concerned that many of "these pitiful unfortunates will be destroyed" by the loss of their only source of livelihood. He is also concerned by the political ramifications because the small landowners formed a sizable group. To Alam, the matter of khorde-malekin is regarded as "a really major problem." Alam reports that he raised the issue with the shah in an attempt to increase compensation to the expropriated owners or to enable them to keep some of the land. The shah became angry and flatly rejected the proposal. According to Alam, the shah also declared that "not one of these owners actually resides in the villages." Alam's only response was to say that His Majesty was "ill-informed," but given the shah's anger, he did not pursue the matter. He consoled himself for having done "his duty" by informing the shah.[30]

Several points concerning this episode are noteworthy. First, the shah's view on small landowners, as reported by Alam, is in sharp contrast with what the shah had stated earlier. In his book, the shah declared that "as a class, the big private landlords are parasites, and as I shall indicate in a moment, their days of feudal control are limited. Quite different are many of the smaller landlords, who may own one or a few villages and not infrequently live in close association with their tenants, . . . many of the best-managed villages in Iran are run by them."[31] In view of Lambton's earlier descriptions, and considering what the shah himself had stated in 1960, the shah's alleged statement that "not one of these small owners actually resides in the villages" is truly astonishing. How could one expect intelligent and compassionate policy under such circumstances? Conceivably, what the shah meant was that by then the small landowners had been forcibly driven from the villages. There is ample evidence of this. Alternatively, the shah's hostility toward the small landowners reflected the political opposition of the latter as evidenced by the numerous pamphlets they had published and the certain involvement of the small landowners in the uprising of 5 June 1963.

Second, there is an astonishing degree of hypocrisy and dishonesty in Alam's seeming sympathy for the small landowners. It is clear that he is trying to exonerate himself and blame the shah for the injustices inflicted on the small landowners. Alam is conveniently oblivious to the fact that it was under his premiership that the so-called Additional Articles, subsequently known as Phase Two, were drafted and approved by his cabinet in January 1963 and implemented by his successors. The minister of agriculture in Alam's cabinet at the time, and the author of the "articles," was none other than Alam's friend, Hasan Arsanjani. It was the provisions of the Additional Articles that had begun the process of the de jure confiscation of the small landowners. The 1963 pamphlet that was cited above, "An Open Letter to the Prime Minister," published by the Population of Small Landowners, was addressed to none other than Prime Minister Alam. In the "letter" there is a litany of the injustices suffered by the small landowners because of the government's policy. Finally, it was Alam who ordered the paratroopers to direct machine-gun fire at the demonstrators on 5 June 1963. Six years later, the same Alam is expressing his "concern" over the fate of the small landowners.

Others were concerned for the small landowners. That the confiscation of the small landowners continued to arouse anger is seen from a 1968 article by Hasan Ali Hekmat, a well-known poet, written for the weekly *Khandaniha*. What is remarkable about the piece is that it was written at a time when even a hint of criticism incurred the wrath of the secret police. Hekmat points out that even by the government's own initial figures, 1.2 million small landowners were subject to expropriation under Phase Three. He denounces the expropriation of the small landowners, and he is especially critical of the compensation offered to those facing expropriation.[32] He deems the confiscation unjust and politically unwise. This article caught the attention of the CIA, which proceeded to translate and distribute it.

American Consular Reports on Small Landowners in Azarbaijan and Khorasan

The contents of Hekmat's article, however, came as no surprise to the CIA. By January 1963, the American government was fully aware of the conditions in Iran and the magnitude of the blunder that had been committed. The proof is found in the confidential American diplomatic and consular reports from Iran. Shortly after the approval of the Additional Articles, Consul John M. Howison discussed some of its provisions in airgram A-52 (dated 26 January 1963):

> The number of people facing direct loss from land reform has been increased many times over. Even if the amendment is liberally interpreted to account many smallholders as "farmers" entitled to keep their land, the affected proprietors will be socially and politically of a social class different from their predecessors in losing land. Both Persian and Turki as used in Azarbaijan distinguish between *khorde-malekin* (petty proprietors) and *arbabs* (latifundists). Although the economic and social role of the petty proprietor has been institutionally just as invidious as that of the *arbab*, their relative poverty and incapacity to adjust to change may impel them to claim greater consideration from the regime than has been accorded to the *arbab*.
>
> Although as long ago as last August a senior official of Azarbaijan implied that this year would see land reform reach the holdings of petty proprietors, the local evidence is that the recent amendment of Land Reform Law was neither part of a preconceived plan nor a purely political action. Governor-General Ali Dehqan on January 22 observed almost ruefully that the new phase of land reform was a "necessity" because "two systems of land tenure cannot exist side by side." This Lincolnesque "house divided" observation may have a broader validity, and suggest to us that reform may breed reform almost spontaneously across the whole spectrum of innovations initiated during the governments of Alam and Amini.

In a long, confidential report to the State Department (airgram A-63, dated 12 March 1963), euphemistically entitled "Azarbaijan Smallholders and the Land Distribution Program," Howison described the desperation of the khorde-malekin in East Azarbaijan who were being "harassed" by peasant cultivators. The consul had also noted that according to Parviz Behbudi, head of the Agriculture Ministry in Azarbaijan, practically every one of the 4,020 villages in East Azarbaijan was affected by the provisions of Phase Two. He had also recorded the rising concern over the "serious increase in urban unemployment" pursuant to the disenfranchisement of the small landowners. Given Howison's previously outspoken support for the program, it was not surprising that he tried to paint a less gloomy picture. Here are some excerpts from Howison's immensely important report:

Discussions with provincial agricultural officials reveal that they are concerned about the enormity of the task of distributing small-holder lands under present arrangements. Engineer Parviz Beh-budi, able Provincial Agricultural Chief for East Azarbaijan, says that virtually every Azarbaijan village is affected by the regulations concerning smallholders and he expects the number of Eastern Az-arbaijan villages directly affected thereby to reach 4,020. He com-mented that by comparison, dealing with a small number of impor-tant landowners had been an easy task. Behbudi reported that every day groups of smallholders besiege his office offering their lands for sale to the government, and he is hard pressed to accommodate them. He attempts to discern which cases are the more grievous and to purchase those lands first, but finds his funds insufficient to pur-chase all of the lands offered. Behbudi seems sincerely concerned about the welfare of the average smallholder, but at the same time seems determined to accomplish in an equitable fashion the enor-mous task before him. While he admits there is some friction be-tween peasants and smallholders over land ownership, he stoutly maintains there is no widespread agrarian unrest, and that with the help of the provincial gendarmerie he and his staff are able to medi-ate these disputes as they arise and stabilize each situation by issu-ing land deeds to the parties involved. The harassment of individual smallholders has clearly hastened the implementation of the Janu-ary 17 amendment to the Land Reform Law, and has caused them to sell their lands directly to the government without dealing with their former tenants. Behbudi and his staff appear to be going ahead as best they can under present regulations. Although minor distur-bances in particular villages are sure to continue, they do not appear to be beyond the capacity of agricultural and Gendarmerie officials to control. The land reform program in Azarbaijan is not in serious trouble. However, the extension of land reform to smallholder lands has for the first time since the beginning of land reform elicited from provincial land reform officials complaints about the difficulty of administrating land distribution. As in the past, Governor-General Ali Dehqan and his subordinates can be expected to carry out their difficult task with quiet determination and expectations of "success."

In discussions about the enforcement of the regulations concerning smallholders' lands, Engineer Behbudi and his assistants have given detailed information about that group which is of interest. Smallholders (*khorde-malekin*) can be divided into the same categories as landlords: resident and absentee. Resident smallholders are those who live on their lands or in the village immediately adjacent to their lands. Normally, they possess relatively limited amounts of land, often inherited from their fathers. Absentee smallholders are such groups as minor bureaucrats, petty merchants, and school-teachers. They have had in the past money to invest, and not having confidence in the security of investments in industry or business, have purchased lands. The agricultural activities of both types of smallholder have been characterized by the utilization of additional labor, either hired or sharecropper, to achieve agricultural production, the difference between the two groups being that the resident smallholders physically take part in farming. (Some resident smallholders farm their lands without assistance.) The majority of smallholders either parcel out portions of their lands to peasants (*rayat*), who pay the smallholders a set share of each crop as peasants did to landlords, or hire laborers (*khoshneshin*) by the day. Smallholders who farm land themselves or hire day laborers, according to Behbudi, are not obliged to sell, rent, or divide their lands to or with others as provided in the January 17, 1963, Land Reform Law amendment. It is the peasants who were forced to give shares of their crops to the smallholder in payment for use of land and productive facilities, who are now to receive land deeds.

Behbudi, who has consistently expressed sympathy for ex-landlords over their financial difficulties, is even more concerned over the plight of the smallholders. He says seventy percent of the land distribution now being carried out in this province is in response to requests from smallholders that the government buy their lands before they begin to suffer from unsettled conditions in their villages. He describes these smallholders as people who depend on agriculture for all or the major part of their income, and is particularly sympathetic towards the resident smallholders, who have no place to live and no other employment by which to gain their living once they leave their lands behind. Behbudi explains that the one-fifteenth of the value of the smallholder's land which would be paid to him upon approval of the sale and the conclusion of the appropriate papers is usually completely inadequate to support him and his family, and he must therefore gravitate to the cities such as Tabriz, where work is so scarce that unemployment is already a serious problem. He hopes that government construction projects can be implemented and industry stimulated in order to provide jobs for these new additions to the ranks of the unemployed. That this increase in the number of unemployed could be extremely serious can be seen from Behbudi's estimate that the distribution of small-holders' lands will affect 4,020 villages in East Azarbaijan alone.

Behbudi admits that in some cases agricultural workers and peasants without lands of their own are harassing smallholders, but denies that there is any widespread agrarian unrest. As soon as reports of such harassments reach his office, Behbudi dispatches an expert to the village concerned to ascertain the nature of the disagreement. . . . He said recently that extensive use of the Gendarmerie is being made and jokingly remarked that he and Colonel Tabatabaii-Vakili now act "as joint commanders of the Gendarmerie." Judging from his remarks about the Gendarmerie, Behbudi is utilizing that tool extensively. Although the Consulate has no way to ascertain how much use is being made of the Gendarmerie, it has received no accounts of serious disturbances in this Consular District.

The distribution of lands belonging to smallholders to the extent it is presently planned is an enormous undertaking. When asked how long it might take to implement the new regulations, Behbudi would not even hazard a guess. His staff and his financial resources are both inadequate to handle the present load placed on them, and it is obvious that he feels the present regulations are both overly ambitious and excessively harsh in their effect on the smallholders. The Consulate believes Behbudi is hoping for a limited relaxation of the January 17 regulations now that Minister of Agriculture Arsanjani has returned to Tehran. There are signs that a group representing smallholder interests is active in Tabriz; this development is being reported on separately.

In Eastern Azarbaijan, where peasants' hopes for lands of their own have received more attention and satisfaction than in other areas of Azarbaijan, it is clear that limited conflict between landless villagers and smallholders has provided the incentive for immediate implementation of the January 17 amendment in some villages at the request of harassed smallholders. It is also clear that in the majority of these cases smallholders have elected to sell their lands to the government rather than become involved in rental, sales, or sharing agreements with their peasants, as provided in the regulations governing the distribution of smallholder lands. The press of events and the urgent needs of the smallholders asking to sell their lands have almost certainly caused land reform officials to be less than meticulous in carrying out the involved procedures prescribed for computing the value of the lands being distributed, and there may be disputes over these hastily made settlements for years to come.

At about the same time, the American consul in Mashhad, J. P. Mulligan, who previously reported on the gathering of the small landowners at the house of Ayatollah Qomi (see chap. 8), sent a confidential report on his meeting with the chief of land reform in Khorasan. In this report (airgram 20, dated 23 March 1963), Mulligan informed Washington that there were a great many small landowners in Khorasan who were affected by the provisions of Phase Two:

> Information obtained from Engineer Abbas Akhavan, chief land reform official and Acting Director of the Department of Agriculture in Khorasan, indicates that approximately 90% of the land distribution scheduled for this ostan under phase one of the land reform program has been completed. According to his estimate, phase one, i.e., the distribution of holdings in excess of one village, will be completed in about one month's time.
>
> In his remarks to reporters present, Eng. Akhavan praised the cooperation of several large landowners, notably Mahmoud Sareme Dargazi (of Dargaz) and the Shadlu family in Bojnurd, including particularly Khanlar Qarachorlu (Shadlu) who retained only 80 hectares of land, which is even less than the amount to which he would be entitled under the Amendment to the Land Reform Law.
>
> He also observed, however, that things had not gone so smoothly in Shirvan, where Amir Hosein and Shapur Negahban, the largest owners in the area, having heard of Dr. Arsanjani's resignation as Minister of Agriculture, refused to sign the required documents of transfer. This act was accordingly performed by Eng. Akhavan, who proceeded then to purchase their holdings and distribute them as indicated above.

Application of Amendment to Land Reform Law

In discussing this information with me on March 19, Eng. Akhavan stated that in comparison with some other regions in Iran, this area did not have a great many landowners who owned more than one complete village and therefore the total number of peasants who had received land was not high. He added that in Khorasan there are a great many small landowners who will be affected by the Amendment to the Law and applicable by-laws.

Concluding Observations

Howison's report again shows that many of the nonresident (absentee) small landowners were members of the lower urban middle classes who were being deprived of their life savings by the so-called land reform. In addition, his description of the plight of the resident small landowners and their desperate attempts to sell their lands to the government in the face of peasant "harassment" indicates that the estimate of 1.3 million expropriated landowners is very conservative and that the actual numbers were much higher. It is in the context of Howison's report that we begin to understand the shah's declaration to Alam that "not one of these small landowners resides in the villages." They had been driven out. Consequently, most of the 1.3 million landowners of Phase Three were nonresident members of the urban middle classes. Little is known about the fate of the resident small landowners. Much more research is needed. Consequently, it is possible that the total number of expropriated landowners exceeded that of the peasant beneficiaries.

Unfortunately, from the beginning, American consular and embassy officials chose to disregard the warnings about small landowners. Crawford's report on Isfahan was soon forgotten. In a long, confidential report on land distribution in Azarbaijan (Foreign Service despatch 53, dated 29 January 1962), the vice consul in Tabriz, Archie M. Bolster, duly reported that Ezatollah Majid, a landowner in Azarbaijan, had sent a telegram to Prime Minister Amini "on behalf of landowners of Azarbaijan." The text of the telegram was published in the newspaper *Azarabadegan* on 12 January 1962. In the telegram, Majid warned that because of the government's land distribution policies and the haste with which these policies were being implemented, "the landowners of Iran and their relations, who constitute one-fifth of the country's population, might be entirely extirpated." The allegation was dismissed by the vice consul and his superiors as pure propaganda. How could such a serious allegation be so easily dismissed? Would the tragedy of Iran's small landowners have occurred if the actual landownership structure had been widely known? If the actual numbers about petty landowners were known to the U.S. government, would the same path have been taken? If the truth about landownership were widely known, could the likes of Arsanjani have had the opportunity to wreak havoc on Iran's society? Of course not. Why was it that, unlike Egypt and Turkey, Iran did not conduct a rural census that provided data on landownership? The reason was simple: the need to hide the extent of the land theft by the two Pahlavis. For the corruption and greed of Reza Shah and his son, the people of Iran paid a heavy price.

13

Toward a Theory of Landownership
in Islamic Iran and Some Consequences
of Land Distribution

The long-accepted view of landownership in Iran has been heavily influenced by the writings of Ann Lambton. Her view was that most of the land was owned by large landed proprietors, and these large estates were cultivated by a multitude of tenants. According to Lambton, small landowners and peasant-proprietors owned relatively little land. This widely accepted view greatly influenced both academic and journalistic writings in the West. But Lambton was in error. While large ownerships cultivated by a multitude of tenants did exist, they were far less numerous than Lambton indicated. Small ownerships were widespread and covered much land. This was the inevitable outcome of the Islamic practices of polygamy and inheritance. Under the Islamic system of dividing the property among all sons and daughters, large estates were broken up relatively quickly. Islam resulted in a continuous redistribution of property and the breakup of large holdings.

What then explained the existence of large ownerships, that is, ownership of one or more villages by one person in an Islamic system? How could the medium ownerships be explained? The most obvious explanation is that the land policies of the state consisted of confiscating land and giving it to individuals. Reza Shah confiscated large areas of the country and dispossessed the owners. In addition, as a result of Reza Shah's land "exchange" policies, some new large estates were created. A more important and subtle explanation was suggested in a pamphlet published in 1959 by the National Agricultural Council. Unbeknownst to the pamphlets' authors, they were proposing a working theory of landownership in Islamic Iran.

Under the Islamic system, all large private ownerships were broken up relatively quickly. In the more arid regions and in those areas where agriculture required qanat irrigation, subdivision of ownership by inheritance resulted in neglect of the irrigation systems and a decline in agriculture. The agricultural decline was reflected in the price of the village. Its price declined to a level that made it economical for an individual investor to purchase the village from its owners and then to redevelop the village. This helps explain the existence of large and medium ownerships at any given point in time. They consisted mostly of former large ownerships that were in the process of being broken up. And so the cycle continued. According to this theory, certain regions of the country were destined for permanent petty ownerships. Other regions were suited to large ownerships. These areas were in a permanent state of flux. A dynamic equilibrium was achieved when the relative shares of the three types of ownership were stabilized. The equilibrium was disturbed as a consequence of government intervention in landownership. This simple and yet elegant reasoning helps to explain the actual structure of landownership in Iran in 1960. Of the 56,000 privately owned villages, the equivalent of 30,000 (54%) were owned by petty landowners. Of these, 20,000 were entirely owned by petty landowners. Some were in a permanent state of petty ownerships, while others were in a transition stage to large ownerships. Only 6,000 (11%) villages had one owner. And the remaining one-third were in the form of medium ownerships.

Sharecropping fulfilled a vital role, combining minute ownerships that resulted from the Islamic system into economically viable holdings cultivated by tenants. In an Islamic system, the number of landowners could easily equal or even exceed the number of tenants. The other purpose of sharecropping was to break up the temporary large ownerships into smaller operational units. It was not surprising that sharecropping was approved by religion and tradition. In the long run, the system was dynamic, efficient, and equitable. This ancient system was completely destroyed by the so-called land reforms. Within a relatively short period, most of the qanats were ruined. Iran, like Egypt, soon became one of the world's largest agricultural importers. I find it significant that, more than forty-five years after Nasser's land distributions, Egypt is now restoring the land to the descendants of its original owners.

Decline of Qanats

A qanat is an underground irrigation channel made by excavation. It brings underground sources of water to the surface using gravity and the natural slope of land. It requires no energy, it creates an equilibrium between precipitation and water use, and it prevents depletion of water sources and environmental degradation. According to official statistics, there were 62,615 qanats in operation in Iran in 1972 at the completion of land distribution.[1] Iran's system of working qanats measured 311,000 kilometers and averaged one qanat per village. Each qanat required an average of 5 kilometers of digging.[2] Iran's landowners built and maintained this system. Within twenty-two years, the number of qanats had shrunk to 28,663.[3] This decline was associated with an increase in the number of wells. In 1972, there were 9,351 deep and 31,810 semideep wells. By 1994, these figures had leaped to 84,322 and 223,274. In practice, an environmentally friendly and sound system had been replaced by one that relied on subsidized energy and capital and that was likely to cause environmental degradation. In contrast to qanats, which do not use any energy and which maintain a balance between precipitation and outflow, wells are heavy users of energy and capital. Most often, private profitability has depended on provision of subsidized cheap energy and capital. The cheap energy and subsidies cannot last forever. Eventually, declining petroleum reserves alone will raise energy costs. The comparison between the two systems involves some interesting issues of private versus social costs and external economies and diseconomies.

I have read that the main reason for the decline in the qanat system is increased labor cost. The validity of this claim should be judged by the fact that the relative cost of labor has fallen in the oil-producing countries since the collapse of oil prices in the mid-1980s. Rapid population growth and the arrival of several million Afghan refugees have enlarged Iran's labor force. In my view, the main reason for the destruction of so many qanats is the removal of the landowners, who built and maintained the system, and the absence of an institutional system to replace the landowners. To compensate for this loss, the government has resorted to providing subsidized energy and capital.

Demise of Cultivation Teams

These changes also doomed Iran's traditional system of cultivation. For centuries, in regions of water scarcity, mostly in central, eastern, and southern parts, cultivators were organized into production teams. These teams were known by various names, depending on the region. In Tehran and Qazvin, the term *boneh* was used. In Khorasan the term *sahra* was observed. In Shiraz, it was *harata*. The number of teams depended on the amount of water available. Each team had an equal share of the village's water and land resources.[4] Each team member had an assigned task and shared in the output. This traditional system was said to solve the prob-

lem of land fragmentation and to significantly improve the efficiency of
water use, the most limiting input. By combining the cultivators into
teams, field size was expanded, land fragmentation was prevented, and
water was used more efficiently. In addition, in the interest of equity,
fields were reallocated regularly, so that fields of different fertility rotated
among teams. The system disintegrated after land distribution. In northern and western regions with adequate water, individualistic mode of
production had prevailed even before land distribution.

The literature has identified two main categories of cultivation teams:
landlord-sharecropper (*arbab-rayati*) and ploughmen (*gavbandi*) teams. In
the arbab-rayati, a landowner or his representative organized the team
and often supplied animal power, tractor power, and seed. By this crite-
rion, the bonehs in Ebrahim Abad and Jamjerd were clearly of the first
kind. In the gavbandi, the team was organized and the plough animal and
seed were provided by an oxen owner (gavband), who often also worked
as a team member. Although it has not been suggested in the literature, it
is clear that the gavbandi teams existed primarily in villages that were
owned by small landowners who exerted little power and control over
village affairs. Safinejad's comparison of the two teams included the following revealing description:

> Usually, if a landowner resided in the village, or was sufficiently
> powerful to control village affairs and supervise the *bonehs'* cultiva-
> tion, he acquired the *gavband* rights [rights to provide oxen power to
> the teams]. But in villages where landowners or their representa-
> tives, for reasons diverse, could not supervise cultivation, nor had
> any knowledge or control over village affairs, the vacuum was filled
> by *gavbands* [owners of oxen]. They became the intermediaries be-
> tween the owners and the village. Under these conditions, many of
> the privately owned villages and nearly all of the *moqoufeh* [en-
> dowed] and *khaliseh* [public] holdings were administered in the
> *gavbandi* mode. The *gavbands* were mostly local inhabitants.... There
> were several classes of *gavbands*. Some possessed a single [ox] or a
> pair of oxen and worked as cultivators on the land. But others ac-
> quired a great deal of wealth and power and became the real owners
> [*arbabs*] of the village.[5]

Under the provisions of the various land distribution decrees, the
gavbands were recognized as cultivators and thus received land. Petty
landowners were expropriated, and their property was given to the
wealthier gavbands. It was termed social justice.

Rising Agricultural Imports

Nearly forty years have passed since the launching of land distribution in Iran. It is now possible to assess some of its economic consequences. It is clear that the destruction of the traditional system of landownership, irrigation, and cultivation teams and its replacement by small-scale owner-occupied farms brought fundamental dislocation to Iran's agriculture. An indication of the measure of performance can be seen from the import figures. The statistics tell their own story. In 1962, Iran was self-sufficient. Its main traditional agricultural imports were sugar and vegetable oils. Grain imports were insignificant: 56,000 tons in 1962, only 1 percent of production and consumption. By 1977, grain imports had increased to 2.43 million tons. Wheat imports had increased from 35,000 tons to 1.2 million tons. Rice imports had grown from 19,000 tons to 600,000 tons. Spectacular increases were also recorded in the imports of meat and dairy products.[6] While government growth statistics indicated that Iranian agriculture grew at one of the highest rates in the world between 1963 and 1978 (4.3% per year), the import figures clearly showed that Iran's agriculture had failed to meet the rising demand.

Many explanations were offered by scholars for the rising imports. Some alleged that agriculture had been neglected by the government. It had failed to provide sufficient price support and protection from imports. Others blamed insufficient investment incentives by the government. Others, including this author, tried to explain the rising imports in relation to rapid population increase, rising per capita income, and the consequences of the oil boom of the 1970s.[7] Subsequent developments showed that none of these explanations were even remotely satisfactory. Upon coming to power, the Islamic Republic declared the achievement of self-sufficiency in food to be a top priority. It increased price supports and subsidies to agriculture. It undertook a crash program of rural road construction and electrification. Yet, despite its efforts and the end of the oil boom since the mid-1980s, Iran's agricultural imports have continued to increase. By 1994, grain imports alone stood at 4.3 million tons.[8] Import levels reflected the structural disruptions caused by the so-called land reform. While oil prices were rising or high in real terms between 1968 and 1985, agricultural imports did not constitute a heavy burden. But with the decline of oil prices since 1986, and the calamitous collapse of oil prices in the mid-1990s (oil prices in real terms in 1998 were at an all-time historical low with no relief likely), agricultural imports have become a heavy drain on Iran's economy.

A fundamental reason for the poor performance of Iran's agriculture since 1960 is the fact that investment in rural Iran is no longer considered safe. The foundation and security of private ownership was shattered by the shah's land distribution program. Historically, investment in farmland has been the investment of choice for Iran's urban middle classes. As shown in this study, such groups as shopkeepers, bureaucrats, army officers, teachers, as well as those in the professions (professors, lawyers, and physicians) put their savings into land by purchasing villages or shares in villages. This capital was obviously a vital source of agricultural growth and rejuvenation. After the expropriation of these groups between 1962 and 1971, this source of capital to the agricultural sector completely dried up, and it is unlikely to resume. It is a lasting legacy of American policy and Hasan Arsanjani.

A Statistical Summary: "White" or "Pink" Revolution?

Land distribution in Iran has been viewed favorably by many writers because it gave land to so many cultivators. Binswanger and Elgin described it as "an outstanding example of a successful land reform." It was considered a progressive measure during which the rights of a few were sacrificed for the benefit of many. Overall statistical results of land distribution show that more than 1.8 million tenants became owners of the land they cultivated: 1.6 million received private land and 200,000 received endowed and government land. When compared with the data found in the 1960 census of agriculture, it is evident that nearly all those eligible to receive land did so. This was further confirmed by data published after the revolution.[9] By the same token, virtually all the private land that was cultivated by tenants was transferred to the sitting tenants between 1962 and 1971. Subtracting owner-occupied land indicates that nearly 75 percent of the land was transferred. Land distribution, undeniably, benefited a large number of people. To the extent that the tenants were able to maintain and increase production after land distribution, and given the fact that the annual installment payment for the land was a small fraction of rent previously paid to landowners, land recipients benefited from land distribution. Not only they were relieved of rent payment but they also became owners of land. Even in the case where the output declined after land distribution, and the decline was greater than the rent previously paid, the former tenants were mostly better off because they could lease out or sell the land and then move to nonagricultural employment.

The results in this study point to a hitherto unexamined side that forces a total reappraisal. Based on the results of the 1960 census of agriculture and much other evidence, it was shown that at least 2.1 million individuals owned land in 1960 and that nearly half of the land was owned by small landowners (khorde-malekin). The huge number of small ownerships and small landowners was the inevitable outcome of the Islamic matrimonial and inheritance practices. Land "reform" resulted in the expropriation of at least 1.3 million small landowners and some 52,000 large and medium owners. The dispossessed landowners and their dependents constituted at least 20 percent of the population. The actual number of cultivators and landowners affected by Phase Three throws light on the redistributive consequences of land distribution. The data show that 1,200,587 cultivators received land under Phase Three.[10] For each peasant who became owner, a landowner was expropriated. However, as shown in earlier studies, one-third of the peasant beneficiaries of Phase Three had also received land under Phase One.[11] Thus, 800,000 peasants received land for the first time under Phase Three. The number of losers under Phase Three, some 1.3 million landowners, far exceeded the number of first-time land recipients. This hardly qualified as "an outstanding example of successful land reform."

The estimated number of expropriated landowners given in this study is conservative. The possibility that the actual number of expropriated landowners was at least as great or exceeded the number of peasant beneficiaries cannot be ruled out. Vast numbers of people were adversely affected by land distribution. Two groups were particularly important. The first group consisted of the urban middle classes, including bazaaris, petty merchants, petty bureaucrats, widows, orphans, etc., who had inherited or invested in land. These groups lost their life savings, retirement nests, and often their only source of income. The second group consisted of small landowners who resided in the villages who were driven away by peasant violence and who lost everything. As described by Consul John M. Howison, these destitute people had nowhere else to go but to the cities, where they joined the ranks of the unemployed. The consequences of this political madness were to be felt almost immediately during the upheavals of 1963.

The disenfranchisement of the huge class of small landowners in Iran had a historical parallel in the form of the disenfranchisement of the kulak class in the Soviet Union under Stalin. Thus, the claim by Mohammad Reza Shah that his revolution was a "white revolution" was not correct. It had a strong tinge of red. Moreover, this affinity with Stalinist rural policies was further shown by the establishment of state-run collective farms that were misleadingly called "farm corporations."[12] All of this had been done with the support of the U.S. government.

The Opposition: Landowners and Ulama

Despite the loss of the endowments, and contrary to reports by American diplomats that the ulama had been weakened because peasants resented them as allies of landlords, the position of the ulama was greatly strengthened by the shah's land policies. Landowners, large and small, including members of Iran's traditional and modern urban middle classes and the population of resident khorde-malekin, were totally alienated from the Pahlavi regime. With alternative organizations and political parties suppressed and silenced, this group looked to the ulama for protection and guidance. A historical opportunity was created for the ulama, and Ayatollah Khomeini seized it.

In reading passages from the shah's 1971 book, *The White Revolution*, one is struck by the depth of hostility that the shah still displayed toward landowners and the ulama.[13] Even though eight years had passed since the uprising of June 1963, and land reform had been declared complete, and the foundations of a new society had supposedly been laid, there was no sign of forgiveness or magnanimity toward the "vanquished" foes. And for good reason. The shah's land reform was perceived as an alien measure that was being imposed by foreigners on an Islamic country. It was conceived as an attack on Iran's Constitution, the laws of Islam, and Islamic institutions and practices. Most damaging of all, it had been portrayed by landowners and Ayatollah Khomeini as a conspiracy by foreigners to destroy Iran's agriculture, make her dependent on food imports, and thus reduce the country's independence. Whether this was true or not is irrelevant. It came to be regarded as the truth by large sections of Iran's population before the Islamic Revolution. Of all the accusations that were made against the Pahlavi regime, none was more damaging and widely accepted than the charge that the shah had destroyed Iran's agriculture at the instigation of his foreign masters.

Faced with the mounting opposition, the Pahlavi regime resorted to intimidation and violence to silence the opposition. It also took extensive measures to cover up the expropriation of the small landowners. It delayed the publication of the 1960 census of agriculture for nearly a decade, and even then little meaningful information was released. It put out misleading and inconsistent figures on landowners expropriated by its land distribution policies. It also tried to erase evidence of Arsanjani and the excesses that were committed during that period. In the 1978 Stanford book *Iran under the Pahlavis*, edited by George Lenczowski, large segments are devoted to land reform but not a single word to Hasan Arsanjani. It was as though he never existed. The sensitivity of the regime can also be seen from its attempt to suppress Lambton's 1969 book because Lambton was sympathetic to Arsanjani and had also mildly hinted at the expropriation of the small landowners.

The confiscation and plight of the small landowners and the alienation of the middle classes help explain why the shah was not able to expand the base of his regime through land distribution. It also explains the depth of the opposition and upheavals that shook Iran in the spring of 1963. The opposition culminated in protests and the uprising of 5 June 1963, a hallowed date in the annals of the Islamic Republic, and a defining event in the history of the resistance to the Pahlavis. After the brutal suppression of the protests, and the emergence of Ayatollah Ruhollah Khomeini as the leader of the opposition, there could be no reconciliation with the Pahlavi regime. It was not a mere coincidence that one year later, a triumphant Mohammad Reza Shah had issued an imperial decree that ordered the government to implement the provisions of the Additional Articles, also known as Phase Two.[14] Similarly, Assadollah Alam could confidently boast of having smashed the alliance of the landowners with the ulama.[15] But the "victory" was transitory. The Pahlavi regime had won a battle, but lost the war.

For fifty-three years, the two Pahlavi shahs struggled almost continuously with landowners and the ulama. Reza Shah's attack on traditional landownership and his secular and anticlerical policies were continued by his son. The struggle ebbed and flowed. Between 1925 and 1941, Reza Shah and the "modernist" elements had the upper hand. The situation changed between 1941 and 1948 when the "traditional" forces were able to reexert themselves. The 1951–53 oil nationalization period was one of chaos, and as a result, landowners and clerics actually allied themselves with the Pahlavi regime and assisted General Zahedi in overthrowing Mohammad Mossadeq. Both Mossadeq and Zahedi were landowners. But the alliance with the Pahlavi regime was short-lived and ended with the dismissal of General Zahedi as prime minister and his exile in 1955. Thereafter, the Pahlavi regime again went on the offensive and was able to reassert its dominance. In the desperate struggle that took place between 1959 and 1964 between landowners and the ulama on one side, and the Pahlavi regime and its domestic and foreign supporters on the other side, the Pahlavi regime had seemingly won again. However, that lengthy confrontation and the resulting disenfranchisement and alienation of the huge middle class and the petty landowners gravely weakened the Pahlavi regime. In the end, neither the support of a superpower nor the oil billions could save it.

Land Policy of the Islamic Republic

With the establishment of the Islamic Republic under Ayatollah Khomeini, the former landowners briefly hoped that the historical wrong inflicted on them would be rectified. Indeed, given the record of opposition by the ulama, particularly by Ayatollah Khomeini, the former landowners expected to regain their property or at least to receive a measure of justice. Soon after taking power, the Islamic Republic nullified the transfer of publicly endowed lands to the cultivators, and all private ownership deeds to these lands that had been issued after 1962 were declared null and void. Nothing was done concerning private land. Soon after the establishment of the republic, in a stunning turnaround, government rhetoric began to attack "feudalism" and the need for a land distribution, as though no land distribution had taken place under the shah. Remarkably, the leadership of the Islamic Revolution and the government behaved as if the events of 1959–64 had never occurred. The fatwas by such personalities as Ayatollah Borujerdi, Ayatollah Hakim, and Ayatollah Khomeini himself were forgotten and ignored. As outlined by Schirazi, a land distribution bill was drawn up by a committee of Islamic jurists in 1979 and approved by the Revolutionary Council in 1980.[16] Under the bill, seven-member committees were set up for each region. The Committee of Seven was given extensive powers to seize land and to give it to the poor. The implementation of the measure was soon halted because of its seeming "conflict" with the laws of Islam.

Next, the leadership of the Islamic Republic moved to deal with the matter of land seizures after the revolution. During the early months of the revolution, with encouragement and support by such leftist groups as Mujahedin Khalq and Fedayan Khalq, there were instances of land seizures by peasants, landless rural residents, and even urban residents. The figures were relatively small. The amount of land involved was said to be 800,000 hectares; those who had seized land were said to be 120,000 individuals. Most of this land had not been confiscated under the shah and had remained with the original owners. These seizures were not officially sponsored by the government. But the response of the Islamic Republic was to "legalize" the seizures, and in practice to confiscate the owners. In 1986, by a margin of 75 percent, the Islamic Consultative Assembly voted to grant the ownership of the land to the squatters who occupied it, on the condition that they paid a "fair" price to the former owners. However, just as in the days of the shah, the entire exercise was a charade because there was no mechanism to force the squatters to pay. In 1988, the Islamic Majlis voted additional legislation that enabled the new owners to obtain title

deeds to the land. Needless to say, thirteen years later, no "compensation" had been received, and none was expected. In effect, what the shah began was completed under Ayatollah Khomeini. The little land that had remained was confiscated. At least under the shah there was a pretense to pay compensation. In Iran, the more things changed, the more they stayed the same.

APPENDIX A

A Sample of Correspondence Concerning
Reza Shah's Foreign Bank Deposits

The following banking correspondence was included in a 1995 article by Reza Farasati in *Contemporary History of Iran*, published by the Institute for Historical Studies. This is the text of a letter from the director general of Pahlavi Bank, Tehran, to the president of the National Bank of Persia. It was written in French, and an English translation follows:

Pahlavi Bank
Confidential
Tehran, 17 August 1931
Mr. President of the National Bank of Persia,
Tehran

Excellency,
   Based on His Majesty's order, I beg you to send telegraphic instruction to Midland Bank in London to deposit $150,000 in His Majesty's account at Westminster Bank, and confirm it by telegram.
   With my highest esteem to you, Mr. President,
   Director General, Colonel Amir Khosrovi

The next day, the following response was received:

National Bank of Persia
Management
18 August 1931
Bank Pahlavi, Central Headquarters in Tehran, to the good care of Mr. Director General, His Excellency Colonel Amir Khosrovi, Tehran

Excellency,
   Following receipt of your instruction number 5170 of 17 August, I have the honor to inform you that yesterday immediately following the receipt of your letter, I gave telegraphic instruction to Mid-

land Bank Ltd. of London to deposit $150,000 to the account of His Majesty at Westminster Bank Ltd., London.

Westminster Bank has received our telegraphic instructions and will inform you of the receipt of the money.

My highest salutation and consideration to Your Excellency,

Dr. Lindenblatt, National Bank of Persia

The manager of the foreign branch of Westminster Bank Ltd. wrote to Reza Shah to acknowledge a deposit:

Westminster Bank Ltd.
Foreign Branch Office
The Manager
82, Cornhill
London, EC3
Reference: GAJ/ML   4 September 1931
His Majesty Reza Shah Pahlevi

Sir,

I have the honour to inform Your Majesty that, in accordance with instructions from Banque Pehlevi, I have received the sum of one hundred fifty thousand dollars with which amount we have opened in the name of Your Majesty a Deposit Account for one year bearing interest fixed at the rate of three per centum per annum.

I enclose herewith the formal receipt sealed with the seal of Westminster Bank Ltd.

I have the honour to remain Your Majesty's obedient servant,

Signed,

Manager

The following is a letter from the chief of the Office of Imperial Estates to the management of Bank Pahlavi:

Lion and Sun
Office of Imperial Estates
Tehran
20 August 1932

Respected Management of Bank Pahlavi:

In response to your letter of 19 August 1932 and on the basis of His Imperial Majesty's orders, you are informed in writing that the Westminster Bank will be instructed that His Majesty's deposit of $150,000 be renewed for six months from 25 August 1932 to 25 February 1933 at a rate of 1.5% interest per year. In addition, His Majesty ordered that two new accounts each for $4,500 from the interest in-

come of last year, plus the interest income of the past six days, be opened and the money be paid when instructed. Of course, these two accounts will be managed according to usual banking practices. Chief of Office of Imperial Estates

The following certificate of deposit was issued:

Westminster Bank Ltd., Foreign Branch Office
No. 378, 25 August 1932
  Received of His Majesty Reza Shah Pahlavi the sum of one hundred and fifty thousand dollars for the credit of deposit account with Westminster Bank Ltd. fixed for six months until 25 February 1933 at the rate of interest of one and one half per centum per annum
Cashier [signature]
Manager [signature]
$150,000 [seal of Westminster Bank]

There are other documents. For example, in a letter dated 19 August 1931, Dr. Lindenblatt of the National Bank of Persia informed Reza Shah that the interest income from His Majesty's $150,000 deposit at the Reich Kredit Gesellschaft for the period 3 June until 3 August 1931 amounted to $743.83, and a check for that amount was humbly submitted. In another letter dated 16 September 1931, Dr. Lindenblatt informed Reza Shah that the interest income for the two-week period of 4–18 August 1931 from His Majesty's $150,000 deposit at Midland Bank in London was $86.30, and a check for that amount was humbly presented. In a letter dated 11 October 1931, Dr. Lindenblatt informed Reza Shah that the interest income from His Majesty's $150,000 deposit at the Union de Banque Suisse from 30 June to 30 September 1931 amounted to $875, and a check for that amount was humbly submitted.

Zavar Document of Exchange, 26 July 1935

Majd retained the document of exchange, dated 26 July 1935, between the government and the owners of the estates of Zavar. By this document, the estates of Zavar, Tonekabon, were exchanged for a group of villages in Qazvin, Zanjan, Karaj, and Arak:

  Lion and Sun
  Ministry of Justice
  Countrywide Office of Registration of Documents and Estates
  Miscellaneous Transactions—Deed of Exchange, 11th Office of Legal Documents, Tehran
  The contents of this document, which have been recorded on

pages 195 and 196, number 8978, in the registry of the notary office, have also been recorded by me as representative of the registration office, on page 164 of the record book of the 11th Office of Legal Documents under the number 7945, on the date 26 July 1935. Parties to the transaction (the exchangers):

1. Mr. Mohammad Qoli Khan Entesar Khalatbari (the former Amir Entesar), holder of identification card number 114, issued in Tonekabon, residing in Qazvin.
2. Mr. Mirza Hasan Khan Khalatbari (the former Amir Momtaz), holder of identity card number 6218, issued in district 2 of Tehran, residing in Tehran.
3. Mr. Gholam Hosein Khan Akbarpour Sheikholeslami, holder of identity card number 13113, issued in Qazvin, residing in Qazvin.
4. Mr. Jahanshah Massoudi, holder of identity card number 31295, issued in district 2 of Oladjan, residing in Qazvin, representing the respectable Fakhr-e Zaman Khanum (Motamedi Gorgi).

Other party to the transaction (recipient of the exchange): His Excellency, Mr. Mirza Ali Akbar Davar, the Honorable Minister of Finance of Iran, in the name of and representing the August Government of Iran.

Items of transaction (to be exchanged):

The entire and total six dangs of the village of Kotra-ye Olia known as Eshrat Abad, six dangs of the village of Kotra-ye Sofla, six dangs of the village of Entesar Abad known as Kat Kaleh, six dangs of the village of Hosein Abad of Mazibon and the pasture, six dangs of the village of Pelet Kaleh known as Qoli Abad, six dangs of the village of Al-e Kaleh known as Abdollah Abad, six dangs of the village of Rude Posht-e Olia and Sofla, six dangs of the village of Habib Abad and the entire sharecropped tea plantations of Habib Abad, six dangs of the village of Ashraf Abad and each and every one of the following pastures of Chaleh Sara, Babulat, Hosein Abad, Lot-e Kotra, Kat Kaleh, Talusarak known as Entesari-eh, and the pasture of Tameshkot, all of which are located in the region of Zavar, Tonekabon (Talusarak and Tameshkot are in the region of Khoram Abad, in the jurisdiction of the village of Gharb-e Siavarz). And the ownership of the parties to the transaction in each of the locations in the above list of names is established and not subject to any liens and encumbrances. All religious, traditional, usual, and legal ownership rights to all the areas and additions in the villages and pastures (dependent or independent), plants, orchards, forests, buildings and constructions, threshers, all kinds of real estate, canals and water rights, all kinds of water flows, all other properties and assets in each of the cited villages, and all other ownership and property rights of the named persons who are party to this transaction, are measured and recognized, be they mentioned or not mentioned in this deed (with the exception of the share of the parties to this transaction in Talesh Mahaleh and Sarbord and the remainder of Mazibon). Such that, with the above noted exceptions, they retain no ownership and possession rights whatsoever in the above-mentioned villages and dependencies. Including all of the two flocks existing in the area, and consisting of 500 head of sheep, and 60 head (large and small) of cattle. (All benefits and all revenues from the estates in this transaction for the current year 1935 are included in the exchange).

To be exchanged in return: All the hamlets and property belonging to the government in the village of Khoramdareh, located in Abhar Rud, Khamseh (with the exception of a government building that houses the Ministry of Post and Telegraph), government share consisting of two dangs of the village of Ardagh and surroundings located in the Dasht-Abi District of Qazvin, four dangs of the villages Najaf Abad and Hasan Abad of Panjeh Kosh located in the Eqbal District of Qazvin (the above-mentioned shares in Ardagh, Najaf Abad, and Hasan Abad Panjeh Kosh that were transferred to the government by the heirs of the late Sepahsalar Khalatbari, are included in this exchange in the same manner as given in the relevant documents), six dangs of the village of Ebrahim Abad located in the Zahra District of Qazvin, six dangs of the village of Nowdeh Lakvan located in the Dasht-e Abi District of Qazvin, six dangs of the village of Khoznein located in the Ramand District of Qazvin, six dangs of the village of Asb-e Mord and the four dangs share of the government in the village of Yarud located in the Rudbar District of Qazvin, and 2.5 dangs of the village of Ebrahim Beigi located in the Savetch Bolagh area of Tehran. The locations of all of these are clearly defined, of which Ardagh and Najaf Abad are the properties of the public treasury, and the rest are assuredly the property of the government and are not subject to any encumbrances and liens. With all areas and contents, and all religious, traditional, and legal rights, in the manner owned and possessed by the government, and without any exception (apart from the above-mentioned government building in Khoramdareh), and all revenues and benefits of the exchanged villages for the year 1935, are part of the exchange and are exchanged.

Note: Of the villages that are exchanged, 700 jaribs of cultivated and noncultivated land, and a share in the sheep flocks of the other villages are the property of Mr. Amir Momtaz, 307 jaribs, subject to the same conditions, are the property of the respected Fakhr-e Zaman Khanum, and 264 jaribs with similar conditions, are the property of Gholam Hosein Khan. The remainder of the exchanged villages, their parts, and conditions are the property of Mr. Amir Entesar. In return for his share in the exchanged villages, two dangs of Ardagh and its surroundings are granted to Mr. Amir Momtaz; two and one-half dangs of the villages of Najaf Abad, and Hasan Abad Panjeh Kosh are given in exchange for the share of Mr. Akbarpour Sheik-ol Eslami; and six dangs of the village of Nowdeh Lakvan are given to Fakre-e Zaman Khanum in exchange for her share. The rest of the exchanged estates (the above cited hamlets and areas of Khoramdareh, one and one-half dangs of Najaf Abad and Hasan Abad Panjeh Kosh, and six dangs each of Ebrahim Abad, Khoznein, and Asb-e Mord, four dangs of Yarud, and two and one-half dangs of Ebrahim Beigi) are granted to Mr. Amir Entesar in exchange for his share. And each of the above-mentioned persons have completed this transaction in the same manner and condition. The settlement contract is complete, and the entire transaction is executed.

"Dated the fourth of the month of Mordad, 1314 Solar, corresponding to 25 Shahre Rabi-ol Akhar, 1354 Lunar [26 July 1935].

Place of Signature: Mohammad Qoli Tonekaboni, Hasan Tonekaboni, Gholam Hosein Akbarpour, Jahanshah Massoudi Tonekaboni, Ali Akbar Davar."

Bojnurd Deed of Sale, 10 February 1940

I would like to greatly thank Reza Azari Shahrezaii of Iran National Archives Organization for making this document available to me. The term *musha* means joint ownership of undivided parts. *Six dangs* means ownership of six shares out of six shares. By this document, the following properties in Bojnurd, Khorasan, were sold by the Ministry of Finance to Reza Shah:

Lion and Sun
Ministry of Justice
Central Registration of Documents and Estates
Document of Miscellaneous Transactions
Type of Document: Definitive and Immovable
Notary Office Three—District of Tehran

The contents of this document that have been recorded on pages 105 and 166, number 8978, in the record book of the head notary have also been recorded by this representative/recorder of the registration office on pages 236 and 237 of the record book of the Third Notary Office of Tehran 17249, under number 16148, on 10 February 1940.

Purchaser: Our Illustrious Master, His Imperial Majesty, Reza Shah Pahlavi, Shahanshah (represented by Hosein Sheibani, who undertook this transaction on behalf of His August Imperial Majesty, the Shahanshah).

Seller: Brigadier Reza Qoli Amir-Khosrovi, Minister of Finance, representing and in the name of the government of Iran.

Items to be transacted: complete and all of the following villages, hamlets, items, and estates located in the region of Bojnurd whose location, identity, and characteristics are given below. 1. Six dangs of the hamlet of Taromi. 2. Six dangs of the hamlet of Amirieh. 3. Six dangs of the hamlet of Dor. 4. Six dangs of the village of Ali Abad, including the garden located therein. 5. Six dangs of the hamlet of Kohneh Kand (located in the vicinity of the town of Bojnurd). 6. Six dangs of the village of Haj Mohammad Esmail. 7. Six dangs of the hamlet of Panbeh Zar. 8. Six dangs of the pasture of Baqer Khan. 9. Six dangs of the hamlet of Koor Cheshmeh. 10. Six dangs of the hamlets of Kaleh Gav and Halqeh Sang, including a garden and 13/30 of a flour mill. 11. Six dangs of the hamlet of Kalateh Beed. 12. Six dangs of the village of Haj Hosein including the garden. 13. Six dangs of the hamlets of Kateh Bashoqi and Takhteh Bashoqi (located in the suburbs of Bojnurd). 14. Six dangs of the village of Joush Khan. 15. Six dangs of the village of Chahar Beed, including six gardens and three mills (located in the District of Shaqan). 16. Six dangs of the hamlet of Kargar. 17. 56/108 musha of hamlets of Okhlizad and Nagol. 18. Six dangs of the village of Sarok. 19. Six dangs of the village of Qarloq-e Sofla, including two mills. 20. Six dangs of the village of Ozoun Bijeh. 21. Six dangs of the hamlet of Qormat-e Baqeri (located in the District of Garm Khan). 22. Six pieces of delineated land known as Zir Kharabeh. 23. One piece of land located in the Fort of Shir Ali, including two gardens. 24. Thirteen pieces of delineated land known as Sabrestan. 25. Three pieces and one-half piece of delineated land known as Posht-e-e Amirieh. 26. 6/14 musha of the hamlet of Sadr Abad, including one garden, one mill, and 4/10 of a stable (all located in the vicinity of the town of Bojnurd).

27. 2 1/24 musha of the village of Garmeh (located in the District of Esfarain). 28. 5/14 musha of the village of sar Cheshmeh. 29. 3/6 musha of the village of Qazal (Qazal Kariq), including one village. 30. 27 and 5/130 musha of the village of Abdol Abad. 31. 2/6 musha of the village of Marzeh Ali Khan Beyk (located in the District of Garm Khan). 32. Six dangs of the garden known as the Garden of Ilkhani. 33. Six dangs of the Garden of Allah Verdi Khan. 34. Six dangs of the garden known as the Garden of Nasrollah (located in the vicinity of the town of Bojnurd). 35. Six dangs of the Garden of Farah Afza. 36. Six dangs of a house known as the House of Ardeshir Shavoli that is near the headquarters of Bojnurd Regiment. 37. Six dangs of each of the forty-six shops. 38. Six dangs of each of the two caravanseraye. 39. Six dangs of one cold storage (located in the town of Bojnurd). 40. 5/14 musha of the mill located in the village of Aziz. 41. 10/30 musha of a mill located in Qordan Loo (located in the suburbs of the town of Bojnurd). 42. Six dangs of the hamlet of Qesti. 43. Six dangs of the village of Shahr Abad Kord. 44. Six dangs of the village of Shahr Abad Khavar, including eighteen gardens and one mill. 45. Six dangs of the village of Haidar Abad, including the garden. 46. Six dangs of the village of Aziz Abad, including eighteen gardens and one mill. 47. Six dangs of the villages of Shah Abad Kord and Khavari, and the surroundings, including fifteen gardens and 12/30 of a mill. 48. Six dangs of the village of Shir Abad, including one mill. 49. Six dangs of the villages of Biar Kord and Khavari, including one cold storage. 50. 4/6 musha of the village of Incheh Olia, including one mill (located in the District of Samlaqan). 51. 10/16 musha of the village of Jajarom, including one garden. 52. Six dangs of the village of Gazi. 53. 6/18 musha of the hamlet of Navazi and one qanat. 54. 5/18 musha of the hamlet of Nayer Abad and one qanat. 55. 5/14 musha of the village of Alyoor. 56. Six dangs of the village of Mirza Baylo (located in the District of Jajarom). 57. Six dangs of the village of Gaz Abad. 58. 5/14 musha of the village of Kalantar. 59. 4/40 musha of Shah Joub Kalantar (located in the District of Maneh). 60. Six dangs of the village of Sar Abad. 61. Six dangs of the village of Bireh (located in the District of Takmaran).

All of the above named are clearly located and recognized, and each and every one is free of all legal, regulatory, religious, and traditional encumbrances and restrictions, including all villages, hamlets, pastures, plants, buildings, mills, all kinds of real estate, qanats, channels, mills, and all other items, be they stated or not stated in

this deed. Each and every one of the above is included in this transaction, so that the government will retain no legal, religious, or traditional rights of use, ownership, and possession whatsoever. In
addition, all incomes and revenues for the year 1940 are also included in this transaction.

Price: 1,718,759 rials, all of which was deposited to the treasury of
the country, and both sides fulfilled their obligations. Be it noted that
in the event any fraud is found in this transaction during the next
fifty years, the government undertakes to repay the price and compensate for all damages incurred. The above transaction was completed and recorded.
10 February 1940
Signed,
Reza Qoli Amir-Khosrovi

Establishing Citrus Groves in Zavar, 1940:
A Case Study in the Management of Royal Estates

As outlined above, Zavar was acquired by Reza Shah in 1935 and became
part of the Royal Estates. Little has been published on the management of
the lands that were acquired by Reza Shah. In my father's private papers,
I found nineteen original duplicates of contracts that had been drawn up
in 1940 between the Office of Imperial Estates of Tonekabon, or an identical contract with the Accounting Office of Imperial Court, and the cultivators in various villages in Zavar, Tonekabon, for the establishment of
orange groves. It is noteworthy that the Imperial Court was directly involved in the management of these estates. These contracts are all drawn
up between a Lieutenant Majlisi, representative of the Office of Imperial
Estates of Tonekabon, and the individual cultivators.

To maintain accuracy, the text of the contract is given below. Thereafter,
the details of each specific case will be summarized in table A1. First, the
contract with information to be filled in:

Emblem of Imperial Crown
Office of Imperial Estates of Tonekabon
Contract for the Establishment of Orchard
    The following contract is drawn up between Mr. _____, repre-
sentative of the Office of Royal Estates of Tonekabon, and Mr.
_____, residing in the village of _____, son of _____, and holder of
identity card number _____, for the establishment and development of _____ jaribs of uncultivated land (each jarib consisting of

1,000 square meters), for the purpose of planting _____ groves in the village of _____, region of _____, which is part of the Royal Estates. The contract has been entered into, and _____ copies are prepared.

1. Mr. _____ undertakes on the basis of this contract and the conditions cited therein to plant and develop an area of _____ jaribs of uncultivated land that has been assigned him in the village of _____, to _____ groves.

2. I, _____, hereby undertake from this date to cut the trees on the above-mentioned land, remove wood, take out the roots, level and plough the land in such a way that the land is developed and no longer in a state of waste, and prepare the land for planting _____ trees.

3. After the completion of the provisions of Article 2 above, I promise to plant the trees from _____ until _____, and complete the planting without any shortcomings or faults.

4. I undertake to maintain the above grove with the utmost care, and I undertake to pay for any damages to the fruits or the orchard that result from my negligence.

5. The above-mentioned cultivator, in exchange for the above undertakings, has received the sum of 40 rials as an outright grant for each jarib of tea gardens or citrus orchards planted.

Addendum: The above-mentioned cultivator has received previously the sum of _____ rials from the Office of Imperial Estates of Tonekabon, on the basis of documented expenses incurred.

6. If the above-mentioned cultivator deliberately leaves and abandons the orchard, he will have no root or plant rights in the established orchards. Second, the Office of Royal Estates will assign the orchard to another cultivator.

7. If the cultivator is for legitimate and acceptable reasons unable to take care of the orchard and is obliged to sell and transfer his root and plant rights, he is required to inform this office and identify his successor.

8. On the fourth year of the planting, the Office of Estates will collect nine kilograms of dried tea from each jarib of tea plantation, and one-half of the crop of the citrus groves as the owner's share of output.

9. This contract has been drawn up in four copies. One copy is given to the cultivator, and the other three are held by the Office of Royal Estates.

Signature or seal of cultivator _____, Regional Accountant _____, Regional Bailiff _____, Head of Accounting _____, Chief of Imperial Estates of Tonekabon _____.

In exchange for clearing forest land, preparing and ploughing the land, and planting the trees, each cultivator was paid 40 rials ($2.50) per jarib of land (1,000 square meters). Thereafter, the tenant had to give half of the crop to the Office of Royal Estates as the annual rent. In practice, with an expenditure of a mere $25 per hectare, the Royal Estates was assured half of the crop during the productive years of the orchard (20–30 years). However, the Addendum to Article 6 indicates that the cultivators may not have received any money themselves. The reason is the mention of "document of expenditure." This would be relevant if the cultivators had employed wage labor,

Table A1. A Sample of Cultivation of Orange Groves on the Royal Estates of Zavar, 1940

Village	Name of Cultivator	Contracted Area (jaribs)	Amt. Received (rials)
Kotra	Baba Ali	2.5	100
Kotra	Gholam Hossein Najaf	6.0	240
Kotra	Yusef	5.0	200
Kotra	Seyed Abol Fazl Bahrami	49.0	1960
Kotra	Zaman	6.2	248
Kotra	Baba Ali	12.0	480
Kotra	Seyed Taqi and Najaf	14.0	560
Kotra	Esmail	3.5	140
Kotra	Moharam Ali	6.5	260
Kat Kaleh	Isa and Rostam	30.0	1200
Kat Kaleh	Rostam Ali	2.5	100
Kat Kaleh	Alijan	3.5	140
Habib Abad	Ali Khan	10.0	400
Habib Abad	Qorban	4.3	172
Tilbordesar	Mehdi Hosein	2.8	112
Tilbordesar	Seifollah Mohammadi	5.7	228
Zavar	Qahreman	5.0	200
Zavar	Jarollah	4.0	160
Ashraf Abad	Najaf Ali	2.0	80
Total		174.5	6,980

Source: Contracts between the Office of Royal Estates and the peasants in Zavar. From the papers of Mohammad Ali Majd.

in which case the money would be paid as wage. The cultivators were liable to pay for all damages due to negligence. It is also noteworthy that the management policies of the Royal Estates had a decisive impact on the formation of a rural "bourgeoisie" and peasant differentiation. For example, Seyed Abol Fazl Bahrami, who was to become a Kotra notable and a wealthy man, had been assigned forty-nine jaribs of land and had received nearly 2,000 rials for the purpose of establishing orange orchards. Another cultivator, Najaf Ali in Ashraf Abad, had been assigned only two jaribs.

APPENDIX B

Text of a letter from the Agricultural Union of Iran to the U.S. embassy in Tehran (translated into English by Arsalan Khalatbari):

16 April 1962
The Embassy of the United States of America

As observed and witnessed by the ambassador, the agents of the Ministry of Agriculture in Iran perforce confiscate people's lands and perforce distribute them. It is beyond credibility that the information bureau of the American embassy is oblivious to the above.

Dispensing with the idea that such actions are sponsored by the wishes and the help of American policy in Iran, however, the publications of the American news agencies and newspapers and the allegations made by some of the high-ranking officials in your government, namely, Mr. Chester Bowles, adviser to the president, make us believe that the confiscation of lands by means of force and torture, the handcuffing and the subsequent display of landowners in the streets and bazaars, the felling of trees, the plundering of granaries, and even the throwing out of the small landowners from their own plots of lands—all these events signify that such are the persistent wishes of the politicians of the democratic and freedom-loving government of America.

That which takes place in Maragheh now coincides with that which Lenin in the beginning of his rule carried out in the vast country of Russia. Lenin allowed the peasants, backed by the Red Army soldiers, to confiscate lands and to drive away the owners from their homes. Today, this actually takes place in Maragheh, supervised by communist leaders whose names are recorded in the archives of the Security Organization.

It is said that the Americans, in order to barricade the way of communism, are planning to clear this danger from Iran by means of the distribution of landowners' properties among peasants, while in actual fact, Iranian communists with the help of communists from the outside are delivering into Khrushchev's hands a part of Iranian soil which is of very little distance from the Soviet border.

The luminous democracy of the United States has been founded upon the following sentence of Abraham Lincoln: "A person who has no house of his own must not demolish another's but rather build one for himself, and by this deed make sure it is safe from aggression." Iranian democracy too has been established on the following saying of the prophet of Islam: "Mankind is ruler of its life and property." This sentence of our prophet has been reflected in the clause dealing with the rights of people in the Constitution of Iran: "Ninth Clause—members of society in respect of their life, property, house, and honor are immune from aggression" also continues "on no condition is a piece of land to be taken from its existing owner unless it be on lawful and legal grounds, and that, only after the fixing and the payment of a fair price."

Please bear in mind that Iran is not in the category of backward and newly independent countries devoid of long years of standing, customs, and civil rights. This country boasts of a civilization 2,500 years old, and has continuously been subject to, and accustomed to carry out religious, codified constitutional and legal laws, and has considered aggression to the property of her people against her institution and her rights. Thus you are compelling our country to neglect her religion and to forgo the rights of her people.

You yourself know better that in a society where the guardian of the heart which is religion and the official police which is law do not reign, the country will ultimately by means of confusion, chaos, and slavery succumb to the elements of communism.

Now, under the leadership of well-known communists, our simpleminded peasants are led to tread upon their religion and to overthrow their country's laws and rules; and these communists then attribute these actions to the persistent demands of American policy in the Middle East, namely, in Iran, and is it not surprising and hypocritical that so unwise a policy should be named "land reform"!

The nation of Iran is that very same nation which assimilated within herself the attacks of Alexander and Changhiz, and is as yet alive and proud; this very nation will sooner or later repel this present danger which threatens us and which is unfortunately strengthened by your financial aid and the leadership of communists. But there is much to regret in that the 100-year-old popularity of your righteous and mankind-loving nation, and your worthy help in troubled times as in the case of Pishevari in Azarbaijan, should now by the mistakes of some of your politicians, or by your being deceived by some of Iran's old enemies, be completely destroyed. Strange and mysterious policies are very ably creating a general hatred toward the American government.

We sincerely hope that these sentences, which have been addressed to you by only a few seekers of truth and faithful patriots, will strike deep down and prove effective and thus enable you to think over your plans and actions once more.

Agricultural Union of Iran

Text of a letter dated 1 March 1962 from Julius Holmes, American ambassador in Tehran, to Chester Bowles, special representative of the president for African, Asian, and Latin American affairs:

Dear Chet,
You will perhaps recall that when we were visiting some of the villages during your visit here a Dr. Hushang Ram spoke to you briefly about some of his reservations regarding the Government's land reform program. Dr. Ram has some experience in this field as he has been in charge of the program involving the lands formerly owned by the Shah. Dr. Ram has requested that I submit to you the enclosed paper setting forth his views as to the most effective means to achieve land reform in Iran.

Sincerely,

Julius

Enclosure: "A Critical Analysis of Land Reform Methods" by Hushang Ram"

Text of a letter dated 26 March 1962 from Orville L. Freeman, secretary of agriculture, to George W. Ball, undersecretary of state, concerning a letter from Hasan Arsanjani:

Dear George,
Enclosed is a copy of a letter from the Minister of Agriculture of Iran which, in light of the conversation we had about Iran the night we were flying together to San Francisco, you might find of some interest.

Best regards,

Orville

Text of Arsanjani's letter to Freeman dated 17 March 1962:

Even if formalities could justify a delay in writing to a friend like you, your kindness and sincerity would certainly discourage any delay in replying to your affectionate letter of January 16, 1962. So, I sincerely apologize for the delay which, nevertheless, had its causes. I mentioned to you in Tehran that in a short while I would take action for the emancipation of our helpless and hungry peasants. I wanted to be able, when replying to your letter, to say that I have effected land reform in Iran. On March 13, for the first time, a group of 520 peasants received their title deeds in accordance with the provisions of Land Reform Law; and thus, I crushed the barrier that feudalism has presented in the way of our nation's progress. With all the humanitarian feelings that I have found in you, I am sure that you will be happy to know about what we have done.

When we met in Rome I felt rather embarrassed among men who had succeeded in serving their countries. But now I can say that I have taken a humble and small step for the emancipation of the people of my country.

Again, I wish to express my sincere gratitude, Mr. Secretary, for your kindness and sympathy. Please convey my sincere regards to Mrs. Freeman in whom I found an example of refineness and human excellence. Wishing you all the success, I am,

Sincerely,

Dr. Hasan Arsanjani

APPENDIX C

Of the 3,218,000 rural households given in the 1960 census of agriculture, 776,700 were described as noncultivating households (*khanevar-e gheir-e bahrebardar*). There are strong indications that most of the noncultivating households were small landowners who resided in the villages. It is precisely for this reason that the Pahlavi regime refused to provide any information on the composition of these households. Two key characteristics of this group distinguish it from the cultivating households (*khanevar-e bahrebardar*). First, there are much higher levels of literacy in this group. Forty percent of males ages ten and older were able to read. This compared with 20 percent for the cultivating households. Also noteworthy is the sharply higher literacy among the females in this group. The second crucial characteristic of this group is the sharply lower labor force participation rate and the high proportion of those ages ten and older who are described as economically inactive. Fifty-nine percent are described as "economically inactive," compared with 48 percent for the cultivating households. Significantly, the ratio of economically inactive or under ten years per employed person was 2.7 for the noncultivators and 1.9 for the cultivators. Given that there is no difference in the age structure between this group and the cultivating households, the higher rate of inactivity points to the ownership of land that had been rented out to tenants. Otherwise, how could they survive? Based on the high proportion of the economically inactive, it can be concluded that of the 776,700 noncultivating rural households, at least 500,000 were small landowners who rented land to sharecroppers and also resided in the villages. The remaining households (at most 200,000) consisted of rural shopkeepers, traders, and rural artisans and professionals who resided in the country's 60,000 villages.

Landownership in Isfahan: Report by the American Consul

The following is an excerpt from a confidential report (Foreign Service despatch 695, dated 30 March 1959), from the U.S. embassy in Tehran to

Table A2. Selected Characteristics of the Rural Population, 1960

	Nonfarming Households	Farming Households	Total
Number of households	776,700	2,441,760	3,218,460
Population	3,334,950	12,095,880	15,430,830
Under 10 years	1,121,700	4,193,629	5,315,329
60 and older	203,400	828,361	1,031,761
Average household size	4.3	5.0	4.8
% of population ages 10–59	60.3	58.5	58.9
Employed in agriculture	177,600	3,742,352	3,919,952
Employed outside agriculture	733,500	399,300	1,132,800
Economically inactive	1,302,150	3,760,599	5,062,749
Inactive as % of age 10 and older	58.8	47.6	50.0
Under 10 or inactive per employed persons	2.7	1.9	2.0
% of 10 and older able to read	26.9	11.8	15.1
% of males 10+ able to read	39.9	19.9	24.0
% of females 10+ able to read	13.7	2.8	5.2

Source: *First National Census of Agriculture, October 1960*, vol. 15, *Summary of Results* (Tehran: Ministry of the Interior, n.d.).

the U.S. State Department. It is entitled "Land Reform in Iran." The section on Isfahan is by Franklin J. Crawford, American consul in Isfahan.

A common assumption of foreigners and even Iranians in Isfahan is that rich and powerful landlords control vast, baronial expanses of cultivable land in this ostan. An examination of the landholding situation, mainly through interviews with landlords, agricultural and irrigation officials, and others presumed to be knowledgeable about landlord-peasant relationships, belies this assumption. Lambton in *Landlord and Peasant in Persia* (p. 268) states that land in Isfahan is predominantly owned by large holders. Rough estimates obtainable locally, however, tend to refute this. They put the number of individual agricultural landholdings in this ostan at 400,000 to 500,000. Even allowing for the fact that these figures are at best mere guesses and further that many landholdings are infinitesimal, amounting to only a few square meters, it nevertheless seems clear that there is a fairly wide distribution of land in this ostan which has a population of about 2,000,000. The Land Registration Department of Isfahan is either unable or unwilling to provide any figures on landholding except to confirm the statements of others that the pattern tends towards small holdings. A number of Isfahanis have volunteered the opinion that there are not more than fifteen or twenty persons in this ostan who are the sole owners of one or more villages. The largest landowner in Isfahan is Akbar Masud (Sarem-e-Dowleh). He controls four villages, two in his own name and one each in the names of his wife and son.

Governor-General Abbas Garzan, Governor-General of Isfahan, pointed out, a propos of all of Iran, that the trend during the past fifty years on the part of landed families has been away from the land to the cities. This, coupled with inheritance laws, has produced a natural distribution of land. Given continued internal security, there is no reason to suppose that this process will stop. Another phenomenon which has occurred is the acquisition of agricultural land by urban industrialists and bazaar merchants. As these people have made fortunes from war-time commodity speculation, from the textile industry, and from urban real estate speculation, they have purchased villages, or shares in villages. There are two reasons for this. Landholding provides prestige in Isfahan. It is also a good investment which appreciates in value along with the general land inflation. It seems generally agreed that the newly rich landlords do not give their properties the paternal attention which the better of the old landed families did. For the former, agricultural land is a purely economic thing; for the latter, landholding has been a way of life.

The collection of feudal dues from peasants has been in decline for many years. While there are still cases of peasants bringing landlords presents of chickens and eggs on No Ruz, the peasantry in the vicinity of Isfahan is pretty knowledgeable about its rights. There are, undoubtedly, still many petty exactions, but the newly appointed Gendarmerie commander in Isfahan reports that his office has had to take very little action to enforce the decree of last fall prohibiting the exaction of feudal dues. It is reported that the payment of feudal dues is still fairly widespread in Charmahal and Fereidan in the Bakhtiari country.

There is no discernible widespread demand for land distribution in this area. The idea of personal ownership of the land appeals naturally to the peasant, of course, but the most responsible observers, including officials who have no vested interest in the land but are nevertheless aware of its problems, maintain that any extensive division of land among the peasants would be economically disastrous. This is for the simple reason that peasants at present have neither the technical skill nor the financial resources to sustain an agricultural economy which is based almost entirely on irrigation. The payment of irrigation fees for Kuh Rang Tunnel water in Zayandehrud, amounting to 8,500,000 rials ($1 equals 76 rials) per year, and the cost of building and maintaining qanats are beyond the means of individual peasant landholders. Village cooperatives do not now exist in sufficient numbers or with sufficient resources to enable the peasants to pool their assets effectively.

The Isfahan Registration Department claims that about two-thirds of the cultivated land in this ostan has been registered, but the Charmahal and Fereidan areas of the Bakhtiari country are pretty much untouched by registration. It is obvious that any general scheme of land distribution if it is to be fair will have to be based on a more complete cadastral survey than is at present available.

The general attitude of landowners is, of course, repugnant to any kind of exploitation. The Islamic regard for the inviolability of private property is cited as an obstacle to this means of land distribution. The idea of an Agricultural Bank which would buy land from its owners on a short-term basis and sell it to the peasants on a long-term basis appeals to some, presumably because this would be an easy way to liquidate their assets. But these people also stress the necessity of increasing and improving assistance to peasants from the Ministry of Agriculture and the Community Development Bongah. Some landowners have even expressed their willingness to divest themselves of their landholdings—provided they are paid for them—if the regime finds this politically necessary or expedient. In general, though, they speak of greater agricultural assistance from the government, the need for more "study," and the need to wait and see if the distribution of the Shah's estates results in a higher standard of living for the peasants residing on them.

The reporting officer has reached the following tentative conclusions:

1. There is no general agitation for land reform in this ostan.
2. Thoughtless land distribution would satisfy no one and would be economically foolhardy.
3. The government can best assist the peasant economically, and at the same time prepare him for eventual ownership, by increased assistance aimed at improving agricultural techniques and by enforcing the collection of the landlord's 5 percent fee for community development villages.

NOTES

Chapter 1. Brief Historical Survey and Introduction

1. This brief historical survey is based on the following works: Ervand Abrahamian, *Iran between Two Revolutions* (New York: Columbia University Press, 1982); Yahya Armajani and Thomas M. Ricks, *Middle East, Past and Present*, 2d ed. (New York: Prentice-Hall, 1986); Homa M. A. Katouzian, *The Political Economy of Modern Iran, 1926–1979* (New York: New York University Press, 1981); Nikki R. Keddie, *Roots of Revolution: An Interpretive History of Modern Iran* (New Haven, Conn.: Yale University Press, 1981); George Lenczowski, "Political Process and Institutions in Iran: The Second Pahlavi Kingship," in *Iran under the Pahlavis*, ed. George Lenczowski (Stanford, Calif.: Hoover Institution Press, 1978), 433–77; Mohammad Reza Shah Pahlavi, *Mission for My Country* (London: Hutchinson, 1961).

2. Iran National Archives, *Iranian Government and German Immigrants, 1931–1938: A Documentary Collection* (in Persian), ed. Reza Azari Shahr-Rezaii (Tehran, 1995). Most disturbingly, it is reported by Armajani and Ricks that for the first time institutionalized discrimination against religious minorities was introduced in the army. It is also reported that the Iranian Boy Scout movement began to resemble the Hitler Youth movement. "Goodwill" tours were undertaken by such individuals as Baldur von Schirach, the Hitler Youth leader. Armajani and Ricks, *Middle East, Past and Present*, 422.

3. One influential writer who chose not to address the constitutional issues is Ann K. S. Lambton. Long regarded as the foremost authority on matters of land and landownership in Iran, Lambton served for many years as a member of the British embassy in Iran. She is the author of *Landlord and Peasant in Persia: A Study of Land Tenure and Land Revenue Administration* (Oxford: Oxford University Press, 1953) and *The Persian Land Reform, 1962–1966* (Oxford: Clarendon Press, 1969). It is shown in this study that some of Lambton's main conclusions concerning landownership are in serious error and have been the source of confusion and inaccuracy as well as inappropriate policy. It is also apparent that Lambton's portrayal of key issues and events is inaccurate. Some of these issues are discussed in chapters 5, 8, and 12.

4. A *qanat* is an underground irrigation channel made by excavation. The qanat system brings underground sources of water to the surface using gravity and the natural slope of land. Not only does it not require any energy but it creates an equilibrium between precipitation and water use and prevents depletion of water sources and environmental degradation. The amount of water flowing from a qanat is measured in terms of "stones." As outlined below, there were 62,000 qanats in Iran at the completion of land distribution in 1972. The length of underground channels was estimated at 311,000 kilometers.

5. A *dang* is one-sixth of a piece of property or real estate. Half-dang ownership corresponds to one-twelfth of a piece of property. Six-dang ownership corresponds to ownership of the entire property.

Chapter 2. Political Career of Mohammad Ali Majd

1. Sheik Karaki was one of the highest religious authorities (*mojtahed*) of his day.

2. Hafez Farmayan and Elton L. Daniel, *A Shiite Pilgrimage to Mecca, 1885–1886: The Safarnameh of Mirza Mohammad Hosayn Farahani* (Austin: University of Texas Press, 1990).

3. Safaed-din Tabarain, *Iran under Allied Occupation: A Documentary Collection, 1939–1945* (in Persian) (Tehran: Resa Institute for Cultural Services, 1992), 87–115.

4. Under Reza Shah, oil revenue was earmarked for arms purchase. As noted below, Mossadeq subsequently claimed that Reza Shah had diverted much of the oil revenue to his personal account in lieu of buying arms.

5. In the version that was published before the revolution, this part had been altered. Instead of the original version in which Reza Shah had said nothing, it stated that as the telephone communication was so poor, Majd had not understood what Shokuh ol Molk had said. It is possible that Reza Shah had suffered a nervous breakdown.

6. Baqer Aqeli, *Zoka ol Molk-e Foroughi and August 1941* (in Persian) (Tehran: Sokhan, 1988), 81.

7. A brief account of Majd's actions as governor of Mazandaran and Gorgan is given in Ruhollah K. Ramazani, *Iran's Foreign Policy, 1941–1972: A Study of Foreign Policy in Modernizing Nations* (Charlottesville: University of Virginia Press, 1975), 94–95.

8. Ervand Abrahamian, *Iran Between Two Revolutions* (Princeton: Princeton University Press, 1982), 186.

9. See Hasan Arsanjani, *The Autonomy of Governments* (in Persian) (Tehran: Organization of Pocket Books, 1963), back cover.

Chapter 3. Acquisition of Land and Wealth by Reza Shah

1. Armajani and Ricks, *Middle East, Past and Present*, 2d ed. (New York: Prentice-Hall, 1986), 421.

2. Donald L. Wilber, *Riza Shah Pahlavi: The Resurrection and Reconstruction of Iran, 1877–1944* (Hicksville, N.Y.: Exposition Press, 1975), 216.

3. As reported in the daily newspaper *Etela-at* on 8 October 1936, the exchange

rate was 16.55 rials per dollar and 80.5 rials per pound sterling. It was also reported in the *Etela-at* on 10 March 1937 that the government revenue for 1937–38 was estimated to be 1,250 million rials, and government expenditure was estimated at 1,248 million rials. The shah's deposit was the equivalent of $42 million at the then prevailing exchange rate, and it was equal to 55 percent of the entire non-oil government revenue for the year 1937–38. To obtain a current equivalent sum, the U.S. Consumer Price Index is used. The index stood at 14.1 in 1941 (1982 = 100) and 161.6 in 1998. Prices rose 11.5 times, giving $481 million.

4. Reza Farasati, "Some Documents on German Managers of the National Bank of Iran during 1932–33," *Tarikh-e Moaser-e Iran* (Contemporary history of Iran), 7th book (1995): 199–275. For a longer discussion of Reza Shah's annual income and its sources, see Mohammad Torkamam, "An Examination of Reza Shah's Liquid and Immovable Wealth," *Tarikh-e Moaser-e Iran*, 7th book (1995): 100–168.

5. See Donald L. Wilber, *Riza Shah Pahlavi: The Resurrection and Reconstruction of Iran, 1877–1944* (Hicksville, N.Y.: Exposition Press, 1975), 215–18. Wilber does not make it clear whether the sum of "at least £35,000" was the total amount transferred to the British bank in Bombay or the amount spent on shopping by the shah's children. Skrine had no way of knowing the total amount transferred to Bombay. However, he makes it clear that the shopping orders were placed through him and he handled the orders. Consequently, it can be safely concluded that the sum of $175,000 represented what the shah's children had spent on shopping in Bombay.

6. Ervand Abrahamian, *Iran Between Two Revolutions* (Princeton: Princeton University Press, 1982), 185.

7. Fakhreddin Azimi, *Iran: The Crisis of Democracy, 1941–53* (New York: St. Martin's Press, 1989), 92.

8. Mansur Gorgani, *The Problem of Land in Turkoman Sahra* (in Persian) (Tehran, 1979), 20–30. Gorgani also describes the 1932 confiscation of Turkoman Sahra by Reza Shah from a large group of small landowners and tribesmen. I have read that the many palaces, hunting lodges, and hotels Reza Shah built in northern Iran and treated as his private property were actually paid for by the Tehran municipality. Tehran mayor Forouzan is said to have paid 600 million rials. Numerous documents in Iran's National Archives show orders from Reza Shah's Special Bureau to various government ministries concerning the salary and benefits of some of the employees of the Office of Royal Estates. The employees were to be paid by the government and treated as "civil servants." It should also be mentioned in passing that the $500 million mentioned by Mossadeq would be equivalent to $6–7 billion at current prices.

9. Sattareh Farmanfarmaian, *Daughter of Persia: A Woman's Journey from Her Father's Harem through the Islamic Revolution* (New York: Crown, 1992), 47.

10. Lambton, *Landlord and Peasant in Persia: A Study of Land Tenure and Land Revenue Administration* (Oxford: Oxford University Press, 1953), 256–57.

11. A few examples follow. Page 6, entry 110: "Village of Joub-Yar, consisting of the following locations: Kolagar Mahaleh, Baghi, Kord Mahaleh, Baghban

Mahaleh, Astaneh Sar, Sadr Abad, Saraj Kolah, including the land on which peasant houses are located. Six dangs [six shares out of six shares] were purchased from small landowners [khorde-malekin], in the year 1934." Page 14, item 269: "Village of Kushk Kala, in addition to the village of Kia Kala, and the village of Sahra Dasht, 6 dangs, purchased from the Ministry of Finance, January 1936, 5.5 dangs, and 0.5 dang purchased from small landowners in February 1936." Page 16, item 301: "Villages of Ramenat and Soltan Mohammad Taher, 6 dangs, purchased from the heirs of Haj Hossein Khan Saidi, July 1936, and purchased from Kazem Kaboli as the administrator of the endowment [mutevalli], and Ali Akbar Baghchian as the representative of the Office of Endowments, 18 July 1937 (2 Jaribs of land). Page 213, item 57: "Village of Hasan Kief and village of Gorg Pas, and the following pastures: Daleh Goosh, Ja Khoy, Kaleh Kat, Shahre Nik, Jir Garan, Saf Kosh, Langeh Nan Darah, Goljaren, Mish Dar, Alashst, Lenari Sara (all of the above villages are part of and known as Hasan Kief), and three buildings." Page 217, item 137: "Village of Kelar Abad, in addition to a tea plantation, 6 dangs, purchased from Ali Asghar Khan Khalatbari, and his sisters." Page 639, item 9: "Village of Gajereh, including the coal mine."

12. Mohammad Reza Shah Pahlavi, *Mission for My Country* (London: Hutchinson, 1961), 201–2. The shah stated that the Crown lands "were acquired and developed by my father, and are now administered by my Pahlavi Foundation." Discussing the sale and distribution of the Pahlavi estates, the shah was adamant that "his" land should not be freely given away to peasants because "this would be psychologically the wrong approach." Later, the shah told Wilber that his father bought land in Mazandaran and Gilan in order to protect the country from communism. Wilber, *Riza Shah Pahlavi*, 245.

13. Amir Abdol Samad Khalatbari, *The Diaries of Mohammad Vali Khan Khalatbari, Sepahsalar Tonekaboni* (in Persian), ed. Mahmood Tafazoli (1949; Tehran: Novin, 1983).

14. Although he probably was the largest landowner in Iran, it is clear that the reports of his legendary wealth are vastly exaggerated. First, when he died, he was undoubtedly one of the largest debtors in Iran, owing vast sums to the Bank of Iran (former Russian Imperial Bank). Second, his obituaries alluded to financial difficulties. On 23 July 1926, *Shafaq-e Sorkh* had a long article entitled "Why Sepahsalar Committed Suicide." It said, "Despite all that property, Sepahsalar was always in financial difficulty. He was surrounded by many sycophants who always took from him, but never gave him support and comfort or peace of mind. For this reason, the premier landowner in Iran was continuously faced by money troubles."

15. Majd provides the following account of the intervention by Nosrat Dowleh. "One day, I was at the royal court [Darbar], and Prince Mohammad Vali Mirza, the brother of Nosrat Dowleh, the minister of finance, was there. He asked me what became of [Sepahsalar's] affair with the government. I replied that we had got nowhere. He suggested that we should appoint Sheik ol Molk Orang as our attorney with extensive powers, and he would reach a satisfactory solution. I tele-

phoned Sheik ol Molk, and he agreed to see Amir Entesar and me at 6 A.M. the next day. At that time, Sheik ol Molk resided at the house of the late Mokhber ad Dowleh located in the Mokhber ad Dowleh Intersection. Sheik ol Molk stated that his fee for settling the affair was 300,000 tomans. After much coming and going, the agreed sum was set at 90,000 tomans. It came to 9,000 tomans per share, and the share of Sepahsalar's widow, Soghra Khanum, was also to be 9,000 tomans. They were to sign promissory notes, and Sheik ol Molk was to be paid after the settlement with the government. Shortly after, Sheik ol Molk telephoned and a meeting was convened at the house of Sadar Eqtedar. Sheik ol Molk informed us that he had settled the matter with Nosrat Dowleh, the minister of finance. As repayment for the 650,000 toman debt to the Russian Bank, the village of Shal in Qazvin was to be transferred to the government. To settle the 400,000 toman tax debt to the government, the heirs were to undertake to pay 40,000 tomans per year for ten years. In return, the estates of Tonekabon, Kelarestaq, and Siarestaq were to be returned and registered to the heirs. We were all very happy with the proposed settlement. But Sardar Eqtedar asked to address the meeting. He said that although Sheik ol Molk's father, Molla Abdol Karim, was a friend of Sepahsalar, he would not accept the settlement. Sheik ol Molk asked why. Sardar Eqtedar said that he was not willing to transfer Shal to the government for 650,000 tomans. The Sheik asked how much he wanted. Sardar Eqtedar replied 250,000 tomans. At this time, Sheik ol Molk exploded with anger. He said that the buyer was proposing 650,000 tomans, and the seller should ask for 800,000 tomans and not 250,000! I asked Sardar Eqtedar why he did not want to transfer Shal to the government for 650,000 tomans. He said that in the previous division agreement among the heirs, Shal had been appraised at 250,000 tomans. If it were transferred for 650,000 tomans, then the agreement would be nullified. Unfortunately, some of the heirs were in contact with the government, and the police were being informed of the proceedings. Consequently, the late Nosrat Dowleh was dismissed from the post of minister and was arrested."

16. Majd then continues, "Concerning Moshar ol Molk's villainy and outright evil nature, I would like to recount this episode. One day, the late Amir Entesar and myself had gone to Moshar ol Molk's house. We informed him that the village of Tilbordeh Sar in Tonekabon was the private property of Amir Zadeh Khanum because it had been bestowed on her many years before by her late father, the Sepahsalar. In his peculiar accent, Moshar ol Molk asked us if we had documentary proof and an ownership deed. Amir Entesar replied in the affirmative. Moshar ol Molk told us to go right away and bring the papers so that he could inspect them. We went to Amir Zadeh Khanum and asked for the deed. She was extremely reluctant and asked us not to do it. But we took the deed and the papers to Moshar ol Molk. He took the material and put it in his pocket and would not return it to us. We learned subsequently that the next day he had ordered that Tilbordeh Sar also be included in the transferred property to Bank Iran."

17. Gorgani, *The Problem of Land in Turkoman Sahra,* 11–19.

18. Sattareh Farmanfarmaian, *Daughter of Persia,* 96.

19. Homa M. A. Katouzian, *The Political Economy of Modern Iran, 1926–1979* (New York: New York University Press, 1981), 109; Keddie, *Roots of Revolution: An Interpretive History of Modern Iran* (New Haven, Conn.: Yale University Press, 1981), 94.

20. Katouzian, *Political Economy of Modern Iran*, 110.

21. Lambton, *Landlord and Peasant*, 241.

22. Often regarded as the most capable and honest administrator under Reza Shah, for many years Ali Akbar Davar served as minister of interior, minister of justice, and minister of finance. His fate was no better than many others who had collaborated with Reza Shah. He committed suicide in February 1937. Wilber, *Riza Shah Pahlavi*, 177. Despite his reputation for honesty, as demonstrated here, Davar was also an instrument of Reza Shah's tyranny and corruption.

23. As reported by Majd, the exchange took place in the notary office of Najmabadi, and the proceedings were recorded on pages 195 and 196, item number 8978, and on page 164, item 7945, dated 26 July 1935.

24. Tahereh Adib-Saberi, "Village of Golsefid: A Study in Community Affairs" (in Persian), Division of Sociology, Publication 81, Tehran University, January 1978, p. 30.

Chapter 4. Background to Land Distribution

1. Mohammad Reza Shah Pahlavi, *Mission for My Country* (London: Hutchinson, 1961), 201.

2. Mansur Gorgani, *The Problem of Land in Turkoman Sahra* (in Persian) (Tehran, 1979), 30–40; Shoko Okazaki, *The Development of Large-Scale Farming in Iran: The Case of the Province of Gorgan* (Tokyo: Institute for Asian Studies, 1968), 14; Lambton, *Landlord and Peasant in Persia: A Study of Land Tenure and Land Revenue Administration* (Oxford: Oxford University Press, 1953), 257.

3. Ali Moarefi, "Distribution of Pahlavi Estates," Country Project no. 3, Food and Agriculture Organization of the United Nations, Center for Land Problems in the Near East (Salahuddin, Iraq, 1955), 1–4.

4. Bank Omran, *The Pahlavi Domain Land Distribution Program: Objectives, Accomplishments, Needs* (Tehran, n.d.), 8. The report stated that as of 1958, a total of 1,980 villages remained in the Pahlavi estates, and they were to be distributed during the next three to four years. Most significantly, the report also adds that as of 1958, the ownership of at least one-third of the Pahlavi estates was subject to litigation in the courts.

5. Amir Assadollah Alam, "The Land Tenure Situation in Iran," in *Land Tenure: Proceedings of the International Conference on Land Tenure and Related Problems in World Agriculture Held at Madison, Wisconsin, 1951*, ed. Kenneth H. Parsons, Raymond J. Penn, and Philip M. Raup (Madison: University of Wisconsin Press, 1956), 58.

6. That the peasants were very unhappy with the practice of dividing land into lots on the basis of the surveyors' drawings is also reported in Lambton, *Persian Land Reform, 1962–1966* (Oxford: Clarendon Press, 1969), 190–91.

7. Ibid., 191.

8. Rahman Qoli Khalatbari is a son of Amir Asad and a grandson of Moham-mad Vali Khan, Sepahsalar Azam and brother of Arsalan Khalatbari. Rahman Qoli had been elected a deputy from Mazandaran to the 14th Majlis. It is remarkable that such individuals, who under Reza Shah had been exiled from Mazandaran, were elected to the 14th Majlis barely two years after the downfall of Reza Shah.

Chapter 5. Founding of the Agricultural Union of Iran, 1959, Land Reform Law of May 1960, and Cabinet Decree of 9 January 1962 and 17 January 1963

1. In many instances, in addition to building a house for the cultivator, land-owners were also responsible for repairs and maintenance. These points indicate a general shortage of labor.

2. Concerning financial and other assistance by landowners to the cultivators, the following specifics are given in Safinejad. "Under the arbab-rayati bonehs, the landlords provided the necessary advances to the boneh members. Before land reform, monthly allowances provided to boneh members by landlords or their representatives varied between 20 to 40 mans [each man equals 3 kgs] of wheat and 20–40 tomans in cash. The advances were given during nine months of the year. . . . Wheat advances were deducted from the winter crops, and cash advances were deducted from the summer crops. Under the gavbandi bonehs, the gavbands supplied the advances." Javad Safinejad, *Boneh: Systems of Collective Production before Land Reform*, 2d ed. (in Persian) (Tehran: Toos, 1974), 138. Bonehs were culti-vation teams that were organized by landowners. For a detailed discussion and explanations of the two types of bonehs, see chapter 13. Miller discusses the same point: "Under the old landlord system, it was in the landlord's self-interest to keep his peasants prosperous. His share was dependent in large measure upon the pro-duction of his tenant. As a consequence, the landlord would lend money at no interest or low interest in times of crop failure, distress or illness. Now that the landlord is gone, this 'insurance' is gone; the government has not established credit cooperatives, so the money lenders are in a dominant position." William Greene Miller, "Hosseinabad: A Persian Village," *Middle East Journal* 18 (1964): 483–98, 495. It is interesting to point out that, although a fictitious name, based on the geographic and regional description given by Miller, "Hosseinabad" was lo-cated in the vicinity of Khoramdareh, Zanjan.

3. Lambton, *Persian Land Reform, 1962–1966* (Oxford: Clarendon Press, 1969), 58. As noted, the Majlis and the Senate approved the land reform law in May 1960, three months after Ayatollah Borujerdi's fatwa. Thus, Lambton's claim that the 1960 land reform law became a "dead letter" because of Ayatollah Borujerdi's fatwa is inaccurate. Given Lambton's fluency in spoken and written Persian, and given that she spent much time in Iran during this period, it is difficult to explain her "error." It is apparently an attempt to justify the refusal of the Amini govern-ment to implement the 1960 law and to provide justification for the 1962 cabinet decree that supposedly "amended" the 1960 law.

4. Willem M. Floor, "The Revolutionary Character of the Iranian Ulama: Wish-

ful Thinking or Reality?" *International Journal of Middle East Studies* 12 (1980): 501–24.

5. In January 1961, he went to London for the wedding of my sister Alieh Majd to Seyed Reza Alavi Shustari. In London, medical tests showed that Majd had a growth in his right lung. The tumor was removed and found to be benign, and Majd made a full recovery. He returned to Iran in April 1961.

6. Lambton, *Persian Land Reform*, 58.

7. Homa M. A. Katouzian, *The Political Economy of Modern Iran, 1926–1979* (New York: New York University Press, 1981), 215.

8. Lambton, *Persian Land Reform*, 51.

9. It has been claimed that Arsanjani was not Amini's first choice for minister of agriculture. His first choice was Arsalan Khalatbari. The shah vetoed Khalatbari's appointment, and Amini then selected Arsanjani. Needless to say, had Khalatbari been appointed in place of Arsanjani, the history of Iran might have been very different.

10. Lambton, *Persian Land Reform*, 63. Her description is the following: "Meanwhile, Dr. Arsanjani had been urging his cabinet colleagues to promulgate new legislation for land reform. Eventually, on 9 January 1962, Dr. Amini and a few of his ministers signed a bill amending the land reform law of 1960. . . . Technically, the bill was merely an emendation of the law of 17 May 1960, but in fact it was a new law."

It appears that Lambton, who had been invited to observe and record the land distribution program, was not quite at liberty to write freely. We learn from Alam's diaries that when Lambton's book was published in 1969, the minister of land reform at the time, Abdol Azim Valian, was so angry that he seriously suggested buying and destroying all the copies, and in 1972 he tried to "persuade her to change her account, leaving out the controversial passages." See Amir Assadollah Alam, *The Shah and I: The Confidential Diaries of Iran's Court*, ed. Alinaghi Alikhani (New York: St. Martin's Press, 1992), 107 and 241.

11. Mahmoud Abdel-Fadil, *Development, Income Distribution, and Social Change in Rural Egypt, 1952–1970: A Study in the Political Economy of Agrarian Transition* (Cambridge: Cambridge University Press, 1975), 1–15.

12. It should also be noted that as a protégé of Ahmad Qavam, Arsanjani was an opponent of Mohammad Mossadeq. Mossadeq was the one who was widely admired by Nasser and Egypt as a true patriot, and by implication, Arsanjani's boss, Qavam Saltaneh, was regarded as a traitor.

13. Lambton, *Persian Land Reform*, 122.

14. An example of this egregious inequity was the case of the villages of Ebrahim Abad and Majd Abad, District of Dasht-e Abi, Township of Qazvin, given in chapter 11. Another example was the villages of Jamjerd and Fatn Abad, District of Qaqazan, Township of Qazvin, also described in chapter 11.

15. The system was illustrated by the history of taxation of the village of Shal, District of Ramand, Township of Qazvin, given in chapter 11.

16. As discussed in chapter 3, as part of Reza Shah's land acquisition during the

1930s and as compensation to the expropriated landowners, government-owned villages had been "exchanged" in return for land acquired by Reza Shah. At the time of the exchange, the tax on these villages was negligible because the government had no interest in taxing itself. The case is illustrated by the history of taxation of the village of Khoznein, one of the villages included in the 1935 Zavar Exchange described in chapter 3. Located in the vicinity of Shal, Khoznein's access to the waters of Khar Rud River was limited, and thus its water supply was considerably less than Shal's. Much less valuable than Shal, its annual tax in 1935 was a mere 1,600 rials, and it had remained so until 1955 when its tax was revised and raised to 60,000 rials. Majd had protested this fortyfold rise in taxes, and they had been reduced to 20,000 rials because Khoznein did not have a working qanat. For greater detail, see chapter 11.

17. A numerical example is illustrative. Suppose that a village is valued at $15,000. The landowner receives $1,000 in cash, and fourteen bonds each with a face value of $1,000 and bearing an interest rate of 6 percent per year. Each year, one of these bonds matures, and the last bond is redeemed in the fifteenth year. To obtain the real price received for the village, the net present value of the stream of future payments is needed. Assuming a market interest rate of 24 percent, and given that the interest rate on the bonds is only 6 percent, the discount rate on the bonds is 18 percent. The present value of a stream of payments of $1,000 per year over fourteen years with a discount rate of 18 percent is $4,600. This is the market value of the bonds. With the $1,000 in cash payment, the total real compensation to the landowner amounted to $5,600, or 37 percent of the appraised price of $15,000.

18. See the case of Soltanabad, Khoramdareh, described in chapter 11. Lambton also reports in *Persian Land Reform* instances where an entire village with hundreds of hectares of cultivated land was "purchased" for 50,000 rials ($650) on the basis of the tax records, and the "price" was payable over fifteen years.

19. Ayatollah Seyed Hasan Emami (died 1979), the Imam Jomeh of Tehran, was a person whose opinions had once been respected by the American embassy. On 4 February 1955, just two months before General Zahedi was dismissed, a "source" speaking on behalf of the Imam Jomeh informed the army attaché, Colonel Bernard P. Major, of Emami's views. The contents of the conversation are given in a lengthy secret report (Foreign Service despatch 390, dated 21 February 1955).

> The Imam Jomeh insisted that he was not against the Shah nor the dynasty, but he did criticize the present Shah severely for wanting to rule as well as reign despite the fact that he is not temperamentally fitted for this role. . . .
> The least cooperative of all Iranians, and the one from whom all lack of cooperation stems, is the Shah. He calls himself the King of Kings, but he doesn't know how to cope with the responsibilities of the position or, for that matter, he doesn't even understand the significance of the position itself. Because of his youth, ignorance, and knowledge of the fact that he is Shah he thinks the way to run the country is by keeping people divided and at each other's throats. This of course preserves his position but at the same

time is detrimental to the welfare and prestige of the people and the country as well as his government. As a result, unfortunately, no Iranian has any real confidence in the Shah and professions of loyalty are only lip-service and not from the heart. This is true of even such people as Brig. Gen. Nematollah Nasiri, Commander of the Shah's own Imperial Guard. . . . He continues to accept advice from the greedy, lying and opportunistic advisors who surround him. He made Qavam Saltaneh and Razmara Prime Ministers without regard for anyone—especially the common people. He tries to act like his father at times but he is not a Reza Shah. If he were, he would not have fled the country and deserted his people in August, 1953. I have also told the Shah this. If it were not for a foreign power there would not have been a 19 August because the Communists were ready to take over when the Shah left. I have heard, for instance, that a large sum of money was given to a religious leader—Behbehani, I think—to buy the people to support the Shah. In speaking to Behbehani, I estimated the amount at 90 thousand but he said "zero it," that is, increase it.

In 1949, I advised the Shah not to take his trip to Europe and the U.S. and make a fool of himself as a playboy and a naive ruler making all kinds of promises in a political realm of which he knows nothing. I said that this would be detrimental to his prestige with the people and advised that he stay in Iran and learn his country and people. But, being young and inexperienced, he said, "Don't try to tell me what to do—I am the Shah!" and he went. The Shah expects me to advise him and I try to, but because he is the Shah he frequently will not accept constructive criticism or advice from anyone. . . . He thinks that since he is the Shah and claims to be benevolent he can get away with anything in the name of democracy. . . . The 19th of August 1953 was another chance for Iran and she must not throw it away, because as things are going, there is sure to be another 19th and if we are not careful the tables will be turned and it will spell our complete downfall.

20. As described in chapter 3, in 1941 when Reza Shah was coveting the Amini estates of Lashte Nesha and Hasan Kia in Gilan, Majd risked his career and more in trying to save the Aminis, and in the process, he incurred Reza Shah's wrath. Having witnessed the mayhem and calamity that were wrought on the Khalatbaris by Reza Shah, Majd had in effect saved the Aminis from a similar fate. Naturally, had Reza Shah remained in power, no one could have saved the Aminis. However, it turned out that Majd's intervention had been crucial. By delaying the process for six months, he enabled the Aminis to be saved by the Allied invasion. Twenty-one years later, this was his reward from Ali Amini.

Chapter 7. Selected Publications and Bulletins of the Agricultural Union of Iran and Organizations of Small Landowners

1. This was a reference to Arsanjani's frequent trips to Europe. See the content of Arsanjani's news conference given in chapter 9.

2. Further detail on this subject is provided in a pamphlet that was published in

1959 by an organization calling itself the Central Agricultural Council (Shoray-e Keshavarzi Markaz). This was an organization of landowners formed in 1941, probably after the departure of Reza Shah. In response to the rumors concerning threats and limitations to private landownership, it met on 20 October 1959 and approved the publication and distribution of an information pamphlet. Several of the arguments in Majd's position paper reflected the views of the National Agricultural Council. In addition, the pamphlet gives information on the land distribution episode in Sistan. Prior to land distribution in Sistan in 1933, the region had 70–80,000 kharvars (21,000 to 24,000 tons) of excess grain, which it exported to India. In 1938, there was famine in the region. A government commission was appointed to investigate. The commission reported that, following land distribution, the new owners had failed to reach agreement over the maintenance and clearing of the irrigation canals bringing water from the nearby Hirmand River. Agriculture had deteriorated, and many had abandoned their fields in search of employment elsewhere. The pamphlet points out that the episode was unrelated to the diversion of water from Afghanistan that took place many years later.

3. Manucher Parvin and M. Hic, "Land Reform versus Agricultural Reform: Turkish Miracle or Catastrophe Delayed?" *International Journal of Middle East Studies* 16 (1984): 207–32. See also Hans P. Binswanger and Miranda Elgin, "Reflections on Land Reform and Farm Size," in *Agricultural Development in the Third World*, ed. Carl Eicher and John Staatz (Baltimore: Johns Hopkins University Press, 1990), 342–54. Parvin and Hic argued that Turkey had substituted "agricultural reform" for land reform. Binswanger and Elgin have also stated that in situations where a land distribution may not be politically feasible, agricultural reform will serve as a substitute for land reform. That is, rural prosperity and welfare are raised without the need to redistribute landownership rights.

Chapter 8. Landowners' Appeal to the Ulama and the Response

1. Ervand Abrahamian, *Khomeinism: Essays on the Islamic Republic* (Berkeley: University of California Press, 1993), 5. According to Abrahamian, Ayatollah Khomeini's paternal grandfather, Seyed Ahmad (died 1868), bought land in Khomein in the 1830s and married the sister of a local notable. His father, Seyed Mostafa (died 1902), owned substantial land in Khomein, and his title was Fakhr ol Mojtahedin. He was also a prominent mojtahed.

2. S. Akhavi, *Religion and Politics in Contemporary Iran* (Albany: State University of New York Press, 1980), 96. Cited in Asghar Schirazi, *Islamic Development Policy: The Agrarian Question in Iran* (Boulder, Colo.: Lynne Rienner, 1993), 68.

3. For instance, Schirazi has declared that the majority of the ulama were not against land distribution. Those who were opposed "agreed not to mention land reform in their protests," and only two "naive" members of the ulama spoke against land distribution. In view of the evidence presented in this chapter, such statements made as late as 1993 are truly amazing. Despite Ayatollah Khomeini's fatwa and many statements denouncing land distribution, Lambton stated that Khomeini's outspoken attacks on the shah were "not, however, on grounds of land

reform." Citing the work of Algar, Walton declared that, contrary to the assertions of the ancien régime, Ayatollah Khomeini was not opposed to the shah's reform package, which included land reform and the enfranchisement of women. His opposition to the shah, it was claimed, was in defense of the Constitution and constitutional monarchy. Similarly, citing Katouzian and Hooglund, Farazmand stated that Ayatollah Khomeini was not opposed to land reform and "never spoke against land reform." Floor's excellent account and discussion of the events and personalities provides documentary evidence of the opposition by some important ulama such as the Ayatollah Borujerdi, Ayatollah Behbahani, and Ayatollah Khonsari. He also reports on Ayatollah Milani's opposition to land reform, because of the adverse effects of government policy on small landowners. But on the critical issue of Ayatollah Khomeini's stance, Floor was unable to provide documentary evidence or opinion. Floor also noted that in a 1979 biography of Khomeini, Hamid Rouhani stated that not only was Khomeini not opposed to land reform but that Rouhani "does not know of any religious leader who opposed land reform." Floor also notes that the Soviet writer Doroshenko stated that Khomeini was opposed to land reform. Faced with the conflicting evidence, Floor wisely noted that more research is needed. Surveying the evidence, Keddie concludes that while some ulama were opposed to land reform, the Ayatollah Khomeini "probably" was not opposed. Subsequently, Keddie stated that Khomeini "did criticize the faults in practice of land reform." In contrast, Abrahamian states that while Khomeini was opposed to land reform, as a shrewd politician he was careful not to leave any written record of his opposition. Bakhash also states that despite their opposition to land reform, the ulama refrained from issuing fatwas because land reform was popular with the peasants. Finally, in the massive collection of Imam Khomeini's writings and speeches, published between 1982 and 1991, there is no record of written or verbal opposition to land reform before 1963. This is in contrast to the declarations and interviews that the Imam gave during the 1970s. See Schirazi, *Islamic Development Policy*, 61–68; Lambton, *Persian Land Reform, 1962–1966* (Oxford: Clarendon Press, 1969), 112; Thomas Walton, "Economic Development and Revolutionary Upheavals in Iran," *Cambridge Journal of Economics* 4 (1980): 271–92; Ali Farazmand, *The State, Bureaucracy, and Revolution in Modern Iran: Agrarian Reform and Regime Politics* (New York: Praeger, 1989), 33; Willem M. Floor, "The Revolutionary Character of the Iranian Ulama: Wishful Thinking or Reality?" *International Journal of Middle East Studies* 12 (1980): 501–24; Keddie, *Roots of Revolution: An Interpretive History of Modern Iran* (New Haven, Conn.: Yale University Press, 1981), 157–58; Ervand Abrahamian, *Iran between Two Revolutions* (New York: Columbia University Press, 1982); Shaul Bakhash, *Reign of the Ayatollahs* (New York: Basic Books, 1984), 28–29; *The Source of Light: Speeches and Writings of Imam Khomeini*, 23 vols. (in Persian) (Tehran, 1982–91).

4. It appears that the shah had a history of "temper tantrums" and trying to emulate his father's behavior. In a confidential report (Foreign Service despatch 4, dated 7 August 1955), entitled "Temper Tantrum of His Majesty the Shah of Iran,"

the U.S. consul in Khoramshahr, Ronald H. Bushner, reported the following incident:

> Reliable foreign sources, including one of the highest officials of the Iranian Oil Refining Company, have told officers of the Consulate the following story. On March 28, 1955, His Majesty Shah Mohammad Reza Pahlavi, during a visit to Khoramshahr and Abadan, made a tour of the Abadan Refinery. His chief guide was Dr. Reza Falah, Director, Production, National Iranian Oil Company, who is the Iranian having the most influence with the NIOC concerning the Refinery. (During the NIOC operation of the Refinery, Dr. Falah was Refinery General Manager; a part of his influence stems from the widespread belief that he is "close to the Shah" whom he sees fairly frequently.) During Dr. Falah's presentation at the Refinery's Training Institute he used a number of foreign technical terms which His Majesty reportedly failed to understand. Apparently angered by this, the latter kicked Falah and hurled him against the wall, shouting that he should learn to use his own language. According to one report, the Shah kicked Falah after the latter had fallen to the ground. . . . Falah was reportedly hustled to jail, where he allegedly remained for two days while the Iranian Oil Refining Company interceded to arrange his release. . . . [This incident] is also of interest in assessing the character of His Majesty the Shah. In view of the healthy respect Iranians have for power, it is unlikely that they were as shocked to see their sovereign abusing one of his subjects (who could neither resist nor retaliate) as foreigners were.

5. Ervand Abrahamian, *Khomeinism: Essays on the Islamic Republic* (Berkeley: University of California Press, 1993), 9.

6. Schirazi, *Islamic Development Policy*, 61–62. Schirazi noted that in early 1962, Ayatollah Khomeini denounced land distribution as a measure intended to open up Iran's markets to American goods and to place Iran's economy under the control of the United States and Israel. Seventeen years later, in his speech at Behesht Zahra Cemetery in Tehran, on Thursday, 1 February 1979, his first upon his return from exile, Ayatollah Khomeini denounced the shah's land reform as a plot by America to destroy Iran's agriculture and economic independence and to enable America to plunder Iran's wealth.

7. It appears likely that the two "naive and misguided" unnamed ayatollahs cited in Schirazi were Khoii and Shirazi. What is most curious is the fact that the source of much of the material on the ulama given in Schirazi is Abol Hasan Bani Sadr, the son of Ayatollah Nasrollah Bani Sadr. As described in this book, Ayatollah Bani Sadr, a major landowner in Hamedan, was a crucial liaison between landowners and the senior ulama from the very beginning of the resistance. He had close ties with Ayatollahs Borujerdi, Khomeini, and Hakim. Either Abol Hasan Bani Sadr was totally ignorant of his father's activities, which is hard to believe, or he was deliberately providing false information to Schirazi and others.

8. Schirazi has stated that Ayatollah Shariatmadari made two statements in the

386 / Notes to Pages 210–46

religious journal *Maktabe Islam* in 1963 and 1964, declaring that the ulama were not against (land) reform. Schirazi, *Islamic Development Policy*, 55. In view of Shariat-madari's 1962 fatwa and the claims about subsequent statements by Shariat-madari, the matter requires additional research and clarification.

9. The one exception was Mossadeq's 1953 referendum in which Mossadeq sought the authority to dissolve the Majlis, which was no longer submissive to his policies. The issue is discussed in greater detail in chapter 10.

10. Lambton, *Persian Land Reform*, 112.

Chapter 9. America's Role As Seen by the Opposition

1. Ahmad Ashraf, "The Appeal of Conspiracy Theories to Persians," *Princeton Papers: Interdisciplinary Journal of Middle Eastern Studies* 5 (fall 1996): 57–87, 57.

2. Nikki R. Keddie, "The Iranian Village before and after Land Reform," *Journal of Contemporary History* 3 (1968): 69–91, 83.

3. Mahmoud Abdel-Fadil, *Development, Income Distribution, and Social Change in Rural Egypt, 1952–1970: A Study in the Political Economy of Agrarian Transition* (Cambridge: Cambridge University Press, 1975), 1–10.

4. Shoko Okazaki, *The Development of Large-Scale Farming in Iran: The Case of the Province of Gorgan* (Tokyo: Institute for Asian Studies, 1968), 15.

Chapter 10. Suppressing the Opposition and Silencing of the Agricultural Union of Iran

1. See Gasiorowski, *U.S. Foreign Policy and the Shah: Building a Client State in Iran* (Ithaca: Cornell University Press, 1991), 183–87. For an account of the events of 21 July 1952, see Fakhreddin Azimi, *Iran: The Crisis of Democracy, 1941–1953* (New York: St. Martin's Press, 1989), 288–92. On 19 July, the shah dismissed Mossadeq and appointed Ahmad Qavam to be prime minister. Qavam's minister for parliamentary affairs was Hasan Arsanjani. On 21 July 1952, massive anti-Qavam and pro-Mossadeq demonstrations broke out in Tehran. At first, the demonstrators were attacked by the army and police. But soon the shah lost his nerve, the army was withdrawn, and the streets were taken over by the protesters. Qavam was forced to resign. Arsanjani was warning the opposition that this time matters would be different and that the army would not be withdrawn.

2. Amir Assadollah Alam, *Diaries of Alam* (in Persian), vol. 1 (London: New World, 1992), 162, 337.

3. The execution of tribal leaders is mentioned in Ann Lambton, *Persian Land Reform*, 113. In 1996, I met a son of an executed tribal leader. I was researching land acquisition by Reza Shah at the Institute for Contemporary Historical Studies in Tehran. During a meeting with Abdollah Shahbazi, the institute's director, he said he was a member of the Qashqaii tribe. Their land was confiscated under land distribution and his father took part in an uprising against the shah in the spring of 1963. His father was executed in 1963, and his survivors were driven from their ancestral homes. The plight of the tribes is also discussed in the memoirs of Manucher Farmanfarmaian. He writes that in 1964 a young man dressed in black

came to see him and asked for his assistance. His name was Hayat Davoudi, and he was a member of the Hayat Davoudi tribe, which had been allied with the Qashqaiis in their 1963 uprising. Subsequently, the young man's father and all his uncles were executed and the survivors were driven from their homes. That young man's words are reproduced in the memoirs of Farmanfarmaian. "My wife and children are hungry and living in the streets. We have become like lepers in this town. What am I to tell them? That no one wants to help me because of my name? Why don't they just get rid of us, rather than leaving me to beg—and at last to die?" Manucher Farmanfarmaian and Roxanne Farmanfarmaian, *Blood and Oil: Memoirs of a Persian Prince* (New York: Random House, 1997), 374–78.

4. The detained leaders of the Agricultural Union of Iran were fortunate in that the chief of Savak was General Hasan Pakravan, whose father, Fatollah Pakravan, had been a friend of one of the detainees, Amir-Teimur-Kalali, a landowner in Khorasan. Otherwise, it is doubtful that the four would have been released so quickly.

5. Roger M. Savory, "Social Development in Iran during the Pahlavi Era," in *Iran under the Pahlavis*, ed. George Lenczowski (Stanford, Calif.: Hoover Institution Press, 1978), 85–127, 105.

6. Ibid., 104; George Lenczowski, "Political Process and Institutions in Iran: The Second Pahlavi Kingship," in *Iran under the Pahlavis*, ed. George Lenczowski (Stanford, Calif.: Hoover Institution Press, 1978), 461.

7. Mohammad Reza Shah Pahlavi, *Mission for My Country* (London: Hutchinson, 1961), 96.

8. Manucher Parvin and M. Hic, "Land Reform versus Agricultural Reform: Turkish Miracle or Catastrophe Delayed?" *International Journal of Middle East Studies* 16 (1984): 207–32.

9. Bent Hansen, *The Political Economy of Poverty, Equity, and Growth: Egypt and Turkey* (Oxford: Oxford University Press, 1991), 341.

Chapter 11. Theory and Practice of Land Reform: Case Studies

1. Efraim Orni, *Agrarian Reform and Social Progress in Israel* (Jerusalem: Jewish National Fund, 1972); Yakir Plessner, *The Political Economy of Israel: From Ideology to Stagnation* (Albany: State University of New York Press, 1994); Ann K. S. Lambton, *Persian Land Reform, 1962–1966* (Oxford: Clarendon Press, 1969), 122.

2. Alain de Janvry, "The Role of Land Reform in Economic Development: Policies and Politics," *American Journal of Agricultural Economics* 63 (1981): 384–92; R. Albert Berry and William R. Cline, *Agrarian Structure and Productivity in Developing Countries* (Baltimore: Johns Hopkins University Press, 1979); Hans P. Binswanger and Miranda Elgin, "Reflections on Land Reform and Farm Size," in *Agricultural Development in the Third World*, ed. Carl Eicher and John Staatz (Baltimore: Johns Hopkins University Press, 1990), 342–54.

3. For a summary of the debate on the relative efficiency of sharecropping, see Mohammad Javad Amid, *Agriculture, Poverty, and Reform in Iran* (London: Routledge, 1990), 8–27.

4. Berry and Cline, *Agrarian Structure,* 26–27.

5. Information on agricultural rents in Mazandaran is contained in a letter dated 30 May 1961 from Arsalan Khalatbari, a respected attorney and a landowner in Mazandaran, to Ali Amini, prime minister, with copies sent to Arsanjani, minister of agriculture, Alamuti, minister of justice, and to the Central Agricultural Council. The letter is reproduced in Majd's memoirs. Khalatbari gives the following figures. In the districts of Babol, Babolsar, Amol, Shahi, and Sari in eastern Mazandaran, the landowner's share of the rice crop varied between one-sixth and one-fifth of the output. Rent per hectare of cotton cultivation was 80 kilograms, or about one-twentieth of output. However, in Babol district no rent was levied on cotton, cannabis, and seifi (summer cash crops). An example cited by Khalatbari was the village of Dahfari, whose owner was Asghar Akhavan. In the Tonekabon region of western Mazandaran, rent per jarib (1,000 square meters) of rice was fixed at 2.5 peymaneh per jarib, or 300 kilograms per hectare. This was between one-twelfth and one-tenth of the output. The low rents indicate a low marginal product of land and a high marginal product of labor.

6. Two such letters are quoted herein. The first is a translation of a letter dated 27 February 1969 from Abbas Mahdavi, a resident of Khoznein, to Mohammad Ali Majd. "His excellency Mr. Majd, With the utmost respect I submit. Since many people were in difficulty due to lack of a water storage, I undertook to construct a water storage and a mosque. However, the completion of the two is dependent on help from you. I am sure you will not deprive me of your great kindness. Please allow us to use the bricks from the arbabi building in the construction of the mosque and a water storage. In addition, I also bought the necessary land from a cultivator. Consequently, your permission and approval is needed so that these actions are not undertaken on usurped land. I trust that you will accept your servant's twin requests, and the buildings can be completed in your illustrious name. I have no other requests. Abbas Mahdavi." It should be added that Majd's house in Khoznein, known as the arbabi building, had been destroyed in the earthquake of 1962 and was never rebuilt. The bricks were from the rubble of the building. The second sample letter given, dated 17 March 1973, is from Abdollah Mohammadi, who is writing on behalf of the residents of Khoznein. "His Excellency Mr. Majd Fatn ol Saltaneh, Respectfully, we your humble servants from the village of Khoznein who have witnessed your generosity in the past, we hope and beg you that to satisfy the Almighty God you will forgive us. Each and every one of us humbly beseech you for your forgiveness. Your devotee, Abdollah Mohammadi."

7. During the summer of 1955, I accompanied my father on a visit to the village of Shal. A large party of men riding horses and armed with rifles and rows of ammunition greeted us several kilometers from Shal and escorted our vehicle to the village. To a nine-year-old boy, this was very impressive. To this day, I still vividly remember my father, my cousin, Jahangir Massoudi Tonekaboni, and I in the back seat, and in the front seat, Abol Qasem Jokar and the driver, Abbas Goudarzi, being followed by a small army of armed riders.

8. Majd recounts in his memoirs that during the election to the 17th Majlis in the winter of 1951, he ended up in Abegarm, near Hamedan, on voting day. Unbeknown to Majd, a group of 250 armed men from Shal had walked seventy kilometers in a snowstorm to protect him because he was running as an opponent of the Mossadeq government. Majd reports that the Shalis took control of the election booths to ensure that voters would only vote for Majd. Highly embarrassed, he felt compelled to stop the practice and send the Shalis home. He easily won the rural vote. Majd states that the government of Mossadeq then resorted to election fraud and placed 12,000 votes in favor of its own candidates. Upon hearing of the vote fraud, as protest, a large group of Shalis descended on Qazvin and threatened to riot. Qazvin's governor came to appeal to Majd at 9 P.M. and begged him to ask the Shalis to disperse and leave Qazvin. Majd took to the streets and asked his supporters to desist from violence. In 1965, many years after he had been driven from office and his property had been confiscated, Majd visited the Qazvin office of the Agricultural Bank. In the courtyard, he encountered some Shalis, who bowed to him. Upon leaving the bank, Majd was met by a large group of Shalis who gave him a standing ovation. Visibly moved, he thanked them for their longtime loyalty.

9. For the record, the villages of Asbe Mord and Yarud in Alamut District of Qazvin were part of the Zavar Exchange in 1935, in which part ownership of the two villages was transferred to Amir Entesar. After he died, they became the property of his daughter and my mother, Shamsol Moluk Khalatbari Tonekaboni, Amir Banou Majd. She retained her partial ownership in these two villages as her "chosen" village; consequently, the villages were not included under Phase One. In 1965 under Phase Two, the two villages were leased out to the cultivators for thirty years. Under Phase Three, the ownership was transferred to the cultivators. However, as the documents show, the formal transfers took place in 1973. This is noteworthy because long after the shah had declared the completion of land distribution in May 1971, the land transfers had continued.

10. Around 1930, Soghra Khanum and her brothers temporarily assigned part of their ownerships in Nashta to a group of Taleqani merchants. The male descendants of Hedayatollah Khan later made a "conditional transfer" to several other individuals. In 1932, these persons with temporary or conditional rights "sold" their rights to Reza Shah. After Reza Shah's downfall, they too laid claim to Nashta. Their claim was dismissed by the court in 1945, but the court ruling provides a great deal of information on the manner in which Nashta had been acquired by Reza Shah.

11. Examining her bank statements for the period 21 August 1953 to 17 March 1954, the initial balance was 24,500 rials, and there was one deposit of 3,000 rials, giving a total of 27,500 rials. This was the equivalent of $860 at the official exchange rate, or $400 at the market exchange rate. Total withdrawals were 21,500 rials, and the balance was a mere 6,000 rials, or $85. This is particularly significant because it occurred only four days from the Persian New Year, Nowruz, a time of heavy expenses, and she had purchased a new outfit. Another indication of her finances

is provided by a bank statement covering the period 11 April to 5 September 1957. The initial balance was 17,000 rials. There had been four deposits totaling 13,020 rials, giving a total of 30,020 rials ($430). Total withdrawals amounted to 23,500 rials ($335), leaving a balance of $95.

12. On 6 January 1967, she paid 30,000 rials to her attorney, Kazem Farhangi. Two weeks later, on 20 January 1967, she paid 47,415 rials ($680) to the Bureau of Registration (receipt number 304366) and 13,080 rials to her attorney. On the same day, she petitioned the Registration Bureau for permission to pay the remaining expenses in installments. She had no income at this time, and she had borrowed money to pay these fees. Moreover, as was often the case, any attempt to register a property brought numerous legal objections by individuals who were professional objectors (blackmailers). They would withdraw their challenge only after the payment of a sum of money. Otherwise, the process could take many years and be tied up in the legal system. In the papers of Soghra Khanum there are many court summons, ordering her to appear in person in court and answer to the objections raised to her ownership claims. She could ill afford this added expenditure.

13. The notice concluded with the following statement: "In addition, you are hereby informed of part 2 of decree number 36104, dated 5 March 1962, which states: 'The Ministry of Agriculture is required to transfer the excess property to the government after announcing the price, as specified by law, and after the lapse of the objection period, and to inform the Highest Commission of the landowner's objection. In the event of an objection by the landowner or the Land Reform Organization to the proposed price, and after the ruling of the Highest Commission, any price difference will be calculated and paid in installments according to Article 14 of the law. In any case, the drawing up of the transfer deed will not result in the termination of the owner's rights in this regard. In cases where the declaration form [ezhar nameh] is drawn up by the Ministry of Agriculture, the landowner has ten days to select the property to be retained in accordance with Article 13 and in compliance with Articles 2 and 3 of the Amendment Law to the Land Reform Law and the relevant addendum. In the event that the landowner fails to make a selection, the decision of the Ministry of Agriculture is final, and the excess property will be transferred to the government in the manner described above."

14. The information is given in a letter from the Ministry of Finance dated 8 April 1969. The letter warned her that unless a tax payment of 15,960 rials plus 10 percent penalty was made within thirty days, the government would move to seize her belongings.

15. In a letter from Mohassess, head of the Land Reform Organization in Shahsavar, to the gendarmerie station in Abbas Abad, dated 3 March 1968, number 1349, Mohassess wrote, "Mrs. Soghra Massoudi Tonekaboni, one of the small landowners of the group of villages of Nashta has contacted this office and has declared that none of the cultivators of the villages of Pasandeh Olia and Pasandeh Sofla have paid their rents. Considering that Mrs. Soghra Massoudi was subject to Phase Two, and has declared her ownership in these two villages as part of the sale of land in excess of thirty hectares, she is entitled to receive the annual rent for the

year 1966." The letter goes on to state that her rent from the village of Pasandeh Sofla was 13,874 rials ($197), and the rent from Pasandeh Olia was 18,610 rials ($265). The gendarmerie was instructed to collect the rent, render it to Mrs. Massoudi, and inform the office of the outcome. It is also clear that the gendarmerie did not collect all of the rent from these two villages. The story is repeated the following year. In a letter dated 10 February 1969, number 5559, the same Mohassess wrote to the gendarmerie station in Nashta Rud (with a copy to the Abbas Abad station), instructing the gendarmerie to collect Mrs. Massoudi's rent for the years 1966 and 1967. The sad saga continued. In a letter from Qoreishi Zadeh, the new head of the Shahsavar Land Reform Organization, to the gendarmerie station in Nashta Rud, dated 29 January 1971, number 5893, the gendarmerie was instructed to collect Mrs. Soghra Massoudi's rent from the villages of Hangu, Rudgar Mahaleh, Marzeh, and Faqieh Abad. That the gendarmerie had not collected the rent is clear. In a letter dated 17 April 1971, Soghra Khanum wrote to the Land Reform Organization complaining that her rent had not been collected because the headman [deh-ban] in each village had refused to supply a list of the tenants in the village. She asked that the headmen be ordered to supply the list of cultivators to the gendarmes.

Chapter 12. Structure of Landownership on the Eve of Land Distribution

1. Ann K. S. Lambton, *Persian Land Reform, 1962–1966* (Oxford: Clarendon Press, 1969); Cyrus Salmanzadeh and Gwyn E. Jones, "An Approach to the Micro Analysis of the Land Reform Program in Southwestern Iran," *Land Economics* 55 (1979): 108–27; Mohammad Gholi Majd, "Land Reform Policies in Iran," *American Journal of Agricultural Economics* 69 (1987): 843–48; Mohammad Gholi Majd and Vahid F. Nowshirvani, "Land Reform in Iran Revisited: New Evidence on the Results of Land Reform in Nine Provinces," *Journal of Peasant Studies* 20 (1993): 442–58. For an alternative interpretation, see Eric J. Hooglund, *Land Reform and Revolution in Iran* (Austin: University of Texas Press, 1982); Afsaneh Najmabadi, *Land Reform and Social Change in Iran* (Salt Lake City: University of Utah Press, 1987); Mohammad Javad Amid, *Agriculture, Poverty, and Reform in Iran* (London: Routledge, 1990).

2. Hans P. Binswanger and Miranda Elgin, "Reflections on Land Reform and Farm Size," in *Agricultural Development in the Third World*, ed. Carl Eicher and John Staatz (Baltimore: Johns Hopkins University Press, 1990), 342–54.

3. Iran, General Department of Public Statistics, *First National Census of Agriculture, October 1960* (in Persian), 15 vols. (Tehran: Ministry of the Interior, n.d.). Volumes 1–14 give the regional findings. Volume 15 summarizes the results.

4. Gabriel Baer, *A History of Land Ownership in Modern Egypt, 1800–1950* (Oxford: Oxford University Press, 1962).

5. Iran, Statistical Center of Iran, *Yearbook of Statistics, 1974* (in Persian) (Tehran: Plan and Budget Organization, 1975), 298.

6. Esmail Ajami, "Land Reform and the Modernization of the Farming Structure in Iran," *Oxford Agrarian Studies* 2 (1973): 120–31.

7. Salmanzadeh and Jones, "An Approach to the Micro Analysis of Land Reform"; Majd, "Land Reform Policies in Iran"; Iran, Statistical Center of Iran, *Yearbook of Statistics, 1976* (in Persian) (Tehran: Plan and Budget Organization, 1977), 252/47.

8. Majd and Nowshirvani, "Land Reform in Iran Revisited," 442–58.

9. See Lambton, *Persian Land Reform*, 198–200.

10. Majd, "Land Reform Policies in Iran," 846.

11. Hasan Ali Hekmat, "The Bill on the Fourth Phase of Land Reform Still Defective," *Khandaniha*, 30 November to 3 December 1968, 12. Translations on the Near East, no. 342, pp. 4–9, JPRS, 7:10, 1968–69, reel 107.

12. Iran, Statistical Center of Iran, *Yearbook of Statistics, 1973* (in Persian) (Tehran: Plan and Budget Organization, 1974), 298.

13. Hekmat, "The Bill on the Fourth Phase of Land Reform Still Defective," 13.

14. Lambton, *Landlord and Peasant in Persia: A Study of Land Tenure and Land Revenue Administration* (Oxford: Oxford University Press, 1953), 266–67.

15. Radio interviews from 20 and 21 September 1961 given by Hasan Arsanjani, minister of agriculture, and cited in "An Open Letter to the Prime Minister and the Council of Ministers," printed in the national daily *Etela-at* on 1 October 1961, and given in chapter 7 above.

16. Lambton, *Landlord and Peasant*, 264.

17. Salmanzadeh and Jones, "An Approach to the Micro Analysis of the Land Reform Program," 113.

18. Ibid., 115.

19. Ibid., 123.

20. Located east of the township of Tonekabon, province of Mazandaran, Nashta was the property of a landowner who had died circa 1925. He had three wives and was survived by six sons and eight daughters. Nashta was inherited by his children. In accordance with the Islamic practice, each son's inheritance was one-tenth of Nashta, and each daughter's inheritance was one-twentieth of Nashta. In 1932, Nashta was acquired by Reza Shah and was restored to its previous owners in 1944. By the advent of the 1962 land distribution, several of the owners had died and their property had been distributed among their survivors. Some had left numerous heirs. Consequently, the land belonging to one man in 1920 was shared by some sixty descendants forty years later.

Court records indicate that by 1945 two of the eight sisters had died, and their ownerships were thus divided among their descendants. By the advent of the land distribution decree in 1962, two of the brothers and two other sisters were deceased and their ownerships had been distributed among their descendants. Some had left numerous heirs. For instance, the oldest brother, Karim, had been survived by five sons and three daughters. All had shared in the ownership of Nashta. Another brother, Parviz, had died, survived by a son and three daughters, two of whom were minors. In contrast, a sister, Om-mol Khaqan, had been childless, and on her passing (ca. 1955), her share of Nashta had been divided among her surviving siblings. For a description of landownership in Golsefid, see Adib-Saberi, "Village of Golsefid: A Study in Community Affairs," 30.

21. Mahmoud Abdel-Fadil, *Development, Income Distribution, and Social Change in Rural Egypt, 1952–1970: A Study in the Political Economy of Agrarian Transition* (Cambridge: Cambridge University Press, 1975), 14–15.

22. Lambton, *Landlord and Peasant*, 278.

23. Two excellent examples where large, medium, and small ownerships existed in the same village and were thus partially included in Phase One are the villages of Shal in Qazvin and Khoramdareh in Zanjan. In each case 3.5-dang was owned by one individual who also owned other villages, and the remaining 2.5-dang was owned by a large number of khorde-malekin as well as peasant cultivators. In the case of Khoramdareh, the small landowners had emerged during the 1950s when the owner had sold land to the inhabitants of the village. These two cases are discussed in detail in chapter 11.

24. The average ownership is a little over one-dang. This allows us to conclude that the number of ownerships in the multiple ownership category was less than six. If it had been above six, then the owners would have been included in Phase One, which we know is not the case. Assuming an average of five villages per owner results in 8,596 (42,978/5) owners with multiple ownerships. Added to 35,425 owners with single ownerships results in 44,021 owners (table 12.5). Again, it should be noted that this is a conservative estimate.

25. Large landowners in Egypt (those with 200 feddans or more) also owned 20 percent of the agricultural land. Abdel-Fadil, *Development*, 15–20.

26. Lars Wahlin, "Inheritance of Land in the Jordanian Hill Country," *British Journal of Middle Eastern Studies* 21 (1994): 57–84, 70.

27. Lambton, *Landlord and Peasant*, 281–82.

28. Ibid., 282.

29. Lambton, *Persian Land Reform*, 100–101.

30. Amir Assadollah Alam, *Diaries of Alam* (in Persian), vol. 2 (London: Swann Overseas, 1993), 131, 135.

31. Mohammad Reza Shah Pahlavi, *Mission for My Country* (London: Hutchinson, 1961), 200–201.

32. Hekmat, "The Bill on the Fourth Phase of Land Reform Still Defective," 13.

Chapter 13. Toward a Theory of Landownership in Islamic Iran

1. Iran, Statistical Center of Iran, *Yearbook of Statistics, 1981* (in Persian) (Tehran: Plan and Budget Organization, 1982), 341.

2. However, because of adequate precipitation and rivers, in certain regions of Iran such as Gilan and Mazandaran, there were no qanats. Some villages such as Khoznein did not have a qanat because attempts to establish one had been unsuccessful. In this case, the village relied on the nearby river for its irrigation. Other villages often had more than one qanat.

3. Iran, Statistical Center of Iran, *Yearbook of Statistics, 1995* (in Persian) (Tehran: Plan and Budget Organization, 1996), 205.

4. Javad Safinejad, *Boneh: Systems of Collective Production before Land Reform*, 2d ed. (in Persian) (Tehran: Toos, 1974). The amount of land cultivated by each boneh was measured in terms of "pairs of oxen," that is, the amount of land that could be cultivated by one pair in one year. For example, it was said that each boneh cultivated three pairs. It meant each team cultivated an amount of land that was cultivated by three pairs of oxen. In dry years, qanat flow declined and cultivation by each team could decrease to two or two and a half pairs. The number of teams per qanat depended on its madar (orbit). The madar itself depended on climatic and soil conditions. Frequently, it ranged from six to twelve days. A madar of ten meant that each team received one day of the outflow from the qanat every ten days. In this case, the qanat could support ten cultivation teams. But since in practice two or three days of water were allocated to orchards and alfalfa fields, the number of teams would be seven or eight, and the number of cultivators between forty-two and forty-eight, assuming that each team had six members. The head of each team was called "sarboneh," a title that commanded considerable social respect in the village.

5. Safinejad, *Boneh*, 95, 132.

6. Majd, "Land Reform and Agricultural Policy in Iran, 1962–78," Cornell International Agricultural Economics Study, A.E. Res. 83–17 (Ithaca, N.Y.: Cornell University, April 1983), 28–32.

7. The issue was analyzed within the framework of the "Dutch Disease." According to this theory, increased oil prices lead to relative price changes in the economies of oil exporters. With plentiful oil income and dollars, the relative price of goods subject to international trade, such as agricultural products, decreases, and the relative price of goods not subject to international trade, such as land and labor services, increases. The agricultural sector becomes less profitable and thus shrinks in relative size. At the same time, with rising real per capita income associated with the oil boom, demand for food increases. The two effects combine to raise imports. It was believed that this theory "explained" the sharp increase in agricultural imports. However, despite the collapse of the oil prices, and thus the disappearance of Dutch Disease, agricultural imports have continued a relentless increase, an indication that Dutch Disease was not the main cause of rising imports. In addition, it was difficult to blame land distribution for the poor performance of agriculture because all the existing theory on the subject indicated the opposite. The theory had predicted greater efficiency and output following a land distribution and "modernization" of the farm structure. At the time, it was not understood that conditions in Iran were very different from the assumptions about the theory of land reform.

8. Iran, *Yearbook of Statistics, 1995*, 294.

9. Mohammad Gholi Majd and Vahid F. Nowshirvani, "Land Reform in Iran Revisited: New Evidence on the Results of Land Reform in Nine Provinces," *Journal of Peasant Studies* 20 (1993): 442–58.

10. Iran, Statistical Center of Iran, *Yearbook of Statistics, 1976* (in Persian) (Tehran: Plan and Budget Organization, 1977), 252/47.

11. Cyrus Salmanzadeh and Gwyn E. Jones, "An Approach to the Micro Analysis of the Land Reform Program in Southwestern Iran," *Land Economics* 55 (1979): 108–27

12. The law for the establishment of farm corporations was passed in 1968. Some have called it the fourth phase of land reform. The avowed aim of the measure was to promote farm mechanization and "consolidation" and to help the peasant population to achieve greater income. In practice, several (often between ten and fifteen) adjoining villages in a region were formed into a "farm corporation" by which the peasant cultivators exchanged their ownership of land for shares in the corporation. They became shareholders and wage laborers. The government took over the management of the farm corporation, appointed the overseers, and provided the machinery and other inputs. Despite its name, the "farm corporation" resembled the collective farms in the Soviet Union. By the advent of the revolution, there were ninety-four farm corporations on land that had been part of nine hundred villages, affecting some 40,000 rural households. Although the farm corporations only covered 2–3 percent of agricultural land, the land was among the most fertile. According to Katouzian, state subsidies per cultivator on farm corporations were eighteen times more than subsidies to regular cultivators. Similar to farm collectives in the Soviet Union, the corporations were inefficient and were dissolved shortly after the revolution. The land was returned to the cultivators. See Homa M. A. Katouzian, *The Political Economy of Modern Iran, 1926–1979* (New York: New York University Press, 1981), 309–11.

13. George Lenczowski, "Political Process and Institutions in Iran: The Second Pahlavi Kingship," in *Iran under the Pahlavis*, ed. George Lenczowski (Stanford, Calif.: Hoover Institution Press, 1978), 455, 461.

14. The text of the edict is given in an undated pamphlet published by the Ministry of Agriculture, Land Reform Organization, and entitled "Complete Text of the Additional Articles to the Land Reform Law, and Land Reform Regulations Approved by the Joint Commission of the Two Houses of Parliament." Although the pamphlet is undated, from the various dates given in it, one may conclude that it was published during the last quarter of 1964. The shah's edict is dated 4 June 1964. In it, the shah had based his action on Supplementary Article 27 of the Constitution. The letter from the prime minister to the minister of agriculture giving authorization for implementing the law is dated 2 August 1964. The pamphlet carefully records the chain of command and instructions received by the Ministry of Agriculture. It was as though the Ministry were trying to absolve itself of any responsibility.

15. Amir Assadollah Alam, *Diaries of Alam* (in Persian), vol. 2 (London: Swann Overseas, 1993), 131.

16. Asghar Schirazi, *Islamic Development Policy: The Agrarian Question in Iran* (Boulder, Colo.: Lynne Rienner, 1993), 161–62, 169–95.

GLOSSARY

The following terms and their meanings are used within a context of agricultural institutions, practices, and land distribution regulations.

abi: Irrigated crop.

alem: A learned person having knowledge of religious laws; member of the clergy.

amlak: Plural of *melk;* estates or properties.

amlak-e dangi-e parakandeh: Scattered partial ownership.

amlak-e khaliseh: Estates belonging to the government.

arbab: Landowner-boss.

arbabi: House and garden of a landowner located in the village.

arbab-rayati: Landowner-sharecropper.

bahrehbardarie melki: Owner-operated or owner-occupied farm.

dang: One-sixth part of any real estate or property.

dastur-e pardakht: Promissory note issued to landowners in lieu of money.

deimi: Rainfed or nonirrigated crop.

ezhar nameh: Declaration form on which a landowner declares the list and extent of his ownership.

faqih: Religious jurist.

fatwa: A religious ruling or decree issued by a competent religious authority, usually by one who is designated a Source of Emulation.

gavband: Owner or operator of plough animals.

jarib: Area corresponding to 1,000 square meters.

kanoun-e keshavarzan: Society of farmers.

khaliseh: Owned by the Iranian government.

khanevar-e bahrebardar: Cultivating or beneficiary household.

khanevar-e gheir bahreh-bardar: Noncultivating or nonbeneficiary household.

kharvar: Weight measure corresponding to 300 kilograms.

khorde-malek (**pl.** *khorde-malekin*): Small landowner.

khoshneshin: Village resident without land or cultivation rights.

malek: Owner.

marja-e taqlid (**pl.** *mara-je taqlid*): Source of emulation; highest religious authority.

martah: Pasture.

mazra-e: Hamlet.

mojtahed: Senior member of *ulama* who is so respected that he has the authority to issue opinion on matters of faith.

musha: Joint ownership of undivided parts.

nasaq: Cultivation rights held by a sharecropper or tenant.

pelak-e sabti: Piece of property with a separate registration identity and tag number.

qanat: Underground irrigation channel made by excavation.

qar-yeh: Village.

rayat: Tenant cultivator.

sarboneh: Head of peasant cultivation team.

sardar: Commander.

sartip: Brigadier.

seifi: Summer cash crops.

sepahdar: Commander of the army.

sepahsalar: Highest military rank.

sharia: Religious law.

tasarof-e odvani: Unlawful usurpation.

ulama: Plural of *alem*. Men of learning and piety. In this book, it denotes members of the clergy, religious authority.

vaqf: Endowed property; endowment.

vaqf-e amm: Property endowed for public charitable purposes.

vaqf-e khass: Property endowed for the benefit of a person or family; private endowment.

INDEX

Mohammad Gholi Majd is the author of articles published in the *Journal of Peasant Studies, Middle East Journal, American Journal of Agricultural Economics, Middle Eastern Studies,* and *Land Use Policy,* among others. He has taught courses in Middle East economics and economic development, most recently in the Department of Economics and at the Middle East Center, University of Pennsylvania.